THE FIRST

Also available in the 'Echoes of War' series:

THE AMRITSAR MASSACRE: TWILIGHT OF THE RAJ by Alfred Draper
A CHILD AT ARMS by Patrick Davis
THE EDGE OF THE SWORD by Anthony Farrar-Hockley
FLYING CORPS HEADQUARTERS 1914–1918 by Maurice Baring
THE FORTRESS by Raleigh Trevelyan
ILL MET BY MOONLIGHT by W. Stanley Moss
THE MASSACRE OF GLENCOE by John Buchan
A PASSIONATE PRODIGALITY by Guy Chapman
TAKE THESE MEN by Cyril Joly
WINGED VICTORY by V. M. Yeates

Echoes of War

THE FIRST
BOER WAR

JOSEPH LEHMANN

BUCHAN & ENRIGHT, PUBLISHERS
LONDON

First published in 1972 by Jonathan Cape Ltd

This edition
published in 1985 by
Buchan & Enright, Publishers, Limited
53 Fleet Street, London EC4Y 1BE

British Library Cataloguing in Publication Data

Lehmann, Joseph H.
    The first Boer War.
    1. Transvaal (South Africa) —— History ——
    War of 1880–1881
    I. Title
    968.04   DT928

Printed in Great Britain by
Redwood Burn Limited, Trowbridge, Wiltshire and
bound by Pegasus Bookbinding, Melksham, Wiltshire
Cover printed by The Furnival Press, London

CONTENTS

ILLUSTRATIONS

PREFACE

THE ANNEXATION of the Transvaal by Britain, and the Boers' subsequent struggle for independence, changed the entire course of South African history. These two factors contributed directly to the outbreak of the Second Anglo–Boer War (1899–1902) and events which followed. Because the second war overshadowed the first in length, scope and numbers of fighting men involved, the first has been generally ignored as a minor conflict. The purpose of this work is to correct this neglect and to restore the First Anglo–Boer War to its rightful place in history.

Reliance has been placed almost exclusively on primary sources. Apart from the books and articles written by correspondents of the great London dailies, the files of lesser journals—the *Natal Witness*, the *Natal Mercury*, the *Cape Argus*, the *Transvaal Argus and Commercial Gazette*, *De Volksstem*, etc.—have been explored. A search for public opinion as reflected in the press, including that of the United States and the Continent, has also been undertaken.

The period is rich in memoirs, but some of the more significant ones have been generally overlooked—for example, those of A. Merensky (*Erinnerungen aus dem Missionsleben in Transvaal, 1859–1882*) and J. W. Matthews (*Incwadi Yami*). Moreover, autobiographical accounts from those men trapped in the beleaguered garrisons, as with the overall story of the sieges, have often been given scant attention.

A travel grant from the American Philosophical Society and leave time provided by De Paul University made possible a trip to South Africa to consult unpublished documents and papers, among them those of the Boeren Voormannen, the Joubert Collection, and the Lanyon Papers in the archives at Pretoria; the papers of Shepstone and Colenso in the archives at Pietermaritzburg, Natal; and at Cape Town the papers of Frere, Merriman and Hofmeyer at the South African Public Library, and the Government House Papers, Cape Archives.

In Britain, I am grateful to Her Majesty the Queen for permission to investigate the valuable papers of the Duke of

Cambridge at the Royal Archives, Windsor Castle. For the political side of South African affairs, the British Museum provided the papers of Gladstone, Dilke and Morley; the Public Record Office provided the Granville Papers. For hitherto rarely investigated papers left by soldiers stationed or fighting in South Africa, there are the Commeline Papers at the Gloucester Records Office, the Craven-Smith-Milnes Papers at the Records Office, Nottingham, the recently declassified Buller Papers, along with the Wolseley papers at the War Office Library and the public library at Hove.

With the helpful assistance of Brigadier J. Stephenson, Director of the Royal United Service Institution, the recently discovered private letterbook of Wolseley (compiled while he was in South Africa), as well as his unpublished memoirs relating to the period, were made available. In addition, the R.U.S.I. library holds Wolseley's voluminous correspondence with his wife, and the regimental papers of the Connaught Rangers.

Most fortunate was the opportunity to consult the private papers of General J. F. Maurice, with the kind permission of his grandson, Mr M. F. P. Maurice, and the papers of Field-Marshal Sir George Stuart White provided by the Hon. Sir. Albert Napier and Lady Napier (daughter of the field-marshal). Nearly every surviving officer of the 92nd who participated in the battle of Majuba Hill described an account of the action in a personal letter to Sir George White. (The White Papers are now to be found in the India Office Library.)

Mrs George Shield, the former secretary and executor of Sir Ian Hamilton's estate, was good enough to disclose information about the general's adventures in South Africa in 1881.

Finally, the Wood Papers acquired by Duke University, North Carolina, have proved an excellent source for the field-marshal's unofficial views.

It is with the deepest gratitude that I mention the help given by Mr D. W. King of the War Office Library in directing me to the somewhat rare and formerly confidential Parliamentary Papers. Further thanks are due to Major G. Tylden, Mr W. J. de Kock, Miss Joan Davies and Mr Hans Panofsky for advice and encouragement, and to Mr P. R. Smit for translations from the Afrikaans. For assistance in research, I wish to express my appreciation to Miss Carol Carbine and Mr Edward E. Gordon.

Financial support, in part, was generously provided by the North American Foundation.

JOSEPH H. LEHMANN

[1]

ANNEXATION

We would rather live for ever in a wilderness than under the Union Jack.

Andries Pretorius

To the Victorians South Africa was a land of surprises, a land of extremes where unparalleled discoveries in diamonds and gold coincided with incredible political and military blunders. It was a land of warfare, endemic ever since Cape Town was surrendered to the British in 1806. While the sun never set on the British Empire, the blood never seemed to dry in South Africa. Britons, Boers and blacks clashed and fought and fought again, in a fashion bewildering to those in distant centres of world civilization.

In the middle of the maelstrom were the Boers (the word means 'farmers'), who had journeyed six thousand watery miles to live in peace and freedom. Detesting all things military, they were nevertheless stubborn warriors. They were made of the same hard stuff as their Dutch forefathers who had successfully defended their homeland against Philip II when Spain was the first power of the world, and their blood was infused with that of exiled Huguenots who had sacrificed home and property in resisting the despotism of Louis XIV. The Huguenots were easily absorbed, for they shared the same strong religious convictions, the same profound love of independence, and the unyielding courage to fight for both against enormous odds. The process was hastened by the Dutch East India Company, rulers at the Cape for 150 years, who proscribed the use of French in religious services and official documents.

The Company were harsh and unsympathetic. They regarded the Cape as a mere halfway house, a seaside tavern on the voyage to the East. The need for provisions persuaded them to send out Jan Van Riebeck with settlers to establish a colony, 'a cabbage garden', in 1652. Oppressive and monopolistic, the profit-hungry Lords of Seventeen, who ran the Company, did nothing to endear themselves to the colonists. Goaded into a state of semi-rebellion, many disobeyed the law by moving to the hinterland, where there was no dictating, taxing, or restricting officialdom.

When the British conquerors came to safeguard the strategic-ally vital Cape, they made even less effort than the Dutch 'Highmightinesses' to win the loyalty of the colonists, a trouble-some and unprofitable ingredient of the cession. The settlers, after the manner of the times, found themselves handed over with the soil, like serfs, to traditional enemies whose sovereignty could not be repudiated. They grew sullen, and when the British interfered on the side of the black, hotter heads resisted. The Boers, a God-intoxicated people with a primitive, Calvinist cast of mind, were ruled by the Old Testament, which taught that people of colour were their inferiors. Bushmen and Hottentots were accursed children of Ham, divinely appointed to be 'ser-vants of servants'. Like Israelites of old, the Boers conquered and killed, and frequently enslaved, the natives. As a slave-owner, the Boer treated the native as a child who was never ex-pected to grow to maturity, who had to be sheltered, fed, and ruled firmly and, if necessary, with severity. But slavery at the Cape, as the English historian J. A. Froude described it, 'was rather domestic than predial; the scandals of the West India plantations were unknown among them'.

In 1815 a Boer named Bezuidenhout was charged with mal-treating a Hottentot servant. When he resisted arrest, he was shot dead by soldiers attempting to seize him. Bezuidenhout's friends and neighbours took up their weapons and resolved to sweep the British into the sea that had brought them. The effort failed. Five rebel leaders were condemned, though none of them had actually shed blood, and hanged at Slagter's Nek. The beam broke under their combined weight before they were dead. De-spite the tearful entreaties of relatives and friends, the beam was repaired and the sentence carried out. The futility of further re-sistance was clearly demonstrated. Outwardly the farmers were loyal, but the rancorous memory of Slagter's Nek ate into their hearts. A proud people can forgive the death of men in battle, but not their execution on the scaffold.*

* Eighty years later, after the Jameson raid, the same beam was brought to Pre-toria with threats that it might be used a third time on British raiders who sought to destroy the Boer Republic.

The new rulers made efforts to anglicize the Cape. The more democratic Dutch form of local government was abolished and English was decreed to be the official language. In 1820 the introduction of thousands of British settlers began. (The Boers called them 'rooineks' or 'rednecks' because they burned quickly under the African sun.) In the name of scientific agriculture, the Government insisted that steel ploughs replace the heavy wooden ones. It was 'Do this' and 'Do that' as the British tried to substitute the new for the old.

English virtues can sometimes be more annoying than their vices. After experiencing what Macaulay described as 'one of its periodic fits of morality', Britain emancipated all the slaves in the Empire in 1834. To the South Africans this magnanimity seemed to be at their expense, for compensation was not only considerably less than anticipated but payable in treasury bonds in far-off London. The untutored farmers, regarding these bonds as practically worthless, sold their claims for a pittance to speculating middlemen. Pride prevented many from seeking any form of compensation.

More vexing was the Government's increasing sympathy for the natives. South Africa, 'a faint telescopic object', was viewed by the British people 'mainly through glasses of the missionary and the philanthropist'.[1] As early as 1828, the natives were declared to be political equals. This declaration included not only the docile Hottentots and primitive Bushmen, who had been easily overcome and scattered, but the fiercely warlike Kaffirs* or Bantu-speaking tribes who crowded in from the north and set the frontier aflame. Punitive measures on behalf of ruined farmers were denied by Englishmen who sentimentally regarded these tribesmen as 'noble savages'. Moreover, it was argued that the cost would be prohibitive. To the Boer it appeared that it was the European who was slandered for disturbing the idyllic life of the native so that British philanthropists and taxpayers could rest more comfortably in their beds.

The old Dutch spirit asserted itself. It was the kind of spirit which had caused their ancestors to tear open the dykes before invaders. Beginning in 1836, over twelve thousand Boers, nearly a quarter of the entire European population, abandoned

* The word Kaffir was borrowed from the Arabs, who called them 'unbelievers'. It became a word of contempt in the mouth of the Boer.

their homes and plunged deep into the unclaimed interior, deliberately cutting themselves off from the outside world. Their
racial pride outraged, they turned their backs on an alien Government whose laws favoured the blacks, and on a civilization that
violated their concept of personal and religious liberty. The Cape
authorities were dismayed by this mass exodus but found no law
that could prevent it. Sir Benjamin D'Urban, the Governor, felt
himself powerless to prevent an evil that was, after all, pre-
cedented by the mass annual migration of Englishmen to America.
'We quit this colony', declared one Boer leader, Piet Retief,
'under the full assurance that the English Government will allow
us to govern ourselves without its interference.'

And there was no interference. Unlike Pharaoh, the Governor
made no effort to pursue these modern Israelites searching the
wilderness for a promised land. It was assumed that danger and
hardship would chasten the survivors of the trek to the point
where they would return willingly to the blessings of British
rule. After all, Britain had just abolished slavery.

They called themselves 'voortrekkers'. To the restless, semi-
nomadic Boers, trekking from one farm to another more inviting
was commonplace. Never before, however, had the journey been
so long and perilous. But these Boers—men and women—were
perhaps the toughest, most resourceful pioneers the world has
ever known. Confronted by overwhelming odds, their confidence
was never shaken, for they 'walked with God'. Their Odyssean
efforts wrote an epic that resembles the American heritage by
containing elements of the story of Valley Forge, the Alamo, the
Oregon Trail, Custer's Last Stand, the Apache wars, and more,
all compressed into the experience of one generation.

Like the Americans who opened the West, they loaded their
lumbering Conestaga wagons with bedding and camp equipment,
furniture and utensils, children and grandparents; chicken-coops
were slung underneath and dust-covered cattle and sheep jogged
alongside. The team of oxen, resembling Texas longhorns, were
pointed towards the roadless north. The pace was slow as the
wagons trundled over the veld, joltingly slow in rough country
where the vehicles had to be constantly unloaded and reloaded.
Sometimes the wheels were removed and the four-ton wagons
were dismantled or pulled like sledges. Boer strength was taxed
to the limit of human endurance, but the Great Trek rolled on.

Men and animals perished. Children were born. When the water ran out, they learned to drink the putrid liquid that remained in the stomachs of their dead cattle. Famine, fever and wild beasts stalked them. Lions often appeared in such numbers that one small party of emigrants counted 249 killed in the space of a few months.

At night and in time of danger the wagons were placed in a circle, or laagered, with thorn bushes crammed into the open spaces. A temporary fortress was thus created to repel any attack by beasts or tribesmen. At first, after they crossed the Orange River, the fertile plains appeared to be free of savages, just as their scouts had reported. Actually they were moving towards a sea of enemies who had 'eaten up' the land before them for hundreds of miles.* Tribes like the Zulus to the east and the Matabele to the north, formed into powerful, well-organized military confederations, killed thousands, taking women as wives, cattle as loot, and boys to be trained with Spartan-like discipline for their merciless military machines. Nothing would soften the hearts of these well-muscled warriors; they seemed to lust for blood for its own sake. In the hard Boer they found their match.

At the laager wall war was a family matter. Women and children fought at the sides of their menfolk to defend the circle of survival. Wives and daughters did not carry a gun but they could load and fire one in need. When attackers tried to climb into the laager, club-wielding women grimly battled to repel them. Many pioneers were massacred. Whole parties sometimes disappeared.

In open warfare the Boers possessed one great advantage, the horse. Startled natives regarded these strange creatures, 'oxen without horns' as they called them, with awe, then dread. A mounted attack was swift and deadly. The Boers approached to within a hundred yards or so of the enemy, fired their muskets from the saddle with unerring accuracy, and retired quickly beyond a cloud of spears to reload, wheel about and charge again. Repeated lightning assaults discouraged even the bravest warriors.

* Quite literally in some instances. According to reports by French missionaries, tens of thousands were eaten by cannibals, who were by no means averse to eating white men. As one man-eater of the Basuto tribe explained, they tasted even better than black men 'because they ate salt, sugar and other nice things, and their flesh would be better seasoned'.[2]

Once the voortrekkers crossed the Orange River they branched off, some settling the region before them to found the Orange Free State, others pressing northward beyond the Vaal into a vast, virtually unknown territory which many believed to contain Jerusalem. Still more, travelling as usual in small bodies of a hundred or so, veered eastward and made the fearful crossing of the Drakensberg ('Dragon Mountains') to descend upon Natal, the land of promise. It was also the special preserve of the Zulus.

Dingaan, the great Zulu king, with false promises of friendship, lured the Boer leader Retief and a party of seventy into his kraal, where they were butchered. Casting aside his role of fox, Dingaan became a lion. He ordered out his impis (bands of warriors), and 500 men, women and children were slaughtered before the survivors could draw together into a laager. The outlook was bleak. Many more were to die under the assagai (spear), but the pioneers persisted until reinforcements arrived. Under Andries Pretorius some 500 revenge-maddened voortrekkers sought out the enemy. On December 16th, 1838 the Boer commando encountered 11,000 of Dingaan's warriors. Forming a powerful laager, they repelled repeated attacks until the blood of 3,000 vanquished Zulus turned a near-by stream red. It was a devastating revenge which smashed the power of the Zulus in Natal. Trailing blood, the survivors retreated over the Tugela River into Zululand proper. The Boers, who lost only six men at the battle of Blood River, felt no undue exaltation from their triumph; rather they were convinced more than ever that God was on their side. It was His victory.

They now parcelled out the land that they had won by conquest and raised the flag of the Republic of Natalia. It was to go down as one of the most short-lived republics in history. An old enemy, the 'verdomde Engelsman', delivered the death blow. Until now, the British had shown no inclination to take over Natal. Time and again requests for annexation by a small British settlement at Port Natal (Durban) were categorically refused. Once the voortrekkers appeared in Natal, the British Government wavered between assertion and abdication. It was the missionary interests that tipped the scales.* Boer treatment of the

---

* It was said at the time that when the secretary of a missionary society visited the Colonial Office, he was received as if he were a minister of state.

'harmless' natives in Natal was reported as cruel and arbitrary, with intentions to enslave. And there was the danger, not altogether exaggerated, that the land-hungry Boers might cause whole tribes of dispossessed natives to begin a dash to Cape Colony. Alarmed settlers at the Cape added their demands for intervention. Strategists argued that the Boers must not be allowed a port which might admit a foreign power and thereby threaten the route to India.

In 1838 troops were sent in ever-increasing numbers to the only good port at Durban. Troops were followed by proclamations prohibiting the sale of powder and lead to the voortrekkers, and declaring that it was not in the power of the emigrants to disclaim allegiance to the British Crown. In 1843 Natal was annexed.

The Boers had sacrificed too much to surrender the land to the British without a fight. Successful at first, they were soon beaten by superior numbers. The majority of the pioneers remained irreconcilable. Once more they abandoned their farms, loaded their wagons and creaked back over the Drakensberg into the Transvaal, beyond British rule. Natal thus became largely British in race and sentiment, as thousands of colonists came from the mother country to replace the Dutch. The number of immigrants was, however, comparatively small because of reports in Europe of the warlike character of the natives.

When Sir Harry Smith, a gallant and aggressive soldier, became Governor of Natal in 1847, a determined effort was made to strengthen British supremacy in South Africa. An old hand at fighting Bantu tribesmen, who had earlier conducted successful operations in the eastern Cape area under Governor D'Urban, Sir Harry Smith beat them again in what was called the Seventh Kaffir War. He kept on going and boldly advanced British supremacy over the Orange Free State. Most of the trek-weary Boers, harassed by Basutos, accepted British protection with little protest, but the fiercely independent Transvaalers, anticipating Sir Harry's effort to capture all of the Great Trek, protested for them. Under the fiery Andries Pretorius, a commando of angry Transvaalers rushed south to encourage the annexed Boers to resist. Sir Harry Smith, whose military reputation extended from Waterloo to vanquishing the Sikhs in India, quickly brought up staunch regulars. After a sharp encounter at Boomplaats in 1848, the recalcitrant Boers recrossed the Vaal. The defeated Pretorius, now with a price on his head, fired one last verbal blast, swearing that he and his supporters would 'rather live for ever in a wilderness than under the Union Jack'. Others, aching for a life without interference, followed him to the far north. The two territories—the Transvaal and the Orange River Sovereignty—were to be separated not merely by a river (the Vaal) but by a well-defined demarcation of temperament.

If the expansion-minded Governor Smith had been permitted a free hand, the little Transvaal Republic planted so audaciously in the middle of the veld would have been swallowed by an Imperial tide. Instead, the home authorities ordered a complete about-face. The onset of another Kaffir war and the defeat of some British regulars at the hands of the Basutos had a disquieting effect in Britain. Beginning with that great moulder of public opinion, *The Times*, the press made a concerted attack upon a colonial policy that perpetuated native wars and drained the country of millions of pounds. The cry was echoed eloquently in the halls of Parliament by exponents, like Gladstone and Bright, of a 'Little England'. The latter spoke of the Empire as 'a gigantic system for providing outdoor relief for the aristocracy'. The doctrines of Manchester—cheap government, peace (at almost any price) and reform—dominated debate. Colonies, it was argued, were a source of weakness rather than strength, for they encouraged wars, tyranny and jobbery. The law of supply and demand was the panacea that would promote prosperity and civilization throughout the world. To oppose it was blasphemy. Even Disraeli, the future imperialist, described colonies as 'millstones round our necks'.

Sir Harry Smith was recalled. The surprised Pretorius, with the price removed from his head, was offered a treaty guaranteeing the independence of the Transvaal. By the Sands River Convention of 1852 the Transvaalers were given their freedom, and, to appease the missionaries, they were told that they would be allowed to purchase gunpowder if they abolished slavery. (It should be noted that despite the allegations of evangelicals, Sir Harry found in his personal investigations no evidence of slavery.)

The Imperial tide continued to ebb. Two years later, by the terms of the Bloemfontein Convention the Orange River Sovereignty was abandoned. There was one lone objector in the

House of Commons and he was taunted by *The Times*. Some missionaries protested on behalf of the natives and begged the Queen to reconsider the step taken. But the restraining force of evangelicalism, never wholly absent from the Victorian scene, was temporarily eclipsed.

Insulated by an international vacuum from a pursuing civilization, the Boers were free to work out their own concepts of liberty in a wilderness. Their Zion was almost as God had originally made it. A vast tableland of veld rising over four thousand feet above sea, broken only by an occasional valley or odd-shaped kopje (little hill), it looked to the traveller the very incarnation of desolation. It seemed to be a part of the geological past where mastodon or dinosaur might be suddenly met. But to the Boers in the far north, an ungregarious people in some ways as strange and rude as the land itself, it was home. On a limitless sea of grass they deliberately sought isolation, even from one another. Settling on farms 6,000 to 12,000 acres and more in extent, they measured distances by hours, not miles.

Their solitary seclusion was rarely disturbed as they squatted in chocolate-red farmhouses made of sun-dried bricks with mud used as mortar and roofed with thatch or corrugated iron. Though rich in land, and with ever-increasing herds, the Boer would have shocked the average English labourer by his lack of comfort and refinement. His home usually consisted of two mud-floor rooms smeared with cow dung as protection against vermin: the kitchen with a sheep-dung fire for heating and cooking, and the bedroom, which often accommodated the entire family, who slept in the home-made clothes they wore all day. Travellers related with Rabelaisian humour how, lacking a spare room, the hospitable Boer offered a share of the family bed.

The frugal frontiersman's simple needs—coffee, sugar, powder and lead—were provided by the wily European pedlar, sometimes his only contact with the outside world. Ignorant in the ways of that world, the unsophisticated farmer was often shamelessly swindled by the shrewd, smooth-talking 'smous'. Those posing as physicians found the Boer a perfect mark for quackery. One travelling 'doctor' was rumoured to have made a fortune vaccinating gullible farmers with condensed milk at a rate of five shillings or more. As agents of 'civilization' these uitlanders hardened Boer suspicions as to the worth of civilization.

Amusements were few, but frequent family reunions offered pleasure and served to tighten bonds of kinship that were already close. With their wagons laden with most of their household goods, a sojourn of many weeks was common. In time, English, Scottish and German storekeepers helped to establish towns where the isolated farmers came to trade and celebrate Nagmaal (the sacrament of the Lord's Supper) every three months. This was the most important social event in their lonely lives. Children were christened, daughters were courted and married, wives purchased cheap imported finery, while the men talked much and sampled the liquor. All munched Scotch sweets by the pound. The Boer did not ask for more.

Unlike America, in Africa there were no waves of immigrants with fresh blood and new ideas to alter the ways of the Boer. His outlook remained parochial and quickly fossilized. There were few schools or books; from the well-thumbed Bible the child was taught the rudiments of reading and writing by his parents. The simple farmers were satisfied if they could understand and sign documents when required, and cull favourite passages from the Scriptures to reinforce their Calvinist dogma. Their religion, however, did not foster the social stratification found in other lands. A class-distinction based upon hereditary leadership or accumulated wealth was unknown to this homogeneous people. And with little aptitude for trading or mining, they continued to follow a semi-pastoral life with equal opportunities for all.

The Transvaal was a country without boundaries. A vagrant disposition inbred among the voortrekkers prompted them to be ready at a moment's notice to search for a better home. Numbering but a few thousand, and depending largely on a natural (and often prodigious) increase, they ranged over a land the size of France. They thrust towards every point of the compass: northward to the lower lands south of the Limpopo until arrested by deadly fever; to the desert-like regions to the west until discouraged by thirst. They pressed the Zulus to the east and even spilled back into the lands south of the Vaal. Powerful tribes often fought them every step of the way. The natives of Africa, unlike the red men of North America, refused to die or disappear. Yet in the end they did little more than divert or delay Boer expansion.

The independent farmers also disputed among themselves.

Resenting control of any kind, their government existed in name
only. A common danger alone would unite them. Tax-collectors
were ignored and magistrates were disobeyed. To the Boer way
of thinking, a man was virtually a State in himself, and he was
prepared to fight whenever he believed that his rights were
violated. His exaggerated notion of individual freedom led to a
puritan anarchy. The land north of the Vaal soon split into at
least four recognizable and bickering Republics that were further
torn by disputes between high-mettled factions.

Chronic unrest was encouraged by religious as well as political
differences. Did a true Christian wear a narrow- or a broad-
brimmed hat, and did he button his waistcoat all the way to his
throat? Was it proper to sing hymns? Should the authority of
the Cape Town Synod be recognized? Unfortunately, virtually
no ministers had accompanied the voortrekkers. The Dutch
Reformed Church, closely resembling the Presbyterian Church
in its form of worship, quickly hardened on the veld and broke
into three major sects, none of which held a high opinion of the
others. The most numerous and uncompromising were members
of the newly formed (1859) Separatist Reformed Church, popularly called 'Doppers' (or 'Dampers') because of their determination to dampen down all thoughts of progress, religious or
otherwise. They were alleged to have approved of Galileo's condemnation by the Inquisition, for they insisted that the earth was
flat. Like the Quakers, the Doppers were easily identified by their
dress and cropped hair, and were strong in their objections to
political or ecclesiastical control.

There were many disorders and comic-opera wars, with much
commandeering of coffee and powder but little bloodshed; the
Boers preferred to fight at a distance with the least possible risk
to themselves. In one such extended 'battlefield', antelope
frolicked in the centre as the cautious warriors patiently waited
for someone to make the first move. The penalty for technical
treason was about the same as that for being drunk and disorderly.
Not until 1864 was reconciliation achieved and a single Republic
established, with Marthinus Wessel Pretorius, son of Andries,
recognized as President, and Paul Kruger as Commandant-
General.

Personal liberties, so jealously guarded by the Transvaaler,
were by no means surrendered to the Republic. The highly flex-

ible Grondwet (constitution), based in part on the American model, was founded on the principle that every man capable of bearing arms had a right to be heard in the Volksraad (national assembly). The President was viewed as little more than a moderator presiding over a people's committee. And there was no hesitancy on the part of these whole-souled democrats to intervene directly in the legislative process by marching to Pretoria, the capital, to make their views known to the legislators.

In one matter there was total agreement: to be a citizen a man must be white. It was written into the Grondwet that the people desired 'to permit no equality between coloured people and the white inhabitants, either in Church or State'.

The discovery of diamonds in Griqualand West and traces of gold in the Transvaal introduced another stormy chapter in the history of South Africa. It was a curious freak of nature that she buried her greatest treasures in the land of pastoral Old Testament people; they regarded these glittering objects as a curse rather than a blessing. To the pious Boer, gems and precious metals were not the materials out of which to fashion a nation. Instead they tried to conceal nature's secrets. The Transvaal Government made it a serious offence, with a £500 fine, for a farmer to disclose the presence of riches on his land to anyone other than the Government. One Dutch prospector was actually paid to return home and tell no one of the gold that he had found. Most Boers would have agreed with Piet Joubert when he warned, 'This gold will cause our country to be soaked in blood.' But prospectors were not easily discouraged. Stopping them, a member of the Volksraad declared, was like 'stemming the tide with a pitch-fork'. However, until the great promise of untold wealth was uncovered at Witwatersrand in 1886, the findings were not sufficiently rich to attract large numbers of uitlanders.

Diamonds were another matter. The Kimberley mines on the borders of the Transvaal proved rich beyond measure. Thousands of eager diggers soon gave the parched angle of land between the Orange and the Vaal an appearance that resembled 'an insane asylum turned loose on a beach'. The territory was claimed by the two Republics; but with the discovery of diamonds, the normally lethargic, anti-expansionist Government headed by Gladstone moved swiftly to preserve order. At the request of the Governor at the Cape a Griqua chief, Waterboer, who was under British protection, laid claim to the diamond fields. The question of ownership was arbitrated with equal promptness by Lieutenant-Governor R. W. Keate of Natal, who awarded the disputed territory to Waterboer. Griqualand was then made a crown colony in 1873, and formally annexed to the Cape in 1880. Later, when it was proved that the Griqua's claims were false, the Orange Free State, which had the best claim, was paid £90,000 by the British to soothe distressed feelings. The sum was a very tiny fraction of the true worth of the land.

The Keate Award awakened suspicion among the Boers. The loss of the diamond-fields did not rankle as much as the assault on the integrity of the Republics. Rooineks were once more encroaching on their lands, possibly scheming encirclement and eventual destruction of their liberties. Not since the Great Trek had feelings run so strong. President Johannes Brand of the Free State, champion of moderation, calmed his people and strove to maintain friendly relations with the British. The Transvaalers' fury turned inward against President Marthinus Pretorius, who had received no authority to arbitrate. He was compelled to resign. There was no serious suggestion to take up arms, but the soreness inflicted by annexation was slow to heal. Years later an old Boer debated with a British administrator as to the possibility of minerals being present in the moon. The Britisher insisted that there must be some there. 'No, Meeneer,' said the contradicting Boer, 'there are no minerals in the moon, for if there were you British would have annexed it long ago.'

In 1872 a most implausible Boer, Thomas François Burgers, was elected President of the Transvaal. A Cape Dutchman and sometime minister of the Reformed Church who had been educated in Europe, he soon made it obvious that he was bent on transforming the Transvaal into a modern state, if not a world Power. Despite his eloquence and charm, the energetic Burgers could never win the complete confidence of the majority of his people. His progressive ideas were totally at variance with their Calvinist limitations. Most damning in the eyes of bigoted Boers were his unorthodox views on religion. Some charged that he believed that the Devil had no tail, though a tail was clearly illustrated in their old Dutch Bibles. A synodical commission had once suspended Burgers from his ministry for the alleged heresy of denying the personality of the Devil, but the Cape

Supreme Court reinstated him in 1864. Nevertheless, the details of the case, which gained considerably in the telling, eventually reached the backveld Boers, to whom the denial of the existence of the Devil was tantamount to denying the existence of God. To them the presence of Satan was quite real. It took no great stretch of their imagination to picture him concealed behind some near-by rock with horns, pitchfork, tail and all. The President was once confronted by an irate farmer who challenged his disbelief in a real Devil, whereupon Burgers gave the disarming reply, 'Do you then believe in the Devil, when the Bible tells us that he was a liar from the beginning?'[3]

The ready wit of the President, however, failed to mollify the opposition when he introduced an Education Act calling for a comprehensive school system without religious indoctrination. Opponents denounced him for advocating 'Godless schools', and for importing hundreds of foreigners, mostly Hollanders, as teachers, administrators and parsons. Political enemies mischievously related how a piano, 'a Godless instrument' in the words of the Dopper leader, Paul Kruger, had been installed in Burgers's home.

Programme for progress can be expensive, and the President had no prejudice against gold. Burgers encouraged the uitlander miners to the point of visiting the diggings in the Eastern Transvaal and treating the miners to his well-received eloquence. Since most of them were Scots like the pretty wife he married while in London, he flatteringly named the gold-bearing district New Caledonia and the leading settlement Mac-Mac. To the Boers these foreign miners were about as welcome as they would have been to an English country gentleman asked to approve digging for coal on his lawn. With a large purchase of nuggets, Burgers ventured to give the nation its first gold currency. The coins depicted the President's fine head, with a flowing beard and the eyes of a prophet, on one side, and a strange new international coat of arms of the Republic on the other. Stern Republicans saw it as a blasphemous act committed by a man who aspired to be Caesar.

Reforms were met by circumvention. Most vital to Burgers' government was an effort to teach the Transvaalers to pay their taxes promptly and regularly. The farmers, however, refused to be taught. Supreme ruler over his own domain, the Boer on his solitary farm either ignored the tax-collector or put him off his land. There was no police force or regular army to enforce the law.

Undaunted, the ambitious President sailed for Europe in February 1875 to borrow sufficient funds to construct a railway that would join the capital with the sea at Delagoa Bay. A Peter the Great among Boers, Burgers envisioned a 'window to the West' that would introduce commerce, immigrants and modern ways to his people.

Progressive ideas of another sort designed to modernize South Africa were germinating in the Colonial Office, where Lord Carnarvon had been installed as Secretary in 1874 in the new Imperial-minded Disraeli Government. The activities of Carnarvon were to represent the first ripples in the returning tide of imperialism. Henceforth there would be a quickening interest among the British people in overseas acquisitions and responsibilities, an interest which was to have its counterpart in other great States during this age of the New Imperialism. The opposition to a colonial empire, sponsored by the Manchester school, had reached its peak in the 'sixties. Its cherished hope that the Empire would disintegrate through neglect never materialized. It had behaved much like the indifferent husband who tried daily to convince his wife that though he did not actually hate her, he would not find it inconvenient if she left his home for good; surely even the most devoted spouse would eventually get the idea and start packing. Taking the opposite approach, Carnarvon regarded the colonies as a helpmate working towards the common goals of security and prosperity.

Carnarvon recognized that no portion of Britain's vast holding had deteriorated more than South Africa, which he described as perilously close to Balkanization, making peace a stranger and exciting the ambitions of rival powers. After sixty years, Britain's vacillating, off-hand, semi-accidental policy had produced examples of almost every variety of colonial government. Cape Colony, the strongest and most advanced, enjoyed a responsible Government, but it had been slow in coming. Natal and Griqualand West were Crown Colonies. Semi-independent locations were to be found in Kaffraria and Basutoland. There were quasi-States of the Pondos, Swazis, Matabeles and Zulus threatening the perimeter of white settlements. Smack in the middle of this assorted clutch of territories, like the hard stone of a peach, were the poorly defined Boer Republics. The only hope for peace and order, Carnarvon decided, lay in federation. The advantages were obvious. Federated self-governing States, including that of the Boers, would encourage greater loyalty and stimulate a flow of European immigrants and capital while reducing the demands for help in the shape of British pounds and soldiers. The pressing need for general union, argued the Colonial Secretary, was a uniform policy in dealing with the formidable native question. A sincere philanthropist at heart, Carnarvon felt an obligation to maintain sufficient Imperial control to thwart the provocative hostility of white colonists.*

The Colonial Secretary was no stranger to federation. He had played a leading role in the confederation of Canada in 1867, a fact which he proudly and frequently proclaimed both publicly and privately. Nor was his proposal new to South African affairs, but it had never been enthusiastically endorsed by the British Government. Brilliant and resourceful, Carnarvon was given a free hand by Disraeli, though he was fully aware of certain weaknesses. The Prime Minister, finding him prone to flattery and self-consciously anxious or fidgety, called him 'Twitters'. Carnarvon's most serious fault was his unyielding ignorance, particularly of the Boers. Moreover, his vanity would not tolerate anything that suggested criticism of what he termed 'my federation policy'.

His first mistake was in selecting James Anthony Froude, the historian, as an Imperial missionary to propagandize the cause of federation and to report his findings, after two flying visits to South Africa, in preparation for a South African Conference. Froude, whom Disraeli described as having written 'more rot on the reign of Elizabeth than Gibbon required for all the *Decline and Fall*', proved to be a clumsy agent. On his second visit to Cape Town on June 18th, 1875, exactly one week after the House of Assembly had rejected Carnarvon's proposal of federation, Froude decided he could coerce and lecture the colonists and the Cape Parliament, which he called 'a collection of pert schoolboys', into changing their minds. Froude intended to make history as he wrote it, with a startling disregard for the facts.

---

* Carnarvon began his career as champion of the oppressed at an early age. When he was seven, he gave a speech to the Society for the Prevention of Cruelty to Animals, of which his father was President.

Undertaking an ill-advised campaign on Carnarvon's behalf, the cocksure academic committed a series of egregious indiscretions which served only to harden prejudice at the Cape against the Colonial Secretary's policy. Nevertheless, Carnarvon's confidence in Froude remained unshaken.

At the moment, however, Carnarvon was far more interested in events in Natal than in the activities of his apostle at the Cape. It was the explosive character of native affairs that initially drew Imperial attention to the other British colony. Increasing numbers of Natal's blacks walked hundreds of miles to the diggings, where after months of labour they could earn enough money to buy a gun, the weapon which they identified with the white man's superiority. Though these guns were usually of the gas-pipe variety, often more dangerous to the user than to the intended victim, the 20,000 colonists feared that the 300,000 natives crammed into Natal would be encouraged to break the power of the conqueror. Accordingly, stringent laws were written to outlaw the purchase and possession of such weapons. Efforts to disarm them provoked a minor rebellion led by Langalibalele, whom the stiff-tongued called 'Longbelly'. Severe reprisals followed, encouraged by Governor Pine, who was already discredited at the Colonial Office by rumours of concubinage. Bishop Colenso of Natal, a powerful champion of the abused natives, went to London to agitate on their behalf.

The activities of Colenso had already gained a notoriety which reached far beyond the borders of Natal. Writing as what would today be called a social anthropologist, he stupefied the Archbishop of Canterbury by suggesting to him that upon conversion a Kaffir should not be required to put aside the practice of polygamy. This was only the beginning. Working with the Zulus, whose language he had mastered, the missionary bishop produced a new translation of the Scriptures with novel interpretations. While collaborating with William the Zulu on a translation of the story of the Flood, the native convert asked, 'Is it all true?' Colenso decided it was not. The sceptical Zulu thereby converted the bishop, who soon dedicated himself to demythologizing the Pentateuch. In a work published in 1862, the iconoclast bishop argued that part of the Old Testament was a pious fraud written by someone other than Moses. The bishop and the book were condemned by both Houses of Convocation,

and an effort was made to buy all available copies of the scandalous work. Colenso's superior in Cape Town tried to depose him,
but the action was declared unlawful. An ignoble and unedifying
spectacle raged in Natal, involving court orders and interdicts
which closed and opened cathedral doors until a second cathedral
with a separate bishop was consecrated. His enemies claimed
that the Pentateuch was played out and that he was now searching for new sensations by taking up the cudgel on behalf of
Langalibalele.

It has never been difficult to stir up feelings in England on
native questions. Colenso, afflicted with an ardour which fed itself, quickly gained supporters and created an atmosphere of
acrimony against the Natal Government. Tales of atrocities
against the black man filled the journals. The Anti-Slavery
Society, the Peace Society and the Aborigines Protection Society
raised great cries of alarm. Questions were asked in Parliament,
and there was talk of an official investigation. The Queen became agitated. She told Carnarvon that native races should be
treated 'with every kindness and affection, as brothers not—alas!
as Englishmen too often do—as totally different beings to ourselves, fit only to be cursed and shot down'.

With federation in mind, Carnarvon needed no prompting to
act. The determined Colonial Secretary dispatched a second
agent, Sir Garnet Wolseley, a man considerably more adroit and
forceful, to serve as Governor of Natal. His mission was to
investigate the chances for federation in general and at the same
time to promote the cause by putting Natal's house in order, an
aim which required, in the main, persuading the colonists to take
the self-sacrificing, retrograde step of remaking their constitution so as to make the Crown the controlling element, especially
in native affairs.

Sir Garnet Wolseley and his 'brilliant staff' (as the Natalians
were soon accustomed to calling them), fresh from their victories
over the ferocious Ashanti of West Africa, created a sensation in
the remote colony. Already dubbed 'our only General' by an
exultant press, Wolseley looked every inch the 'budding Wellington'. A slight, wiry man, brimming with self-assurance,
Wolseley radiated a sense of power. Here was a man, Froude
declared, to 'follow to the world's end'.

Possessing a soldierly disdain for politics, Wolseley would

have preferred tearing the constitutions to shreds, but Carnarvon
warned him that such action would be neither prudent nor legal.
The celebrated general actually played the role of politician with
great skill. Gay, gallant, charming yet masterful, Wolseley campaigned tirelessly to disarm hostility. The new Governor and his
equally beguiling staff entertained lavishly at Government
House, with dinner every night and a ball every fortnight. The
London season was drab by comparison, one giddy guest asserted.
The liquor bill alone outpaced the Governor's salary. Wolseley,
observed a local judge, 'drowned the independence of the colony
with sherry and champagne'.[4] In reality, many of the colonists
were flattered into submission by the extravagant concern that
Carnarvon and the mother country displayed in sending so distinguished a general to woo them. (Privately, Carnarvon described Natal as 'that wretched little colony'.)

Wolseley did not win without a fight. He suffered some anxious moments during the three nights of robust debate in the
Legislative Council over his proposed constitutional changes. All
the clever men, he complained, were on the Opposition side. The
tone of debate, remarked Major William Francis Butler of the
general's staff, reached a level that compared favourably with
that in much larger colonies such as Canada. After several pre-
liminary addresses, the principal arguments for constitutional
modification were delivered by Colonel George Pomeroy-Colley,
the Chief of Staff who was respected and esteemed by all. 'Wait
until you hear Colley, the star of the team,' was the intimidating
taunt the Opposition heard from the Governor's supporters. To
cordial cheers, Colley rose and carefully arranged his elaborate
notes like weapons for legislative combat. The renowned soldier
was the cynosure of every eye as he addressed the assembly in
stately tones of persuasive argument. All went well for a few
minutes, then he hesitated in the middle of a sentence, stuttered
and stopped. His hand swept his brow as he looked blankly at his
notes. There was a flutter of encouraging applause as he un-
comprehendingly faced his listeners. Turning to the Speaker,
Colley mumbled an apology and sat down. Throughout the rest
of the debate his face remained gloomily buried in his hands in a
gesture of self-reproach for having failed the chief.* Why did

* Confusion seemed contagious. One able leader of the Opposition became so
flustered that he cast his vote for the Government's bill by mistake.

Colley break down? A cultivated man, he spoke readily and well
on many subjects. Proud, sensitive, and burning for achievement,
Colley obviously set his goal of oratorical performance too high.
He cracked under the strain. It was a personality flaw his critics
would remember.

The Bill was approved by a narrow majority at the end of
May, 1875. 'No man in England', boasted Wolseley, 'could have
got more out of the Council than I did.'[5] Carnarvon was pleased.
He hoped that the changes wrought in Natal would give him 'a
very fair base of operations as regards other questions of South
African policy'.[6] Uppermost in his thoughts were conditions in
the Boer Republics. The delicate mission of reconnoitring the
Boers was entrusted to two superbly intelligent members of the
'Wolseley gang'. Colley was dispatched to the Transvaal, and
Butler, who had successfully performed a similar mission for
Wolseley in Louis Riel's Republic of the North-West during the
Red River expedition, was sent to the Orange Free State.

The mission was a welcome change for Colley. After the
passage of the bill, he had returned to his duties as Treasurer.
Shocked by the muddle in which he found the colony's finances,
he worked on the books around the clock, setting standards that
no successor would ever quite attain. Freed from his desk, Colley
was refreshed by the mid-winter climate (June and July) of this
region of Africa. Travelling first to Delagoa Bay before making
for Pretoria, Colley joined a small Boer commando escorting a
diplomatic mission to Swaziland. It was an excellent opportunity
for the 'tourist' to assess the military system of the Boers. The
professional soldier was astonished by their unmilitary bearing
and slipshod methods. The future fighter of the Boers came away
with the unfortunate impression that their worth as fighting men
would be virtually nil if they were opposed by regulars.

In Pretoria the British colonel was amused to find gold-seeking
uitlanders digging in front of the home of the absent Burgers. If a
law were not passed soon, he suggested, the house would be
destroyed. There was a warm welcome for Colley from the diggers and townspeople, who were mostly British or pro-British.
He was pleased to learn that the prayer for the English Church
took precedence over that for the President, and that on the
Queen's birthday most shops were closed and the Union Jack was
boldly displayed.

In a carefully phrased report to Wolseley, Colley dwelt on the resentment and suspicion awakened among the Boers by Britain's annexation of the diamond-fields; but he introduced a note of optimism when he observed that British influence was increasing and—a good omen for Carnarvon's scheme—appeared 'likely before long to become dominant'.[7] Nevertheless, he stressed the absolute necessity of acquiring Delagoa Bay in order to seal off the Republic's access to the sea before the Boers could be induced to surrender their political independence. Acquisition would prove difficult, for at the very time Colley was writing his report, the President of France, Marshal MacMahon, was arbitrating the Delagoa Bay dispute and awarding the entire region to Portugal.

Before leaving Pretoria, Colley met with Acting President Piet Joubert, ostensibly to discuss postal communications between Natal and the Republic. They spoke mostly of federation. While Mrs Joubert served the polite young English officer with her best cooking, her husband spoke words of encouragement to Colley. Colley returned to Natal convinced of Joubert's future co-operation in furthering Carnarvon's programme. It was later said that Colley was taken in by the 'slimheit' ('craftiness') of Joubert. His flirtation with federation was a stratagem to forestall what he feared would be an effort by Wolseley to seize the Transvaal. 'By cleverly stroking the Strong Arm of the army while within reach,' his supporters boasted, 'Joubert adroitly postponed annexation of his country for two years.' Wolseley, of course, had no authority to make such a move, but Boers like Joubert were understandably apprehensive when they saw how the English colonists of Natal were pressured into surrendering control of their Government because of alleged maltreatment of rebellious blacks.

Major Butler's report was strong and straightforward. Because of the Keate Award, he found the Free State staunchly anti-British. He described the Boers as 'a homely, sober, quiet, dull race of beings, full of faith in God and fair dealings between man and man as this holds sample of'. Butler's pro-Boer sympathies never diminished and eventually blighted his career. On the eve of the Anglo–Boer War of 1899–1902, his efforts to prevent Imperial forces from trampling down the independence of a free people led to his dismissal as commander of the British Army in

South Africa. At home, he became 'one of the best abused men in England'.

Wolseley, meanwhile, toured Natal. The general insisted that the rest of his hard-working staff should accompany him 'to prevent accidents', for these dashing officers had become involved in a series of romantic affairs with susceptible young ladies and wives that bordered on the scandalous. To guide him, Wolseley had the services of Theophilus Shepstone, Secretary of Native Affairs for Natal. The sphinx-like Shepstone had lived among the Zulus since childhood, and was regarded as the greatest living authority on the natives of the region. He repeatedly warned the Governor against Exeter Hall* propaganda which convinced insular Englishmen that when one of their brethren migrated to the colonies all sense of justice and humanity towards the native was immediately replaced by cruelty, greed and oppression. Shepstone shared the fears that haunted the European settlers, fears of being overwhelmed by black hordes or of race suicide through integration. He would segregate the natives and preserve their customs, except for such practices as polygamy and witchcraft, and as a safety device he would reduce the power of the hereditary chiefs to vanishing point. On returning from his tour, Wolseley publicly endorsed Shepstone's views, thereby stirring the wrath of the sharp-tongued Colenso, whom Shepstone at the time was suing for slander. The bishop complained to Carnarvon of how he had been 'cold-shouldered' by the new Governor and was 'painfully disappointed' by his policies which were contrary to his lordship's instructions.

'The bishop is mad on one subject,' Wolseley angrily told Carnarvon, 'and thinks that unless everyone sees as he does, they are cruel oppressors of the black man.' Wolseley believed that it was impossible for the two races to live together in perfect equality. The great native majority should be taught, he warned, not to confide in the white man's justice, but 'to realize and acknowledge his superiority'. Policy shaped by philanthropic sentiments, he argued, had made Natal 'the weakest and most dangerous point in the Empire'; if the British Government had dealt with the natives as the Boers did, the majority of blacks in the territory would have migrated elsewhere. [8]

* A meeting place in London for humanitarian societies that indiscriminately championed native races.

With Shepstone, Wolseley talked privately of shooting Zulus.
Shepstone assured him that with a thousand men he could cross
the Tugela and easily depose Cetewayo, the Zulu king, and annex
Zululand. Enamoured by military solutions to political problems,
Wolseley wrote to Carnarvon for consent, pointing out that
annexation was inevitable and would, according to Shepstone, be
approved even by the Zulus, who feared and hated their cruel
chief. Thus even philanthropic forces would support an act 'of
humanity and of civilization' that was also 'beneficial to British
interests in South Africa'.[9] To make the proposal more tempting,
Wolseley suggested that a pleased Transvaal would become more
amenable to federation if Britain removed 'the standing menace'
on its border.

The cautious Colonial Secretary, alarmed by Wolseley's harsh
and daring methods, refused to approve the plan. Wolseley, with
no chance to draw his sword, then asked Carnarvon to make good
his promise that his Natal assignment would not last longer than
six months. As to a successor, Wolseley apprised Carnarvon of
the 'admirable qualities' of Colley. The Colonial Office appointed
Sir Henry Bulwer instead; Colley went on to India to join his
regiment.

At a final outgoing stop at Cape Town, Wolseley held long
interviews with Prime Minister John Molteno. So long as this
man was at the head of the Government, Wolseley advised,
federation with Cape Colony was impossible. But once the
Colonial Secretary got an idea into his head, he obstinately refused to abandon it. At the end of October 1875 he blithely
announced that public discussion on federation had accomplished
all that a proposed conference of States in South Africa could
have done, and that the next step would be a conference in
London. Carnarvon's plans were introduced into the Queen's
Speech at the opening of Parliament. In an address at the Lord
Mayor's banquet at Guildhall in November, Disraeli spoke
glowingly of 'every prospect of success' in establishing a South
African federation.

The South African Conference that assembled in London in
August 1876 was a fraud. It was a Downing Street affair dictated
by Carnarvon which subverted the broadly representative government that confederation was claimed to promote. The only
politically independent members were President Johannes Brand

of the Free State and the Colonial Secretary himself. Brand, born
a British subject and son of the Speaker of the Cape Assembly,
and, moreover, married to an Englishwoman, was animated by
the warmest feelings towards Britain. But the President of the
so-called 'model Republic' was in London to settle the injustice
of the Keate Award, and in obedience to his own Volksraad
threatened to withdraw if the subject of federation arose. Shortly
after his arrival, he was flabbergasted when the Colonial Secretary unfolded a pocket-map of South Africa and politely asked him
to point out the exact location of the Free State.* Molteno, the
absent Hamlet of the conference, as the *Standard* dubbed him,
did not even have the authority to attend. To the more prosperous Cape Colony, union with the other states spelled economic
catastrophe, especially with war and rebellion threatening. The
Transvaal refused to send a representative. Burgers was sympathetic, but the Transvaalers anticipated the loss of individual
independence and increased taxes. In the absence of any special
delegate from Griqualand West, Carnarvon designated Froude
to represent the colony, but as soon as that community learned
of his selection, they repudiated the well-meaning mischief-
maker. The large Natal delegation was an anomaly. Messrs John
Akerman and John Robinson of the Natal Legislation Council
had no formal position and attended to make a show. Shepstone
was more or less a representative of the Colonial Office. A dis-
gruntled Wolseley, who had hoped to be rewarded with command in a 'little war' in Burma, served as Vice-President. He
privately predicted a fiasco.

At the opening session, Carnarvon ostentatiously announced
that Shepstone had been granted a K.C.M.G. for his faithful
services. This was done at the suggestion of Wolseley, who
thought that by parading Sir Theophilus before the delegates
they would provide an example of how colonial statesmen were
rewarded for their co-operation. The conference met seven times
and adopted nine resolutions dealing with native affairs; these
resolutions were never carried out. Confederation, Carnarvon's
chief aim, was not even discussed. The best that could be said of

---

* Lack of geographical knowledge was not unknown among officials at the
Colonial Office. When at a banquet Sir John Pakingston was asked by a lady to state
the position of the Virgin Islands, he answered, 'As far as possible, dear lady, from
the Isle of Man.'

the conference was that it brought together for the first time a number of prominent persons to discuss the mounting danger of South Africa's problems. Nevertheless, the Colonial Secretary called it a success. Parliament obligingly passed a permissive Act; but there was no response from South Africa.

After Carnarvon's feeble, almost pathetic attempt to gain the backing of the conference delegates, he responded more readily to the suggestion of coercive methods advocated by his chief adviser, Wolseley. Suffering acutely from federation fever, 'Twitters' listened to the imperious general as a patient does to his physician. The cure that Wolseley prescribed was the annexation of the Transvaal, by force if necessary. Together with diamond-rich Griqualand and Natal, with its great port of Durban, it could be moulded into a federation that would in time absorb the intractable Free State and the refractory Cape Colony. Annexation would immediately obviate the Delagoa Bay difficulty and eliminate the danger of foreign intervention. (Germany, where the demand for colonies was rising, was feared most.) Robert Herbert, described as 'the first expansionist Under-Secretary', wholeheartedly endorsed this strong remedy to his cousin Carnarvon, with whom he enjoyed a close personal relationship.

Events in the Transvaal played into Carnarvon's hands. When the visionary Burgers returned from Europe after securing a loan of £90,000 from Dutch bankers at usurious rates, he found that conditions had greatly deteriorated. The railway plant he had purchased in Belgium was seized for freight on its arrival at Lourenço Marques, where it was left to rust while narrowly pious Boers inveighed against it as ungodly; if the good Lord had wanted railways, some declared, He would have created them. Moreover, much of the territory to be traversed by the projected railway line was seized and held by the wily old chief Sekukuni and his Bapedi warriors.

War was declared on Sekukuni in June 1876. The forces of the young Republic, supported by Bapedi-hating Swazis, were captained by the inexperienced President himself. Burgers had invited Kruger, the nation's leading campaigner, to join him, but Kruger refused on religious grounds, saying, 'With your merry evenings in laager and your Sunday dances, the enemy will shoot me even behind a wall; for God's blessing will not rest on our expedition.' The commando was ignominiously defeated before Sekukuni's mountain stronghold. Burgers tearfully tried to rally his men, even begging them to shoot him rather than disgrace him. The Boers shrugged their shoulders and went home. It was one thing to fight in defence of their homes, but quite another to risk their necks fighting for the Government, especially one headed by a godless President. Kruger's presentiments were psychologically disturbing.

To contain the marauding Bapedi, Burgers constructed a chain of forts and manned them with a band of mercenaries from the gold-fields commanded by a Prussian adventurer, Captain von Schlickmann, who had been driven into exile by a tragic love affair. Such measures were costly. Burgers was forced to levy a special war tax to pay for the defence of his feeble country. Many a burgher, however, ignored the tax and stolidly retreated to self-rule. The Volksraad refused to co-operate; instead they debated such matters as adding a gnu to the arms of the Republic. The *Illustrated London News* at the time gleefully printed a sketch of the dilapidated thatched structure where the legislators met which included several donkeys grazing just outside. 'At least in Boerland', ran the caption, 'they keep their asses outside Parliament.' Burgers was not so sure.

The Republic became hopelessly insolvent. It was said that there was barely a 'Scotsman' in the Treasury.* The value of Government pound notes dropped to a shilling, and I.O.U.s circulated freely as currency. Salaries of officials went unpaid or were paid in stamps. Creditors at home and abroad clamoured for payment. The well-intentioned Burgers sacrificed his own personal wealth to lubricate the wheels of state. Kruger (recently elected Vice-President by the Volksraad) and his supporters announced that these misfortunes were an act of God, who was angered by the irreverent behaviour of the President.

As burgher confronted burgher with acrimony, the Bapedi, the Bechuanas, the Swazis and other tribes appeared to be plotting revenge on their old enemy. The gravest threat came from the Zulus, led by the cunning and warlike Cetewayo. He could

---

* A 'Scotsman' was the name given to a two-shilling piece. In the early days, as the story goes, Scottish traders would pass the piece off as a half-crown to unsuspecting blacks and Boers. Actually the Treasury had 12s. 6d. The national debt was £215,000.

mobilize over forty-thousand fighting men, many of whom were celibates yearning to take a wife, a course of action denied the individual warrior until he had washed his assagai in blood. In London, Shepstone convinced Carnarvon that the Zulus were likely to combine with other tribes in blotting out the Republic. Wolseley warned that all South Africa could blaze with a native uprising if a man such as Burgers was allowed to continue his blunderings. Once more he urged annexation in the name of 'progress and prosperity'. Surely 'no shade of political thought', he added, 'would oppose putting and end to such a dangerous condition of affairs.'[10]

The menacing sword of conflict cut both ways. It was said that the European colonists were threatened by rampaging tribesmen, while a large segment of the press printed exaggerated atrocity stories of natives being butchered and enslaved by the Boers and their mercenaries. The Queen, reacting to the Boers in a way that was not uncommon among many of her subjects, exclaimed, 'The Boers are a horrid people, cruel and over-bearing.' Wolseley advised Shepstone that 'public opinion in England will always back a policy that is "evidently intended" to defend the native against European aggressors.'[11]

Together they assured Carnarvon that the discontented Boers themselves would welcome annexation in preference to chaos. Carnarvon had another attack of fidgets—and then decided to annex. Disraeli, who was more concerned with the growing crisis in the Near East, gave his consent. On the eve of annexation, the wily Prime Minister told Lady Bradford that he chose his henchman from among those who were 'not too scrupulous'. Three years later, Carnarvon swore to the House of Lords that 'in annexing the Transvaal the question of Confederation never entered my head.'

Who would administer the *coup de grâce* to the unstable Republic? Robert Herbert suggested Wolseley to Carnarvon, but it soon became obvious that the general wanted no part of the South African assignment. Moreover, the Colonial Secretary was a little timid about sending anyone whose methods might prove too forceful. Shepstone suggested Sir Henry Bulwer, but in a roundabout way Wolseley eliminated him by telling Carnarvon that the Governor of Natal was 'fanatically just' and had a far abler brother in the War Office. Instead, Wolseley recommended Shepstone as the best candidate. Shepstone was given the assignment the next day.

Sir Theophilus, though on his honeymoon and suffering from a sore throat, left immediately, carrying little more than his commission and a photograph of Carnarvon and another of his bride. The commission, giving him the dignified title of Her Britannic Majesty's Special Commissioner to the South African Republic, instructed him to annex the Transvaal if he found that 'the inhabitants of such territory or portion thereof, or a sufficient number of them ... desire to become British subjects'. But Shepstone's secret verbal orders were to annex the Republic in any case.

To ensure Shepstone's success, efforts were made to isolate the Republic financially. Cape bankers were asked not to offer credit, and Carnarvon put pressure on Brand not to lend money from the Free State. By withholding clothes from the Transvaal, remarked one observer, the Republic could be arrested for being indecent.[12] To weaken the Transvaalers further, an embargo was placed on ammunition that had been purchased abroad by the Republic.

Shortly after Shepstone made his hasty departure, a strong battalion was sent out, ostensibly to relieve the 32nd Regiment, but actually—in the words of Carnarvon—'to be available for all purposes'. The seven companies were soon increased to seven battalions. Shepstone was delayed by the wreck of his mail steamer outside Cape Town; then the transport, as he jokingly wrote to Wolseley, followed his example by getting wrecked itself.

The nature of this man Shepstone is still a subject of controversy. Son of a missionary, reared an Afrikaner, he created an aura of mystery by being wholly self-contained and undemonstrative, never saying a word or using a gesture that was unnecessary. His writings are curiously vague and scant. Shepstone's detractors describe him as arrogant, hypocritical, ambitious and priggish, with little regard for either the Boer or the Bantu whom he was reputed to know so intimately. For over thirty years he was the virtual dictator over Natal's natives, placing them in semi-autonomous reservations where their customs were preserved but where they could not vote, despite the demands of the humanitarians who insisted that the native should be made as much like the white man as possible. His influence over the Zulus was enormous, for he had personally placed the crown on Cetewayo's head and administered the coronation oath. Cetewayo and the natives revered him as 'Somtseu' ('mighty hunter'). The Boers gave him the less complimentary nickname of 'Slypsteen' ('whetstone'), but found it hard to resist his friendly manner and courteous speech, which was delivered in perfect Taal.* There is no evidence that he was unsympathetic in his dealings with burghers or blacks, but it is clear that his allegiance, as a loyal citizen of Natal, was to Britain and the Empire.

Shepstone was not a man of action. Once in South Africa, his predilection for caution and deliberation took hold of him. He seemed content to 'wait for the pear to ripen itself and fall into his mouth'. Wolseley, who was in constant communication with him, urged speed. Carnarvon grew impatient. The time for harvest was growing late, for it was reported that the Sekukuni War, which provided much of the necessary justification for the take-over, was languishing. Wolseley began to entertain the fear that Burgers might be too formidable a foe. Knowing that the President was chronically ill, he hoped that the excitement and overwork brought on by the present crisis would give Burgers a personal opportunity to test his theory as to whether the Devil had a tail or not! (Carnarvon had already wished for Burgers's death two years before.)

While the dilatory Special Commissioner remained poised on the Republic's frontier, Wolseley—who was said to have an almost hypnotic influence over Shepstone—offered sound and sometimes Machiavellian advice. He suggested that Shepstone take a regiment and march on Pretoria, and make it appear that he was there 'for the purpose of securing life and property from Kaffir attacks'. But he cautioned against entering the Transvaal as a conqueror; such a move might 'prove far too drastic for

* The Bible and official business were written in Dutch, but the Boers spoke the beloved patois called Taal (i.e., 'the language') or Afrikaans. Limited education, amalgamations with foreign elements and adaptations derived from speaking to native servants produced a simple and quaint dialect with eroded grammatical forms. Folksy and whimsical, it easily lent itself to humour. Olive Schreiner relates the story of two South Africans whose laughter disturbed their fellow lodgers in an Edinburgh boarding-house. On inquiry, the landlady discovered that they were amusing themselves by translating the book of Job into Taal.[13]

John Bull's stomach'. If the Boers rejected federation, Shepstone's knightly mentor advised exploiting their fear of the Zulus
whose fingers fidgeted on their spears. 'Were I in your place,'
Sir Garnet slyly suggested, 'I would use Cetewayo as a powerful lever to influence wavering spirits.'[14] Assured of Britain's
neutrality, Cetewayo would willingly have gone to war with the
Boers.

The general tried to teach Shepstone the game of divide and
rule, and how to place his troops on the frontiers so as to carry
out a policy pursued by the British in India 'and which is still
followed by all Russian Generals in Central Asia'. And remember, Wolseley told his friend, that you can count on the support
of the English press 'and with that mighty power behind you,
what is there within the range of human possibility that you
cannot accomplish?'[15]

After a ten-week delay, Shepstone, accompanied by a staff
consisting largely of friends and relatives, and escorted by
twenty-five mounted police, ambled towards Pretoria. He carried
Wolseley's invigorating letters in his pocket and his bold ideas
in his head. Taking his cue from Wolseley's success in Natal, he
also took with him a large supply of bottled persuasion. Journeying for thirty-five days over rough roads, he stopped at every
shop and farmhouse to chat. These were friendly meetings with
much hand-shaking and drinking with people who had not the
slightest notion of his true mission. In Pretoria he was greeted
with cheers and volleys. His animals were unhitched and a human team drew his carriage through streets gaily festooned with
flags. A camp was pitched in the Market Square. Shepstone,
whose face was normally passive, beamed as the Union Jack was
raised. There was singing and more cheering—mainly in English, for there were 'scarcely five Boers present'. Burgers welcomed Shepstone as a 'friendly adviser'. Champagne and sherry
diplomacy followed, with the Special Commissioner attending
fifty-nine social functions in a little over two months. Between
the popping of corks, 'Slypsteen' distributed trinkets among the
children. (The British Government later refused to compensate
Shepstone for 'unauthorized expenditures for which no vouchers
have been produced'.)

The reason for Shepstone's visit was soon made clear to the
not unsuspecting President. The Special Commissioner told

Burgers he would stay his hand only if he would introduce re-
forms. Lacking any popular support and thwarted by an unruly
Volksraad, there was nothing the President could do—and
Shepstone knew it. Some Boer leaders actually intrigued against
Burgers, hoping to find themselves a place under British rule.
Kruger, the real strong man of the Republic, remained aloof.
Burgers was allowed to make a face-saving protest against
annexation. There was no resistance when the Union Jack was
raised on April 12th, 1877. The young man who performed the
deed was Rider Haggard, Shepstone's secretary, later to gain
greater fame as a writer with such novels as *She* and *King
Solomon's Mines*. The sole casualty in Shepstone's bloodless campaign was Burgers, who came down with an acute attack of
gout from all the wining and dining. Shepstone sent a message
to Carnarvon in which he declared, 'Great majority of Boers
welcome change.'

Shepstone became the idol of the Empire. Notes of congratula-
tion poured in to Pretoria. Wolseley, who experienced a secret
feeling of satisfaction in witnessing the fulfilment of plans he had
helped to formulate, sent a long, complimentary letter to Shepstone. 'What a General you would have made,' he concluded.
The English press gave the event much attention, though copy
had to be squeezed in between the Russo–Turkish War and
Schliemann's latest discoveries at Mycenae. They jubilantly described how barbarism had been vanquished and a new, though
admittedly unpolished jewel had been added to the Crown. The
World proposed that Sir Theophilus be appointed Secretary of
State for Foreign Affairs. The *Graphic* 'immortalized' Shepstone
by publishing his likeness. The *Saturday Review* was almost alone
in describing the annexation as 'an inopportune and untoward
event'. (Gladstone agreed by predicting that this act would 'involve us in unmixed mischief'.) The foreign press took little
notice, but *Kladderadatsch*, the Berlin comic weekly, observed
that Britain had pocketed the Transvaal while the rest of Europe
was absorbed with the Turkish question.

Except for Piet Joubert, who had resigned his office, virtually
all the old officials were kept on, including Kruger. Burgers, the
unpractical President who looked forward to the millennium,
retired under protest to the Cape with his wife and four children,
and continued to write books. The British gave him a pension—

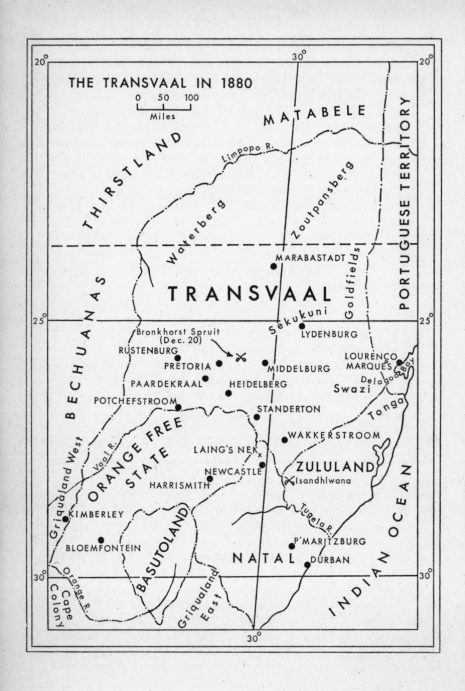

THE TRANSVAAL IN 1880

0   50   100
Miles

THIRSTLAND

MATABELE

PORTUGUESE TERRITORY

Limpopo R.

Waterberg

Zoutpansberg

MARABASTADT

Goldfields

BECHUANAS

TRANSVAAL

Sekukuni

LYDENBURG

Bronkhorst Spruit
(Dec. 20)

RUSTENBURG

PRETORIA

MIDDELBURG

LOURENÇO
MARQUES

PAARDEKRAAL

HEIDELBERG

Delagoa Bay

Swazi

POTCHEFSTROOM

STANDERTON

Tonga

Vaal R.

ORANGE FREE STATE

WAKKERSTROOM

LAING'S NEK

ZULULAND

NEWCASTLE

HARRISMITH

Isandhlwana

INDIAN OCEAN

KIMBERLEY

Griqualand West

BASUTOLAND

Tugela R.

BLOEMFONTEIN

P'MARITZBURG

NATAL

DURBAN

Orange R.

Cape Colony

Griqualand East

others called it 'hush money'—on condition that he never returned to the Transvaal. A bitter and grief-stricken Burgers
paused at the Orange River on his journey south. It was the eve
of Queen Victoria's birthday (May 24th), the day before the
official proclamation of annexation was read. Burgers angrily
registered his protest by inserting into a bottle a piece of paper
bearing the words 'God damn the Queen'. He corked it and cast
it into the river, shouting, 'Let it journey the universe!'[16] He
spent much of the remainder of his life in bed. His last wish before he died on December 9th, 1881, was that he should be buried
in front of a sheep kraal, where all trace of his remains would be
trampled into oblivion.

⌜2⌝

RETENTION

Wherever we go, you English always follow us.

Piet Joubert

To JUSTIFY the annexation, Blue Books documented the misconduct of the Boers towards the natives. It was a shocking catalogue of wanton cruelty, slavery, and traffic in 'black ivory'. No less a person than Burgers himself, who had actually struggled to improve the lot of the native, was said to be a slave-dealer. The Government accepted as evidence anonymously written items in anti-Boer journals and material contributed by the Aborigines Protection Society, whose officers were often anxious to justify their employment. The Society refused to reveal the names of its informants, understandably so, for it was later discovered that among them was an unfrocked clergyman being held for swindling; another was a trader imprisoned for gun-running.

An opportunity to substantiate these charges was provided when the British took over the Transvaal. But to the great disappointment of the philanthropists, no slavers or slaves were found, despite the offer of ten pounds by the Anti-Slavery Society as reward to anyone who could produce evidence that a single slave had been liberated as a result of annexation.[1] It was then claimed that an 'apprentice system', which largely involved destitute or deserted children, was virtually slavery in disguise. But under Shepstone the 'vicious' system was not abolished; instead eight hundred more were apprenticed to Europeans in less than two years. As to the charge of maltreatment, there is no gainsaying the fact that these uncompromising Calvinists regarded the dark races as condemned by God to perpetual servitude, and that certain Boers were rigidly harsh in their dealings with them. It is possible, however, that Boer brutality was considerably exaggerated. In their defence, Bishop Colenso, the most dedicated of missionaries, pointed out the simple fact that 800,000 natives lived under the Transvaal Boers without fleeing to Natal. 'To all appearance,' he concluded, 'they even prefer the Boer rule to our own.'[2] Two weeks after annexation, Chief Magato contributed £60 to defray expenses for a deputation to protest against Shepstone's high-handed act. The Boers not only repudiated the allegations of slavery, they retaliated by claiming that it was they who were being enslaved by the British.

True justification for the annexation lay in the fulfilment of Shepstone's proclamation promises: a substantial measure of representative institutions supported by a generous financial settlement. But contrary to Boer expectations the Volksraad was never convened, nor were fresh elections held. Instead, Shepstone became an autocrat. Redcoats were brought across the brown veld and a special native police force was raised to maintain order. The administration carried on with no allowances made for the Boer character and prejudices.

After his cleverly engineered coup, the Special Commissioner was strangely inept. He sat tight and said nothing, proudly claiming that 'silence is golden'. He appointed friends and favourites who often proved irresponsible, swaggering about the land demanding strict obedience to the law from burghers they regarded with contempt. Much of his time was spent labouring for signatures to petitions requesting federation, though he confided to Herbert that many of the ignorant farmers did not understand what federation meant. Cecil Rhodes later ascribed subsequent troubles in the Transvaal to the 'shocking misgovernment by the Imperial Commissioner who conducted business on lines of a second-rate line regiment'.

Once the bankrupt Republic was added to the Empire, a parsimonious British Government resolved to run it on the cheap. A niggardly £100,000 was allotted to Shepstone. Even then, what funds the out-at-elbows colony possessed were so badly managed that the Colonial Office found it necessary to send out a financial officer to assist. (The few pennies Rider Haggard found in the Treasury at the time of annexation disappeared shortly afterwards.)

When the unpopular war tax was repealed, it was replaced by a native hut-tax, which averaged £1 a year for each adult male.

A special advantage was claimed for this act, in that it provided an incentive for the natives to work. In practice, it meant that the native women were worked harder while their men continued to idle. There were no complaints from the humanitarians.

The debt, nevertheless, continued to mount under a costly military occupation and the creation of sinecures enjoyed by Shepstone's friends, though old Boer officials were denied their back pay.

The British hoped for a great increase in gold production. Prior to annexation, Shepstone told Carnarvon that the mineral wealth of the Transvaal could 'scarcely be overstated'. But for those motivated by cupidity there was only frustration. The great gold strikes were another decade in coming. What little gold was found provided limited profits because of transportation costs and primitive mining methods.

Pretoria itself enjoyed prosperity. The I.O.U.s which circulated freely before, even to the point of finding their way into the church collection box, were replaced by coin and currency introduced by soldiers, speculators and place-hunters. The annexation was virtually an expansion of Natal as hundreds followed Shepstone, the colony's greatest son, over the border to the Transvaal. Many found lucrative posts as 'carpet-bag' administrators and 'were decorated for their services—to themselves!'[3] Others, including Shepstone's son-in-law, speculated profitably in land and in a proposed railway to Durban. New places of business were established, and the only saloon, 'The Transvaal Bar' (formerly called 'The Hole in the Wall'), soon had competitors.

Basking in the popularity of fellow Englishmen, Shepstone presided over all with the same bland, pompous dignity he had employed so successfully as Native Commissioner. He continued to dispense trinkets and sweets to children, and occasionally saddles to young men. The Special Commissioner and his personable Chief of Staff, Colonel Brooke, were in great demand as godfathers. To accommodate the female sex, the infants were baptized with the less than euphonious combination, 'Theophila Brookiana'.

Distinguished visitors from England (such as the novelist, Anthony Trollope, who had a new drink named in his honour) were impressed by the capital of Britain's most recent and lusty progeny. They reported flourishing commerce by day and a rapid rotation of balls and other gaieties at night, with handsome young officers in scarlet coats the leading attractions.

It was far easier to anglicize the towns, where the annexations were concentrated, than the country. *De Volksstem*, Pretoria's leading journal, counted only a handful of farmers at Shepstone's reception. When the Union Jack was hoisted, one backveld Boer was heard to mutter, 'O Father and Grandfather and Great-grandfather, rise from the dead and drive away these wretches who have come to take our land from us.'[4] Later, Paul Kruger's fiery brother Tjaardt offered to fight a duel with 'Slypsteen'. If he won, the country would be restored to the Boers. Shepstone merely laughed.

The vast majority of burghers remained apathetically acquiescent. They were a patient folk, children in the art of government. But as Shepstone's guarantees failed to materialize, suspicion deepened. As was their custom, the burghers talked a great deal, argued and drew up petitions. The Boers had an extraordinary fondness for petitions, which they circulated and debated before sending them on to the capital. They were ignored. When an Englishman explained to a protesting Boer that the might of Britain was so great that the sun never set on her vast Empire, the simple farmer replied, 'It shows that God Almighty cannot trust you rascals in the dark.'

As feelings of injustice mounted, Paul Kruger came to the fore. He was pre-eminently a Boer among Boers, whom some called 'the Colossus'. As his role as patriarch became manifest, he was referred to affectionately and respectfully as 'Oom Paul' ('Uncle Paul'). (Deference to age and experience was traditional among the Boers.) None could match the richness of his deeds, already legendary, which contributed to the most vital chapters of his people's history. Of direct German descent, a racial ingredient not too far behind French among the Boers, he was ten when the Kruger wagon joined the Great Trek. He began fighting the tribesmen when only thirteen, and fought in almost every subsequent native war and civil war, rising to the rank of Commandant-General of the Republic. Kruger's decision to play prophet rather than soldier in the disastrous Sekukuni War strengthened his image as God's chosen leader among his co-religionists. Occasionally, like a Mosaic intercessionary, he vanished into the veld for long periods to commune with God, subsisting on insects and bark. Some of his followers were said to believe that he was bullet-proof.

Other tales of his great strength and daring on the veld pressed the bounds of credulity. Beginning at the tender age of fourteen, young Kruger killed more lions than any other man in his community; unarmed, he was credited with outdistancing a pursuing lion. As a runner he had no peers. During a long-distance match with native champions, Kruger found time to stop for coffee and shoot a lion, and still win the race. He was able to long-jump twenty-three feet, wrestle buffalo to the ground rodeo-style, and ride a horse like a Cossack, shooting game with deadly accuracy whether sitting backwards or forwards. While hunting a rhino, his gun exploded, severely injuring his thumb. With a hunting knife he calmly amputated part of it to lessen the danger of infection.

Tough and fearless, resourceful and shrewd, Kruger carried these veld-sharpened traits into politics. Bismarck saw in him the greatest natural-born statesman of his time; Gladstone, who had the opportunity to test his skill, declared him the most astute politician in all of Africa; Disraeli, annoyed by his uncompromising determination, called him 'an ugly customer'.

Kruger was all the more remarkable because he was an anachronism. Essentially a man of the seventeenth century, he had no formal or modern education to confuse his preconceptions. He learned to read one book, the Bible, which he committed to memory. His was a primeval mind of natural wisdom and narrow prejudice, supported by a belief in Divine Guidance. His single-minded tenacity in argument was attested by General Nicholas Smit. When Joubert asked Smit to join him against Kruger, Smit answered, 'Old friend, it is like this, I *do* stand against him. I know he is wrong and I tell him so. But first he argues with me and, if that is no good, he goes into a rage and jumps about the room, roaring at me like a wild beast, and I cannot hear myself talk. And, if I do not give in, then he fetches out the Bible and— ach de liebe Gott!—he even quotes that to help him out. And if that fails, he takes my hand, cries like a child and begs and prays me to give in. Say, old friend, who can resist a man like that?'[5]

The Boer leader shared his people's mistrust for the English. He branded the annexation as 'an entirely iniquitous act' which

violated the Sand River Convention in which the English had
promised, in his presence, never to encroach upon the land north
of the Vaal. Once more the Egyptians had taken his people captive. Strangers were pouring into the Promised Land: unscrupulous traders who would sell knives and forks to cannibals, publicans and gamblers, the like of whom, in the words of Major
Butler, made Kimberley look like Monte Carlo on top of Sodom
and Gomorrah. In that ungodly city, Kruger heard, prostitutes
conducted public auctions in which they offered their services to
the highest bidder. (One bidder paid £25 and three cases of
champagne.) There were soldiers of Pharaoh who amazed the
Boers by marching out of Pretoria and firing on a herd of game
with cannon! The Boers complained that as a result the buck
deserted the high veld completely.

To test the stock expression 'British fair play', Kruger decided to go to London to plead the case for Boer independence.
Shepstone found it difficult to take Kruger seriously until he
eventually succeeded in borrowing enough travel money for
himself and his party. When Kruger left on May 10th, less than
a month after the take-over, Shepstone sent a letter to Carnarvon
suggesting that the 'Protest Committee' could easily be reconciled to annexation because Kruger was merely disappointed by
his failure to succeed Burgers as President. (An election was to
have taken place in May.) On the grounds that Kruger continued
in office after annexation, Shepstone hinted that he could be
bought off. To Kruger, however, the Republic had never ceased
to exist; it was temporarily in abeyance.

In the company of Kruger were Dr Edward Jorissen and Dr
William Bok, educated young Hollanders whom Burgers had
brought to South Africa to assist in governing his less sophisticated people. The Boers, including Kruger, had little use for the
superfine, smooth-talking, black-coated imports, but they toler-
ated them for their zeal and talents. Jorissen had a reputation as a
'man of epigrams'. At one of Shepstone's balls given on the eve
of his coup, he quipped to Colonel Brooke, 'We are dancing on
the grave of the Republic—but then we all believe in the glorious
resurrection.'

As a traveller, Kruger appeared comically grotesque in the
company of the stylish, spare and intellectual-looking Hollanders. He was a big, barrel-like man, with shoulders broad and

bowed, and one leg and one thumb shorter than the other. He was dressed in the country costume of a Dopper: a broad felt hat, short jacket, wide and flapping moleskin pantaloons, and shoes of untanned leather. The face was no less startling, with baggy, hooded, cunning eyes, a large mouth and a prominent nose. His wide nostrils, big ears and low, heavy brows gave him somewhat the look of a gorilla. The effect was heightened when he grew a fringe-line, off-the-face beard which extended from ear to ear. Misled by appearances, the polished and urbane gentlemen he met in England probably felt inclined to crown him with a dunce's cap.

To properly impress the rustic malcontent, the English took Kruger on a tour which consisted largely of viewing military establishments. Interviews followed with an affable and condescending Carnarvon, whom Jorissen described as a 'conceited aristocrat'. As 'guests from Africa' in Carnarvon's palatial residence, they were served with his home-brewed beer. As he sipped, the Colonial Secretary insisted that it was 'altogether impossible' to reverse the annexation. After all, he pointed out, it was the great wish of the majority of Transvaalers. However, the Colonial Secretary sent the delegates away with a promise of self-government 'as soon as practicable' within the confederation.

Returning home at the end of the year, dressed in ill-fitting ready-made clothes and a stove-pipe silk hat (paid for by the British Government), Kruger found Shepstone travelling about to receive addresses staged by his agents to demonstrate the popularity of British rule. This artificial display of support provoked hostile agitation on the part of the burghers, who were now further disappointed by Kruger's failure in London to undo what they called 'an act of violence'. Independence committees were formed throughout the land. When a group gathered in Pretoria to sign a petition, Shepstone had cannons menacingly pointed at them. They ignored the guns. Then, claiming that the signatures were obtained by intimidation, Shepstone issued a proclamation threatening condign punishment to the promoters. He made matters worse by doing nothing more than fume as 6,591 signatures opposing annexation—out of some 8,000 voters in the country—were collected. Those backing the Act obtained only 587, though 3,000 were supposed to have petitioned for annexation before the event.

Early in April 1878 a combined meeting of protesters was held, and after three days of deliberation the decision was made to send a second deputation, which included Kruger, Joubert and Bok. When Kruger declared his intention to continue the struggle should this mission fail, an angry Shepstone dismissed him from office. Shepstone also deprived Jorissen of his office. Compensation was offered to him but he refused it. He hoped to join the second deputation, but the burghers preferred to rely on one of their own kind and replaced him with the popular Joubert.

Piet Joubert's background was similar to that of Kruger. His family, of French Huguenot blood, joined the Great Trek when he was six, and settled in Natal. Ten years later, he fled with his destitute and widowed mother to the Transvaal. Because of a disputed boundary settlement that favoured Natal, Joubert trekked again as a young man to a farm in the Wakkerstroom district. Small wonder that after the annexation he angrily declared, 'Wherever we go, you English always follow us.'

Hard-working and largely self-educated, especially in law, Joubert prospered. Surpassing fellow Boers in education and oratory, he rose in prominence as a politician and soldier, a combination not uncommon among their leaders. As Chairman of the Volksraad in 1873 and Acting President during Burgers' European visit, Joubert developed a thirst for political prominence. Upon Burgers' return he was no longer content to be merely a member of the Volksraad and he resigned all his political and military posts. Patriotism and ambition brought Joubert out of retirement only when the British annexed his country.

Although they recognized a common enemy, Joubert and Kruger were often antagonistic. More tolerant of new ideas and uitlanders, Joubert became a leader of the smaller and more progressive faction. 'Slim' Piet, as he had been called since youth, had a reputation for cant that proved to be a weakness as well as an advantage. He tried to remain on good terms with everybody, and in the end displeased his supporters and opponents alike. While Kruger remained steadfast, Joubert would vacillate. Nevertheless, he was respected for his generosity and kindness, his love of peace and country.

Joubert's features were well known. A propensity for being photographed soon made him the most easily recognized person

in South Africa. He was a better-looking man than Kruger, with
a high forehead, a well-shaped nose and bright, alert eyes. His
hair was long and he had a black moustache and a grizzled
beard. Square-shouldered and strong, he appeared dignified and
composed, but was actually excitable and quick-tempered.

As Boer discontent mounted, the chances for federation grew
slim. Shepstone had plucked a prickly pear. The disenchanted
Carnarvon could not be persuaded to create an independent legislature which would in all likelihood become, like the Cape Parliament, obstructive to Imperial policies. The Free State was more
resistant to federation than ever, and their Volksraad formally
expressed the hope that Kruger and his party would succeed in
their mission. Irked by Carnarvon's clumsy tactics, Disraeli
told Lady Bradford that 'every day brings forward new blunders by Twitters.' Carnarvon, in turn, was disturbed by the
Prime Minister's Eastern policy. When Disraeli sent the British
fleet to the Bosphorus in January 1878, Carnarvon resigned to
sulk in political exile. At the bottom of this abrupt decision was
discouragement over the failure of his South African policy. In a
ministerial reshuffle, Sir Michael Hicks Beach was given the
Colonial Office.

Hard, dour and tart-tongued, Hicks Beach was commonly
called 'Black Michael'. One colleague held that he 'habitually
thinks angrily'. When a Liberal annoyed him during a debate in
the Commons, Hicks Beach instructed his secretary, 'Go and tell
him he is a pig.'

The new Colonial Secretary did not share Carnarvon's interest in South Africa and certainly had little enthusiasm for federation. A loyal 'Disraelite', Hicks Beach regarded his office as a
sinecure which would allow him time to devote himself to party
politics and his Gloucestershire estates.* Vexed by the increasing
demands the office made upon him, Hicks Beach often behaved
peevishly. For his education in department affairs he relied on
Robert Herbert, who bemoaned the fact that the office was no
longer 'a happy family'. The latter told him that the Boer leaders he was about to receive were 'bitterly anti-English' and could

---

* In those pre-Chamberlain days, the Colonial Office was still very much a
third-rate department with more than its share of time-servers and eccentrics. One
top official, on discovering that his mind functioned more efficiently on horseback,
had a saddle installed in his office to improve his thinking.

not be civilized; Kruger in particular was 'weak and cowardly like a true Boer'.[6]

Armed with its petitions, the Boer delegation was greeted coldly by the tall, austere, well-dressed Colonial Secretary. The petitions were quickly rejected and all hope for the revocation of Shepstone's act discouraged. Privately, however, Hicks Beach wrote to Shepstone advising the desirability of granting 'a sort of self-government'. But rather than liberalize his regime, Shepstone still sought to popularize British rule with arbitrary administrative acts. He told Hicks Beach that it was Kruger's intransigence and ambition that was at the bottom of his troubles. A year later, when Hicks Beach was out of office, he wisely observed, 'Improving people against their will seldom succeeds in anything but exciting ill-will and obstruction to reform.'[7]

While Sir Michael busied himself with 'more important' matters, the Boer leaders were treated to the usual routine of tours and receptions. They found little public interest in the Transvaal, but some Liberals, sensing an opportunity to fashion new political missiles, expressed sympathy for the Boer mission. It was not difficult for the Boers to discern that mounting Irish and Imperial troubles could bring down the English Conservatives and reverse their policies. Kruger advised his followers at home to 'sit tight'. During his visit, Kruger received from an English admirer a gold ring with the inscription: 'Take courage, your cause is just and must triumph in the end.'

Returning to South Africa, Kruger and Joubert met three-thousand burghers at Wonderfontein on January 10th, 1879. After four days of discussion in which many expressed the desire to shoot the British, the moderates won the day. Kruger, supported by Joubert, persuaded the burghers that there was still hope of regaining their freedom by peaceful means. Joubert was sent off to the Cape to plead the cause of independence with Sir Bartle Frere, the new British High Commissioner for South Africa.

It was apparent that the intractable Shepstone's personal rule had failed. Financial difficulties, complicated by costly efforts to contain Sekukuni and the antagonism which he inspired among the Boers, led to an order that Shepstone should travel to London for consultation at the end of January. Shepstone's leave of absence proved to be his recall and he returned to Natal as a private citizen. Though another Imperial administrator, William Owen Lanyon, would soon replace him, Transvaal affairs were placed more directly under the supervision of Sir Bartle Frere.

Frere was the great pro-consul of his day. His experience as an administrator was rich and varied. In India, where he attained the post of Governor of Bombay, his work was described as brilliant. An aggressive, cool-headed imperialist, Sir Bartle combined a powerful intellect with a persuasive personality which he used to charm a wide circle of friends, among them Queen Victoria and the Prince of Wales.

Among South Africans, however, little enthusiasm was exhibited when his appointment was announced. It was felt that though the High Commissioner was an expert on Indian affairs, he had a lot to learn about Africa. A popular story that circulated at the time of his arrival told how he and his son had got lost while hunting in the forests of Zanzibar several years before. After roaming about for hours, they came upon a native hut and claimed the occupant's hospitality. As the woman of the house began to prepare an omelette for the starving men, Sir Bartle spotted some 'mushrooms' which he promptly tossed into the pan before the protesting woman could stop him. When the husband arrived home some time later, he was furious and denounced the white men for having eaten his prize trophies—the ears he had lopped off his vanquished enemies!

Arriving in Cape Town a few days before annexation, Frere was astonished by the coup. 'Good heavens!' he exclaimed, 'what will they say in England?' He was quick to recognize that the move would be inimical to federation, and that the initial mistake was compounded by Shepstone's failure to 'substitute a better system'. When Shepstone refused to heed his advice to engage competent officials and consult with Boer leaders on the promised liberal constitution, Frere warned him that Kruger was a leader of 'considerable ability and shrewdness under his somewhat clownish appearance'. A man of great personal integrity himself, Frere saw the Transvaal Commissioner as 'a singular type of Afrikander Talleyrand ... skilful in that sort of diplomacy which defers decisions and evades difficulties by postponing action'.

Frere's policy was dynamic and decisive. At the time of the Wonderfontein meeting, he told the Boers that annexation was

irrevocable, but he held out the promise of redeeming the pledges
that Britain had made.

From the very outset, Frere shared Wolseley's view that the
native problem must be settled first. Predisposed by training and
temperament to a forward policy, the High Commissioner suppressed the traffic of alcohol and arms, disarmed entire tribes,
and proclaimed protectorates. Native risings and border brawls
were frequent but suppressed with no great effort. South Africa
was introduced to what he described as the Indian tradition of
firm and just rule in dealing with belligerent races.

The conviction grew in Frere's mind that at the root of native
unrest was the Zulu chief, Cetewayo. His hand was detected in
inciting several chieftains and encouraging the continued rebellion of Sekukuni. Most of the colonists were already 'seeing
black' and feared, along with Frere, the possibility of a general
native uprising. Cetewayo and his 'magnificent animals', Frere
announced, 'were a threat to the peace of South Africa'.

Most nations have an army; the Zulu army had a nation. All
men capable of bearing arms were warriors. Shepstone informed
the High Commissioner that out of an estimated population of
250,000, nearly 50,000 were at that time in the army. Thousands
of women and boys, acting as carriers, provided for their simple
needs in the field.

Good relations with Cetewayo deteriorated quickly after the
English took over the Transvaal. Hitherto the Boers had been
the imaginary enemies against whom the Zulu evolutions and
spear-wavings were directed in their annual military exercises;
the English, at least by comparison, were their friends. On the
eve of annexation, Cetewayo willingly obeyed Shepstone's request to mass his impis on the Transvaal frontier. But once
'Somtseu' established himself in Pretoria, he did a complete
about-face and supported the Boers against the Zulus. For fifteen
years Shepstone and the British Government had backed Zulu
claims to disputed territories on the Transvaal frontier. Now he
told Cetewayo his claim was without foundation. The furious
chief called Shepstone a liar. Steadily Cetewayo's demeanour became more warlike.

The colonists of Natal had a saying: 'If you must live next
door to a tiger, you must draw its teeth.' The High Commissioner
claimed that the Zulu chief had deliberately violated the promise

of good government that he had made to Shepstone at the time of
his coronation. Moreover, he charged the 'demon King' with
exhibiting a barbarian's disregard for human life. When unmarried girls refused to accept as husbands celibate warriors
from two regiments composed of men over forty, they were
massacred.* Sir Bartle related to the Duke of Cambridge how
their corpses were 'placed on the highways by hundreds as a
warning to other disobedient women'. Refugee women were
pursued into Natal and taken back to be executed. White settlers
in the disputed territory were threatened. Missionaries were
compelled to leave Zululand, and their converts were murdered.
Clergymen made no effort to conceal their hope that the 'godless
despot' would be deposed; only Colenso and his few supporters
defended the black king, claiming that he was misunderstood. As
the atrocities continued, remonstrances addressed to Cetewayo
were returned with insolent replies.

Frere always skirmished far ahead of opinion in London, even
more so now that Hicks Beach had replaced Carnarvon. The
Liberal leader, Harcourt, was at his satirical best when he later
read to the House an imaginary letter from Hicks Beach to his
high-handed Commissioner: 'Dear Sir Bartle Frere. I cannot
think you are right. Indeed I think you are very wrong; but after
all I feel you know a great deal better than I do. I hope you won't
do what you are going to do; but, if you do, I hope it will turn
out well.' Only when an Afghan war seemed imminent did the
Colonial Secretary, on November 7th, 1878, insist that a Zulu
war, in addition to other troubles, was out of the question. Too
late! The veto arrived on December 13th, two days after Sir
Bartle had sent an ultimatum to Cetewayo which would expire
in thirty days. (This is another instance in history where direct
telegraphic communications might have averted a war.) Frere
purposely made the ultimatum unacceptable by demanding, among
other things, that the Zulu armies be disbanded, knowing that
the military system was the pride and cohesive element of the
Zulu nation. The ultimatum went unanswered as Cetewayo
mobilized his impis. Frere had his war.

* A Zulu wife was a slave to her husband, treated as chattel or a beast of burden.
The day after she arrived at her husband's hut, she was allowed, even encouraged,
to tax her imagination in calling her new master every vile name she could think of.
Having once delivered her most abusive and provoking insults, the wife was never
again permitted to talk or act independently.

Kruger was asked by Frere to join the invading force as an adviser. The Boer leader answered with a counter-offer: he would conquer the Zulus with five hundred burghers, in exchange for the independence of his country and his people. Many Boers displayed what the English called 'a very disloyal spirit' by hoping for a Zulu victory. Some suggested an alliance with Cetewayo to throw off the British yoke, but to Kruger any support given to savages against civilization was not Christian. A few Boers fought on the side of the British. Formed into a corps of irregulars and guides, they performed gallant service under Colonel Evelyn Wood. The majority, however, remained aloof. Even the generous offer of five shillings a day and rations could not induce them to enlist.

The Zulu War, properly planned, should have been over after thirty minutes of fighting; one crushing blow might have sufficed to destroy Zulu power for ever. Instead, the war dragged on for eight months, owing to the incompetence of the British commander, Lord Chelmsford.

Chelmsford had demonstrated some administrative talent, but until now he had never had an opportunity to show what he could do in the field. As a player of *Kriegspiel* at Aldershot, he had won an enviable reputation; unfortunately Cetewayo and his Zulu warriors, knowing nothing of this sophisticated table-game, did not play according to the rules. Three years before, Wolseley had warned Carnarvon, 'I feel convinced that troops handled according to Regulations can only succeed against a Kaffir enemy after very great losses in money, men and prestige.'

With overweening self-confidence, Chelmsford promenaded through Zululand with 5,000 British troops, 1,200 mounted colonists and large bodies of native allies. He assured Frere that the conquest would be quick and easy. More than once, Chelmsford scorned the advice of Boers to prepare against a surprise attack by forming the wagons into a protective laager. Moreover, he committed the tactical blunder of splitting his force in the face of a resourceful enemy. On the morning of January 22nd, Chelmsford took half of his column (one of three invading columns) out of camp at Isandhlwana to support a reconnoitring party. In his absence, the Zulu generalissimo, employing the strategy of stealth, surprised the camp with a force of some

20,000 men. With ancient weapons—knobkerries and assagais—
the trained impis annihilated a modern British regiment.

What began as a picnic turned into a panic. On his return
Chelmsford left his dead comrades without burial and fled the
grisly scene totally unnerved by his defeat. Natal huddled in
expectant terror behind frantically built barricades. Bishop
Colenso provided no consolation when he declared, 'We richly
deserved it.' Fear spread to the Transvaal. In Pretoria wild rumours prompted a call for volunteers and the construction of a
laager. Tension was relieved by the calm confidence exhibited
and the subsequent news that the Zulus had been checked.

The disaster startled the people of England like a thunderclap. Heated invectives were hurled in the press and Parliament.
How could a savage horde defeat a British force supported by
artillery? Why was Frere allowed to provoke a war? The Cabinet was prepared to submit to popular demand to dismiss Frere,
but Disraeli, influenced by the Queen, who made no secret of her
sympathy for Frere and Chelmsford, forced a compromise. The
High Commissioner was censured for exceeding his instructions;
however, in the same dispatch, he was told of the Government's
confidence in his ability to bring the whole affair to a successful
conclusion.

The Zulus were not the only problem. Frere had assured Hicks
Beach that a show of strength would win strong support for
annexation among the Boers; instead, the Isandhlwana disaster
created a great contempt for the British mode of warfare. With
grim satisfaction, the Boers made capital out of the 'good news'
of Britain's reverses by calling for another mass meeting near
Kleinfontein, thirty miles outside Pretoria, on March 17th. Some
4,000 Boers assembled, though, according to Rider Haggard,
many were coerced into attendance by the threat of being converted into 'biltong'—strips of meat dried in the sun. In the
absence of regulars, loyal Transvaalers raised a corps of the Pretoria Horse as a defence measure, and when armed Boers moved
close to the capital, a cannon was placed in Church Square. One
night the gun was moved by practical jokers who trained it on
Owen Lanyon's residence with a pumpkin over the muzzle.

Frere, who was soothing nerves in Natal, was invited by the
defiant Boers to attend the meeting. Stung by his recent censure
though hardly repentant, the High Commissioner travelled to

Pretoria. Until his arrival on April 12th, Lanyon tried to fend off the protesters with talk of incorporating the Vierkleur into the Union Jack. Frere was astonished by the vehemence of Boer demands for independence, and it took more than a little courage to ride into the sullen malcontents' camp. But the Boers soon reverted to their traditional hospitality by offering him champagne. The High Commissioner quickly warmed to Kruger, though he could not overcome his dislike for Joubert, with whom he had conferred earlier. Meeting in and out of Pretoria over the next few days, the mild-mannered and soft-voiced Frere stated categorically that the annexation must stand. Before the Boers dispersed, Frere did promise to submit their memorial to London. In a covering letter he told the Colonial Secretary that the Boer spokesmen were, 'with few exceptions, men who deserve respect and regard for many valuable and amiable qualities as citizens and subjects'.[8] Nevertheless, Frere left no doubt at home that if he had had the men and guns he would have scattered the rebels.

Before leaving Pretoria, Frere instructed Lanyon to make Dutch an official language and to prepare for greater local self-government. The Boers respected Frere for his honesty, but some of the more excitable burghers advocated taking Pretoria and then hanging him by his heels. However, the 'wait a bit' policy of their leaders prevailed. With heavy reinforcements pouring into South Africa and the end of the Zulu War imminent, this was not the time to cross swords with the British.

Frere's days as High Commissioner of the Transvaal were numbered. As he parleyed with the Boers, the Disraeli Government experienced another crisis. The prolongation of the costly Zulu War at a time of acute distress in industry and agriculture led to another round of bitter attacks on policy in South Africa. For the first time the Liberals attacked confederation and suggested that the annexation was a mistake. To quiet the protests, the ministry decided to sacrifice that 'prancing pro-consul' Frere and 'the cowed and confused' Chelmsford, as Disraeli put it. The popular Wolseley, with the whole-hearted approval of the Liberals, was selected to play a dual role: to replace Chelmsford as the military commander, and to replace Frere as High Commissioner of South-East Africa, which included Natal, the Transvaal and Zululand. Frere was left the truncated post of High

Commissioner over the territories to the south. To the surprise of his supporters and of his detractors, Frere did not resign.

The impatient Wolseley, who had been eating his heart out serving as Governor in newly acquired Cyprus, rushed to the scene of action. He arrived a few days after July 4th, when a British square broke the back of Zulu power at Ulundi. Chelmsford's failure to exploit the victory fully left Sir Garnet with the distasteful task of chasing down Cetewayo and preparing for a political settlement. Busied by Zululand problems, Wolseley left the administration of the Transvaal to Lanyon.

Colonel William Owen Lanyon was the worst possible choice to govern the Transvaal. He had the appearance and manner of an arrogant, blimpish martinet. Goggle-eyed with a monocle, a drooping moustache, and hair plastered on his domed head, he stood tall and erect in sartorial splendour. The Boers called him 'Lang Jan' ('Long John'.) They resented the appointment of a soldier who obviously preferred to rule by the sword. It was common knowledge that in his former post as Governor of Griqualand West he had been disposed towards despotic methods, and it was not long before the Boers discovered that during most of his career as a professional soldier he had been in charge of black troops, first in Jamaica and then in the Ashanti War in which he commanded a West Indian regiment under Wolseley. Far worse, the more they looked at his unusually dark complexion and coarse-textured hair, the more convinced they were that Lanyon had black blood. Frere, Wolseley and others tried to explain that the administrator was merely a swarthy Irishman, deeply tanned by his many years of service in the tropics (in truth, his family, of Cornish origin, had lived in Ireland for generations), but the Boers remained unconvinced. The foolish slander as to how they were governed by a Kaffir was told and retold throughout the land. Many insisted it was a deliberate insult on the part of the British.

Other tales, not without some foundation in fact, found their way into the veld, of how 'Lang Jan' used a church organ to play waltzes and how he took on airs when meeting Boer visitors, refusing to shake hands. Moreover, he was a thirty-seven-year-old man without a wife! And Lanyon had no intention of taking one in Boerland. Should he take a Boer wife, he wrote to his father, she would in all likelihood 'be flabby, limp, and draggletailed, and speaking a tongue which is as like Dutch as Lancashire talk is like English'.[9]

Lanyon despised the Boers as a 'semi-civilized people who think of leniency and forbearance as a sign of weakness and fear'. He gave little heed to their wishes and devoted most of his time to what he assumed was his forte, the collection of taxes. A tax collector is rarely popular in any land; to the Boers he was anathema. Lanyon was undismayed. 'Colonists are like a glass piano,' he wrote; 'they require most careful playing, but a skilful operator can get harmonious music out of them by gentle touches.'[10]

Though distant and overbearing in his dealings with the Boers, Lanyon was regarded as honourable and warm-hearted by his friends. As a soldier, Lanyon won Wolseley's highest praise in Ashantiland, where he contracted fevers that shortened his temper. Sir Garnet was delighted to place the dull chores of local government in 'Billy's competent hands' while he attended to affairs of greater moment. Wolseley offered his eager assistant one word of advice: despite all failures, Downing Street would pronounce any administration an unqualified success as long as it proved solvent.

By now it began to appear to the British taxpayer that all of South Africa was taking part in a plot to exhaust the Imperial chest. A Parliamentary Return in July 1879 indicated that the costs of military expenditures alone had increased tenfold since 1870. *The Times* angrily asked why the colonists were not made to fight and pay for their own wars. It was charged in some quarters that the South Africans deliberately provoked unrest so as to profit from military expenditures.*

Lanyon needed no instructions in the art of tax-gathering. As Governor of Griqualand West, he had won favour with the Colonial Office by transforming a long-standing deficit into a healthy solvency. Anxious to prove that the Transvaal was financially sound, Lanyon worked minor miracles. Delinquent taxes were soon paid in excess of estimates. By 1880, his arbitrary arm-twisting methods had produced the first surplus in

* To defray the expenses of the Zulu War, P. T. Barnum asked that Cetewayo be given into his charge as the star attraction among the Zulus he already had on display at the Aquarium. The fabulous showman was prepared to pay half the admission price of one shilling into the British Treasury. The vulgar suggestion was ignored by the British Government.

history. Lanyon's achievement in squeezing revenue from the notoriously tax-resistant Boers lent strong support to the argument that the Transvaal was reconciled to British rule. Rather, it was the presence of the super-efficient Wolseley, chief troubleshooter of the Empire, which temporarily tamed the Boers. Having captured Cetewayo after an exciting chase, he hastily set up thirteen Zulu kinglets and then bullied his way into the Transvaal, sending the 80th Regiment before him 'to ensure loyalty'. Wolseley hoped a show of strength would be all that was necessary because, as he told Hicks Beach, if even the smallest fight should take place, 'English opinion would force the Government to withdraw from the Transvaal, or would bring about a change in ministry at home which would lead to the same result'.[11]

Travelling over the veld in a straight line to Pretoria, leaving a trail of broken wagons behind him, the 'man of action'—a role which Wolseley played to the hilt—paused wherever possible to impress the burghers he met on the way. As the farmers clustered in sullen silence, the new High Commissioner pointed to the sun and told them in his big, firm voice that 'as long as the sun shines, the Transvaal will remain British territory.' He asked Lanyon and Frere to make similar solemn assurances, and proposed that Hicks Beach announce it in Parliament. He wrote to his wife that it was the Government's failure 'to put its foot down and make its power felt' that encouraged sedition.[12]

Administration was never Wolseley's speciality. The task of pacifying the Transvaal was most distasteful. The master of little wars dreamed of a command in India where he could enhance his reputation by walloping the Afghans. 'I confess I don't like colonies,' he confided to his sister Matilda; 'they are mostly peopled by a money-grubbing people devoid of all higher feelings for the mother country.'[13] Worst of all were the Boers, 'who imagine the country is their own special property, ignoring altogether the English settlers'.[14] He described the Boers as 'the most incorrigible liars' and by far 'the most ignorant white people in the world'. The 'half-civilized Dutchmen' appeared so crude and unpolished that he could well believe the story that their tattered and filthy clothes never came off their bodies until they dropped off. Some were so stupid, he told the Duke of Cambridge, that they believed that all of the English soldiers had been killed by the Zulus and that Britain had no more to send.

One Boer asked a British officer if England could be seen from Cape Town. One and all, family, friends, officials, Wolseley told of his desire to leave South Africa by the end of the year, hoping never to return again.

At Standerton, where he was welcomed by the English settlers, Wolseley met Joubert. The High Commissioner found the Boer spokesman polite and deferential, though Frere had reported Joubert to be insolent and threatening in their spring meeting. Then, of course, Joubert had thousands of armed Boers at his back, while Sir Bartle had none. Now all the guns were on the British side.

After a pleasant lunch a verbal duel took place which surprised Sir Garnet and his staff, for Joubert spoke earnestly and well in fluent English. Wolseley tried to coax Joubert into supporting his administration, but the Boer leader refused to play what he called the role of a traitor. When Joubert hinted that greed was behind Britain's annexation, Wolseley pointed out that though the Zulus were conquered, they continued to enjoy independence. Joubert retorted that it was a great insult to make such a concession to savages while the Boers were not permitted the right to manage their own affairs. The High Commissioner appeared to regret his allusion to the Zululand settlement. Concluding the interview, Wolseley hinted that Joubert would be foolish to carry on his opposition. Later Colley, his Chief of Staff, cynically observed that 'the maxim that every man has his price would apply to him if we had a sufficiently high price to offer.'[15] (It was widely rumoured that when Joubert served as acting President of the Republic, he promoted his own pecuniary interests.)

Before reaching Pretoria, a message was received from Lord Lytton, the Viceroy of India, asking for the services of Colley as his personal military adviser. Wolseley very reluctantly agreed to the request, for he would 'miss Colley's good sense and sound judgment *very much*'. He was by far the most talented officer he had ever had and he felt that 'any sensible Commander-in-Chief would make him a general.' But, he concluded, 'H.R.H. [the Duke of Cambridge] does not come under that category.'[16] The Duke, for his part, resented the way Wolseley always pushed Colley's name forward while there were so many senior officers no less deserving. 'When certain officers are constantly brought to the front,' he advised Wolseley, 'the whole body of officers suffer in their *esprit de corps*.'

For a quarter of a century, Sir Garnet and the Duke fought their own private little war over army reforms. Almost single-handed and with rare courage, Wolseley battled to lay the foundations for a modern army by driving home the lessons he had learned while fighting the Queen's enemies of every kind and in every clime. A battering-ram of flesh and blood, he tried to breach the walls of inertia, prejudice and unreasoning conservatism. Leading a determined rearguard action against change was the Duke of Cambridge, that 'grotesque shadow of the Duke of Wellington'. With a strong sense of personal authority, responsible to the Sovereign (his first cousin) rather than to Parliament, the 'Royal George' clung tenaciously to the traditional ways, bitterly resenting the actions of a reform-mad, pushing upstart.

According to Wolseley, the army should be run as a business; if it were run according to the old-fashioned principles that His Royal Highness cherished, it would be bankrupt in a year. The Duke, he told Lady Wolseley, had a one-track mind—one which always ran in the wrong direction. 'He has cost the nation millions', he estimated, 'by his ignorance—thick ignorance of war and how to prepare for war.'[17]

The defects of the old military system were pitilessly exposed by the Crimean War, but reform was delayed until the Gladstone ministry (1868–74), when political and public support was heightened by the Prussians, who represented a modern system, swiftly and dramatically defeating the French. Under Viscount Cardwell, Secretary of State for War, who relied upon Wolseley for advice, the structure of the army was altered. Most fundamental were the elimination of the purchase of commissions, which had kept the army 'in pledge' to aristocratic officers, and the introduction of a 'short-service' system, based on the Prussian model, which originally provided for a service period of six years with the colours and six in reserve. In addition to being more economical, it would attract more recruits and would provide the nation with a larger emergency force in times of crisis. The traditionalists, however, decried the substitution of callow youths for seasoned, long-term professionals. The controversy raged for over a decade. In subsequent military campaigns, jaundiced critics waxed exultant when to their satisfaction they found Cardwell's 'children' wanting in courage, stamina or discipline. The Duke and his supporters were quick to attribute the defeats and deficiencies attending the Zulu War to the new-fangled system.

In Pretoria the conqueror of the Zulus was greeted by Englishmen waving banners and solemn Boers waving petitions. Given to hyperbole, Wolseley picturesquely spoke of how the Vaal River would flow back into the Drakensberg before the Transvaal would gain independence. He added that now that telegraphic communications—which preceded his arrival by nine days—linked the Transvaal to the outside world, the land was bound to the Empire more firmly than ever.

The brusque and unconciliatory High Commissioner deeply offended the burghers. His swagger and brag, and reports of how he gave special authority in Zululand to John Dunn, the notorious gun-runner and polygamist who boasted of some sixty wives and over a hundred half-caste children, fanned the smouldering unrest. Outside Pretoria, farmers bullied shopkeepers into selling them ammunition, sales the Government had forbidden without a magistrate's permit. Never one to hem and haw, Sir Garnet immediately dispatched a troop of cavalry to Middelburg, where the disturbances were centred. Once order was restored, the general moved the bulk of his infantry into the Lulu Mountains to subdue the mischievous Sekukuni.

After vanquishing the Zulus, Wolseley had assumed that Sekukuni, 'Cetewayo's dog', would have the good sense to capitulate without further ado. In June, when he arrived in South Africa, Wolseley immediately ordered Lanyon to suspend his attacks on the stronghold of the Bapedi chief; he could not risk another reverse to British arms. Now in October, with the Boers at his back threatening the peace, the High Commissioner decided to play diplomat. He offered Sekukuni undisturbed rule over his territory if he allowed the British to build a fort there and paid a fine of 2,500 cattle. The pugnacious Sekukuni rejected the offer and continued to raid and plunder. He boasted that his 'Fighting Kopje' was impregnable against all comers. After all, he had thoroughly repulsed Burgers and the Boers, and when the parson President hired a miniature foreign legion, united by a love of adventure and strong drink, they too were vanquished, and their leader, von Schlickmann, received an assagai under his Iron Cross. When the British inherited the war from the dead Republic, a force of native police and rowdy volunteers, giving Shepstone a few anxious moments by threatening to throw him into a river if whisky were not included in their rations, was ingloriously routed. In the summer of 1878 Sekukuni saw the backs of the British redcoats when Colonel Rowlands failed to penetrate his defences because of an unprecedented drought.

Regretting that he had wasted his time negotiating with that 'bumptious chief', Sir Garnet organized the Transvaal Field Force, consisting of 1,400 British infantry, 400 colonial horse and nearly 10,000 native warriors, mostly Swazis, who would take the place of regulars left behind to deal with a possible Boer uprising. Moreover, as Wolseley explained to the Duke of Cambridge, why shed 'good Saxon blood' when more expendable blacks could do the job?

The campaign involved much more than the suppression of a band of marauders. Wolseley saw it as a means of restoring British prestige in the Transvaal, and, further, in the whole of South Africa. To demonstrate that the 'red soldiers' could fight would reduce the chances of future conflict with either Boer or black. During the Zulu War every action had been fought on the defensive, awaiting impi assaults in laagers or from behind shelter-trenches. The Boers were, therefore, amused by the notion that the British could successfully storm the 'Gibraltar of the Transvaal'. Wolseley confidently welcomed the challenge to exhibit the fighting qualities of the British soldier on the offensive, not only to the Boers, but to the 'old-fogey clique' who still regarded 'short service' as a mistake. He would show them how 'the much abused young British soldier' would follow his officers without hesitation and maintain his discipline under fire as well as any long-term soldier in the past. The behaviour of the reserves in the Zulu War, Wolseley told the Duke, was 'not a question of young soldiers, but of bad leading'.

To reduce the risk of unfavourable publicity such as Chelmsford suffered in Zululand, Wolseley tried something unique in the history of war reporting. Before leaving London, the general arranged for the members of his staff to represent as many of the leading newspapers as possible, rather than for them to send out their own correspondents. (Reporters were often offensive in their conduct as well as in their stories. F. R. Mackenzie of the *Standard* was accused of beating out the brains of a fallen Zulu.) With the departure of independent correspondents after the close of the Zulu War, Wolseley came close to having a mono- poly of news sources in the Transvaal, especially before under- taking the Sekukuni campaign. The one reporter who remained behind, however, was potentially the most dangerous of all: the father of modern war correspondents, Dr (later Sir William) Russell, affectionately called 'Billy' by all arms of the service.

Russell was a power to reckon with. Perhaps no single news- paper correspondent in history ever wielded such extraordinary influence. His letters from the Crimea to *The Times*, which brought the British public behind the scenes of war to witness neglect, abuse and mismanagement, did more to cause the downfall of the Aberdeen ministry than any other single force. During the Indian Mutiny Russell's letters were instrumental in establish- ing a more humane policy towards the rebels there. And when reporting the American Civil War, his descriptions of the dis- graceful acts committed by Union soldiers at Bull Run provoked such a storm of anger in the North that his life seemed in danger. The celebrated correspondent had a knack for starting trouble. Moreover, he was on intimate terms with the great men of his time, from Bismarck to the Prince of Wales. Russell was courted and petted—and often feared—wherever he went. During the Franco–German War, Matthew Arnold sarcastically pictured him being hoisted into his saddle by the old King of Prussia while the Crown Prince held the stirrup and Bismarck the horse's head.

Wolseley firmly believed that it was not the politicians, the heads of military departments, or the circumstances of war, even when they involved victory or defeat, that made or destroyed a soldier's reputation, but rather the scribblers who recorded their deeds for the press. So far, Russell had sided with Wolseley's foes. Since the Cardwell days he had opposed reform and backed the reactionaries. In South Africa, Russell aligned himself with Colenso and favoured the Boer cause. When Russell wrote for permission to join the Transvaal Field Force, Wolseley sent the note home to his wife so that she might see by the tone of it what 'a half-fawning and half-bullying snob he is'.[18] But the

general dared not refuse Russell's request. He answered 'Billy's'
letter in gushing terms, telling him how happy he would be to
have him as a guest at his table. Knowing, however, that the
journalist hated tea and could not do without his grog, Wolseley
tried to discourage him by writing about the short supply of
liquor at his 'tea-drinking mess'. Russell went all the same.

As he did in all of his campaigns, Wolseley predicted the pre-
cise moment of victory. On the afternoon of November 28th, he
boasted that he would have his tea in Sekukuni's hut—and he did.
With astonishing speed and skill, Wolseley smashed the robber's
stronghold and dragged the 'wily old savage' off to the jail in
Pretoria. Disraeli declared, 'Sir Garnet has not disappointed me.
He is one of those men who not only succeed but succeed quickly.'
Even Russell scribbled his unqualified praise, despite the mishaps
and ragging he endured. At the outset he lost his dentures while
crossing a mountain stream. Later his horse fell upon him and
left him lame. The staff, refusing to treat this intimate of princes
with proper deference and respect, needled him with sarcasm and
told the toothless Irishman fantastic yarns to relate to his readers. The horseplay reached a climax when 'Baby' McCalmont put
an ape into the stout old gentleman's bed. The victim nearly
suffered a stroke. Wolseley declared he was as much relieved by
the departure for London of the celebrated correspondent as he
was by the capture of Sekukuni.

Throughout the campaign, Wolseley was vexed by Boer
threats and by their determination to hold a mass protest meeting on December 10th at Wonderfontein. While engaged against
Sekukuni, he employed 'Boer tactics by giving currency to
alarming rumours of fearful engines of destruction lately issued
to our artillery'. As a partial reward to the Swazis, who were not
allowed to take women, he ordered them 'to carry off cattle
from all the farms where are found owners to be absent at the
monster meeting'.[19] Surely, he told Hicks Beach, this would have
the effect of keeping many Boers at home.

To Lanyon, Wolseley suggested that before the Boer meeting
means should be found to buy off the leaders with posts in the
Government. Why not make Kruger a political agent with the
Swazis 'at a salary of say £600 or £700 a year'? And since
Marthinus Pretorius was 'a needy man', why not offer him a
seat on the Executive Council? 'I would be glad to give him a

bonus down to a year's salary of £300.'[20] Lanyon dangled the carrot with no success. At the same time, he organized what was called a 'Bow-Wow' counter-meeting in Pretoria on November 17th, at which a number of English settlers declared that they would fight if necessary to keep the Transvaal British.

Wolseley suffered no illusions as to the nature and extent of Boer discontent. Where Shepstone, Frere, Lanyon and other officials had assured the Colonial Office that most Boers did not really wish for independence but were cowed by a few aggressive and designing leaders into opposing the British, the eminent soldier, Wolseley, astonished Hicks Beach with the assessment that the annexation was a great political blunder. 'We are hated', Wolseley told him, 'by nine out of ten of the Boers with intense hatred.' To continue, at great annual expense, to hold an unwilling nation of European extraction by force of arms, he warned, might prove very unpopular in England. On the other hand, Wolseley pointed out that it was too late to contemplate the 'abandonment of friends, whether Dutch or British, to the tender mercies of the malcontent Boers, and of the native population to their old oppressors'.[21] Besides the loss of dignity and reputation to the Disraeli ministry, an independent Transvaal might prove fatal to British interests, including federation, and give rise to further native wars. With extraordinary foresight Wolseley predicted that the mineral wealth of the Transvaal would soon attract enough British settlers to outnumber the Boers. He felt that it would be far wiser and cheaper, in the long run, to maintain a small garrison in the land for the next few years so as to avoid the peril of more serious complications in the future. The Colonial Secretary agreed.

As for the Boer threats, Wolseley declared that they were all smoke and no fire. 'They are given to more boasting and tall talk than the Americans,' he confidently told Hicks Beach, 'but at heart they are cowards, and cowards that would be relentless to a fallen foe. They have all the cunning and cruelty of the Kaffir without his courage or his honesty. They know they could not stand up against our troops for an hour.'[22]

The general also expressed a strong sense of foreboding. South Africa was already notorious as a graveyard where the reputations of British statesmen and soldiers were buried. So far, his successes against the Zulus and Bapedi went unheralded, the

latter being overshadowed by Roberts's brilliant handling of the
Afghan War. 'I have been very successful in South Africa hitherto,' he told Hicks Beach with extraordinary candour, 'and I do
not therefore wish to associate myself with failure in my last
public service here.'[23] His anger mounted as Hicks Beach maintained that he must remain at his post. Referring privately to the
Colonial Secretary as 'Hicks Bitch', Sir Garnet told his wife of
'the supreme contempt' he had for his intelligence. Wolseley
described him as 'one of those well-born-looking men with high
principle, very little genius and a character of obstinacy and
variety which is feminine ... There is no virility about him.'[24]

All efforts to discourage the Boer rally failed. The High
Commissioner's warning that those in attendance would be tried
for high treason only added spice to the occasion. On the same
December 10th, the general concentrated his returning force in
Pretoria. The captured Sekukuni was exhibited as striking proof
of British power. A sham battle followed with a thousand redcoats in open order thrusting their gleaming bayonets into the
bodies of a thousand imaginary foes. Artillery fired blank rounds
as the Dragoons, sabres drawn, thundered along in a ferocious
charge. At a political banquet given in his honour a few days
later, Wolseley stated emphatically that, regardless of what
party was in power, Britain would never relinquish her hold on
the Transvaal. He spoke of the ingratitude of the Boers after
having had the Sekukuni thorn plucked from their side. The
assault on the stronghold, he continued, was 'essentially a Boers'
battle', but no Boers were present. Instead, some actually incited
the Bapedi to resist. One in particular, Abel Erasmus of the
Lydenburg district, he denounced as 'a fiend in human form'. The
general impulsively blustered that he was guilty of high treason
and promised to hang him when he got his hands on him.

Equally strong statements were made among the six thousand
Boers who were meeting under the old flag of the Republic at
Wonderfontein. Few were lukewarm. Young women were reported as 'rendering their sweethearts savage' with such taunting remarks as 'You talk a great deal always of what you will do,
but it invariably ends in your doing nothing.'[25] But the Boer
leaders kept the men in check. With the lack of gunpowder and
the presence of so many British soldiers, this was not the time for
war. The Boers, a people noted for their normally equable dis-

position, were calmed by Kruger's favourite expression: 'All shall come right.'

Before taking to their wagons, the burghers passed resolutions to the effect that they wanted their independence, and that they were prepared to unite for that purpose and fight to the death. Another gathering was scheduled for April. Until then, a Boer committee was instructed to take the measures necessary to recover independence.

On December 15th a report reached Pretoria from the chain of sentinels surrounding the city that a body of 150 Boers was marching to attack the capital. 'I feel I can walk over them easily,' Wolseley told his wife, 'but at the same time the killing of them would be unsatisfactory work, extremely distasteful to a soldier, and would be extremely embarrassing to the Government.'[26] The alarm was false. The armed Boers were merely returning home from the meeting.

Assured of the support of the Colonial Office, Wolseley took a strong stand. When he received the Boer committee's demand for independence with a request that it be communicated to the home Government, he immediately ordered the arrest of the two men whose names appeared on the document, Pretorius (Chairman) and Bok (Secretary), on a charge of high treason. In Wolseley's opinion, this would instil fear into the disloyal. After the arrest several hundred armed Boers gathered with the intention of releasing Pretorius, but they were dissuaded by Kruger and other leaders who preached passive resistance.

While Pretorius awaited trial in 'a miserable, dirty cell', Wolseley offered him a seat on his Legislative Council in exchange for his co-operation. To have a Boer with his reputation for sincerity and patriotism sitting among his nominated nobodies, even though he was 'a poor creature', would be a distinct advantage. Pretorius, whom Wolseley regarded as slow-witted, cleverly parried the offer. He asked the High Commissioner to give him a conveyance to journey about the land and explain to the people 'their favourable prospects of happy government under British rule'. If his mission prospered, he would accept a seat on the Council. Thus, instead of being tried, Pretorius was given a mule and a wagon. He never came back. It is difficult to say which had the worse effect, his arrest or his release. One Boer was overheard to say, 'Yes, it appears you must be first placed in

prison before you can get a good appointment.' Bok was also
released, but without a mule.

Vain threats have a way of backfiring. One fine day, Abel
Erasmus strode into the office of the military secretary and
declared that he had come to be hanged. As no one wanted to
make a martyr of him, no formal charges were made. The whole
affair made the High Commissioner look a little silly. Regarding
the malcontents, Wolseley somewhat lamely told the Duke that
he 'did not think it would be desirable to try them until after the
next monster meet' in April.[27]

The autocratic groove was cut a little deeper with the promul-
gation of a sham constitution framed by the Colonial Office along
lines originally proposed by Frere, but falling far short of his
modest suggestions. In addition to the Executive Council which
had already been announced, there was to be a Legislative Council
composed exclusively of British officials and their nominees. Not
only could the Governor remove members of both bodies at will,
he could act, if necessary, without their consent. It was hardly a
safety valve for discontent. The only possible apology that could
be offered for such a document was that it was temporary. The
Constitution was 'laughed and jeered at by nearly the entire
country, both Dutch and English'.[28] If there was any open-
mouthed expectancy regarding the deliberations of the Council,
it was dispelled by the first issue of the eagerly purchased *Gazette*,
which announced that the first measure passed prohibited the
dynamiting of fish in the rivers.

Wolseley's soldiers were attacked that South African summer,
but from a wholly unexpected quarter. The day after Christmas,
the general reviewed his old regiment, the 80th, and told the men
that 'he would not allow them to enter on their homeward march
without expressing his sense of their soldierlike bearing and
conduct'. With the tune of a lively quick march still ringing in
his ears, he settled down to read the latest news from home. It
was only then that he learned of a letter written by 'Billy' Russell
on October 10th, which was printed in the *Daily Telegraph* on
November 21st, stating that the young soldiers in the Transvaal
were responsible for the grossest misbehaviour. Russell told how
detachments marching through Boerland were guilty of drunkenness, housebreaking, assaulting good citizens, and causing decent
women to fly before them and flock into towns for protection.

Russell quoted an inhabitant of Heidelberg who alleged that soldiers 'cleared out the poultry-yards, broke into all the canteens, and most of the stores, ransacked the houses and stole even the church clock, so that nothing more was left in Heidelberg to take or destroy'.

Wolseley choked with rage: 'that arch snob ... scoundrel ... ingrate!' To think that Russell was living at his expense when he wrote his 'infamous letter'. Not once did he speak a word impugning the soldiers' conduct to Wolseley or his staff. Obviously he calculated his time so that copies of the newspaper which carried his criticism would reach the Transvaal after his departure. 'What could have made him so treacherously vicious?' Wolseley's first impulse was to blame McCalmont and that confounded ape he had put into the reporter's bed. Further thought led him to conclude that Russell had dipped his pen in gall in order to discredit the short-service system; it was a diabolical effort 'to injure or break down the present Army system'. He confided to his wife that if Russell stirred Englishmen to the intensity of indignation that he had on other occasions, he might succeed.[29]

The general ordered an investigation, but, without waiting for the results, he telegraphed in hot haste to the War Office that Russell's statements were such 'gross exaggerations and transparent untruths' that he must have been hoaxed. He would be the first to admit that the troops in South Africa had not been angels and that they sometimes indulged in certain 'gross irregularities'. There would always be soldiers, he told the Duke of Cambridge, who would misbehave 'when they return to a town after a campaign where they could obtain no liquor, but the statements made by Dr Russell are simply and literally *untrue*'.[30] Suggestions that women flocked to towns as if flying from the embraces of Zulus, and that Tommy Atkins would steal a church clock, of all things, as a souvenir of 'the sack of Heidelberg', were 'grotesque absurdities'. Wolseley suggested that Russell must have been ill when he wrote the letter.

A paper war followed. Russell's invectives appeared in the *Daily Telegraph* and the *Army and Navy Gazette*, which he owned and edited. Wolseley was at a disadvantage, for he had to request permission from the Secretary of State for War to publish his denials. The controversy, however, failed to stir a public whose attention was absorbed by affairs in India and by the coming election. Wolseley, for his part, assumed that his 'crushing answers' had extinguished Russell, for those who showed any concern generally accepted his denials regarding the journalist's charges.

What conclusions may be drawn from the jumble of charges and counter-charges? No doubt there was some foundation to Russell's assertions, but they were exaggerated and based upon hearsay. His biggest mistake was to fail to fortify himself with sound evidence to present in case he was challenged. Officers, magistrates, innkeepers—some of whom had actually supplied damaging information in the beginning—obligingly testified before the High Commissioner's investigators with improbable unanimity as to the impeccable conduct of the British soldier. In the end, Wolseley demonstrated that only seven soldiers had been convicted of civil offences. How many had committed outrages with impunity would be difficult to prove, least of all by Russell in London.*

The army in South Africa was also a source of friction between the two High Commissioners, Wolseley and Frere. Sir Bartle, undeterred from his aggressive programme, devoted most of his time to suppressing unruly natives in Basutoland and Pondoland, which he hoped to annex along with other native territories. Since Sir Garnet commanded the army in South Africa, Frere needed his permission to use regulars against the natives. To Wolseley's way of thinking, Frere seemed to be gripped by some kind of 'Napoleonic delirium'. (Wars during his term in office cost some 30,000 native lives.) Wolseley advised Hicks Beach that Frere's plans for furthering federation would stand a better chance if 'his fighting instincts were calmed down'.[32] He told his wife that 'Sir Bottle Beer's' real aim was to worry him into resigning so that Frere might be allowed to revert to his former position as High Commissioner over all of South Africa. And if, as Wolseley feared, Frere and his wife succeeded in influencing the Prime Minister into giving him a peerage, he would resign and leave Wolseley out in the cold, forced to remain as High Commissioner over all the territories. It was an absurd political

---

* Sir Garnet and Sir William met at a banquet two years later. When the Prince of Wales caught sight of them chatting amiably, he declared that he was happy to see that they were friends. Wolseley turned to Russell and said, 'I wonder what he means.' Russell replied, 'I'm sure I don't know.'[31]

compromise which allowed two mutually antagonistic High Commissioners, both enjoying exclusive powers, to work at cross purposes.

Having lost his wager that he would return home after the first of the year, Wolseley grew more irritable. To keep him happy, Hicks Beach advised him that his chances for the post of Commander-in-Chief in India would be improved if he remained at his South African post until after the Boer meeting in April. To keep him profitably employed until then, the Colonial Secretary asked him to go to Natal to squeeze a large contribution out of the Government to help discharge the enormous debt accumulated during the Zulu War.

A sojourn in Natal in pursuit of revenue was 'dirty work', and there was little chance of success. The official who had drowned their legislative liberties in sherry and champagne, Wolseley advised Hicks Beach, was not the one to win their co-operation on such a sensitive matter as finance. Not having caused the Zulu War, the citizens grumbled, why should they be made to pay for it? When the High Commissioner requested that they at least share the customs dues with the Transvaal, they refused to share one penny.

In Pietermaritzburg, Wolseley renewed old enmities. Colenso, 'that crotchety philanthropist', chafed over the fate of his poor friend Cetewayo and claimed that the atrocities committed by the British in Sekukuniland rivalled those committed by the unspeakable Turk in Bulgaria. In addition to this, the good bishop now campaigned for Transvaal independence, and delighted in showing Wolseley articles written by Russell supporting his position.

The only possible good that resulted from his stay in Natal, according to Wolseley, was that some of his more amorously inclined officers had been removed from Pretoria. Worst of the lot was St Leger Herbert, his legal secretary, who gave frequent picnics for all the unmarried women of the capital, and then fell hopelessly in love, in his 'usual immoral fashion', with an apothecary's daughter. But 'Sanky' did good service writing for *The Times* under the anonymous title 'Our Own Correspondent', for he vigorously—and sometimes viciously—attacked Sir Bartle and his policies. When Frere angrily remonstrated against 'false accusations', Wolseley somewhat piously told Hicks Beach that he would be the last to interfere with the freedom of the press by calling a correspondent to account for his views. (Herbert later died a hero's death as a correspondent with the Gordon Relief Expedition.)

To ensure the offer of a higher post—and possibly the reward of a peerage—Wolseley returned to Pretoria determined not to leave any stone unturned to demonstrate the success of his mission in the Transvaal; 'it would be', he wrote his wife, 'the greatest feather in my cap that I have ever been able to place in it.'[33]

In an effort to gain greater solvency, Wolseley urged Lanyon to redouble his efforts. A ten-shilling hut-tax was imposed, and despite the Boers' advice to resist, was obediently paid. The outcome of the Sekukuni War helped the natives in their decision to comply. Wolseley was so pleased with Lanyon that he recommended him for the K.C.M.G., which made Sir Owen (he dropped the name William which he hated) the youngest knight of the order. And as a mark of personal gratitude Wolseley ordered a silver cup, which he would present on his departure.

While Lanyon collected money, Wolseley collected non-Dutch settlers and some 'renegade Boers' and organized them into a political body which he dubbed the 'Progressive Party'. To contradict the pro-Boer *Volksstem*, the High Commissioner subsidized a Dutch newspaper in which Government views were advocated for £600 a year.[34]

To reduce expenditures further, the High Commissioner disbanded all colonial volunteers, who earned up to five shillings a day, and reduced his force of regulars 'to the bone', on the grounds that his earlier arrests had the admirable effect of turning the disloyal into loyal subjects. Reversing his earlier estimate to Hicks Beach regarding the widespread character of Boer opposition, Wolseley now declared that the dissidents had been reduced to a manageable minimum. Those still in opposition were 'tall-talk-and-do-nothing cowards'. Many of the Doppers, who were the most intransigent, as he told Hicks Beach, were physically and mentally degenerated because of frequent intermarriage. With sanguine vaticination, Wolseley suggested that the April 6th meeting might never take place.

And he was right. As a general election was pending that promised the advent to power of Gladstone, who had repeatedly condemned annexation, the Boer committee postponed the scheduled meeting at Paardekraal indefinitely. They agreed instead to send Joubert and Kruger to Cape Town as lobbyists against federation.

On learning of the postponement, Wolseley pounded his desk with enthusiasm and immediately wrote to Hicks Beach that it was 'a better result than anticipated'.[35] He wrote to the Duke declaring, 'The Transvaal may now be said to be supremely quiet.'[36] All danger of insurrection had passed and the forces of law and order appeared to have triumphed. Lanyon reported that there was also a great increase in material prosperity. Frere gloomily wrote that such optimism was unfounded, but by now his opinions were generally ignored.

Leaving Pretoria on April 4th, a full two weeks before his official orders arrived, Sir Garnet, together with Major Herbert Stewart, his Chief of Staff, raced for Pietermaritzburg with horses replaced every ten miles. The High Commissioner's departure could not be fast enough for the Boers.

Wolseley was detained an additional week in Natal by the ceremonial responsibilities attending on the pilgrimage to Zululand of the Empress Eugénie, who wished to place a cross where her son, the Prince Imperial, had been slain by the Zulus. The visit was far less of a chore than Wolseley had anticipated. The Empress was captivated by the general's celebrated charm and fell in love with him. Sir Evelyn Wood, who accompanied the party during the entire journey, later told Sir Garnet how he and others chaffed the Empress about him as a consequence.

The day he left Pietermaritzburg, Wolseley wrote to his brother Dick, saying, 'I succeed beyond my deserts and far beyond expectations.' Could any man in the Empire, he asked, have done a more complete job in so short a time?[37]

To succeed him, Wolseley insistently urged the appointment of his most trusted and able friend, Colley. When Colley arrived in July, Wolseley promised that things would 'begin to smoke'. It proved to be a most unfortunate choice of words.

[3]

REBELLION

Away with you, you Government officials; we don't recognize you.

Piet Cronje

THE ANNEXATION had excited little interest and virtually no sympathy for the Boers in Britain. Only a handful of Radicals, the left wing of the Liberal Party which saw the Empire as 'half blunder and half crime', opposed the destruction of a small nation's independence. Leonard Courtney, Member for Liskeard, who delighted 'in flouting the herd', became president of a South African conciliation society which sought to enlighten the British public on the subject. More important, as champions of the 'innocent' Boers, Courtney and his ring of remnants from the Manchester school communicated directly with the disaffected Boer leaders and encouraged them to resist and to look forward to the fall of the Conservatives. As a final act at the Wonderfontein meeting, the Boers endorsed a resolution thanking Courtney for his support. Wolseley angrily and repeatedly denounced 'that pestilent M.P.' as doing 'much mischief here'.[1]

But it was the words of the great and powerful Gladstone which caused Boer hopes to soar. When the question of annexation first arose in Parliament, Gladstone remained silent. He later defended his conduct with the weak excuse that he did not want to induce the Boers to 'spend their blood' in a vain struggle for freedom. However, in November 1879 the septuagenarian statesman, fresh from a tree-hewing retirement, had no reservations about fulminating against 'the invasion of a free people'. During the Midlothian Campaign, the Liberal leader publicly repudiated 'the insane and immoral policy of annexation'. With frothy allusions to the Transvaal, Gladstone harangued Conservatives who were 'drunk with imperialism'. Ever the defender of the weak against the strong, the 'Peoples' William righteously condemned the despotic oppression of a free and tenacious Protestant community. 'If Cyprus and the Transvaal were as valuable as they are valueless,' he stated with impassioned histrionics, 'I would repudiate them because they are obtained by means dishonourable to the character of our country.' The titular head of the party, Lord Hartington, along with other Liberals, joined in raising Boer expectations by declaring that no 'false dignity' should stand in the way of retrocession.

The thunderous oratory of vehement anti-imperialists was clearly heard in South Africa. A great party in England, with a leader who seemed to invoke the wrath of heaven, had pledged itself to the Boer cause. Transvaal and Free State newspapers published their speeches, which soon circulated throughout the veld. On March 18th the Boer committee sent Gladstone a warm letter of thanks for his support.

Boer patriots had every reason to expect independence when the Liberals took over the Government on April 23rd. In their simple way they believed that Gladstone would lose no time in honouring his promises, but their jubilation was short-lived. On May 12th the new Colonial Minister, Lord Kimberley, advised Frere that under no conditions could the sovereignty of the Queen be relinquished. Gladstone, writing directly to the Boer committee on June 8th, rejected their pleas with the abrupt statement that obligations had now been contracted, especially towards the natives, which could not be set aside; however, the Boers would enjoy the fullest liberty to manage their local affairs through confederation. The Boers were stunned. It was as if the Liberals had reversed every one of their promises and were taking up the old Conservative position. Kruger and Joubert were convinced that further meetings and protests would be useless, and they advised their followers to prepare for the worst by quietly purchasing arms and ammunition.

South African policy was determined primarily by the Cabinet, which Disraeli derisively described as consisting of twelve persons representing seven parties. It was a patchwork mosaic of striking contrasts, with independent-minded Whig patricians holding three-quarters of the offices; restless Radicals, who claimed allegiance of three-quarters of the party in the Commons, were awarded the remainder. Gladstone, though outwardly imperious, often allowed himself to be intimidated and overruled by

colleagues who seemed 'almost as well pleased with contention
as with harmony'.[2] In colonial affairs, the ill-fitting coalition
followed a policy Salisbury once described as 'drifting lazily
downstream, occasionally putting out a boat-hook to avoid a
collision'. Crisis bred hesitation and indecision, with prospects
of chopping and changing of policy in the near future.

If Gladstone was intoxicated by his own eloquence, as Disraeli
claimed, he was sobered by the demands of high office. Having
courageously retreated from Afghanistan, he was persuaded by
Lord Kimberley and Lord Granville, the Foreign Secretary, to
keep 'two-thirds of the wages of sin' by holding on to Cyprus and
the Transvaal, an act which excited little public interest one way
or the other. If anything, the public was more concerned with
costs, a subject close to the heart of the Prime Minister. Gladstone was obsessed by the enormous debt he had inherited from
the previous ministry, and he insisted on combining his office
with that of the Exchequer to exorcize a moral evil.*

Kimberley had little difficulty in convincing Gladstone that
plans for federation should survive the election, federation being
still the most economical solution to South African problems and
one which would provide greater protection for the blacks. The
Colonial Secretary was given staunch backing on the native
question by W. E. Forster, who was in charge of Irish affairs.
Known as 'Buckshot' Forster for having advocated the use of
buckshot in dispersing mobs in Ireland, he was very sensitive
where the welfare of the blacks was concerned. Ever since he had
served as Under-Secretary of the Colonies during Gladstone's
first ministry, Forster had acted as a spokesman for the philanthropists who feared the brutal proclivities of the Afrikaner.
Gladstone encouraged him, for he was not above pitting the
humanitarians against the pro-Boer Radicals.

An indignant Courtney, leading a large body of Radicals,
conducted a vigorous attack in the Commons against what was
in essence 'the old South African' programme, one which still
retained 'that author of disaster', Frere, in office. 'Pushful Joe'

* The extreme in economy was attained by Labouchère, who had been repri-
manded while in the diplomatic service for travelling too luxuriously at the Government's expense. He was told to travel, henceforth, the cheapest way possible. On
his next trip, from St Petersburg to Vienna, he decided to walk! He spent three
summer months on a leisurely walking tour, much to the consternation of his
Government.

Chamberlain, a Radical holding a minor post in the ministry, added his strong voice in protest. He predicted that sooner or later the Boers would 'worry this country into granting independence'. Gladstone was willing to sacrifice Frere, who was recalled in September, but he refused to give ground over the Transvaal. As for the fine phrases of the Midlothian Campaign, the Prime Minister explained with hair-splitting verbal adroitness that though he repudiated the annexation, he did not advocate retrocession.

In defence of Gladstone, Sir Charles Dilke (the Radical new Under-Secretary for Foreign Affairs) declared that Gladstone always passionately believed in what he was speaking about at the moment. It was a kind of self-deception that made his moral strength inviolate. A godly man, who believed himself accountable to the Almighty for his every thought and deed, Gladstone saw himself as the upright man battling against his wicked opponent. In the words of Lord Macaulay, he was 'plausible when most in error'. It was a unique power that excited faith and adulation among his admirers, and provoked his enemies to level charges of casuistry and hypocrisy against him. While his self-assurance was immovable, his mind was usually in a state of flux, with ever-changing views on the issues of the moment. He avoided a decision on a given subject until his instinct, rather than his reason, assured him that the hour was right—a sense of political timing which was often labelled opportunism by the Opposition. It then became a matter of high principle which he courageously defended, often against disagreeable facts.

The time was not right for the Transvaal. Absorbed by more pressing matters—Indian policy, the enormous deficit, Parnell and the Irish imbroglio—Gladstone, like Disraeli, had neither the inclination nor the spare hours to concentrate on a remote fragment of the Empire. He was happy to leave South African affairs in the hands of his Colonial Minister.

Lord Kimberley was a patrician Whig thoroughly loyal to Gladstone, but he nevertheless shared the prejudice of his political clan by regarding him as 'Oxford on the surface; Liverpool underneath'. Essentially he was a second-string politician with little talent and even less interest in colonial affairs. Unlike Carnarvon, he pointedly disdained entertaining colonials at Kimberley House, nor did he share Carnarvon's obsession with federation. His appointment was frankly dictated by Gladstone's need to bolster the party's strength in the House of Lords. Mediocre, garrulous and lacking in imagination, Kimberley was yet respected by Gladstone and his colleagues for his prudence and conscientious attention to his responsibilities. The Colonial Secretary's great weakness was that he was content to accept conditions as he found them. He might, if possible, try to improve on an accomplished fact, but he would never fight to change it. He left the initiative to others.

As for South Africa, Kimberley's first concern was to rid the ministry of the embarrassment of Frere, for the Radicals were insistently demanding his resignation. The High Commissioner's allowance was reduced by £2,000, but still he refused to resign. When the Cape Parliament, influenced in part by Joubert and Kruger, predictably refused to participate in a conference on confederation unless the Transvaal Republic was restored, Kimberley found the pretext for Frere's recall. Returning to London, Sir Bartle went directly to the Colonial Office and urged, as he had done in his reports, self-government for the Transvaal. 'Otherwise', he predicted, 'there will be trouble.'

Why interfere in Transvaal affairs, asked Kimberley, when the reports of officials on the spot were uniformly optimistic? Wolseley's convincing dispatches, which carried great weight, were re-read. Agitation, it was felt, was subsiding and the Boers were becoming reconciled to the inevitable; abandonment would promote civil war and anarchy. Hicks Beach, before turning his office over to Kimberley, insisted that 'prospects never looked so bright.' In August, Lanyon found that 'after careful investigation', the inhabitants were 'satisfied and content'.[3]

Nevertheless, Kimberley was enough of a realist to recognize in his report to Parliament that 'the great majority of Boers are *now* against it [annexation].' But when Joubert and Kruger indicated that they might be prepared to settle for a representative Government as liberal as that of the Cape Colony (provided the British flag were hauled down for a single day as an apology for annexation), the Colonial Secretary made it apparent that a legislature dominated by stubborn Boers would be prejudicial to Imperial interests, as well as to the black masses. Kimberley was in no hurry. Time, he believed, was on his side. He was prepared to let the Transvaal drift towards a more propitious future.

The British press continued to display little interest in South Africa. There was an occasional article by Russell giving his view of the annexation as 'an incurable and criminal blunder... in direct opposition to the principles of liberty, justice and sound policy'; or a protesting letter by Bishop Colenso, who was regarded as a mischievous schoolboy who delighted in shocking his elders. Courtney's Parliamentary objections were given scant attention. *Vanity Fair* poked fun at the doctrinaire Radical with the observation, 'He will speak or write on any mortal thing.' Courtney's true audience was in the Transvaal. He advised the rebuffed Boers to persevere. With watchful antagonism and little hope from a Government that had misrepresented itself, the slow-moving burghers continued to distribute bullets and rifles.

An obvious indication that no changes in policy were contemplated was the retention of Lanyon and his subsequent elevation to Governor. Lanyon, who had feared dismissal, was delighted. Kimberley, in his eyes, was a distinct improvement over 'Hicks Bitch' (he had picked up the expression from Wolseley), 'that incomparable noodle and muddler'.[4] And he was happy to be out from under the thumb of Wolseley, whose precipitate manner he resented.

Headstrong, with the stiff manner of a guardsman, Lanyon remained callously indifferent to burgher susceptibilities. Like Wolseley, he refused to employ an interpreter. When he learned somewhat tardily that articles in the pro-Boer organ *De Volksstem* had pricked his conceit by describing him as an 'emperor' who did as he pleased, Lanyon proved the point by placing restrictions on the publication of newspapers. Perversely ignorant of the gathering storm, he continued to confuse his success as Governor with that of a tax-collector. He also succeeded in convincing Kimberley that an increase in payments was a sure sign of contentment. The surplus was such that Lanyon asked for a substantial salary boost (he received £3,000 per annum) for himself and his Governmental assistants so that they might live in a style that befitted their office. In addition, since the land was peaceful, Lanyon anticipated being able to take some leave. Up till then, Sir Owen, a lonely man, had merely asked his father to get some pretty girls he had known as a child to send him their photographs so that he might peruse his album and be able to say, 'I used to kiss that girl when [I was] a child.'[5]

Sir George Pomeroy-Colley, the new High Commissioner, was given a banquet at the Colonial Office on his departure. Kimberley spoke glowingly of how 'a new South Africa' would 'arise out of the mists and vapours of the past'. The same theme was incorporated into warm speeches of welcome when Colley arrived in Durban on July 1st. He was fondly remembered throughout Natal for his quiet charm, and he was esteemed for the administrative reforms he had introduced during the time when Wolseley had concentrated on clipping the colonists' legislative powers. Though designated as High Commissioner for all of South-East Africa, it was stipulated that his authority in the Transvaal was dormant, only to be exercised in case of an emergency. The administration remained in the hands of Lanyon, and so long as Lanyon assured him that all was well, Colley devoted his efforts to improving Natal's Government. A first-rate administrator of tremendous energy, he soon 'worked his A.D.C. nearly stupid with copying'.

As a soldier, Major-General Colley began his career at Sandhurst at the tender age of thirteen. The scion of a prosperous Anglo–Irish family with a great military tradition, which included the Duke of Wellington as a distant cousin, Colley developed a gnawing hunger for undying fame. He graduated at the top of his class. On active service, he began a distinguished record, first against Bantus in the Transkei country, and later in the China War of 1860, where he helped put the torch to the Summer Palace near Peking. Colley returned to enter the Staff College and took his examination after nine months of study, instead of the normal two years. He passed with the highest marks ever yet obtained. Master of several languages, contributor to the *Encyclopaedia Britannica*, equally at home in science and the arts, he gained the reputation of being one of the most intellectual officers in the service. Sir Evelyn Wood called him 'the best instructed soldier I ever met'. But staff officers in those days did not enjoy popularity among most senior officers. The gruff old Duke of Cambridge called them 'bastards' to their face. He once complimented a general by saying, 'Brains! I don't believe in brains. You haven't any, I know, sir.'

Wolseley, a soldier of considerable intellectual attainments himself, insisted that a bookworm could be a fighting soldier. He asked the scholarly Colley to join his staff during the Ashanti

War. Placed at a critical juncture in charge of transportation, Colley seemed to be everywhere; he was found burning villages to discourage desertion by native carriers, hiring thousands of women to replace losses, and generally infusing a new vitality into the life-line of the advancing army. The 'coming man' had arrived. One London journal called him a 'Pillar of Empire'. Wolseley described him as the 'Most loyal, warmhearted of comrades, the most lovable of true men', and he regarded him 'as my successor', the best qualified soldier 'to command an army in the field'.[6] Colley's one 'serious defect', Wolseley conceded, was that he always believed he could succeed with far less than the number of troops necessary. As military secretary to Lord Lytton, Viceroy of India, Colley boasted that 'a thousand men with Martinis could march anywhere in Afghanistan.' His exaggerated optimism as to the capabilities of a small body of British soldiers pitted against a resourceful and courageous enemy contributed to disaster in the Afghan War.

In appearance and manner, Colley was a gentle warrior, much like his hero, Robert E. Lee. His short, slight, well-proportioned body had the upright bearing of an English gentleman and suggested youth (he was forty-four) and endurance. His face was strong and well-modelled, with a large, straight nose and full, dark brown beard. A rapidly receding hairline exposed a massive brow, giving him the look of an intellectual. His eyes were soft and kindly, completing the overall picture of thoughtful sensitivity, modesty and deep integrity. What Colley's mild exterior did not reveal was that he was a proud perfectionist, full of ambition, yet handicapped by 'a disproportionate sense of shyness' and the torment of self-doubt. Under pressure, he was nervous and tense, prone to self-punishment if he fell short of the lofty standards he had set for himself. To relax, he escaped into his books or the clear, mournful notes of the flautina which he always kept near at hand.

Two years before his last assignment in South Africa, Sir George married the strong-willed and attractive Edith Hamilton. A 'cub' of the fiery and terrifying Colonel Meade Hamilton, known throughout the service as 'the Tiger', she seemed no less redoubtable than her father. Intimate friends noted how Lady Colley steadied her husband's tendency to vacillate and stoked his ambition. Witty and personable, she held court at her weekly

'at homes' and stimulated a new sense of social competition in a
capital unaccustomed to the presence of a Governor's wife. When
the first locomotive steamed into Pietermaritzburg on October
21st, 1880, Lady Colley was at the throttle while her husband
stood on the footplate nodding to startled onlookers.

The Governor's duties quickly multiplied. Natal required a
new constitution; the native question in Zululand was becoming
troublesome; a war was brewing among the Basutos; his presence was required at Kimberley; and as overall commander of the
forces in the Transvaal, it was necessary for him to inspect the
military posts. He decided on a flying visit to the Transvaal,
returning by way of Kimberley and Bloemfontein (where he
would consult with President Brand) in time to open the new
Natal Council in the latter part of September.

In the main, the fifth British official responsible for the
Transvaal since annexation admired the character of the Boers.
'Sir George', wrote one colonist, 'does not seem to be violent
and contemptuous in his attitude towards the Boers.'[7] Briton and
burgher alike found him 'a pleasant gentlemanlike man'.[8] In
contrast to the swaggering Wolseley and the oppressive 'West
Indian bastard', Lanyon, Colley's unpretentious ways baffled the
Boers. They saw him as a good man, but any hope for sympathetic
understanding was dashed when the High Commissioner un-
critically accepted Lanyon's political assessment. The situation
in the Transvaal 'is still somewhat uncertain', Colley wrote to
the Duke of Cambridge, 'but the country generally is becoming
rather tired of this agitation; and many who at first held aloof
from us are now becoming friendly'.[9] Lanyon confirmed the
opinion Colley had formed on his last visit in 1879, namely that
troubles originated with 'a small and noisy section' of office-
seekers who hoped to profit through the restoration of the Republic. It was believed that they were abetted by foreign adven-
turers, notably Hollanders, said to be imbued with German
Socialist Republicanism, who fanned discontent among the
lethargic, simple-minded farmers.

Since Shepstone, officials in the Transvaal had pointed to the
professional agitators, the Boks and the Jorissens, as the true
authors of unrest. They were often used as convenient scape-
goats whose alleged machinations provided editors with sensational copy which attempted to explain why the Boers were so

slow in appreciating the blessings of British rule. The most 'evil
spirit', exposed by Frere, was Alfred Aylward, alias Murphy,
alias Rivers, alias Nels, who according to Scotland Yard was 'a
born traitor and conspirator', who would 'betray and conspire
with anyone and anything'.[10] A man of learning and considerable
ability, credited with being a solicitor and a surgeon, Aylward
began his journalistic career on a New York paper, the proprietor
of which was in a lunatic asylum. After his brief stint editing
newspapers in America, where he boasted he had once been a
slave-dealer in West Africa, the firebrand returned to his Irish
homeland to begin his life as a professional agitator, one which
is best traced through police reports which referred to him as
'dynamiting Irishman', 'suspected Fenian', 'traitor', 'drunk and
disorderly'. Accused of murdering a Manchester policeman, he
escaped punishment, it was said, by turning informer, for which
he was rewarded with a free passage to Cape Town. With
astonishing audacity, he asked Frere to employ him in Government service, and when he refused, Aylward joined the staff of a
Cape journal, through which he proceeded to abuse the High
Commissioner's person and policies. From there he moved on to
the diamond-fields to found a daily paper of his own. In a short
time Aylward fomented a rebellion among the diggers which
necessitated the dispatch of troops by the High Commissioner.
Aylward seemed to be at the centre of every disturbance, an-
tagonizing officials and readers alike. To escape retribution, he
once printed his own obituary; on another occasion he held some
irate readers at bay with a revolver as he retreated through a
back window. After a brief imprisonment for homicide, the
irrepressible Aylward popped up in the gold-fields of the Transvaal, where he joined Burgers' foreign lances battling vainly
against Sekukuni. He took command when von Schlickmann was
killed. Following the annexation, Captain Aylward returned to
Britain to write the highly readable and pro-Boer work, *The
Transvaal of Today*.

According to testimony given later by Major LeCaron (a
British agent who masqueraded as a Fenian) before the Parnell
Commission, Aylward was sent back to South Africa by Irish
rebel societies with instructions to start a rebellion in the Transvaal. Arriving during the darkest days of the Zulu War, the
daring Irishman first offered his services to Chelmsford as a

secret agent. At the same time it was rumoured that he was urging the Boers to exploit Britain's predicament by staging a revolt. He finally settled down in Pietermaritzburg as an outspoken editor of the *Natal Witness*, advocating the Boer cause. Frere and Lanyon, prodded by the sharp point of his pen, would have enjoyed seeing the 'Irish traitor' hanged, but Wolseley found the questionable Aylward 'brilliant and charming' and repeatedly invited him to dine at his table. The general vigorously defended him against all allegations of disloyalty. Colley, too, refused to heed the warnings of Lanyon and others, insisting that he found Aylward useful as a source of information.

In October, a disappointed Aylward agreed—for the first time—with the 'frivolous West Indian' that the Boers would not strike a blow for freedom. 'Independence', he wrote, 'has ceased to be a question of practical politics.' As he saw it, Joubert had left the country in the hands of God; Pretorius seemed to have gone over to the enemy while Kruger was no longer followed by the people.[11]

Convinced that the danger had passed, Colley agreed to a further reduction of forces in the Transvaal. After the lavish expenditures of the Zulu War, when over ten thousand men were stationed in South-East Africa, imperative instructions carried off regiment after regiment. Now the new Liberal Government called for further cuts.

The widely separated Transvaal garrisons were by far the most costly posts in the Empire. Each station required ordnance, medical stores and supplies. Almost every article had to be transported great distances from Durban, over difficult mountains, rivers without bridges, and miserable roads, leading to a heavy toll of animals and wagons. Added to this were the problems of theft and deterioration. A shortage of maps at the War Office contributed to the confusion. The story was told of a military chaplain who was directed to give a service at one post in the morning and then on the same Sunday to read prayers at a second post five hundred miles away. The Treasury, concerned with costs, once officially asked the War Office to justify the importance of maps to the military. Sufficient maps of the Transvaal only arrived from Germany one month after hostilities commenced against the Boers.

Wolseley reduced the Transvaal force to three infantry bat-

talions and a cavalry regiment. Under Colley, the King's
Dragoon Guards were shipped off, leaving the land without
cavalry to engage a race of horsemen. (Their horses were sold
to the Boers.) Then in September, Colley ordered the 57th Foot
to be withdrawn. The Transvaal was left with some 1,800
regulars. Pretoria had a garrison of 500 men, four guns and
sixty mounted men; the rest were scattered in five outlying
posts, now regarded as stationary because most of the transport
service was gone. Small posts separated by a short march had
proved useful in native wars, but without cavalry or transport
these feeble garrisons up to two hundred miles apart were hardly
suited for conflict with the Boers. Lanyon, nevertheless, insisted
that their mere presence in a district, no matter how small, was
enough to intimidate the burghers.

Responsibility for the depletion and fragmentation of the
Transvaal force later became a subject for hot recrimination.
Rivals of Wolseley and his 'ring', whom they described as 'that
mutual buttering society', accused him and, to a lesser extent,
Colley. But Colonel Bellairs, locally in charge and no particular
champion of either, blamed Lanyon, the soldier turned civilian,
for sending sanguine reports deemed reliable by the Imperial
Government. Wolseley, Bellairs pointed out, was consistently
'averse to the imprudence of breaking up a regular force'.[12] The
reduction was conducted under specific orders from the Government, orders which were later omitted from the Blue Books,
although the dispatches of acknowledgment from Colley were
included. Colley's sin, if any, was one of omission. Unlike
Bellairs, who unceasingly deprecated the whittling away of forces,
Colley did not protest and made no serious effort to combine the
dispersed companies. He merely reduced the isolated forts from
eight to five. Lanyon, who tried so hard to impress the Imperial
Government of the success of his administration, grumbled privately that London acted 'very unwisely in removing troops at this
present juncture'.[13]

The Transvaal garrisons that Lanyon called 'visible emblems
of authority' were even more of a paper tiger than the stated
official strength would indicate. The young soldiers, faultless in
dress and drill, were woefully unschooled in the art of shooting.
Worse, morale was sapped by the deadly dreariness of isolated
camp life in the midst of a vast, monotonous plain under an

unchanging sky. Army pay seemed smaller than ever. A soldier
could not afford to supplement his meagre and unchanging
rations. One deserter left a note on his bed: 'i am going to see if
i can get a little better dinner somewhere else than i got here
to-day—old Bully meat!'[14] Colley ordered extra rations, but they
arrived too late.

It also cost a lot to get drunk. An ordinary pint of beer selling
for a shilling in Pietermaritzburg cost three-and-six in Pretoria.
'Cape smoke' and 'square face' (gin), which the Zulus called 'the
Queen's tears', were cheaper, and offered a quick though temporary escape from boredom. Drunkenness was a common sight,
and a disgraceful one in the eyes of the more abstemious Boers.

Isolation made the Transvaal the most unpopular station in
the service. Even secluded St Helena, no soldier's paradise, had
greater contact with the outside world if only because of an
occasional passing ship. The desertion rate, which had been
steadily declining throughout the army, rose to alarming propor-
tions. (It rivalled that of the Canadian garrisons during the
American Civil War, when hundreds were lured by large boun-
ties to join the armies across the border.) Most often it was the
veteran, or the soldier with some education or skill, who deserted,
in hopes of finding a better life as a tradesmen or tutor in the
near-by Free State.

The Boers were prepared to furtively encourage and assist the
desertion, particularly if the soldier paid them with a rifle or a
mount stolen from an officer. One sergeant absconded with £200
from the troop and canteen funds. A certain ingenious Madame
X, who used her brothel at the first station in an 'underground
railway' to smuggle out fugitives, later claimed that if she had
begun her activities earlier 'there would not have been a private
left in the King's Dragoon Guards'.[15]

It was 'the terrible amount' of desertions that worried Colley
into accepting drastic reductions. In August alone seventy men
deserted, and by December he learned that the loss numbered at
least 260 for the year. In addition, nearly a hundred were caught
and returned. Conviction resulted in a year or two of imprisonment. (The further punishment of tattooing the chest with the
letter 'D' was abandoned during the Cardwell era.) Those who
did not desert spent much of their time guarding or searching
for those who did. The Transvaal garrisons were obviously los-

ing their fitness for war. Lanyon blamed it on the fact that there
were too many 'Irish rascals' stationed in the country.

Advocates of the old order, fearing another round of army
reforms under the Liberals, said with a sneer, 'I told you so.'
These short-service 'infants in arms' without the 'cat' to keep
them in order, were unfit even for peacetime service. (Flogging
in peacetime was abolished in 1868 and on active service in
1881.)

Misbehaving soldiers were a perennial source of friction with
the Boers. Bellairs complained that his men 'looked upon themselves as in an enemy's country', assaulting citizens, rifling
stores, stealing horses, shooting cattle, and generally exceeding
'the limit of unsteadiness'. Young or newly arrived officers were
often negligent, as Russell charged, or set a bad example. They
treated the Afrikaner with contempt, mocking him and making
him the butt of their practical jokes, considered acceptable behaviour among officers in order to dispel boredom.* As sportsmen,
they trespassed on his land while chasing buck and occupied his
house while the farmer and his family trekked to the low country
during the winter to seek grass for the cattle. Officers and men
alike found most of the women 'ugly, square-shouldered, without
waist or ankles, and due to the unwholesome, insanitary condition of the Boer dwellings she appears in the complexion of the
Jerusalem artichoke'.[16] But they ogled and leered just the same,
and assumed that any girl who lived 'so primitive and unrefined
an existence would not be averse to their overtures'. To their
surprise they were not only rebuffed but found themselves involved in a vendetta with the girl's male relatives.

'The marvel', wrote one young officer, 'is that our fellows do
not kick over the traces entirely. Life here is provocative of every
vice, not for vice's sake, but by way of protest against the
aggressive morality not only of the Boers, but of the British who
are only different from them in name and birthplace. They have
all the narrowness of Scottish elders without their good qualities.
Of course it is not morality that prompts this solicitude, but a
genuine belief that all British officers are scoundrels at heart,

* Their behaviour was never quite as outrageous as that of certain bored Tsarist
officers of the time who played 'Russian roulette', or 'Coo Coo', in which two officers
would closet themselves in a dark room and take turns shouting 'Coo Coo' at one
another and firing their pistols in the direction of the sound.

particularly those sent by the British Government to the Transvaal.' The British officers, he complained, 'live in the full glare
of the limelight here, and a man has only to say "damn" to be
looked upon as a blasphemer whose mouth needs washing with
Condy's, or to chaff a Boer wench to be reported as a libertine'.[17]

What this officer of the 21st Fusiliers failed to mention were
the thriving brothels which outraged the upright burghers' strict
concept of morality. And when it was explained to the unsophisticated Boer that this was a normal concomitant wherever
soldiers were stationed, they were convinced that the British
soldiers were utterly depraved. Denunciations from the pulpit
told of how the worst of 'bible sins' were committed by the
licentious rooineks, even on the Sabbath. One congregation of
Doppers was so moved that it secretly planned 'raiding the
houses and meting out Biblical retribution upon the propriet-
ress'.[18] The plot was discovered before any such punishment was
inflicted.

The Boers were keenly aware of the weakness of the truncated
and dispersed British force. Gone were the cavalry and much of
the artillery which they feared most. Desertion and lack of
discipline nourished the belief that many of the British might
even support their fight for independence.

They saw too how Britain's strength was further eroded by
native unrest. In September 1880 the Basuto tribe rose in revolt
when the Cape Government demanded that they surrender their
rifles. Unlike the Zulus, they were well armed and were excellent riders, and they understood the art of fortifying their mountain positions. This 'Gun War', which proved costly and difficult,
had a disquieting effect on the tribes of Pondoland and Griqualand East. Though a colonial affair, it was not certain whether it
would continue so to the end. Colley detained the 58th in Natal.
Lanyon was induced to raise a force of three hundred volunteers
under Commandant Ferriera. Colley permitted them to take two
field-guns and rifles from ordnance stores.

The absence of veteran volunteers and experienced leaders
who might have acted as a mounted levy in the event of war with
the Boers was a serious loss. Rifles sent from Natal to replace
those supplied to the volunteers were delayed and never reached
Pretoria. The Boers were delighted by the volunteers' departure.
Lanyon informed Colley that that element in the Transvaal

which was still favourably disposed to British rule was 'mixed up
with and dependent on the Boers in trade and other pursuits', and
could not, therefore, be relied upon to give assistance in time of
trouble.[19]

The Boer committee called another mass meeting for January.
The British officials scoffed. Five monster meetings had already
taken place and the result was nothing but loud talk. After long
periods of silence, Lanyon explained, the churlish Boers liked to
gather and 'gas' and indulge in 'tall talk'; they talked too much
ever to come to a conclusion. To the weak, explained Lanyon,
the Boers were insolent, brutal, and overbearing; but 'they won't
stand against the redcoats.'

Colley, somewhat more concerned, sent a loyal Boer to the
retired Shepstone to suggest that they should meet to discuss the
measures that might be taken. Shepstone, still regarded as an
expert on Transvaal affairs, merely laughed and dismissed the
matter as trivial. No one disputed this view. Officials, soldiers,
civilians—colonial born and bred—were unanimous in declaring
that the Boers were too supine to fight. They quoted with amusement Colonel Tucker of the 80th, who, remarking on the unrest
a year before, had said, 'You need not worry your head about
the Boers fighting. I undertake to lead my regiment through
South Africa from one end to the other, armed with only pick-
handles.'

It was stated again and again with an air of stand-offish superiority that the Boers were cowards. Anyone suggesting a contrary
opinion 'would be regarded as something worse than a simple-
ton'.[20] Their behaviour in the Sekukuni War left little doubt that
the warlike spirit of the old voortrekkers was dead. And because
of the scarcity of game, the contemporary Boers had grown fat
and sluggish; they had even forgotten how to shoot as well as
their grandsires. Literary indiscretions written for the British
press by Transvaal officials, often drifting back to the Boers by
way of Dutch journals, ridiculed them as dirty and dastardly, and
asserted that incest was common among them. In the towns
taunting epithets as to their ignorance and lack of courage were
flung at the farmers.

Kruger and Joubert resolved that the time had come to fight.
It was not the ridicule or the concourse of opportunities provided
by troop reductions and the Basuto War that prompted their

decision. Rather, it was their perusal early in November of a
dispatch by Lanyon tucked away in the middle of *The Times* in
which he argued that the Boers must be contented, because increased taxes had never before been collected with so little
difficulty. 'These English', they agreed, 'cannot understand our
love of freedom.'

To give the lie to Lanyon's report, it was arranged that Piet
Bezuidenhout, at Potchefstroom, should bring the issue of unpopular taxes to a head. Bezuidenhout bore a fateful name. It
rekindled memories of his kinsmen who had led the rebels in
1815, and were consequently hanged twice at Slagter's Nek.
Living up to his heritage, Piet Bezuidenhout had already served
a week in jail rather than pay a small fine for obtaining gunpowder without a permit. In November he was summoned as a
tax-delinquent by the landdrost (local magistrate) of Potchefstroom and ordered to pay arrears of £27 5s. Unlike his earlier
kinsmen, Bezuidenhout behaved legally. He proved his contention that he owed only £14, but he was then ordered to pay
'costs' which by an odd coincidence amounted to £13 5s., thus
bringing the total up to the amount of the original claim. (The
'costs' had been stipulated by the Pretoria Government, which
had been consulted by the landdrost during an adjournment.)
Bezuidenhout, seeing no justice in his paying costs to rectify an
error made by the Government, especially one in which he had
no representation, refused to pay. His wagon was seized by the
sheriff and offered for public sale in Potchefstroom.

Lanyon, under pressure from Kimberley (who complained
that the accounts of the Transvaal were 'more in arrears than
those of any other colony with the single exception of the Falk-
land Is.'.[21]), had resolved to deal sternly with the residue of
trouble-makers in order to ensure future collections and tran-
quillity. That many of the demands were ill-advised, not to
mention illegal, did not concern Lanyon and his assistants. Sir
Owen would have done well to heed the advice of one of the
greatest tax-collectors of all time, Jean Baptiste Colbert, who
said, 'The art of taxation consists in so plucking the goose as to
obtain the largest amount of feathers with the least amount of
hissing.'

To try conclusions with a man named Bezuidenhout was a
mistake; to attach his wagon and put it up for auction was an

egregious blunder. To the Boer, with his semi-gypsy way of life,
the covered wagon was capital invested, an institution, part of
his very existence. Now it became a symbol of resistance.

The auction, set for eleven o'clock on the morning of November 11th, never took place. A boisterous crowd, with over one
hundred armed Boers, had assembled for the occasion. When the
sheriff mounted the wagon to announce the conditions of sale, the
Boer leader, Piet Cronje, hurled him aside and kicked him, saying, 'Away with you, you Government officials; we don't recognize you.' The wagon was removed in triumph to the Bezuidenhout farm.

Lanyon was not ruffled by this first act of rebellion. He
promptly sent troops from Pretoria. However, he did not anticipate their employment because, as he told Bellairs, their presence
was designed primarily to lend moral support to civil officers. In
the meantime, the latter tried to persuade the ringleaders to
submit to arrest. Backed by armed supporters, they respectfully
declined. The wagon remained where it was, in the midst of a
district alive with agitation.

The crisis gave Kruger the opportunity to request that the
January meeting be advanced by a month to December 8th.
When Jorissen, his legal adviser, arrived in Paardekraal, the site
selected for the meeting, Kruger greeted him with the ominous
words, 'It is ready.'

On learning that the great meeting had been moved up on the
calendar, Lanyon decided to offer the Boers a sample of his power
and determination. He arrested C.F. Cellairs, editor of *De
Volksstem*. On November 16th Cellairs had published a notice
subscribed to by 113 inhabitants, in which they denounced the
illegal robbery of the quitrent and the tax on a railway which did
not exist. Henceforth they would only pay taxes to the lawfully
constituted Government of the South African Republic. The
editor was fined £25 and sentenced to one month's imprisonment. Cellairs appealed against the verdict; he won and was set
free.

With smug incredulity regarding Boer intentions, Lanyon
advised Kimberley that there was no real threat to the Queen's
authority. On November 19th he wrote, 'I do not think there is
much, if any cause for anxiety'; and on November 28th, 'I believe that the law can be quietly carried out without bringing

about a collision.' However, to help ensure that there was no
breach of the peace he had asked Colley on November 25th for
the return of the 58th. Colley replied that he could ill spare the
battalion, owing to 'alarming reports from Pondoland'; however, on second thought, he promised half a battalion. Again on
December 5th Lanyon told the Colonial Secretary, 'I still do not
think there is much cause for anxiety.'[22]

An unperturbed Colonial Office took little notice of the Boers
except to joke about their resemblance to that other nuisance, the
Irish. But by December Kimberley grew suspicious. His political
instinct warned him that Lanyon's assurances were too pat.
Brand, the President of the Free State, gave substance to Kimberley's fears in an anxious warning which he telegraphed on
December 6th to Sir George Stahan, acting administrator of
Cape Colony. The wise President urged that means be devised
to avert a collision which, in his opinion, seemed imminent. The
message reached the Colonial Office on December 30th, eleven
days after news of the outbreak; Stahan sent it by an ordinary
weekly mail-steamer instead of by telegraph!

Meanwhile, Lanyon denounced the meeting at Paardekraal as
illegal. Proclamations were distributed warning that 'misguided
men' who attended would be punished. The threat was ignored
as biltong was made at farms throughout the land. The Boers
were mobilizing: boots being greased, rifles oiled and beards
trimmed. Down every trail and Bantu path, rifles glinted amid
clouds of dust as the Boers converged on the farm called Paardekraal. Boer individualism, bred by nature and environment, was
submerged in a common cause. Three years of arbitrary British
rule, against which patience and protest had been of no avail, had
given birth to a new sense of patriotism.

In the rocky mounds surrounding Paardekraal some four
thousand burghers rose as one to demand the restoration of the
Republic. Until the Volksraad resumed its functions, they elected
a Triumvirate to govern them: Kruger, who seemed ubiquitous
in his top hat and black frock coat, became Vice-President (no
President was chosen); Joubert, despite his protests that he had
no talents as a general, became Commandant-General; and ex-
President Pretorius, son of a mighty man of war, was included
as something of a figurehead. With the religious solemnity that
had marked their entrance into battle ever since Blood River

exactly forty-two years before, each man cast a stone on a great heap, pledging to sacrifice his life for freedom.

The women, arriving in great ox-wagons, were no less resolute. Aylward declared that they were 'more patriotic and more determined to be free than even their men'.[23] Boers and Britons alike agreed that the conflict that ensued was in large part instigated and sustained by the women. Knowing how to use their tongues and capable of other, more gentle means of persuasion, their influence was said to be paramount in decisions affecting war and peace. Boer women in the Free State and in the more distant Cape Colony encouraged sons and husbands to go to the support of their fellow Afrikaners in the north. Though living in an ostensibly patriarchal society, the women enjoyed an equality that was rare in the Victorian Age. Married or single, they had absolute property rights, and the 'vrou' always had much to say in the affairs of her husband—a husband who was a good father and an uxorious mate. If one of the tests of a strong society is the status of its women, the Boers qualified with honours.

As the women and children returned to their homesteads, the men divided into commandos: one to lie close to Pretoria, another to take Potchefstroom, and a third to establish a temporary capital at Heidelberg, a strategic point between the Natal border and Pretoria some sixty miles to the north. Heidelberg, a solid-looking little town on the slope of a hill overlooking a river (hitherto famed for a family of dwarfs), was taken without a struggle. The Scottish merchants who had settled there in large numbers were far more interested in showing a profit than in favouring one side or the other. And profit they did as Heidelberg became the supply centre for the Republic's forces.

A copy of the proclamation of independence was forwarded to Lanyon with a statement assuring him that the Boers had 'no desire to spill blood'. They were, in fact, prepared to accept some form of federal union, with the British in control of foreign policy; but they would fight to restore complete domestic freedom. Lanyon was given twenty-four hours to hand over the keys of the Government offices.

The Republic's proclamations and official documents, all written in semi-religious style, were already on their way to the printer in Potchefstroom. To see to it that the job was done without interference, Commandant Piet Cronje took an armed

body of four hundred men. Cronje was a small, delicate-looking
man, described by a British correspondent as having a 'Christ-
like face' with an expression of 'sorrowing kindliness, of a wist-
ful desire to live at peace with the world'.[24] But appearances were
deceptive. Cronje was a stubborn firebrand. This *enfant terrible*
of the Potchefstroom district, one of the first openly and vehemently to defy the tax-collector, quickly gained a national reputation for his hot belligerence.

Drawn to Potchefstroom by the Bezuidenhout affair were
nearly two hundred Royal Scots Fusiliers under Colonel Winsloe, who promptly ordered defensive measures. To safeguard a
town which straggled for over a mile on an extensive plain
would have been an impossible task for even a considerably larger
force, so Winsloe constructed an earthwork thirty yards square
about a thousand yards from the brick courthouse, which in turn
was fortified and held by twenty regulars and forty-six volunteers. Another twenty men were allotted to a near-by stone
prison. It was pleasant duty, with tea provided in the afternoon
by a sympathetic English element, and dancing at night. One
large home was 'a great meeting-place for the officers and the
beauty and the chivalry of Potchefstroom'.[25]

On December 15th hundreds of dust-covered, grim-looking
Boers rode into town. Disregarding protests, they took over the
printing works. There was no dancing that night. The next morning a group of horsemen rode defiantly past the Fusiliers confined in the fort. One of them shouted in English, 'Why don't
you fight, you damned cowards?' Nettled by the insult, Winsloe
exclaimed, 'We cannot stand this,' and sent a patrol after the
jeering Boers. The Boers retired behind a stone wall and shots
were exchanged. One burgher was wounded. A controversy immediately arose as to which side had fired first, as if somehow
the blame for the conflict that followed could be attributed to the
side responsible for the first shot—even if one man had acted on
his own authority. But in reality the war did not originate with
that single shot; it was the natural consequence of the blunder-
ing and broken promises which had followed annexation.

The fighting in Potchefstroom became general. The small garrison at the prison was forced to fall back on the fort. The men in
the court-house surrendered after two days, when the thatched
roof was set on fire. When Kruger arrived on December 22nd,

it was unanimously agreed that a close siege of the civilians and
soldiers in the small fort would press them into submission. The
Boer strategy was to besiege the isolated British garrisons of
half battalions and odd companies, while Joubert with a large
commando rushed to the Natal frontier to take up a strong position, holding the narrow front door of the Transvaal against relieving forces approaching through the Drakensberg.

On the eve of the Paardekraal meeting, Lanyon conveyed to
'those inflated toads' (as he privately described them) the
hackneyed promise of granting 'any reasonable requests in the
direction of representative institutions'. The Boers ignored the
offer. On December 11th Lanyon told Colley, 'They are incapable of united action, and they are mortal cowards, so anything they do will be but a spark in the pan.'[26]

On December 17th an astonished Lanyon received the Boer
ultimatum. Cursing the men who delivered it, he ordered that
no armed burghers should be allowed to come within a mile of
any town. Defensive works were raised in Pretoria, and volunteers were drilled in a 'rather farcical' fashion, for everyone still
'pooh-poohed' the Boers' 'loud talk'.[27]

Learning of the outbreak of hostilities at Potchefstroom, Sir
Owen, with a more melancholy expression than usual, proclaimed
that the province was in a state of rebellion, and called up Her
Majesty's forces to quell the insurrection. Though hemmed in by
hostile forces, Lanyon kept his composure. He wrote to Colley
that he could not conceive of what had caused the Boers to behave as they did, but he was certain that they acted on 'an impulse'. 'I do not feel anxious,' he added, 'for I know that these
people cannot be united.' Colley was not so sure. The belief
that the Boers would never be so foolish as to challenge the
might of Britain began rapidly to dwindle. Hitherto he had devoted his attention to Basuto and Pondo troubles; now he was
startled to find his responsibilities enlarged by a rebellion in the
Transvaal. Exercising his dormant instructions, Colley gathered
his small army, which he considered 'sufficient for the Transvaal'. A true Victorian, Colley never doubted the military prospects when the fighting commenced.

Reduced to being just another besieged civilian, Lanyon spent
much of his time fretfully writing and smuggling out messages
vindicating his complacency to the Colonial Office. Before

November, he explained, there had been no intention to rebel. 'It was a moment of temporary insanity' which the Boer leaders themselves did not anticipate. It was absolutely the wrong season for them to fight: the crops, which were rapidly ripening, could not be harvested if the breadwinners were on commando; the grass was plentiful for the cattle in besieged towns and forage was available for relieving columns; and it was the sickly season for horses, thus immobilizing the irregular cavalry with which the Boers hoped to succeed.[28] Moreover, not one report from the military officers in charge of stations, the landdrosts, or the clergy of all sects and quarters, suggested anything but 'the general desire for peace and quiet'. Even Sir Gordon Spriggs, Prime Minister at the Cape, had laughed at the monstrous suggestion of a revolt. According to Lanyon, it was the 'extreme credulity of the Boer character', exploited by Fenians, Dutch carpet-baggers, and unscrupulous leaders like Kruger and Joubert, which fomented 'a human stampede'. 'They lied to the ignorant Boers, telling them that their Church and language would be abolished; and that their sons would be forced to fight in India, for the British had only twenty-five men left to guard the Queen.' These 'scoundrels' even succeeded in convincing large numbers of Boers that Cetewayo was still unconquered. Finally, Lanyon hinted darkly that gold was an insidious persuader, for a certain Mr Johnston had sent a shipment of £25,000 in a coach from the gold-fields to Kimberley, 'which passed within a half an hour's walk of the December 8th meeting'.[29]

But Lanyon promised that 'the collapse will be as sudden as the outbreak.' This was confirmed by 'all the prisoners', who stated that they were 'ordered to camp and told to fight and forced to do so'. Those who would continue to fight were few. In fact, many Boers, like the son of Abel Erasmus (who was later killed by his own countrymen), were wholly committed to the British cause.[30]

The views of Lanyon no longer carried much weight at the Colonial Office. His inane optimism had put the Office in an awkward position. Herbert intimated to Kimberley that the short-sighted Sir Owen, who was after all a military man, had deliberately provoked a revolt so that he might employ the army to purge the unrest. Kimberley, by placing Imperial loans and military expenditures unfairly on the debit side of the balance sheet, concluded that the self-satisfied Governor had been miserably remiss in achieving solvency. But it is doubtful if even Gladstone with all his financial wizardry could have done much better. Lanyon's fatuity offered a convenient explanation for all that had gone wrong in the Transvaal, but it did not excuse seven months of masterly inactivity. The Government's sole concern seemed to be that of saving a few thousand pounds at the risk of creating a South African Ireland.

The solution to the problem rested with the Government, not Lanyon. The Liberal ministry, feeling that Imperial responsibilities were already too large, could easily have ended the costly occupation by granting self-government. There would have been little opposition in Parliament, and virtually none in the nation as a whole. Only after the Boers demonstrated a willingness to fight and, if necessary, die for their independence were political concessions considered.* The British could not help but admire their pluck. Herbert grudgingly conceded that 'when a sufficiently strong cause stimulates them their "Dutch courage" is apparently equal to great deeds.'[31] Kimberley, too, suddenly developed a great respect for the Boers. Without waiting for a requisition from Colley, he dispatched reinforcements. Calculating the expenditure involved in suppressing the rebellion and in the retention of a larger garrison after the conflict, the Colonial Secretary began to search for a way to withdraw gracefully from the Transvaal. It was a tragic commentary on modern civilization that a people, no matter how legitimate their claims, had to resort to a medieval concept of trial by combat to bring justice to their cause.

* One official in the Colonial Office suggested expiation of the original sin through payment of compensation money to the descendants of Boer slave-owners who had not put in a claim after the emancipation of 1834.

[4]

BRONKHORST SPRUIT

War cannot be made with rosewater.
Colley

ON PAPER, the Boer forces were hopelessly outnumbered and
outclassed. To call them an army was a travesty. With less than
seven thousand men, any one of whom might decide to go home
at any time (and many did), they were pitted against an Empire
at the very zenith of its wealth and power. The British could
muster tens of thousands of men who were accustomed to fighting
a great variety of enemies in every corner of the globe, and who
could be transported with ease by a vast fleet. The Boers had no
artillery or regular commissariat. They even lacked a fundamental martial spirit which could inspire men to die for honour and
glory. Yet these apparent deficiencies proved to be their strength.

Boer mobilization was swift. No other nation in the world
could muster its entire fighting strength in so short a time. The
Triumvirate, having issued orders commandeering all able-
bodied males from sixteen to sixty regardless of nationality,
could expect to take the field within forty-eight hours. Even
those with one arm or a wooden leg were called. Only officials,
clergymen and schoolteachers were exempt from service, though
they were required to contribute towards the expenses of war.
Those men who tried to avoid service risked the confiscation of
their property, and possibly death. The women assisted by preparing and packing food into saddle-bags and managing the farms
during the absence of their men. Each man, a self-contained unit,
arrived at his appointed time and place on horseback, carrying a
rifle, bandoliers of cartridges and several days' rations. Little
was carried in the way of extra clothing. Thus an entire nation
became an army and the army was the entire nation.

The Afrikaner approach to war had its origin in the early Cape days and was an integral part of life on the frontier. The uprisings and raids of the ever-present tribesmen required the Boers to band into mounted field forces called commandos. As they were unable to rely on the Dutch East India Company or the British for help, a simple but effective system had developed, one admirably suited to changing circumstances and terrain.

At the time of the war for independence, the Transvaal was divided into a dozen electoral districts (presided over by a landdrost), each of which provided a commando led by an elected commandant. Each district was subdivided into two or three wards headed by an elected veld kornet (field-cornet) with minor judicial powers in peacetime, but extensive authority in time of war, when he became what one Englishman described as 'a veritable Pooh-Bah and Lord High Everything'.[1] Responsible for mobilization, the veld kornet deputed the carrier of the summoning commando-brief—rarely a welcome figure to men required to leave their families alone on isolated farms while on dangerous service without pay. The veld kornet, the closest thing to a career soldier, also had the power to requisition property to furnish whatever food, wagons, blankets and supplies were deemed necessary for the campaign. The transport, though humble by modern standards, was exceptionally well organized and operated efficiently over roadless country, usually with the assistance of native labour. During the absence of the commando, the wagons and animals were guarded by the sick, the lazy and the unmounted.

The veld kornet's greatest concern was ammunition. The Boers began the war with only fifteen rounds per man. Normally, ammunition was the responsibility of the individual, but the requirements of a major war were beyond his means. The burghers remembered only too well how in the last fight with the British at Boomplaats, Sir Harry Smith pressed them so hard that they ran out of bullets. In December 1880 many messages were exchanged with regard to a cache of ammunition and the possibility of seizing British stores. Meanwhile, the diligent burghers at the arsenals in Heidelberg were soon delivering as many as 2,500 rounds a day.

Uniforms were no problem. The Boers turned out for war in their everyday, ill-fitting and often-patched farm clothes. They appeared in odd combinations of flannel, woolly duffel and

coarse corduroy, and often in the uncomfortable, undressed animal skins which abounded among the less prosperous. Some wore
fine-spun clothes taken from the British; though forbidden, this
was often too great a temptation to resist. The prevailing shades
of dun blended with the veld and provided a natural camouflage.
Their only resemblance to soldiers was provided by the bandoliers slung over their shoulders.

To the smartly dressed fighting men from abroad, the Boer
looked like a cross between a bandit and a music-hall caricature.
One amazed Highland officer found the typical Boer specimen to
be 'a dirty unkempt-looking fellow, with long hair and beard,
very much tanned, his face the colour of mahogany, a generally
broad-shouldered, hard-looking man, his dress of all sorts and
conditions—usually a coat that will just hold together, and a pair
of baggy corduroy trousers. The chances are he had one spur on
upside down, his head covered with a broad-brimmed felt hat,
high in crown, and a dirty flannel shirt.'[2] They laughed at the
Boer's ungainly carriage—'about as graceful as a dromedary';
they were repelled by the young men from wilder parts 'addic-
ted to wearing their greasy yellow hair quite long and straight
down their backs', and their tangle-bearded elders who looked
like tramps in cast-off clothes.[3]

Yet the Boers were admired for their imposing physique and
the enormous number of children they sired (Kruger had sixteen). Tall, big-boned and muscular, they were declared by
seasoned travellers to be the most gigantic race that they had
ever seen; even the Zulus could not match them. A perpetual out-
of-doors life of protracted hardships, combined with an invigorating climate, gave them exceptional powers of endurance; in the
saddle the Boers were the equals of the best mounted men. Sir
Arthur Cunynghame, a former commander of British forces in
South Africa, wrote that he never saw 'men more fit for the
Grenadier Guards'. Testifying to their toughness, he told how
he saw one giant burgher, who had lost part of his hand from a
bursting gun, direct his son in 'shaping off' his fingers with a
hammer and chisel.[4]

Every Boer was his own general. The army was run by ballot,
with every choice of decision (ranging all the way from things as
trivial as promotions to the all-important matters of tactics and
strategy) submitted to a vote. In the Kriegsraad (Council of

War) a fledgling private might take exception to the views of the commandant himself. And since the elected veld kornet and corporals (in charge of anywhere from ten to seventy men) were subject to quick dismissal, they were very careful to sound out their men before committing themselves. Theoretically, the commandant or commandant-general (who was selected for five years by popular vote) could make a decision entirely on his own, but in any undertaking, no matter how small, he had to have sufficient volunteers. If they did not appear in large enough numbers, he was then free to call off the operation. In practice, no order could be enforced, even when supported by a clear majority. Refusing to surrender his individual freedom, the Boer acted on his own initiative, joining or leaving the commando as the mood took him. With morale totally dependent on the collective desire of individuals, the commando could destroy itself, as it did in the Sekukuni War, or go to the other extreme and perform astounding feats.

Every war was undertaken with certain fixed conditions which were essential in a broad, empty terrain where the enemy was numerically superior. With few or no reserves of men, and frequently none of ammunition, every burgher recognized that casualties must be kept to an absolute minimum, and that every bullet must find its mark. To offset these disadvantages, the Boer relied on horsemanship and marksmanship.

'Horses are as necessary to us as bread,' declared Jan Van Riebeck, the first South African. The Boers were born horsemen and they rode only stallions. They rode light; it was said that a five-pound piece of biltong could stay the pangs of hunger for ten days. The commando, with spare ponies whenever possible, covered incredible distances. In action, the Boers fired their rifles from horseback; the well-trained horses did not bolt, and thus every available rifle could be utilized on the firing-line. If necessary they used their mounts and the primitive skin-and-fleece saddles as shields.

To the English eye, the Boers were 'firm but awkward-looking riders', on animals that seemed ill used and poorly kept. But no Tartar lavished more love on his steed than did the Boers. They pampered their mounts, travelling at an average speed of only six miles an hour, and it was not unusual for the Boer to share 'his last handful of mealies with his horse and tear his only blanket in half to cover it'.[5] Captain Tomasson, who had a great deal of experience in observing the Boers, wrote that their horses were of the best. Their speed could always keep them out of range of the British cavalry, whose carbines usually had a range half the distance of Boer rifles. 'On being charged,' Tomasson noted, 'they disperse and fly, and their knowledge of the country will always enable them to avoid being trapped.'[6] The artillery found its target a mere cloud of dots, always widely scattered and in motion.

In and out of the saddle, the Boer was an admirable marksman. The story was often told how as a boy the individual Boer was sent out to hunt for meat with no more than a single bullet. If he missed, the young hunter might expect a beating or no supper. Hoarding cartridges like gold nuggets, the frontiersman became deadly accurate. To qualify as a marksman, 'a man must hit the small knuckle-bone of an ox at eighty paces.'[7] The irresistible and fascinating rifle became the inseparable companion of the Afrikaner, not unlike the medieval English archer and his longbow. Though rarely immaculate himself, the burgher would not permit a speck of dirt to cling to his rifle. He used no other weapon for any purpose.

Though staunchly conservative and suspicious of anything new, the Boers were quick to purchase the most modern and expensive rifles that science could provide. They armed themselves with fancy Winchester repeaters, Enfield Sniders, Martini-Henrys and Westley-Richardses; their ammunition was of the very best kind. A few long-bearded patriarchs still placed their trust in the long-barrelled 'roer' or elephant gun—a miniature cannon that fired a ball weighing a quarter of a pound. Most preferred the Westley-Richards, which was very accurate up to 600 yards. The manufacturers wisely provided steel plugs, which permitted the more sceptical to convert the weapon into a muzzle loader. The Martini-Henry, issued to the British solider, was considered superior in loading rate and range—up to 1,000 yards in the hands of an expert. Though the action was simple, the Martini had a vicious kick that bruised shoulders and often caused nose-bleeds. A flinching anticipation of the kick put the rifleman off the mark. And because fouling lodged easily in the mechanism and in the square-cut, deep rifling of the seven grooves, it was prone to jam.

The secret of the Afrikaner's devastating fire-power was in his ability to judge distances. Hardly a day passed when he did not mark a stone or tree, measure the distance with an acute eye, and then verify it by the pace of his horse. Many disdained the backsight, using thumb and forefinger around the barrel instead. Some fired a sighting shot at a mark each morning after breakfast. When shown sketches of the fighting at the siege of Sebastopol, Marthinus Pretorius asked why the Allies had not hired a few hundred Boers to pick off the Russian gunners in the batteries, and thereby conclude the war. Like his fellow Afrikaners, Pretorius was convinced that few Europeans knew how to shoot straight.[8] As an excuse, many English marksmen complained that the clear air of the high veld, which made objects appear closer than they were, caused them to mistake the range.

Anticipating what was called 'the new German school', the Boer took great care in availing himself of every fold in the terrain which could afford cover against a bullet or assagai. Even with many miles between himself and his enemy, the Boer would never expose himself unnecessarily. Advancing or retreating, he had the huntsman's lifetime habits of stratagem and stealth— habits not easily taught on systematic lines to large bodies of 'short-service' soldiers. Even Boer women often possessed superior knowledge in these matters.

Combining the speed of Tartar cavalry with the precision of fire common to the backwoodsmen of America, the Afrikaners were undoubtedly the most perfected mounted infantry in the world. Ever ready to take the field in a saddle that was their cradle, travelling light but complete in their meagre needs, they moved with celerity and caution. They preferred to fight on the defensive, which offered greater religious justification and fewer casualties, and on foot, unless it was to their advantage to remain in the saddle, as in the case of a charge by spear-wielding impis. On the firing-line, though united by a common purpose, they fought independently, each relying on his own superb experience and broad common sense. They sought positions which afforded as clear a field as possible without sacrificing concealment. A hundred will-o'-the-wisp sharp-shooters, more widely spaced because of their rapid-fire breach-loaders and their confidence in hitting the target at greater ranges, might hold a line of several miles, usually without reserves. This wide dispersion, not

practised by regular armies, misled the British into exaggerating
the size of the forces opposing them. Conventional tactics such as
outflanking or surprising the enemy were mingled with decep-
tions tested in various native wars. If their safety was threatened,
the Boers would either take their near-by mounts from dead
ground and change positions, or flee, without damaging their
morale. Some might enjoy a dinner at home before rejoining
their comrades.

There was no shame in flight. The Boer did not enjoy fighting;
he valued his life too highly. There was no glamour in dying for
a cause if it meant that his wife and children would face the dangers of the veld alone, possibly at the mercy of hostile natives.
Moreover, to be *hors de combat* greatly injured his cause. The loss
of one man to this thinly populated nation was equivalent to the
loss of fifty or more to the British. Theirs was a unique military
philosophy which they explained with the simple observation,
'You English fight to die; we Boers fight to live.' Thus the Boers
had a decided preference for 'long-shot' warfare, and they avoided combat in which the victors as well as the vanquished were
sure to suffer heavy losses. The sword and the bayonet were absolutely foreign to the experience and disposition of these frontier
riflemen. 'What sort of a fool do you think me when you offer me
a bayonet?' a Boer later asked an Englishman. 'I can have two of
your men down before they can get even a few yards towards me
with their bayonets!'[9]

The etiquette and conventions of 'civilized' warfare made no
sense to the Boers. Warriors by necessity rather than choice,
they fought to kill with the least possible risk to their own lives.
Schooled for six generations in the harsh realities of Kaffir wars,
they could hardly appreciate the rules of fair play observed by
fox-hunting English gentlemen. The British, for example, later
complained that the Boers often disregarded their flags of truce,
or employed them themselves as a convenient means temporarily
to halt the fighting when the firing became uncomfortably warm.
Nevertheless, the Boers, who always had a strong distaste for
killing whites in a land of numerous, warlike blacks, often tem-
pered their tactics with scruples. But they could hardly be expected to change their mode of warfare by adopting European
standards which most of them had never before experienced.

When William Francis Butler stated that the Boer was anything but a soldier, he expressed an opinion that no British officer would have disputed. The Duke of Cambridge called the Boers a mere 'army of deerstalkers'. Colley referred to them as 'undisciplined rabble'. Wood, when asked just before the Zulu War what he thought of the Boers as fighting men, replied that he preferred regulars; the Boers were good only for shooting natives and driving cattle. Obviously many of them were capital shots, announced another British officer, 'but let the animal have a rifle and know how to use it, and they will go without venison for that day'.[10] This contempt was heartily reciprocated by the Afrikaners. The British method of warfare—crossing the veld on foot dressed in bright uniforms and weighed down with a pedlar's pack full of accoutrements, then fighting in the open according to certain fixed rules and utilizing useless bayonets and rifles that they hardly knew how to fire—seemed to the Boers to be the very height of folly.

The burghers' confidence was buttressed by a simple but profound faith in God which put a fine edge to their fighting qualities. They were gripped by the old Puritan spirit of quiet fanaticism. 'They felt', wrote an English woman living in the Transvaal, 'that God's arm was aiding them in this accursed war that was being waged against them.'[11] And God was more powerful than the British Empire. He had the might, in the words of Joubert, to say to the British, 'Thus far and no farther.'[12]

Until reinforcements could be brought up from Natal, the British forces in the Transvaal had no choice but to fight on the defensive. At the first hint of trouble on November 23rd, Lanyon requested that the central force in Pretoria be strengthened by garnering soldiers from the more isolated garrisons. When hostilities commenced, two detachments of reinforcements were still on the road. Colley, who had approved the move, became 'a little uneasy'. He ordered 'B' company of the 58th, which was marching to Pretoria by way of Standerton, to take refuge in the latter post and reinforce the garrison there. The larger detachment, comprising headquarters and two companies of the 94th en route from Lydenburg, appeared to have a better chance of reaching safety in Pretoria.

But for a series of unfortunate delays, the soldiers of the 94th would have been ensconced in the capital before the war started. The first untoward event was a delay in transmitting the order to march. After it missed the weekly post-cart by less than an hour, two days were lost before a special mounted messenger arrived in Lydenburg, More precious time was lost in replacing the transport that had been eliminated, for reasons of economy, in September. Forced to rely on unfriendly farmers who demanded exorbitant prices, it took some time to purchase the twelve wagons *or less* authorized by the commander in Pretoria. Colonel Anstruther then violated his instructions by insisting that an additional sixteen be purchased. Not only was more time wasted, but once on the road the column was to be handicapped by an extraordinary number of impediments. Then, though admonished to brook no delay, the colonel amused himself with an accelerated social life and a farewell ball before departure.

According to Wellington, 'there is nothing so stupid as a gallant British officer.' Colonel Anstruther, 'the very personification of kindness and courtesy', repeatedly laughed off the very specific warnings from English inhabitants and friendly burghers that the rebels were plotting to attack his column. 'The Boers', he declared, 'will turn tail at the first beat of the big drum.'

The big drum boomed and the soldiers, delighted by the change of quarters, sang lustily as they merrily marched out of Lydenburg on December 5th. The townspeople and the small garrison left to guard the stores lined the road to cheer and to wish them Godspeed. They had no idea, least of all the colonel, that they would soon be passing through enemy territory. They thought of it as a leisurely journey of a peacetime garrison detachment. The detachment consisted of nine officers, 254 non-commissioned officers and men, three women and two children. There were large wagons carrying up to two and a half tons of baggage and drawn by sixteen or eighteen oxen. In addition, five mule carts (later to be used as ambulances) carried water and food supplies. As they moved out, the column trailed out unevenly for well over a mile along the miserable road.

There were discomforts and difficulties all along the way. It was the summer season, and rainfall and heat would reach their highest levels. The heavy wagons often sank into the mire, and a great deal of effort and strength was expended in freeing them. Anstruther's 'flying column' averaged less than ten miles a day. Bellairs, alarmed by reports that Boer commandos were operat-

ing in the area, sent a half-caste mounted policeman with a message to Anstruther on December 15th, advising him to take
precautions against a surprise attack, although no hostilities had
yet actually occurred. He referred specifically to the danger of
an ambuscade in the hilly country just outside Pretoria, which
he believed should be carefully scouted before an advance was
made.

Reassured by apparently friendly Boers whom he met on the
way, Anstruther ignored the warning. His four mounted infantrymen, acting as scouts, rarely ventured more than a few thousand
yards from the column, and often passed the time conversing with
soldiers on the march. A literal man, Anstruther was apparently
waiting for the appearance of the hills that Bellairs had spoken of
before he extended his scouts any great distance. With the bare
plains of the high veld extending in every direction, the likelihood of a sudden attack seemed out of the question. But the veld
was deceptive. A gentle rise or a hollow created by a hidden
stream could easily provide concealment for a sizable force.

The Boers, as a British officer later discovered, had 'a system
of spies and scouts equal to the Zulus'. The Boer leaders, anticipating how difficult it would be to concentrate the scattered
British units, were kept marvellously well informed. Unobserved,
the scouts kept the long, straggling, happy-go-lucky column
under close surveillance. 'Jumping Jerusalem!' exclaimed the
Boers, 'they don't move without bringing the barracks with them
... They can't put their finger in my eye.'[13]

As the column jogged along towards Pretoria, the patriots
gathered swiftly to halt its progress. The interception was entrusted to Commandant Frans Joubert, a white-haired, slightly-
built relative of Piet, with about 150 men. Riding at the head of
the party with Joubert was Nicholas Smit, veteran of many
native wars and the future Vice-President of the Republic. He
was easily distinguished from the rest of the party by the fine cut
of his clothes, his huge grey beard and his bell-shaped top hat.
Sometimes he wore a long frock coat. His dress, despite its un-
suitability for the hot season, was the sole concession to social
superiority among the burghers, and was generally accepted as
appropriate for high-ranking officers.

Singing their favourite psalms as they rode across the veld, the
Boers arrived by moonlight at the farm of Solomon Prinsloo.

Frere, from his visit to the Transvaal, remembered Prinsloo as
the turbulent hot-head who urged that he be 'shot or put over the
border'. The farm was located near a place where the small stream
called Bronkhorst Spruit ('Watercress Creek)' intersected the
Pretoria–Lydenburg road thirty-eight miles from Pretoria. It
was a good spot, said the Boers, to waylay the 'rotten eggs'. In
its approach to the spruit, the track dipped down between slopes
of high grass. To the left was a long, low ridge with gnarled
thorn trees forming a thicket about a hundred yards or so from
the road. On a more gradual slope to the right was a farm with
outbuildings, surrounded by groves of trees. These trees and the
ravine behind the ridge on the left afforded a screen for men and
horses. Bellairs and other Englishmen later claimed that the
Boers used the morning before the attack to mark out distances
with stones 'to suit their rifles for point-blank range'. To suggest
that such precautions were employed against a moving column
of soldiers seems senseless; to suggest further that the Boers,
capable of shooting the eyes out of a buck at two hundred yards,
found it necessary to measure the relatively short distances involved, seems insulting. The true purpose of these remarks, it
appears, was to establish that what followed was a cold-blooded
slaughter and anything but a fair fight.

On the morning of December 20th the British uncoiled from
their laager near Honey's farm where they had camped for the
night. Later in the morning they outspanned for breakfast near
a farm that they had heard was the home of the veld kornet of the
district. Wandering about, some soldiers found a peach orchard
and proceeded to commandeer the fruit. Swarming about the trees
like mischievous boys, they crammed their mouths and haversacks with ripe peaches. Some sergeants chased the delinquent
men out of the garden while a pair of officers went to the farmhouse to convey the apologies of the colonel and to compensate
the vrou for the loss. Though they saw no men around, they were
struck by 'the unusually large number of saddle-horses standing
about the premises'.[14] They thought little of it at the time, for
they had been told on the 18th that they might meet a body of
'friendly' Boers on the way. Shortly before noon, crisp orders
were shouted and repeated down the line as the dishevelled
column got under way. The colonel mounted his great white
horse and took his place with his party of four officers behind

the point, two mounted infantrymen riding a thousand yards
ahead. A forty-man band followed. Amazingly undeflated by the
long march, the puffed-up drum-major brought his long stick
down sharply; the big drum covered with tiger skin boomed; the
small drums, carried by boys, rattled; the fifes piped; and soon a
succession of gay tunes wafted back along the trail of redcoats,
who caught up the tunes and whistled and sang. The eighteen
soldier-prisoners, under the eye of the provost guard, seemed no
less sprightly than the soldiers who skipped alongside the wagon
train. It was a hot day with an unblinking sun blazing from a
molten sky. The soldiers loosened their red jackets, and many
tossed their rifles on to the wagons.

Winding into the sunken road before the spruit, beyond
which they were to camp for the night, the band struck up a great
favourite: 'Kiss Me, Mother, Kiss Your Darling'. The Boers, of
course, were watching them: the colonel on his prancing horse;
the bandsmen without a single rifle among them; the party of
some 150 men around the carts, preceding the wagons, munching
peaches. There were no flankers anywhere. To the burghers, they
seemed pathetically feeble. 'God help them!'

The merry tune ceased abruptly. Some of the bandsmen had
spotted armed and mounted Boers to the ridge on the left. The
sudden silence made the colonel halt and look about. 'My God',
he cried to an officer close by, 'look there.' The colonel then
wheeled about and spurred his horse into a gallop. He shouted
an order to halt and close up the men and wagons. An unarmed
Boer messenger with a white handkerchief tied to his rifle came
out of the thicket and gave a sealed dispatch to Conductor Egerton, the senior warrant officer. When Anstruther came up, the
dispatch was turned over to him. The message, in English, informed him that the Transvaal was now a Republic, and that the
movement of foreign troops was prejudicial to its interests. If
the British advanced beyond the spruit, it would be regarded as
an act of war. The Boer emissary gave the British commander
two minutes to make his decision. As the band switched to playing 'God Save the Queen', the gallant colonel declared that
though he had no wish to fight the Boers, he had been ordered to
Pretoria, and 'to Pretoria I am going'. 'Very good', said the
Boer, who returned to the thicket. Anstruther immediately returned to his men and ordered them to extend in skirmishing

order, while Egerton was told to serve out the ammunition, since the men carried only five rounds apiece. Frans Joubert interpreted these moves as hostile and he ordered his men to charge. They advanced to within two hundred yards, dismounted and fired.

As axes chopped into the screwed-down lids of the ammunition boxes, a hail of fire poured down on the exposed road. The Boers, standing or kneeling behind trees on rising ground, shot down the officers, who, as one officer observed, 'could always be trusted to know how to die'. The men who sought shelter by lying in the grass by the roadside or under the wagons soon found that at such short range the Boer sharp-shooters could easily nick an exposed hand or foot. The Boers seemed to be circling around them, for the fire came at them from all sides. In the confusion the British shot some of their own men.

Seeing that all his officers were down and that the men were falling fast, the heavily wounded colonel ordered the survivors of the luckless 94th to throw their white hats into the air and to wave handkerchiefs as a sign of surrender. In less than fifteen minutes the battle was over. One wounded private continued to fire until the Boers, who had warned him to desist, shot him dead.

The carnage was sickening. The entire column was a shambles. Dead and dying men, horses and oxen were strewn all about and there were pools of blood in the white road. The little band-boys and drummers had the appearance of lifeless red dolls. From the confusion of mangled and torn bodies pitiful moans were heard. The Boers were too sobered by the sight to be elated by their victory. The gruesome spectacle made so terrible an impression that many who fought in the brief action could not bear ever to speak of it. One burgher told his corporal that he could say what he liked, but he had had his fill of fighting and he was going home to mind the farm.[15]

The Boers formed a cordon around the bleeding and broken ranks. Those still standing were told to put down their rifles and helmets and to 'squat down like Kaffirs'. They were soon put to work raising tents for the wounded. Joubert ordered the wagons, which included 30,000 rounds of ammunition, to be removed to the Prinsloo farm. He gave leave to his men to take what rations they pleased. Victor and vanquished alike were to be

seen eating peaches. Though the officers were permitted to keep
their baggage, the Boers began looting and stripping the dead of
boots, coats and whatever else appeared to be of value. One
British soldier noticed the landlord of the Lydenburg Bar among
them. He had been in the camp of the 94th the night before,
drinking in the sergeants' mess.

All the survivors testified to the kindness and great humanity
displayed by Frans Joubert's men and by the staunch Republican residents in the vicinity. The latter provided them with food
and other comforts. Expressing regret for the extent of the
slaughter, especially for the wounding of a women and a child,
the Boers put aside their weapons to bandage the wounds of
their enemies.

Assisting the wounded was the wife of the dead bandmaster,
Mrs Marion Smith, who tore her wardrobe into strips to use as
bandages and compresses. Though slightly wounded in the
head, as was also her little daughter, she insisted upon giving aid
to the more seriously hurt. She served as a nurse until the end of
the war. For her heroism and devotion, Mrs Smith was later
decorated. When she died, years later, she was accorded the
honour of a military funeral.

The extraordinary skill of the Boer riflemen appalled the regimental surgeon, Dr Ward, who was himself slightly wounded.
In his report to the medical authorities he stated that the average
number of wounds was five per man. One private named Duffy
received no less than nine distinct wounds; counting the places
of entry and exit, Ward found eighteen holes in him. Duffy not
only survived, but lived on to become a member of the Gordon
Relief Expedition, and at the battle of Abu Klea he was wounded
again.

Joubert was persuaded to allow two volunteers, Conductor
Egerton and Sergeant Bradley, to walk to Pretoria for medical
assistance. They used the errand of mercy to smuggle out the
regimental colours. The colours were first hidden in the bed of
Mrs Fox, who was severely wounded but survived. When the
Boers searched and inquired after the trophies, they were given
a couple of banners that were used for decorative purposes in
connection with garrison balls and theatricals. The Boers were
delighted. Meanwhile, Egerton managed to wind the sacred
prize round his body under his clothes. In Pretoria the banners

were maintained by the 21st Royal Scots until the regiment was reorganized.* Egerton was subsequently rewarded with a commission in the 94th.

Medical aid was promptly sent but many men soon died of their wounds. At the close of the action, fifty-seven of the British were dead and slightly over a hundred wounded. Some twenty more died within a few days.† All the officers were either killed or wounded, an unprecedented occurrence and one which caused the British to conclude that the best marksmen had been selected for the purpose of picking them off. The Boer losses were two dead and five wounded. 'I fear our men shot infamously', Lanyon later commented. Many of the soldiers' rifles inspected after the battle were sighted at 500 yards.

British pride found the statistics of battle difficult to swallow. They insisted that the Boers numbered about 1,000 to 1,500 men, though the Boer figure was 'about 200'. The British further claimed that the enemy had deliberately concealed their piles of dead. The provost-sergeant testified that he counted twenty-seven dead burghers on one farm and seventeen awaiting interment on another, thus supporting the belief that 'if the 94th had had the slightest chance a different result would have been shown.'[16] But no further evidence was ever supplied to corroborate the sergeant's story.

The British dead were buried near where they fell, singly or in mass graves, on the solitary veld far from church or habitation. Many more would be buried in nameless, neglected graves in all parts of South Africa, the details of their deaths long forgotten. The memory of those who fell at the battle of Bronkhorst Spruit remained uniquely green. Because the soldiers were buried as they stood, the peaches they carried in their haversacks and pockets were buried with them. In due course, peach trees grew forth from the graves. An officer named Marling, who served in the First and again in the Second Boer War,

---

* During the Easter Rebellion in Ireland in 1916 the colours were stolen from the museum of the Connaught Rangers. They were never seen again.

† One of the soldiers wrongly counted among the wounded was Private Miskimmin. He came through the battle without a scratch. On learning that the Boers were going to march all unwounded prisoners away, he got a friend to bandage his arm and put it into a sling. To further ensure the success of his masquerade, he hobbled about with a stick to support him. The 'disabled' private evoked a great deal of tender solicitude from the unsuspecting enemy.

marched through the area in 1901 and found 'two uncommonly
fine orchards' growing in the burial grounds. 'I suppose the poor
fellows' corpses made jolly good manure.'[17]

Anstruther had been one of the first to go down, riddled with
five bullets in the legs. Shortly after the action, Frans Joubert
put on his top hat and sought out the colonel. On seeing Anstruther, he extended his hand and expressed sorrow at his being
wounded. The colonel told Joubert that what had happened was
not his fault. He told the interpreter to say that 'all he did against
me was honest.'[18] The wounded officer then ordered the mess-
sergeant to bring a bottle of champagne. When the glasses were
raised, the Boer leader proposed a toast: 'I drink to the health of
the Queen of England—and I hope all the soldiers will leave the
Transvaal and give us back our Dutch Republic.' Several days
later, the colonel died from shock following the amputation of a
shattered leg. He and his regiment had paid a high price for his
over-confidence. His body was placed on a stretcher supported by
four sergeants, all but one of whom had been wounded. Most of
those who followed his remains to the grave were also wounded.
Some wore splints, others bandages on their heads. Those who
could not manage with crutches were carried on the backs of
more fortunate soldiers. 'At the grave not a dry eye was to be
seen,' wrote Dr Crow in his official dispatch, 'and one and all
seemed to think a friend, a good man, and a soldier, in the
widest and best sense of the term, was gone from their midst.'[19]

The unhurt survivors, except for a small party retained by the
Boers to help the wounded, were marched off to Heidelberg
alongside the many captured wagons. Captain Elliott, the pay-
master, who had received only a slight facial wound, was told to
join them. The prisoners asked for a few instruments to cheer
them on their long journey. Marching from the scene of catastrophe, they played 'Rule Britannia' on instruments wiped clean
of blood but sadly dented from the battle.

The British prisoners were soon released on parole, including
Captain Elliott, on condition that he crossed over the Vaal into
the Free State. He was joined by Captain Lambert of the 21st,
who had been captured on his way back to Pretoria after purchasing horses in the Free State for the volunteers engaged in
operations against the Basutos. Together the officers were escorted directly from Heidelberg to the Vaal. Recent floods, how-

ever, had made the crossing impossible save for a tiny punt that would not accommodate the officers' horses and carriage. When the paroled officers insisted on searching for a suitable ford, the escort deserted them. According to Lambert's account, they spent the next two days looking for a safe crossing. The Boers, who kept them under surveillance, suddenly rode up and stopped them. They were given an official letter which expressed surprise at their having violated their parole, and were told to leave the land immediately or return to Heidelberg as prisoners of war. That night an armed party of eight burghers took them down to the river and ordered them to cross. The British officers complained that the current was too swift, but the escort nevertheless forced them into the water. The vehicle was soon overturned. Realizing that the Boers intended to shoot them if they returned, they decided to swim for it. At that very moment a volley was fired from the bank, killing Elliott. Lambert swam to safety as bullets sprayed into the water around him. Eventually he succeeded in reaching Natal. Elliott's body was later found floating down the Vaal; bullets had passed through his temples, back, wrist and leg. His body was buried by a farmer in the Free State, and was later removed to its final resting-place in the military cemetery in Pretoria.

Throughout the war, Colley regarded Boer 'atrocities' as exaggerated or maliciously fabricated. But the sworn statement of Captain Lambert, a fellow officer, moved him to an indignation which he openly expressed in a letter to the Triumvirate on January 12th. However, he was confident in the belief that the Boer leaders would undertake a full-scale inquiry into the outrage and would punish the perpetrators.

Bok, the State Secretary, when informed of the outrage described by Lambert, promptly replied with an emphatic expression of horror and disgust on the part of his Government. Subsequent inquiries by the Boers during and after the war failed to unmask the culprits. The incident, however, was not forgotten. Rider Haggard dramatically revived the episode in his novel *Jess* by putting the hero and heroine in the position of the two officers.

The destruction of Anstruther's column was a great boon to the Boer cause. The insurgents had won more than the first round. Except for the beleaguered garrisons, all of the Trans-

vaal was firmly in their hands. Waverers at home were now emboldened to join the zealots, and throughout the rest of South
Africa people of Dutch extraction were stirred by their initial
success. Though President Brand was determined to preserve a
strict neutrality, it was beyond his power to prevent large parties
of volunteers, led by Commandant Cornelis de Villiers, from
supporting the cause of their neighbours. Wagons loaded with
supplies and munitions followed them across the border. Among
the anti-British in Natal and the Cape the slogan 'Africa for
Afrikaners', encouraged by the recently organized Afrikaner
Bond, was no longer merely whispered.

But there was little exultation among the Boers. They attributed their victory to the intervention of the Almighty rather
than to their own prowess. Kruger seemed to speak for all of the
Boers: 'Inexpressible is the gratitude of the burghers for the
blessing conferred upon them ... bowed down in the dust before
Almighty God, who had thus stood by them, and, with a loss of
over a hundred of the enemy, only allowed two of ours to be
killed.' Though convinced that God was on their side, the Boer
leaders had no illusions regarding the future. Piet Joubert, who
was making preparations to prevent the British from forcing an
entry into the Transvaal, observed, 'Now the English will no
doubt fight to show their supremacy. But they must first kill all
Boers.' His men, he reported, had adopted the bitter battle cry:
'Rather a ruined country than no country.'

Piet Joubert's force arrived at Laing's Nek (where the road
from Natal cut through the Drakensberg and entered the Republic) on the first day of the New Year. Just west of the hills,
at Coldstream, the main party took up its quarters while scouts
periodically crossed the border to reconnoitre. The only resistance was that offered by an English shop-keeper in Coldstream
named Meek, who, despite his name, knocked down a couple of
Boers with his fist before escaping into Natal.

Urging Colley to move to the assistance of the beseiged British was a surprised and shaken Lanyon. The report of the destruction of Anstruther's force had 'the effect of a thunderclap
upon one and all in Pretoria'. The day before the disaster, an
English shop-keeper had galloped some thirty miles to warn the
dark, mannerly governor that an ambush had been prepared. Sir
Owen laughed good-naturedly and dismissed the warning with his

stock answer: 'They will never stand against the British.' When
Conductor Egerton stumbled into the capital and related the
tragic details of the ambush, Lanyon put the entire country under
martial law. Preparations were made to withstand a protracted
siege. Because of the large, sprawling character of the town, the
inhabitants were ordered into a more easily defended laager
around the jail. The residents of the camp quickly recovered their
optimism and began to walk about 'with their noses elevated in
the air, feeling pity for the enemy to be shortly exterminated'.[20]

While Bellairs directed soldiers and civilians in building redoubts, Lanyon busied himself with writing memoranda and dispatches in defence of his policies. But he no longer spoke of the
Boers as 'cowards'—they had now become 'barbarians'. He described in every detail how Englishmen had been 'robbed of
everything, flogged, and murdered'. At Potchefstroom, he related, the rebels had used explosive bullets with terrible effect.
The dead were shamelessly robbed; a Hollander secretary of
Cronje 'wore the rings of a fallen British officer'. The 'unpro-
voked attack' at Bronkhorst Spruit, carried on 'under a flag of
truce', was described as the kind of 'incident rarely mentioned in
the annals of civilized warfare'. The kindness and attention
shown to the wounded, Lanyon attributed to the Boers' clever-
ness, 'for they well know that such action would obtain sympathy
at home'.[21]

As time went on Sir Owen's dispatches became more infre-
quent. The final 'act of reprehensible barbarism' which he
mentioned was the destruction of telegraphic connections. Not
content with merely cutting the wires, the Boers, 'with characteristic wantonness', uprooted and burned the poles, which had been
carried over rugged mountains into a land with little indigenous
wood. It was as if the Boers had renounced civilization for ever.
The last official dispatch from Natal was smuggled through Boer
lines by a young Irish immigrant girl who hid the document in
her bosom while travelling as a passenger on the last coach
allowed to enter Pretoria.

Cut off from the outside world, Lanyon would have been
pleased to learn that his views were prevailing in the British
press. In raging terms, the 'deliberate treachery' of the Boers at
Bronkhorst Spruit was denounced as 'cruel' and 'uncivilized'.
Parallels were drawn with Glencoe, Cawnpore and Lucknow,

with words such as 'dastardly', 'unsporting' and 'overwhelming numbers' abounding. Much of the denunciation concerned
itself with the Boer action of firing on doctors and on a wagon
clearly marked with a Red Cross flag. (The Boers, ignorant of
the European code of military etiquette, later explained that they
thought the ambulance was an ammunition wagon.) Unsub-
stantiated details related how all the food and medical supplies
were looted and later sold at high prices in near-by markets. A
Zulu driver who was with the rearguard was said to have witnessed the shooting of all the wounded men in his party before
escaping into Natal. The prestigious *Times* declared that Bronkhorst Spruit was not an act of war but of 'cold-blooded murder of
British troops ... a deed worthy of savages'. Tales of the bat-
tered 94th were followed closely by 'the horror of the infamous
murder of Captain Elliott' and other acts of 'barbarism'. *Vanity
Fair* took an exceptionally sober view by pointing out that it was
'not fair to hold the Boers as a body responsible for a base and
cruel act'. Since the rank-and-file Boers accepted no discipline,
a worthless few might easily blacken the name of a whole race.

Disturbed by the slander in the press against the Boers, Colley
issued a general order to check 'violent revengeful feelings'
among his soldiers. Borrowing a phrase from Napoleon, he
expressed the opinion that 'war cannot be made with rosewater.'
He told Kimberley, 'I hate this "atrocity-manufacturing" and its
effect on the men, tending to make them either cowards or but-
chers.'[22] But the general's honourable views were given scant
attention in the press.

In January most journals intensified their denigrations of the
Boers, often using information supplied to Parliament and later
found in Blue Books. What the Turks were to the rest of Europe,
they asserted, the Boers, with their 'atrocitarian manner', were
to South Africa. Unkempt, ignorant 'as the black inside of a dog',
'with a freedom of nicety of a vulture', they were not unlike their
European counterpart in their determination to remain 'stranded
in the rapid stream of progress'. It was wittily observed that the
Boers sailed for Africa in the seventeenth century and had been
travelling backwards ever since. Ostensibly Christians, the
'holier than thou' Boers were totally out of step with all educated Christian peoples. They were devoid of morals; readers
were told how the shocking crime of incest was widespread in the

Transvaal. In the words of Bennet Burleigh, the noted war correspondent who later served with the *Daily Telegraph*, 'your
Boer is a fervent hypocrite.' Several writers pointed out that the
Turks, at least, were intrepid warriors; the Boers, on the other
hand, could muster little more than 'Dutch courage'. This common phrase of contempt, once applied to their forefathers, now
descended to the expatriated race in South Africa.

The illustrated papers published again pictures which had been
drawn while Wolseley was on the scene, and others by artists
who exercised their imaginations in sketching the Boer mode of
fighting. Invariably the rebels were represented as huge, grim-
faced, shaggy-bearded ruffians, usually lying in ambush behind
the crest of a hill, while their horses were held by the bridle close
to the firing-line, sometimes in clear view of the British soldiers
below. (Actually the Boers, who valued their horses as much as
themselves, would never have dreamed of bringing the horses
into the line of fire.) Other illustrations depicted mounted Boers
firing revolvers—while in the act of flight, of course. One English
officer later testified that he never saw a revolver in any ordinary
Boer hand; even if he had such a weapon, 'I am quite sure he
would not fire it from horseback.'

The consensus, as expressed by a leading illustrated, the
Graphic, was that now that the sword had been drawn, 'the
struggle must go on, either till the Boers conquer their independence or till we reduce them to submission.' Even those papers
which had regarded the annexation as a mistake generally agreed
that 'insurrection must be put down, at whatever cost.' It was
the same principle enunciated by George III in dealing with the
American colonies—'rebels must be made to obey.' The fact that
the Boers had exhausted every peaceful means of gaining redress
before resorting to arms was ignored. To the Victorians, who
never doubted their mission to extend British rule and to introduce a superior way of life, Boer behaviour was incomprehensible.
What audacious perversity, asked *The Times*, caused the Boer to
reject 'the blessings of his adoption into the British Empire and
prefer to be left in his original squalor and barbarism'? Perhaps,
as it was suggested by the more scientifically minded, the hot
African sun awakened 'strange ferments' in the normally placid
blood of these misplaced Frisians.[23]

Several journals adopted Sir Bartle Frere's view that the re-

volt was a Fenian plot designed to create a diversion on behalf
of comrades in Ireland. Their readers were told that it was that
scoundrel Aylward and men of his ilk who had stirred the simple-
minded Boers to rebellion. The devil-may-care Hibernian was
known to have left his newspaper offices in Natal to join the
Boers as a correspondent. Rumours soon trickled back that he
was serving Piet Joubert as military secretary. It was said that
he had instigated the ambush at Bronkhorst Spruit, and raised
many a stiff tumbler while uttering his favourite toast: 'Death to
the Saxon!' It was also widely reported that Aylward was none
other than James Stephen, the Fenian Head Centre.[24] Respected
citizens of Natal spoke openly of lynching 'Joubert's Irishman'
if he should return.

There is no question that Aylward's behaviour outraged Victorian respectabilities, but to suggest that he was the main-
spring of rebellion was absurd. In concentrating on Aylward's
alleged subversive activities, Frere and others found a convenient means to gloss over the mistakes that had followed annexation.

But the war in South Africa provoked little interest among the
reading public, especially as the outbreak had coincided with
the Christmas season. Conflict in that burdensome portion of the
Empire had become commonplace: if it was not the Zulus, it was
the Pondos or the Basutos. Colonial affairs generally, in the
opinion of Rider Haggard, were a tiresome subject, and though
disaster might be imminent, it 'did not excite the English public
nearly so much as did the "exodus of Jumbo".'[25]

The commonest question Britons had put to each other since
Christmas, observed the *Illustrated London News*, was, 'What
is the Transvaal?' The confusion was compounded by the use of
words like 'dorp' (town), 'kopje' (hill), 'kop' (peak), and
'slim' (sly or clever). Names such as Potchefstroom and Bronkhorst Spruit proved difficult to pronounce. *Punch* later waggishly
asked, 'Why the dickens don't these Boers give some sensible
names to their towns such as Brixton, Hampstead or Peckham
Rye?'

The public found no reason to be alarmed. Complacency was
nurtured by the view that when the British Lion swished its tail,
the rebellion of these ungrateful Boers, who had neither discipline nor training, would be swiftly terminated. *The Times* con-

fidently pronounced: 'It is needless to enlarge upon the illusion
that can persuade 40,000 rude farmers of their ability to resist
British arms.'

Sympathy for the Boer cause was confined largely to the foreign press. From Moscow to San Francisco, the struggle was
interpreted as that of a coerced people rightfully determined to
be free. Comparisons were made between the Boer rebellion and
the American War for Independence; more odious comparisons
were drawn regarding the differences in British policy towards
the Bulgars and the Boers. The accusation that the Afrikaners
had transgressed the rules of civilized warfare was ridiculed.
Anstruther, with his overweening self-confidence, was simply
another Chelmsford, a man who had also paid dearly for his folly.
The French press took pride in the fact that the Jouberts, along
with many other Boers, were of French descent.

Foreign Governments, on the other hand, usually maintained
officially correct attitudes. However, Léon Gambetta, President
of the French Assembly, characterized the behaviour of the
British in South Africa as 'ignoble'. In the United States, resolutions expressing sympathy for the Boers were passed by several
state legislatures. And later, on February 7th, the House of
Representatives expressed the hope 'that there will be no more
bloodshed, and that Her Majesty may see fit to accord independence to the Transvaal if it should be found that the people
have no desire for annexation to Great Britain'. In Germany,
Bismarck, though he ignored petitions from pro-Boer groups,
privately told Viscount Goschen that the British 'ought to have
done anything rather than fight the "white man" in South
Africa'.[26]

Reactions abroad, as the *Graphic* pointed out, were often due
'to a malicious pleasure of seeing England in a fix', rather than
from any sense of outraged justice. But Britain's success in creating a great world Empire excited more than mere envy; there
was also the conviction that the Empire was totally undeserved.
The numerous accretions, ran the argument, were largely the
result of bluff and bluster, greed and cunning. Moreover, though
formidable in appearance, the Empire was fundamentally weak. A
British defeat prompted exultant predictions abroad that it was
the beginning of the end.

The most sincere sentiments on behalf of the Boers were to be found in the Netherlands. 'It is a long time since any event occurring abroad', wrote the respected *Nieuwe Rotterdamsche Courant*, 'has aroused such deep interest within the limits of our fatherland as the rising of the Boers in the Transvaal.'[27] Under Professor Pieter Harting, a distinguished physiologist from Amersfoort, committees were set up to assist the cause of their fellow Dutchmen. Similar organizations were founded among the Flemish inhabitants of Belgium, and even among people of Dutch descent in far-off New York. Over a thousand pounds was collected by the Dutch Red Cross Society for medical aid to the Transvaalers. This was followed by five thousand francs from the Berlin Red Cross. (The Red Cross Society of France was also asked to co-operate in assisting the sick and wounded in the Transvaal, but declined on the ground that the Boers, being in revolt, could not make war.) There were also rumours of a project afoot among the Dutch to form a rifle corps to assist the Boers.

A petition with thousands of Dutch signatures expressing support for the Boer cause was sent to Queen Victoria. Lord Tenterden answered for the Queen, pointing out that it was 'contrary to established usage' to place petitions from subjects of foreign nations before Her Majesty; however, they were advised that the petition would be relayed to the Secretary of State for the Colonies.

As petitions poured in from the Continent, the Cape and the United States, the Workmen's Peace Society in London adopted a resolution early in January. This resolution condemned the fraudulent means by which the annexation was accomplished and urged that the Liberals live up to their campaign promises by granting the Transvaalers their independence. A deputation from the Society requesting a pacific policy was received by the Colonial Secretary on January 13th. Kimberley told them that arbitration had at one time been considered, but the recent massacre of British soldiers now made it imperative to support the present position. If, however, the rebels put down their arms, he indicated that some satisfactory arrangement could be found.

Organized opposition, though still small, was beginning to develop on the Government side of the House, led by Courtney, now Under-Secretary of the Home Department. Consisting mostly of Radicals, this opposition not only viewed war itself as a curse, but claimed, according to Sir George Trevelyan, that it

provided an opportunity for the aristocracy to gain commissions
in the armed forces for their incompetent relations. A section of
the Liberal press, which entered a phase of greater independence, began to echo these views. The *Pall Mall Gazette*, a twopenny evening paper 'written by gentlemen for gentlemen', began to wage a spirited campaign against the annexation policy
and the inexcusable inaction of the Liberal ministry after seven
months in office. On the Opposition side, the 'Fourth Party' of
Lord Randolph Churchill ('half genius and half naughty boy')
and a small body of admirers sensed an opportunity to make mischief. They protested against the waste of British lives which resulted from an unjust effort to reduce the Boers into submission
after the initial error of annexation.* Though the opposition was
still small, most men in public life, Liberal and Conservative
alike, privately began to wish that the annexation had never taken
place.

Another war in South Africa, in addition to that with the
Pondos and Basutos, could hardly have come at a worse moment
for the Liberal ministry. In the whole of South Africa there were
only five battalions and those were ill-disciplined and weakened
by desertions. A very considerable portion of the British army
was still on service in Afghanistan, though the decision to evacu-
ate was becoming definitive despite strong objections voiced by
the Queen. Turkey and Greece were on the verge of another war,
and there was talk in official quarters of sending the Greeks a
naval force. Another crisis appeared to be in the making in
Egypt. Worse, the situation in Ireland had steadily deteriorated.
Agrarian outrages became common. In Parliament, Parnell and
his phalanx of Irish Nationalists launched an unparalleled campaign of convulsive obstruction. One sitting in January lasted
twenty-two hours, and another which began on the last day of
January was prolonged for forty-one hours.

Contrary passions racked the ill-matched Cabinet. Herbert
Gladstone, son of the Prime Minister and 'a very junior Lord
of the Treasury', declared that the situation looked like 'war to
the knife'. 'Buckshot' Forster, the Irish Secretary, demanded
coercive measures in John Bull's 'other island'; Whig leaders

---

* After a visit to South Africa a few years later, Lord Randolph Churchill hope-
fully predicted that the 'unintelligent Boer would pass away unhonoured, unlamented,
scarcely ever remembered, either by the native or European settler'.

like Hartington threatened resignation if Forster was not supported — and Radicals Bright and Chamberlain threatened to resign if he was. Only Forster's indecision saved the ministry.

It did not take long for the Irish and Transvaal difficulties to become interwoven, with Parnellites joining Radicals in the House to block strong Whig measures pertaining to either land. The ministry itself was torn into factions over the Transvaal. Chamberlain, Dilke, Courtney, and to a certain extent Bright, favoured the Boers, while the Whig peers, including Kimberley, insisted that the cause of humanity and the prestige of Britain must be maintained against the rebels. Forster, as leader of the small surviving party of evangelists and humanitarian imperialists (who ignored the Irish), sided with the Whig peers so as to protect the tribal communities against the Boer white supremacists.

Gladstone hesitated. He was confronted by problems in every quarter. 'What we hoped would be a Government express', remarked his son, 'lumbered along like a blocked and half-empty train.'[28] The Prime Minister, inclined on principle to restrict Imperial expenditures and to favour self-determination, nevertheless finally decided to leave the matter in the hands of his more knowledgeable Colonial Minister, who assured him that British authority could be reasserted in the Transvaal in a matter of weeks. Gladstone, whose practice it was to concentrate on one political issue at a time, was free to turn his attention to what he regarded as the more pressing situation, Ireland.

Kimberley wrote to Colley on December 30th that reinforcements had been ordered out and that 'every support which may be necessary' to restore the situation would be given him. On the same day he rejected as 'inopportune' a proposal by Cape legislators that a special commissioner (preferably J. H. de Villiers, Chief Justice of the Colony) should be sent out to inquire and report on the true state of affairs in the Transvaal. President Brand sent a second message on January 10th urging that efforts should be made to prevent further bloodshed, but Kimberley answered that a satisfactory settlement could not be made until the Boers put down their arms. But the Colonial Secretary's reply to Brand was preceded by a public act far more memorable. As Parliament reassembled on January 6th, the Queen declared in her Speech from the Throne: "A rising in the Transvaal has recently imposed upon me the duty of taking military measures with a view to the prompt vindication of my authority; and has of necessity set aside for the time any plan for securing to the European settlers that full control over their own local affairs, without prejudice to the interests of the natives, which I had been desirous to confer."

'Seldom', commented John Morley, 'has the Sovereign been made the mouthpiece of an utterance more short-sighted.'[29] Morley failed to add that Her Majesty's ministers had put a lie into her mouth by implying that it was the insurrection which had caused the British Government to postpone plans for local self-rule. Unless a mixture of carelessness, neglect, broken promises and lack of wisdom could be defined as a plan, the Government had no plan. The Queen's words only confirmed the mistrust and contempt that the Boers felt for British statesmen.

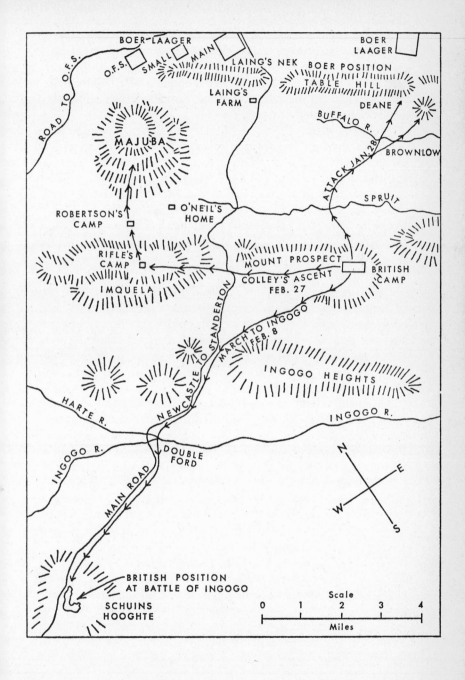

[5]

LAING'S NEK

Thus far and no farther.
Joubert

COLLEY was in a quandary. The sudden uprising of the Boers created an emergency automatically putting him—with barely fifteen hundred men—into a position of responsibility for the pacification of the Transvaal. If the Basuto and Pondo wars had not been simultaneously on his hands, Colley explained to the War Secretary, Hugh Childers, the soldiers at his disposal would have been 'sufficient to maintain the peace' under any circumstances; or if the first encounter had been favourable, a single additional regiment would have been enough to restore the situation. But the defeat of the 94th, 'like Isandhlwana on a smaller scale', had handicapped him.[1]

Ordinarily, with reinforcements on the way, Colley would have been able to 'sit back and smoke' and wait until his numbers were sufficient to overwhelm the rebels. But time, reasoned the general, was against him, for there was considerable doubt in his mind as to whether the isolated garrisons could withstand an extended siege. 'Our weak point', he wrote to Wolseley, 'is Potchefstroom.' Because of scanty provision, the hundred and fifty Fusiliers located there could not be expected to hold out for more than six weeks, and no important reinforcements would reach South Africa before that time.

By moving immediately, Colley believed that he could at least prevent raids into Natal and that he could relieve the pressure on the garrisons by forcing the Boers to face their more active assailants. The loss of one fortified town such as Potchefstroom would, he believed, greatly prolong the war, and a protracted conflict in the Transvaal might easily lead to increased racial tension between Briton and Boer throughout the remaining provinces. 'There are ugly rumours about', he told Childers, 'of very strong feeling among the Dutch inhabitants of South Africa generally.'[2]

To prevent any hatred from arising on the English side, Colley issued a general order to his troops on December 28th in which he described the foe as 'in the main, a brave and high-spirited people ... actuated by feelings that are entitled to our respect'. However, the general was determined that 'the stain cast on our arms must be quickly effaced, and the rebellion put down.' In describing the action at Bronkhorst Spruit to his soldiers, he implied that the Boer victory was not so much attri-butable to the enemy's fighting qualities as it was to the faulty disposition of Anstruther's column. Recalling that British sol-diers ever since Minorca had been inspired by disaster, Colley reminded his men that they possessed 'the incalculable advantage which organization and trained skill give them ... advantages which have been repeatedly proved, and have never failed to command success in the end against greater odds and greater difficulties than we are now called on to contend with'.

The first units of the relief column began the move towards the frontier before the end of the year. The general planned to have his entire force hurried across the border and relieving Standerton—400 miles from Pietermaritzburg—by January 25th. Then, depending on the strength of the Boers opposing him, he would have to decide either to risk battle by pushing on to Pre-toria, or to wait another month until the newly landed reinforce-ments could join him.

When reports reached Colley that the Boers were collecting a large commando to dispute his crossing into the Transvaal, he feared 'the news is too good to be true.' He wrote to Childers, 'It will be very good-natured of them if they will thus give me the opportunity of meeting them close to my base ... '[3]

A modest man, Colley was not given to boasting. He was well aware that he commanded an absurdly small and motley force, composed largely of 'mere boys', but he seriously ques-tioned the capabilities of the Boer irregulars. Their fathers and grandfathers, obviously made of sterner stuff, had been broken by redcoats at Boomplaats, and these same Boers had been ignominiously driven off by Sekukuni's poorly armed warriors. As the present Boers were ill-supplied and easily discouraged,

Colley imagined that they would soon grow weary of campaigning. Despite the efforts of their leaders to hold them together, he
told Childers, 'their numbers ... are probably decreasing instead
of increasing from day to day.'[4] Colley was inclined to agree with
The Times correspondent at Durban who stated that at least two
thousand intimidated Boers 'were serving through fear'.

To inspire in the Boers an even greater fear of the British,
Colley relied on cannon. 'Artillery have a great moral effect
among the Dutch,' insisted Colley, and a battery of artillery
could do more to keep the peace than several regiments.[5] It was
no secret that the Boer leaders themselves were anxious as to
whether their burghers would stand or run under shell-fire.*

Undoubtedly, had his force been even smaller than it was,
Colley would still have preferred the greater risks of advance to
those of delay. He admitted to the Duke of Cambridge that if he
met with a check, 'it will do immense harm'.[7] The Commander-
in-Chief suffered 'the gravest anxiety' when he learned that
Colley was determined to 'advance *at once* ... before any of the
reinforcements can reach him . . .'[8]

Though this was merely one of some eighty-two wars fought
during the reign of Victoria, there was 'agitation and fuss' at the
War Office to hurry troops to South Africa—considerably more
than Colley had requested. The Duke and his staff worked
through Boxing Day. 'The fluster in Pall Mall is such', commented one observer, 'that a stranger might imagine that never
before had troops been sent out of England.' Officers and officials
spoke of Colley's advance as hasty and ill-considered. Sir George
White, the future field-marshal who would successfully defend
Ladysmith in a later Boer war, remembered Colley as the most
enthusiastic advocate of the 'forward' policy in India because of
his 'dangerously high idea of what a few British soldiers can
do'.[9]

The decision to advance immediately with all the troops available caused considerable alarm among the British settlers in
Natal. To many it was 'madness'. The defeat of the 94th was
known to have made an unfavourable impression on the near-by,
aggressive Pondos, but nevertheless Colley quietly removed

---

* The Zulus, who had been taught to fear the cannon, called it 'umbyembyee',
because when a Zulu working a Durban wharf first saw a field-gun and asked its
name, the men landing it replied, 'We will tell you bye-and-bye.'[6]

units to bolster his small force. More frightening still was the danger of a Boer invasion supported by a large number of disaffected Natal Dutch, who in Colley's own words 'warmly sympathized with them'. The resources of the Cape Colony were too heavily taxed by the Basuto War to be of any help.

Though the colonists always prided themselves upon being English in origin and instinct, they wanted Natal to remain neutral. Many had close business connections with the Transvaal that they did not want to see disturbed. The panicky resident magistrate in Newcastle, acting 'as the mouthpiece of the Governor of Natal', sent a letter on his own to the Republicans, reminding them that Natal was a neutral state. He received a prompt and courteous reply on January 7th in which Joubert pointed out that, neutral or not, the colony was being used as a base for operation against them and was therefore inviting invasion.

Memorials requesting the preservation of Natal's neutrality were sent to the Governor, while in the Legislative Council a motion was passed to the effect that the colony would in no way be held responsible for the costs, or any portion of the costs, of the war.

The Governor was quick to correct the behaviour of his magistrate, who was told to write a second letter to Joubert which would repudiate the first. Colley made it clear that since Natal was a part of the British Empire, no subject loyal to Her Majesty could remain neutral in a contest between Imperial forces and rebels against the Crown. Moreover, the Natal Mounted Police, whose employment in the conflict was strenuously objected to, was the Governor's sole responsibility and would be used in such a manner as would best serve the protection of the colony.

In practice, Colley was studiously careful in limiting the committal of Natal and its colonists to an absolute minimum. He wisely reasoned that since the people of Natal and the Transvaal would have to live side by side, the more he made it appear that the struggle was one between the Boers and the Imperial Government the better.

Natal did not lack for volunteers. Many had served in numerous quaintly named irregular corps during the Zulu War: Shambuckers' Horse, Raafs' Rangers, the Buffalo Border Guards.

Volunteers were currently fighting in the Pondo and Basuto wars. But Colley had no intention of using them against the Boers, except for a small select body to serve as a personal escort. Volunteers were useful in other ways, most of all to relieve the Mounted Police, which were below strength. As a professional soldier, Colley was sceptical of irregulars because often they shunned discipline and hankered after loot. 'There is always in South Africa', wrote Major Scott Turner of the 42nd Highlanders, 'a floating population of loafers, mostly of men who have made Europe too hot for them, who are ready to join any corps raised for any service.'

The Natal Mounted Police, well-trained and disciplined, had been recruiting a superior type directly from Britain. Many, however, still looked very 'irregular', with bandoliers over loose cord tunics and garish hats festooned with long ostrich feathers; they wore their beards long and their hair curled inward in the French style, tamed with coconut-oil. They always looked forward to being drafted, for the Crown took over the expense of supply and rationing. When they were drafted in the Zulu War, it was 'the first time in their corporate existence that the men were all out of debt'.[10]

A large party of Mounted Police were sent to Newcastle and Ladysmith to watch the border and collect information regarding Boer movements. Others joined the mounted force under Major Brownlow of the King's Dragoon Guards. It was a queer mixture. In addition to the Mounted Police, there were time-expired and convalescent Dragoons, drivers from the Army Service Corps, and volunteers from two infantry battalions with little or no knowledge of horsemanship. Considering that they numbered only 120 men, and were opposed by a large body of mounted Boers, Colley decided they must be 'carefully used and nursed'. One half were designated to join the advance-guard on the march and to engage in scouting; the other half were to bring up the rear. Colley was painfully aware that his infantrymen on horseback were advancing to engage an overwhelming force of expert horsemen who were capable of mounting and dismounting rapidly, and shooting with deadly accuracy in or out of the saddle. Unless the Boers were vastly superior in numbers, the best chance for success, he concluded, was to attack and to fight at close quarters; the Boers had little skill at hand-to-hand combat,

nor were they armed for it. Colley, therefore, had swords issued
to his men. He later conceded that 'the want of good mounted
troops counted very heavily against us ...'

The guns in which the English put so much of their faith
numbered only six: four nine-pounders and a garrison battery of
two seven-pounders. Each seven-pounder was drawn by a two-
mule tandem, and was manned by a gunner, with two infantrymen from the 58th and two from the 60th Rifles, the entire unit
being commanded by a subaltern of the 21st. It was a strange job
lot, popularly known as 'The Royal Ass Battery'.

In addition to the standard artillery, the Royal Navy offered
two Gatlings and three rocket tubes, which Colley believed would
be 'very useful' at the front. Gatlings had been in service in the
Zulu and Afghan campaigns, but, because of certain unaccount-
able malfunctions, it was fashionable to decry the weapon and to
disparage its range and execution. 'All very well, you know, to
sweep a bridge or defend an outpost, but it is of no use in the
open, and of less behind walls.'[11] Nor was service opinion favourable to rockets, which seemed more spectacular than effective,
and were employed in a sporadic and very minor way since first
being introduced in the Napoleonic Wars.* Now in the closing
days of their existence, rockets were used almost exclusively to
teach the 'less civilized' a terrifying respect for the Queen's
name. Colley had seen them used to good effect in China (where
they had been employed for war purposes a thousand years before) and against the Ashanti. He hoped these novel engines of
war would have a psychological effect on the Boers and cause their
horses to bolt.

The Royal Navy co-operated further by landing 120 bluejackets from H.M.S. *Boadicea* to join Colley's army. With
their characteristic swagger they marched through the streets of
the pretty little capital singing a tune with merry enthusiasm.

'Maritzburg is alive with uniforms,' declared one soldier.[12]
There were sailors dressed comfortably for work in deep blue;

---

* The rocket was instrumental in routing the Americans at the battle of Bladens-
burg, which opened the way to Washington during the War of 1812. The eccentric
behaviour of the rockets, however, made them inherently treacherous. Wellington,
who was nearly killed by boomeranging rockets while watching a demonstration,
declared that he preferred nine-pounders to missiles that were 'undisciplined and
ungentlemanly'. This mistrust was reflected in a naval regulation which stated that
if ever the rockets should hang fire, the crew must jump overboard at once!

officers of the Royal Engineers and the Royal Artillery and staff
officers in dark blue Norfolk jackets; Mounted Policemen in tan;
detachments of the 60th Rifles (many of whom had recently
served against the Pondos) in green; and portions of the 58th,
21st and 94th (consisting in the main of several large drafts who
had just disembarked) dressed in the traditional single-breasted
red serge tunic and blue serge trousers. Nearly all had in common the cork sun helmet covered with white canvas and decorated with a regimental badge, and heavy ammunition boots shod
with iron heels. Once again, as in the Zulu War two years before,
the capital of Natal had a colourful, light-hearted air of martial
confidence and splendour.

The townspeople may have entertained some doubts about
this Lilliputian army, which even in its smallness lacked cohesion,
but the soldiers and sailors never questioned their ability to
vanquish the despised enemy. 'It will only be a picnic,' was the
prevailing attitude. And because the British army was still little
more than a collection of regiments, each man had a special—
almost childlike—pride in his unit and in its regimental dis-
tinctions; their uniforms were covered with facings, badges and
buttons, and, most important, the sacred colours were crowded
with inscriptions of heroic encounters throughout the world.

As his army marched off to war, Colley remained behind,
intending to overtake them at Newcastle. His dual role as
Governor and general made enormous demands on his time.
Chronically anxious, Colley continued to behave outwardly in a
manner he described as 'stolid'; 'I play tennis and hold receptions
and visit schools and hospitals just as usual,' he wrote.[13] He
regretted the war; a short time before the outbreak of the conflict,
he expressed to Wolseley his hope that the Transvaal would be
granted 'as free a constitution as might be consistent with continued connection with the English Crown'.[14] A sensitive, deeply
conscientious man, he reproached himself for having largely
ignored the Transvaal since his arrival, and for having contributed
to the annexation by reporting (after his mission in 1875) that
the Boers would welcome British rule.

Rather than work in the executive office, Colley spent most of
his time in the study of his official residence. Here he was surrounded by his many books (on a wide variety of subjects) and
his collection of contemporary art, his favourite being a water-

colour of a skirmish with the Ashanti. Seated in the same American-style swivel chair which he had occupied during his trying days in India, he attended to the more pressing administrative problems. Other problems were not so pressing, such as that of Colenso, who had found a new cause. The busy bishop now pleaded for the exiled Langalibalele who wanted to return one of his more troublesome wives to Natal.[15] (Not granted.) As general, his concerns ranged from the construction of new ammunition boxes to a request sent to London that the Boers should be given belligerent rights—'they have acted with courtesy and humanity in the matter of our wounded.' (Granted.) But strong objections were raised in England to treating rebels as belligerents. 'If we hang every one of them,' declared *The Times*, 'we should be no more than acting in accordance with recognized rules.'

Remembering that Sir Arthur Cunynghame had once moved the 80th with 'ease and celerity' by way of the Capetown–Beaufort–Kimberley route to the Transvaal, Colley suggested to the War Office that reinforcements arriving from England should be sent by this route. This would distract the attention of the Boers and take them from behind, which would be better than having the reinforcements coming up in the rear of his own force over a line already strained by the demands for supplies and transport. (The Boers, anticipating such a move on the western frontier, stationed a party near Fourteen Streams to observe the border at Griqualand West.) Wolseley called the proposal unwise. The Quartermaster-General argued that the route in question actually passed through Free State territory, and there was every reason to believe that President Brand would refuse permission to enter. The physical difficulties involved in traversing this immense distance during the dry season, he wrote to Childers, were enough to render the proposed march nearly impossible. Moreover, Wolseley assumed 'that the lesson taught us in the Zululand would have made us hesitate before again proposing to act on two or more lines with columns having no power of supporting or even communication with one another'.[16] The War Office also received unconfirmed reports that Boer sympathizers were plotting to destroy the railway bridges if Cape lines were used to carry British troops to the north. The proposal was cancelled.

Meanwhile, when Colley ascertained that reinforcements from England would not arrive much before those from India, he was no longer interested in suggesting a change of base. But others were. General Alison advised Childers that rather than 'running our heads against the strong passes of the Drakensberg', a British force operating in the west could turn that 'formidable obstacle ... and cut in like a wedge between the Boers and their best means of supply and reinforcements, the Orange Free State'.[17] Frere gave his support to this plan and Cambridge was sympathetic. Childers, however, was unmoved. The town of Kimberley offered to raise volunteers and deliver Potchefstroom, but Colley deprecated such action because it might arouse 'hostility between the white races'.*

The road through Natal to the border was difficult. It was the height of the South African summer; the intense heat made the soldiers' dress thoroughly inappropriate to the climate. As they struggled under loads of over fifty pounds, whirling clouds of red dust rose from the unpaved road to sting their eyes. The blistering sun caused their noses to peel and turn a copper colour. Some of the men 'fell out all over the place—too much beer overnight, most of all during celebrating the New Year'.[18] It became necessary for the officers to carry rifles for some of the men. Transport arrangements were insufficient: the mules were bad, the harnesses rotten, and the native drivers, the only ones who could manage the oxen, were 'cowardly, sometimes disaffected, always avaricious'.[19]

It was a tedious, dragging march through a country rising in successive terraces. A breakdown could detain the column for hours; one delayed them for two days. Heavy rains turned the roads into quagmires, and narrow streams became swollen rivers. Wagons stuck in the mud until the only way to move them was to hitch all the mules and oxen to one vehicle and lay on with the long whips while the men pushed. All calculations of time were upset. On January 16th the men were put on half-rations. The storms became more severe. Night and day, the thunder was continuous, as 'deafening crashes, synchronizing

---

* Some people in England entertained the absurd notion that a force could be landed at Delagoa Bay and marched to Pretoria. The path was wholly impracticable, most of all during the summer season when swamp and fever would doom any such venture to failure.

with blinding flashes of light, filled the air.'[20] Men and animals
were stunned or killed.

It took nearly a month of hard marching to get the small force
and its transport into Newcastle. The men, who had not been dry
for days, were hungry and near exhaustion. As they approached
the town, they began to sing as they had done so often on the
march. Old favourites, such as 'My Grandfather's Clock', were
sung to the accompaniment of twopenny whistles and improvised drums, a mess-tin and two sticks.

Almost overnight Newcastle became the focal point of the
war, with refugees and soldiers pouring in from different directions. In the midst of the original scattered collection of corrugated iron shacks and the two hotels and Fort Amiel, canvas
houses and tents mushroomed. 'About as utterly unsightly a combination', observed one visitor, 'as ever received the distinction
of being called a town.'[21] The inhabitants of this frontier district were not highly thought of by those in more settled areas.
They were spoken of by more 'civilized' South Africans as being
'of use for only four things—jawing, lying, drinking and horse-
jumping'.[22]

The night before Colley left for Newcastle to take personal
command, a dinner and dance were held at Government House,
which, save for the sentinel on duty, must have had the look of a
quiet country rectory. To one soldier it was 'a sort of colonial
parody of the ball at Brussels before Waterloo'.[23] The local press
expressed the hope that the general would demonstrate that he
had inherited some of the great qualities of the 'Iron Duke'. It is
quite sobering to reflect, however, that of the thirteen guests at
the dinner table, nine would be dead in a few weeks—eight soldiers and one woman.

On January 10th, the very day Colley left for Newcastle, the
Imperial Government began to incline towards conciliation. Negotiations for a fair settlement were initiated by Brand, who was
unceasing in his efforts to bring about a rapprochement. He
bombarded Colley, Kimberley and Sir Hercules Robinson, successor to Strahan as Governor at the Cape, with increasingly
urgent telegrams to prevent further bloodshed. At the same time
he battled to keep his own Free State strictly neutral.

Replying to a pleading telegram from Brand on the 10th,
Kimberley stated that his Government did not 'despair of mak-

ing a satisfactory arrangement', provided that the Boers would desist from their armed opposition. Brand immediately repeated his earlier suggestion that not a moment be wasted in sending a commission ('with a clear and definite proposal for settlement') to end the conflict. Kimberley still felt that the burghers should put down their arms first. Brand reiterated his pleas on January 16th and again on January 26th. Similar proposals emanated from the Dutch party at the Cape, led by Jan Hofmeyer; and behind the scenes Donald Currie, founder of the famous Castle Line, was in constant private communication with his close friend Brand, transmitting the President's appeals to Gladstone through the ready medium of the latter's son Herbert. In his unofficial correspondence Brand warned that if the war continued, he would not be able to restrain his own burghers.

In reply to a suggestion made by Brand on January 26th that Robinson be appointed as special commissioner, Kimberley wired the same day to Robinson asking him to tell Brand that if armed opposition ceased, the Government 'would endeavour to frame a scheme as, in their belief, would satisfy all enlightened friends of the Transvaal community'.[24]

Despite the vagueness of the Colonial Secretary's statement, Brand was encouraged and he urged that these terms be clarified and sent to the Transvaal before Colley launched an attack.

Kimberley's responses were characteristically non-committal and ambiguous, but Herbert Gladstone maintained that Brand's words suggesting that the war might easily spread to other territories 'at last weighed in against official experts in South Africa', and produced a change in ministerial policy. The Cabinet, according to young Gladstone, decided that the 'facts of conciliation were right', but in 'the absence of a spur of public opinion', no intimation was given to the public of a reversal in policy.[25]

On January 21st Mr Rylands, a Radical back-bencher, proposed a resolution in the House of Commons condemning the annexation as impolitic and unjustifiable, and, therefore, viewing with regret a policy designed to assert British supremacy over a people who rightly claimed their national independence. Gladstone, suffering from the lingering effects of a cold, testily defended his policy by speaking of 'contracted obligations'. He lectured the House on the subtle difference between condemning the annexation of the Transvaal and abandoning the annexation altogether. However, he added, he hoped that it might be possible to achieve the ends that Brand so earnestly sought. He favoured the granting of free institutions to the Transvaal, but this was not the time for 'specific declarations'.

Rylands tried to withdraw his motion but was refused. A large majority, including most of the Conservatives, voted against it, but Radicals like Bright, Dilke, Chamberlain and Courtney deliberately walked out on the Transvaal division. A delighted Lord Randolph Churchill observed that the Transvaal issue split the Liberals 'by a sharper and more insuperable line than the Irish question'.

Obviously Kimberley and a ministerial majority anticipated a decisive military success that would place them in a strong position when negotiations began. Colley confidently assured his superiors that the defeat of the Boers was 'only a matter of time'. His chief concern was with how the Boers would react to a military reversal. He hoped that they would 'accept their defeat and curse the leaders who have misled them', rather than prolong the conflict through guerrilla activities. To reconcile them to defeat, Colley urged that a post-war settlement should include a limited form of representation. To chastise former rebels, he advocated a war tax of ten pounds per farm. 'The punishment of the leaders', Colley privately advised Kimberley, 'would be the confiscation of property, for they are all men of property.'[26] The Colonial Secretary agreed to study the matter but denied Colley the right to offer any terms. He was allowed to go no further than to promise protection to the inhabitants of the occupied territory.

No other instructions were given to Colley. He was kept in complete ignorance about the exchange of messages with Brand. Not until February 3rd did he have any inkling of these negotiations, and then only from Brand himself. Childers, who was in a position as War Secretary to co-ordinate political and military developments, failed also to enlighten him. On January 17th Colley complained to his wife, 'Lord Kimberley has simply sent me his replies to various deputations wihout comment ...' He began to fear that 'continued inaction' might do considerable harm. Since there were no instructions he felt free to act at his own discretion. And Colley was bound to advance, for he considered it his 'plain duty' to vindicate the Queen's authority against the armed men who had assaulted it.[27]

On January 23rd Colley sent an ultimatum to Joubert ordering the Boers to disperse, informing him that large reinforcements were already arriving, and promising him that if they disbanded he would forward any statement of Boer grievances to London. Joubert decided that he would not be justified in replying to a document of such weight himself, so he sent it on to Heidelberg for consideration. But the distance was great and the roads were almost impassable through incessant rains. The Boer commander, therefore, was foolish to assume that Colley, now only a few miles away, would wait indefinitely for a reply to his ultimatum.

The answer, dated January 27th, was that the Republicans were prepared to co-operate with the British desire for federation; they wished only for the invalidation of the annexation and the restoration of the Republic under the protection of the Queen, which could be symbolically expressed by hoisting the Union Jack in the Transvaal once a year. 'If your Excellency resolves to reject this,' read the closing sentence, 'we have only to submit to our fate; but the Lord will provide.' In essence, the reply was similar to the December proclamation, though it was more emphatic. This proclamation was never received by Colley because the Boer party which was sent to have it printed in Potchefstroom was fired upon. Nor did Colley receive the second message until intervening events robbed it of much of its significance. Joubert claimed that he was about to relay the document to Colley when he was attacked, on January 28th. And for some reason, never fully explained, no copy was actually sent across the lines until February 15th.

If the Republicans had not destroyed the telegraph line between Heidelberg and Laing's Nek, their Government would have been in easy touch with Joubert. But it would have been difficult in any case to restrain the Boers, who broke all connections. Knowing that Lanyon used the wire for his dispatches, they angrily told a visitor, 'This thing has lied enough.' They then tore it asunder.[28]

On the day he dispatched his ultimatum, the general held a review of his little army. The exact strength of his force, which was further reduced because large detachments had been left at various points to guard communications, was not revealed for some time so as to conceal its paucity of numbers from the enemy.

The twelve hundred men who marched before the general looked fit and seemed well-handled. The review concluded, the soldiers formed into a square around the commander.

Standing before them was an erect, dignified man. His face was grave and he looked about with clear, penetrating eyes. In a manner perfectly unobtrusive and modest, the general began to speak, at first with his characteristic slight hesitation, of how the men impressed him with their efficiency and good character. Then in a more spirited voice he announced his intention of moving to the aid of the beleaguered garrisons without waiting for reinforcements. Waiting would involve the delay of a month, 'a month of suspense and suffering to their fellow soldiers and the women and children', which would 'in some cases necessitate surrender'. He trusted, therefore, that they would not begrudge the extra fighting and effort. Surely, he added, they 'would be rewarded by the shouts of the brave comrades they had relieved, and the gratitude and blessings of the men, women, and children they had succoured'. With a slight stammer, the general declared that he was proud of the position he held, and that if they could have the same confidence in him as he did in them, all would go well. The speech was applauded; ringing cheers could be heard from one end of Newcastle to the other. As the troops marched back to camp to the stirring music of two bands, Colley rode about on his dapple-grey charger to say goodbye to those who had come to witness the departure of the force.

Colley was a man of upright character and great ability, but he had virtually no experience of commanding troops in the field. He had passed up his one opportunity for an important combatant position in the Ashanti War when he had taken on the difficult and crucial but comparatively uninteresting assignment of organization and command of transport. He wrote to his wife that, despite the good luck that had always favoured him in winning every honour and achievement, he faced his supreme opportunity of command—which would determine his entire future—with considerable apprehension.

Early on the morning of January 24th the advance from Newcastle began. The men had dyed their helmets and belts brown with cow-dung and coffee grounds so as to be less of a target, though they were 'pretty odoriferous for a day or two'.[29] The track to the north was in a deplorable state, and the large convoy

of wagons stuck fast every few yards. Navigating across the
deep and difficult valley of the Imbazane River cost them a good
part of the second day out. Boer patrols were occasionally visible,
but no opposition was offered. On the third day, they toiled up a
long and steep ascent to an eminence known as Schuins Hooghte.
The plateau was dotted with oddly projecting flat slabs, which at
a distance resembled tombstones. From there the land sloped
gently towards a level grassy plain, about a mile long, beyond
which was the deeply cut course of the Ingogo River. They
crossed under cover of infantry and artillery to an area full of
dark clumps of trees. Beyond, the men were treated to the magnificent sight of the majestic Drakensberg Range, guarded, as if
by a solitary sentinel, by the square-topped hill called Majuba.
From the eastern slopes of Majuba ran a low ridge known as
Laing's Nek—now pierced by a railway tunnel—which terminated steeply at the bed of the Buffalo River. Halfway between
Laing's Nek and Schuins Hooghte, some twelve miles out of
Newcastle, Colley established his camp on Mount Prospect in an
area surrounded by cypress trees. As scouts searched the country-
side, a laager was formed with the wagons. Colley felt it was too
late in the day to move on to the Nek.

It was an eventful night. The rearguard had a narrow escape
when lightning shattered a telegraph pole along the road. The
army dined miserably on cold rations in the rain and no man was
permitted to remove his accoutrements. Shortly before midnight
two shots were fired, signalling an alarm. Outlying pickets
crashed into the laager at the double and were nearly fired upon
by frightened sleepers. All the troops stood to arms the rest of
the night, but nothing happened. It was later rumoured that a
bored sentry had fired the two shots to liven things up. The army
remained inactive the next day because of rain and heavy mist
which completely enveloped the Nek.

The British had only a vague notion as to the size and disposition of Joubert's force. Captain Lambert estimated to Colley
that the Boers had mustered 16,000 men, which was the current
view in Natal; but Colley offered a more accurate estimate of
between 5,000 and 7,000, of whom no more than 2,000 had
opposed him at the border. Thus, with anything close to an
equality of forces, a passive defence would be wholly inadmissible
to a British general. Actually, there were barely 1,000 Boers

facing Colley. Their numbers were subject to fluctuation as fresh burghers appeared from day to day or others decided to go home—they could not be 'urged to the front like slaves by the whips of innumerable penalties'.[30] When it appeared that the British intended to fight their way through the Drakensberg, the Transvaalers began to recall their outlying patrols.

At the Boer encampment near Coldstream, from where they could easily move to occupy any of the passes, hundreds of wagons were drawn up in orderly lines for defence, while cattle and horses grazed on the veld outside. The men slept in the wagons or in the tents placed between them. Tents and wagons were decorated with strips of biltong. There were a few wagons marked by flags, indicating that they belonged to commandants or veld kornets.

'Silence and smoke reigned supreme,' wrote Aylward when he visited the camp. The men busied themselves with cooking or drawing on their pipes. There was no drill. Before and after meals the silence was broken by fervent prayers. At night, after the oxen and horses were assembled, psalm-singing accompanied prayers as the men stood reverently attentive. Sometimes they sang songs of protest. The *North German Press* recorded one of them which began:

> Leave us alone! Leave us alone!
> You shall not rob us of our own;
> We will be free! We will be free!
> Our birthright shall our standard be.

But never, observed Aylward, 'have I heard a word of anger or recrimination amongst them'.[31]

Now in his late forties, Joubert had the look of a farmer, but his abrupt military bearing, his grim mouth and quick eyes which narrowed into a squint as he inspected posts and terrain, combined to give him the appearance of no ordinary burgher. Patient, cautious and crafty, he was never brilliant or dashing. Though intelligent in war matters, he had an aversion to bloodshed, and disliked firing the first shot. His gentle nature was such that he was said to have wept at the outbreak of the Second Boer War; later, at the battle of Magersfontein, he would not allow his men to fire on retiring forces. 'They are white men; they are retreating. You must let them go.' His detractors, however, alleged that he was very severe on the blacks—including women—while leading expeditions against them in the early days of the Republic.

Colley and other British officers regarded him as more moderate and less bold in spirit than other Boer leaders, but they were mistaken if they believed Joubert to be wavering in decision or purpose. His mind was cast from a stern mould and shaped by deep religious convictions. His Bible was as indispensable as his field-glasses and wooden pipe. (He carried no weapon in the field.) 'Now and then', wrote a visitor to his camp, 'I caught him droning out some old Dutch psalm to his wife as they were seated together, in a quiet corner.'[32] When he believed the Lord was on his side, Joubert was inexorably tenacious.

Confronted with artillery, Joubert favoured a defensive position which required little or no additional shelter apart from what Nature herself could provide. Familiar with the terrain since childhood, he chose for his Thermopylae what the Boers mistakenly called 'Lang' ('Long') Nek; it was in fact named after Henry Laing whose farm lay just below. Boer scouts frequently visited the region, and on January 27th some of the men began to occupy the ridge, but not until the following morning did Joubert send forth eighty or so burghers under Commandant Greyling to occupy the Table Hill that dominated the position. A single trench and sod bank about 150 yards long was dug across the roadway. Only at the time of the attack did more Boers ride up, taking an extended position behind the best cover they could find. At the onset of battle there were only 250 burghers present; they were reinforced later by another 170.

The strength of the position was apparent at a glance.* The pass over the Nek lay in the centre of a rough crescent of stony hills, six miles in length, with the tips pointing towards Newcastle. It could be approached only from the front. There was no way of approach from the west, the British left, where the ridge culminated in the lofty and forbidding Majuba; the right was protected by the Buffalo River running through a deep gorge. The ground within the semicircle was an undulating grassy plateau, broken by several ravines. No part of the Boer stronghold could be attacked from the front without a steep ascent which would

* For the plan of the positions from Laing's Nek and Ingogo held by the Boers and the British, see map on p. 131.

provide no cover. The reverse slope, on the other hand, was gentle, and would allow rapid movement by mounted Boers.

Having waited five days for a reply to an ultimatum that might easily have been given in as many hours, Colley attacked on January 28th. It was a clear day, and no effort was made to conceal the bustle indicating the preparation for an assault. After breakfast, shortly before 7.00 a.m., Mounted Police were sent out as an advance-guard. Five companies of Rifles followed, covered by two guns. Then came the sailors with rocket tubes and two mountain guns. The rear was composed of ambulances and the 58th, covered also by two guns. Altogether, there were 56 officers, 1,158 non-commissioned officers and men, and 196 horses. The camp itself, surrounded by earthworks, was left in charge of an infantry detachment one hundred strong from the 21st, thirty bluejackets with two Gatlings, and some fifty army service and transport men.

The approach to the Nek was slow. Some of the guns got stuck in the muddy low ground. At 9.15 the column halted at the amphitheatre of hills, still out of range of enemy rifles, and took up an extended position. Few Boers were to be seen and the general belief was that the imposing array of British troops had had a discouraging pyschological effect. On a rise in the bottom, the 58th moved to the right in front of the mounted infantry; the guns stood in the centre; a company of Rifles extended to the left with the Naval Brigade and the rockets. Colley remained with the reserve, composed mainly of Mounted Police and three companies of Rifles.

The action began with the shelling of heights and ravines which might conceal the enemy. Artillery officers wagered that they could clear the entire Nek in fifteen minutes. Shells burst on the hills in every direction. A number of Boers, unaccustomed to bombardment, scattered for better shelter. The noise and confusion in their position was something fearful. A splinter passed close to Joubert's head. Then the bluejackets, protected by a company of Rifles which had found cover behind a stone wall of Laing's farm, pushed out some 500 yards in front to deliver a rocket attack. The erratic flight of these fiery-tailed projectiles was, as always, spectacular. One went off course and burst near the Rifles; the rest dropped with seemingly good effect on the ridge and among the Boer reserves beyond. Clouds of smoke on the skyline caused some to believe that the enemy camp was ablaze.

There was little firing from the Boer side and horses were seen bolting in every direction. Some mounted men galloped over the ridge. 'Everyone cheered madly, thinking the enemy on the run,' wrote one Mounted Policeman, who along with the rest of his comrades mounted his horse 'to be ready for the pursuit'.[33] The officer in charge of the telegraph sent a telegram to the Colonial Office stating that the enemy had abandoned the Nek so as to be out of the reach of the guns.

The morale of the defenders was shaken. One of them later asked a correspondent of the *Natal Mercury*, 'Were you short of ammunition so soon?' None, however, had been smothered by shrapnel, for the shelling was badly delivered. The missiles had either gone over the concealed burghers or had been wrongly directed altogether, bursting in areas where there were few defenders. There was no retreat; instead, the lurking defenders were being reinforced. As the Boers moved into line, they were reminded of Joubert's words: 'Thus far and no farther.'

After twenty minutes of ineffectual bombardment, Colley ordered the advance of the 58th on the Table Hill to the right of the Nek (what he called 'the key of the position') so as to out-flank the defenders. The supporting mounted squadron was sim-ultaneously directed against the hill's eastern extremity, where the slope was less steep and more accessible for the horses. The gunners were instructed to give the attackers covering fire. There was no subtlety in Colley's tactics—but then it hardly seemed necessary in dispersing such rude militia.

'It was carefully impressed upon every officer', wrote one soldier who stood before the Nek, 'that as soon as he found himself in the presence of the enemy, his business was to charge.' Boer marksmanship, it was argued, would be far less deadly when confronted by 'an oncoming line of bristling bayonets'.[34] The traditional superiority of British bayonets, demonstrated on so many battlefields, supported an exaggerated reliance on shock tactics. Major Poole, a highly regarded staff officer who had reconnoitred the approaches to the Nek the night before, insisted that the position could be taken with bayonets. But bayonets need an objective point, and this was exactly what the burghers' tactics did not provide.

Though mostly untried conscripts, the stormers came into line, one correspondent noted, as if in imitation of the charge of the heroic six hundred immortalized by Tennyson. The 58th, or 'Steelbacks',* a unit with a fine regimental history, was commanded by Major Hingeston, but Colonel Deane, intelligence officer on Colley's staff, usurped the duties of the regimental officer by riding impulsively forward with four others of the staff to head the charge. Colonel Deane, recently arrived from command of the Pondo War, had never been under fire. Thoughts of glory seemed to crowd into his mind as he stiffly rode his fine charger and drew his sword. When Mr Sanderson, inspector of roads, told him to beware of Boer sharpshooters, Deane confidently pointed to the cannon and declared, 'But we have these little children to talk to them.'[35]

Regardless of past accounts showing how the enemy carefully picked off officers, no effort was made to disguise their insignia of rank, even down to the swords and shiny scabbards, which were clearly visible at great distances. For fear of being thought wanting in courage, officers would not quit the saddle, or if on foot, they refused to imitate their men by taking advantage of cover. The two unfortunate subalterns selected to carry the colours of the battalion into action were almost certain to be downed; and those rushing forward to pick up the 'soul' of their unit would in all probability suffer a similar fate. After a battle Kipling described the colours as looking like 'the lining of a brick-layer's hat on a chewed toothpick'.†

As the artillery concentrated its fire on the brow of the hill, the 58th dashed towards the ridge in close formation rather than in the drill-book 'attack formation'—a thin, waspish line of skirmishers. There was little fire from above on the solid mass of redcoats, for the incline was so steep that the Boers were unable to bring grazing fire against them. Moreover, the attention of the Boers was soon directed to the flank attack by the mounted men. Advancing on the trot with the officers well in front,

---

* Since Peninsular days, they were called 'Steelbacks' because of the way they endured the lash.

† In the opinion of Wolseley, any general who condemned an officer to death by ordering him to carry a standard into battle against high-powered rifles 'should be tried for murder'.[36] Largely because of his influence, the two standard-bearers at Laing's Nek would be the last to appear on the battlefield; henceforth (after March 1882) the colours were left at home when battalions went on active service.

the mounted men under Major Brownlow suddenly wheeled to the right, spurred their horses into a gallop, and charged in two blue lines, their swords flashing. Without pause they moved on through thickening fire. Because the infantrymen were unable to keep abreast of them, the formation began to veer to the left in compensation, thereby exposing themselves to fire from the ridge as well as from the Boers before them. Near the top, the invisible Boers suddenly made their presence felt. A cloud of smoke and a shower of bullets came forth from a ravine, emptying a score of saddles in a few seconds. Those still mounted faltered and tried to re-form with the second line to charge again. Some bluecoats 'came so close', wrote Joubert, 'that the powder burned each other'. Only Sergeant-Major Lunny got in among the Boers, killing one and wounding another with his revolver. He fell with six bullets in his body.

Then the horsemen were in retreat, followed by unsettling shouts of triumph from the burghers. Most were either killed or wounded or, at best, unhorsed. Riderless horses, their trappings bloody and their bridles swinging loose, rushed wildly downward. The crippled squadron lost seventeen wounded, killed or missing; thirty-two horses were lost. Lieutenant Linmitte, a thrifty Scot of the 21st who had his horse shot from under him, was the last one down. He described his experience: 'I got up and, seeing no one about, I turned and legged it down the hill. My helmet had fallen off, my sword dropped out of my hand, and I lost my field-glasses. It was a dashed expensive day.'[37]

If only the seventy had been regular cavalry on trained mounts, observed Colley, they would have persisted and 'the position would have been ours, without much loss.'[38] According to Joubert, the British were beaten by a picket of twelve men under Commandant Bassa. Bassa's men now turned their guns to support some sixty burghers who were waiting for the charging redcoats. Other Boer reinforcements, meanwhile, were rushing up from the rear.

It was too late to recall the infantry. They were already three-quarters of the way up the Table Hill as they glanced over their shoulders to watch the reeling and breaking bluecoats. At any rate, to a gallant soldier like Colonel Deane, who was riding well ahead of his men, retreat was unthinkable. The men behind him, scrambling and panting up the steep slope on foot through entangling long grass, were approaching exhaustion. Some were vomiting from exertion; many were finding it difficult to hold their rifles steady. Perspiration ran into their eyes. But there was no pause until an ear-splitting volley of concentrated Boer fire caused the front line to waver. The artillery suddenly ceased. The attackers now saw rows of Boers crouched or lying on their stomachs, firing at them. Dead and wounded began to fall before the destructive fire from front and right rear. Half a company tried to check the flanking fire; soon only one man was left standing. The colonel shouted 'Charge!' but only those close to him could hear the command above the deafening noise. Deane was unhorsed. Springing to his feet and still waving his sword, he turned and shouted to his men, 'I am all right.' Then he fell again and rolled over in agony, mortally wounded. (A large monument later marked the spot where he fell.) Lieutenant Inman, his orderly officer (who had earlier caused much comment when he became the first combatant officer to rise from the ranks) fell dead behind him.* Major Poole, the brigade-major, was dead before his body hit the ground.†

Colley's young A.D.C., Lieutenant Elwes, who had failed to keep up with the other staff officers, shouted to another Eton boy, Lieutenant Monck, 'Come along Monck! *Floreat Etona!* We must be in the front rank.' He was shot dead the next moment. It was a cry that exemplified the spirit of enterprise among British officers and which made war appear to be little more than a dangerous sport. Lady Butler, whose brush had done for the British soldier what Kipling had done with his pen, described the action in a painting which was precisely detailed, historically accurate and emotionally appealing. 'Floreat Etona', depicting a daring subaltern charging with sword in hand towards his death, was placed in army messes and club rooms throughout the Empire. It was to be found in nearly every boy's room at Eton, to inspire emulation.

Major Hingeston tried to rally the 58th for a bayonet charge.

---

* Inman had had an éxtraordinary career, serving as a midshipman on board a blockade-runner during the American Civil War, as a corporal with the French in Mexico, and as a member of the 3rd Bengal Cavalry during the Afghan War.

† Poole, one of the most promising officers in the army, had been entrusted with the custody of Cetewayo after the Zulu War. A warm friendship quickly developed between jailer and prisoner. When the old chief learned of Poole's death, he placed his robe over his head and refused to eat for two days.

He was soon shot dead. Captain Lovegrove, acting field-officer, was wounded. At one point, related Joubert, the British 'came so close that the dead on both sides fell in among each other. One of the officers even fired in among our men with his revolver before he was shot—but then the Lord helped us!'[39] As the fire from the reinforced burghers increased, the men lay down to avoid the storm of bullets sizzling towards them. The young soldiers fired quickly and without aiming. Ammunition began to run short. Cartridges had dropped from their pouches during the run up the hill, and now supplies failed to reach them. Many died and were destined to be buried where they lay.

After thirty minutes of this unequal struggle, Major Essex, the last of the staff (who had his horse killed and his helmet knocked off) and one of the few officers left standing, ordered a bugler to sound 'retreat'. (Essex was one of the 'lucky four' who had survived the calamity at Isandhlwana.) As the men ran back down the hill, the Boers left their cover to swoop after them and pick them off. The artillery opened up to discourage the pursuers, firing so close that the shells wounded many of the British as well. A small party of Boers moved in from the far left to drop the sailors operating the rockets. The Mounted Police vedettes, who were waiting with drawn swords, also came under fire. But the burghers were soon checked by the Rifles.

The retirement of the shattered regiment became more orderly. One company re-formed on the way down and helped to keep the pursuers in check. The Rifles moved up behind a stone wall to assist them. Lieutenant Jopp ('Little Jopp'), a subaltern of only three years' service, brought the regiment out of action. 'The 58th', according to Colley's official report, 'marched back in position in as good order, and with as erect and soldierly bearing, as when it marched out.'

On reaching the plain, the survivors of the 58th turned about to face an assault. The artillery continued to discourage the pursuers, and the Boers decided to abandon the chase. (Among them was young Christiaan De Wet, whose name was to become world-renowned in the South African War at the turn of the century.) Some Boers paused to retrieve horses on their return. One of the sons of Nicholas Smit, who was in charge of this section, made off with Deane's charger. The battle ended, as it began, with a shelling.

Even in defeat there was heroic action. During the retreat, Lieutenant Baille, who carried the black silk regimental colours, was wounded. He was succoured by Lieutenant Peel, who carried the other standard. 'Never mind me,' Baille exclaimed, 'save the colours.' Taking both flags, Peel fell into an ant-bear hole. Thinking him dead, a sergeant took the colours to a place of safety. Meanwhile, Lieutenant Hill rushed back to pick up Baille and carried him down in his arms, until Baille was shot dead. Hill returned to pick up another wounded man with a horse, and returned a third time to rescue another. All this was done under heavy fire. Not only did Hill receive the Victoria Cross, but his horse was posthumously honoured by having two of its hoofs mounted in silver, later to be used as ashtrays in the 58th mess.

The last shot was fired shortly after noon. Red dots lay stark on the green hillside. Under a flag of truce, Colley requested that he might be allowed to look after the wounded and bury the dead. Joubert agreed.

In his report to the War Office, Colley stated his losses as being severe: seven officers and seventy-six non-commissioned officers and men killed, two men taken as prisoners, and 111 wounded. The men were buried in four mass graves close to where they fell. The dead officers were brought back to camp and buried with military honours, along with those who died afterwards of their wounds. It was rumoured that some of the wounded had been butchered by the Boers, though quite the contrary was true. Joubert sent parties to assist in caring for the wounded (which Colley gratefully acknowledged), and distributed brandy and water among them. They did, however, take weapons and other articles of value as legitimate spoils of war.

Joubert reported to Kruger, 'The opportunity for the English cannon was great, and we suffered heavily. Twenty-four of our best men were disabled.' He claimed, that with God's help, 'three hundred of the enemy were put *hors de combat*'. To have continued the pursuit of the British, he added, might have cost many more lives, for it 'would have been in the very mouth of their cannon'.[40]

Assisting the wounded Boers was Dr Alexander Merensky, a pioneer Berlin missionary who had established a station near Middelburg. He was regarded with deep suspicion by the burghers because of his previous relations with Sekukuni and because he had supported the annexation, which he had believed would establish peace and order. When the war began, Merensky declared himself neutral, but he could not refuse Joubert's request for assistance. Arriving four days after the battle, he found that the Republicans had fourteen dead and twenty-nine wounded, eight severely so. A German apothecary from the Free State had been enlisted to amputate two arms and a leg, but the job was poorly done. Merensky, therefore, found it necessary to make further amputations on each of the three men. The manner with which the wounded withstood the pain and recovered caused him to marvel at the Afrikaners' stamina. During the two-month period which Merensky served in the Boer camp (which eventually numbered over two thousand men), the German doctor treated only five or six men for sickness. Moreover, he found that camp life was orderly and quiet, with little indulgence in drinking. In all that time he encountered only one burgher who was intoxicated—and he had come over from the Free State.

Merensky set up a hospital in Meek's abandoned home. He was assisted by the German apothecary, an English physician from the Transvaal, a mission-colonist named Schulz, and a young native who had frequently assisted in operations at the mission hospital. Merensky was amused by the perplexity displayed by some of his Boer patients when they were placed under the care of a black. A Red Cross flag, which Colley had given to the German physician during a truce, was flown over the hospital. It became an object of curiosity to many of the Republicans, so Merensky explained to them that among civilized nations this flag was respected as a sign of neutrality. The Boers replied that 'they had had enough of civilization and wanted to know nothing more about it'.[41]

Boer losses were greatly exaggerated among the British. With 200 shells fired at the Nek, they were sure they had given as well as they had received—and more. This was 'confirmed' by an officious gentleman who appeared at Mount Prospect the day after the battle. He represented himself as having escaped from the Boers, and stated with great authority that their losses were 200 killed and 300 wounded. With his own eyes, he claimed, he had seen twenty wagons loaded with casualties returning to the Transvaal. He also claimed that Kruger had a force of 4,000 men not more than twelve miles from the Nek.

On returning to camp after the battle, Colley had all the troops drawn up, and with a voice choked with emotion he briefly addressed them. The general declared that the blame for the failure rested entirely on him. He congratulated all ranks on their steadiness and courage, and assured them in an almost pathetic voice that they had 'not lost one atom of the prestige of England'. When reinforcements arrived, they would certainly 'take possession of that hill eventually'. Every sentence had been followed by a cheer, with one ringing cheer at the end plainly saying, 'We still have confidence in you.'

It was a miserable night. All the bread had been eaten, and the biscuits—full of fat weevils—were so hard they had to be soaked first. One soldier broke a tooth. Those near the hospital tent lost their appetites when they saw an amputated arm, which an orderly had neglected to bury, being eaten by vultures. Private Brennan of the 58th went round to the various groups of men huddled by camp fires and boasted that he was the only man to have bayoneted a Boer, producing as proof a bayonet covered with gore. Brennan afterwards confessed that he had invented the story; he had acquired the gore by probing a dead . horse. The weary men got little sleep. All night long the wounded groaned and cried out with pain.

Major Hingeston and two others were buried the next morning. Major Brownlow recovered, but he would not speak to the men of his command for days.

Some of the men insisted that they had seen blacks fighting alongside the Boers. On the strength of these reports, several newspapers ran the story that hundreds of natives were being pressed into military service with the Republican forces. Colley, recognizing that the Boer army employed blacks (as did the British) as drivers and leaders of oxen, ignored the charges. A second charge was widely circulated that the enemy had used bird-shot and explosive dumdums—flat-nosed expanding bullets. (The same allegation had been made against the Boers during the Sekukuni War, but was never proved.) The British themselves, of course, did not hesitate to use dumdums against fanatical tribesmen. At the Hague Conference of 1899 the British delegate vigorously defended the use of flat-nosed bullets in fighting savages. Winston Churchill related that during the Second Boer War he was carrying ten rounds of 'soft-nosed' bullets when the enemy captured him. He got rid of them without detection.

To preserve the health of his men, Colley moved the camp several hundred yards to an equally strong position on Mount Prospect. In order to protect Newcastle, where there were continual alarms (each night the residents took refuge in laagers), he sent the Mounted Police back in haste. They manned forts newly built to guard the approaches to the town. Rather than maintain twelve miles of communication route to Newcastle, Colley could have retired from his exposed camp to the town, but he reasoned that such a move would have an adverse effect on the morale of his troops. Until reinforcements arrived, he hoped to keep the Boers under close observation. He was sure that the Natal Police was strong enough to discourage enemy patrols.

Two days after the battle, Colley wrote to his mentor Wolseley—who felt as though he had 'lost a battle himself'—that he had underestimated his opponents. 'There is talk of the Boers attacking me,' he continued, 'but I fear I cannot expect such luck.'[42] At the same time he told Childers that during the truce many Boers had admitted to his officers that they were serving entirely against their wills. Clearly even now Colley did not fully appreciate the superior mobility, good shooting and—above all —determination of his adversaries.

Whatever secret doubts the Boers might have entertained before this encounter with 'the fancy-dress soldiers', they now had unquestioned confidence in their own superiority. More volunteers flocked in from various parts of the Free State. On February 7th the Triumvirate issued a proclamation appealing to all Afrikaners: 'Freedom shall rise in South Africa like a sun from the morning clouds, as freedom rose in the United States of America. Then it shall be Africa for the Afrikander, from the Zambesi to Simon's Bay.'

It was the first time since the Crimean War that British troops had fought and been repulsed by an enemy of European blood. What made it worse was that the Boers were considered a primitive enemy, one which had barely attained that level of civilization which could avail itself of the advantage of modern rifles. But in England there seemed no cause for alarm. With so many disasters preceding victories in the past, the British could hardly be depressed by one defeat. *The Times* correspondent dismissed the seriousness of the event with the observation, 'The engagement was not a defeat. We simply failed to take the position.' The journal went on to comment that the real danger was that a warlike spirit might be aroused, causing the nation to fling itself into the conflict with 'an eagerness and determination out of all proportion to the possible value of the results'.

Responsibility for a reverse is naturally visited upon the general, but officialdom and the press viewed the whole matter as a mild tactical blunder on Colley's part. In a small section of the press and in certain military circles Colley was disparaged as 'a mere theorist', unaccustomed to the practical business of war. The confidence of the Cabinet remained generally unshaken. Colley's action, though perhaps hasty, was judged with the utmost generosity. Childers believed that cavalry squadrons now well on their way to South Africa would completely alter the situation. The Duke of Cambridge suggested to Colley that it would have been more prudent to await reinforcements, he conceded, however, that this could 'only be judged on the spot, and criticisms at a distance without knowing all details are premature'.[43]

Gladstone, still suffering from his wavering indecision on the Transvaal matter, appeared annoyed by Colley's effort to solve the problem through an affirmation of the supremacy of British arms—and failing. He complained to Kimberley that Colley 'counts his chickens before they are hatched', as he had done in India. With thorough disapproval, he concluded, 'His line is singularly wide of ours.'[44]

[6]

INGOGO

It won't do for us to be continually beaten by the Boers.

Kimberley

THE DIMINISHED force camped at Mount Prospect could no longer be regarded as a relief column. The action at Laing's Nek demonstrated that Colley's experiment with mounted infantry was a failure and that his batteries were not as overpowering as he had imagined. While he waited for vital reinforcements, the initiative passed to the Boers. Behind his entrenchments, Colley prayed that the enemy would be bold enough to attack him. Guns and Gatlings were located with great care. Every man knew his exact position if the alarm was sounded. A sharp repulse of the Boers would be gratifying and might even allow Colley to have a second chance at the Nek immediately afterwards.

Though greatly elated by their victory, the burghers had no stomach for charging earthworks. They merely kept a careful watch over the British camp. As more Boers crossed the Drakensberg almost daily to support them, Joubert sent patrols into neighbouring districts, penetrating nearly as far as Ladysmith and threatening Newcastle from the direction of Utrecht and the Orange Free State. Cattle were lifted. The postal service was threatened. The telegraph service still functioned, but the single wire between Mount Prospect and Newcastle was in danger of being severed at any time.

By the end of January, British reinforcements began to pour into Durban and to move inland.* Boer intelligence, which was quite sophisticated, had alert agents and excellent means for transmitting the news of every new arrival and the exact location

---

* Within twenty-four hours of learning of the battle of Laing's Nek, two thousand of Australia's local forces volunteered to fight in South Africa. The offer was not accepted.

of each detachment and gun on the roads of Natal. Their reports
were confirmed by stories written by enterprising correspondents of the great London papers. Wolseley, who regarded
journalists as 'the scourge of modern armies', urged Childers to
demand some form of censorship. The Secretary for War finally
mustered enough courage to bring the matter to the attention of
the House of Commons, claiming that certain published passages
sent home by 'specials' would give the Boers 'information of certain importance'. But the legislators refused to sanction any
move that would curb the freedom of the press.*

A peaceful settlement seemed more remote than ever. Brand
was discouraged. On February 1st he wrote to de Villiers, 'I do
not see how I can do more than I have already done without
seeming officious, and doing more harm than good.'[1] As head of
the Government in the Free State he was increasingly embarrassed by the trans-shipment of munitions through his country to
the Transvaal. He replied evasively to British protests, but he
could not deny that hundreds of his countrymen had joined the
Republican ranks. Brand formally asked the volunteers to return
home. None responded to the invitation.

Meetings were held throughout the Free State and the Cape
Colony with the purpose of sending help to the wounded and
provisions and arms for the fighting men in the Transvaal. Resolutions and petitions were sent in the other direction—to London,
Cape Town and Bloemfontein—declaring that the Transvaalers
would never have resorted to arms if they had been given a fair
hearing, and requesting that a settlement be arranged through
negotiations. Respected political leaders at the Cape, like Jan
Hofmeyr and John Merriman, urged Brand to renew his efforts
lest the conflict spread. Alarmed and distressed by rising tempers in South Africa, Brand responded by becoming more im-
portunate than before. He widened his circle of correspondents by
including more members of the Government and other persons
he regarded as influential, such as Froude.

There was also a growing uneasiness in the Colonial Office
among those of Kimberley's advisers who normally supported
strong measures. They were reminded of the words of their for-

* The following year, during his campaign in Egypt, Wolseley introduced his
own censorship, despite a howl of protest; when he supplied correspondents with
information, it was often false, so as to mislead the enemy.

mer head, Hicks Beach, who warned as early as May 1879 that
the Transvaal could not be held 'by a force of bayonets against the
wish of a large majority of the white population. Public opinion
here would probably not sanction such a policy at all, and would
certainly not pay the cost it would entail.'[2] Edward Fairfield, a
young clerk, had these words in mind when he told Kimberley on
February 5th, 'I fancy it was always recognized that if they did
brave death and destruction for the sake of independence, it
would go far towards securing a political victory of the survivors.'[3]

Three days later Colley was instructed by Kimberley to inform Brand that if armed opposition ceased, a commission would
be appointed which would be empowered to develop a 'permanent friendly scheme'. Colley interpreted these words as a demand for unconditional surrender. He relayed the message to
Brand, and in response to Brand's early request that the Boers
should not be treated as rebels, he added, 'I fear I can give no
such assurances as your Honour proposes, can add nothing to
Lord Kimberley's words. Cessation of armed resistance must
precede everything.'[4] Kimberley later complained that his words
had been interpreted too rigidly by the general. But when Brand
asked, again and again during the rest of February, for specific
details (especially about a 'permanent friendly scheme') so as to
transmit them to the Republicans, the Colonial Secretary failed to
provide them.

Napoleon observed once that the secret of war lies in communications. The line of supply is as essential to the survival
of an army as the heart to the life of a human being. On the
morning of February 7th a mail detachment of mounted post-
boys (natives) and their escort of Mounted Police was intercepted by a band of 'rough-looking Boers' as it was crossing the
Ingogo River. It was compelled to return to Mount Prospect. It
came back with the tale that nearly a thousand Boers were mus-
tering at Schuins Hooghte (the heights round which the Ingogo
flows) with the intention of severing the communications of the
column with its Newcastle base, which was not only the source of
Colley's supplies but the station from which his indispensable reinforcements would come. The very next day, a convoy of forty
wagons laden with badly needed ammunition and stores was
scheduled to start for Mount Prospect. Colley correctly con-

cluded that Boer spies had alerted Joubert to the opportunity of
seizing the convoy, as the cargo would be as valuable to the Republicans as to the British. But because large parties of mounted
burghers were observed hovering about the heights and roads
near Newcastle, the commander at Fort Amiel, who could muster no more than one hundred and fifty men (mostly invalids),
determined to wait until reinforcements from Pietermaritzburg
could provide a suitable escort. The decision was communicated
to Colley by telegraph. As the wire was not cut, it was suspected
that the Boers had someone clever enough to tap it. Henceforth
all messages were sent in cypher.

Colley called for an immediate 'demonstration in force' to
clear the road of raiders. He felt that it was imperative that the
Boers should be prevented from establishing themselves athwart
his lines.

With a column consisting of thirty-eight mounted infantrymen (under Brownlow) and four guns and five companies of
the Rifles (273 men), Colley moved towards Newcastle the
following morning. The 60th Rifles were commanded by Colonel
Ashburnham, an old veteran of the Indian Mutiny who was
partial to port and who stroked his large grey-ginger whiskers as
he drank it. To his men he was affectionately known as 'Old
Bristles'. Ashburnham appeared somewhat annoyed at the fact
that the general insisted on commanding the force himself.

Obviously Colley did not expect that he would be gone for
long or that he would have to engage in hard fighting; he ordered
his men's dinner to be ready in camp at 3.30 p.m. Not even a
water-cart was to be taken. 'Everyone was in good spirits',
wrote one of the three correspondents who accompanied them,
'at the prospect of an outing.'[5]

With his four guns, Colley could not imagine that the Boers
would dispute his passage. The artillery, however, was viewed
as a great prize by the Boers; they could see from a great distance the bright rays of the sun reflected off the barrels. The
burghers had two guns of their own at the Nek. One was a very
small brass ship's gun; the other was undependable, for every
time it was fired it flew up in the air.

The Boers, numbering some two hundred and fifty men, retired before the British advance, intending to decoy them on to
the high and unsheltered plateau at Schuins Hooghte. The com-

mando was led by Nicholas Smit, the man who had suggested to
Joubert the feasibility of cutting Colley off from his base at
Newcastle. Smit was easily distinguished by his enormous beard,
which partly concealed a stern face and brawny chest. His military talent was of an exceptionally high order. Butler described
him as 'one of the ablest leaders of mounted infantry that appeared
in modern war'. The greatest tribute came from Colley, who
when writing to Kimberley declared, 'There can be no doubt
that the Boers have some good and determined leaders … and
Smidt (*sic*) seems an intelligent and fine man, courteous and
humane in everything connected with the wounded, and gallant
in action.'*[6]

Smit's first interception on the morning of February 8th was
made on an ambulance train consisting of five mule-wagons,
under a dresser named Smith, carrying twenty wounded to Newcastle. Assuming that the Boers would not disturb the disabled, Colley had sent them forward a couple of hours before
his own advance. They were halted by a Boer patrol at Schuins
Hooghte. Smith later alleged that the burghers were drunk as
they dragged him off his horse, stole his tobacco, and rode off
with his mount. The train started up again, but it was stopped a
second time by the Boers, who this time tore up the Geneva flag
and drove off the mules. The dresser complained; Smit gave him
a safe pass and allowed him to obtain fresh animals so that the
train might continue its journey. Local newspapers embellished
the tale by asserting that some of the Boers, 'specimens of the
type who murdered Captain Elliott', proposed the atrocity of
murdering all the wounded Englishmen; but, after a wordy
altercation with their leaders, they were persuaded to let them
pass unharmed.

Colley's force, meanwhile, began an easy downhill march,
bathed in warm sunshine. No Boers were sighted. The general,
riding in the van among the mounted infantry, spent much of his
time conversing with his wife's brother, Lieutenant Bruce Hamilton ('a real fighter with an iron constitution'), only recently
arrived in South Africa to serve on the staff. They discussed
Lady Colley's work in raising money for the patients at the

---

* Though recognized by both sides as the Republic's most outstanding soldier
in the war, not a statue nor any other memorial was raised to preserve his memory
or to record his deeds.

military hospital in Newcastle. Afterwards they talked about horses. A fellow officer later commented that Hamilton, a future general in the Second Boer War, 'loved horses more than women'.[7] He never married.

When they reached a hill overlooking the road at the point where it began to descend steeply into the valley of the Ingogo, the two seven-pounders were detached along with a company of Rifles. From this commanding height the guns could sweep the rocky ground surrounding the road below and the gently rising ground beyond the river which led to Schuins Hooghte, the 'slanting heights'. The road crossed the knee-deep river by two fords a hundred yards apart. The whole valley was overlooked by spurs and ridges strewn with rocks and boulders. Just the spot, thought the general, that the enemy might select to ambush the column. But there was no sign of the enemy as the column cautiously forded the river and briskly followed the winding road towards the plateau where the mail had been stopped the day before. As the scouts approached the top of the plateau, a sizable party of Boers, most of them mounted, suddenly came into view. They galloped forward to dispute the ridge from cover. Confronted by a formidable firing-line, the vedettes fell back.

The column halted as Colley decided to give battle. He had great confidence in the Rifles; they had played an outstanding role in the Zulu War, earning a reputation for rapidity of movement and steadiness under fire. Selecting the plateau as his position, he extended the Rifles in skirmishing order, with mounted men on the flank and the two nine-pounders rattling up the road to a central position. Advancing to the top, the British were treated to the sight of dispersing Boers. Then the Boers suddenly wheeled about and advanced towards them from the south west as if they meant to seize the four-acre plateau. The Rifles deployed smartly to the right and left, taking up their positions around the edge of the high ground. The nine-pounders were unlimbered and let drive at the advancing foe, but the elevation was at first too high to do any damage. Though less fearful of shell-fire than they had been at Laing's Nek, the burghers broke for shelter and prepared to hold their ground.

The terrain favoured Boer tactics. In the manner of the Zulus, they extended their 'horns' until they encircled the British except for a small patch to the rear. The ground around the plateau

sloped away into little dongas (ravines) covered with thick am-
bookie grass four feet long and studded with large rocks. The
Boers swarmed everywhere, creeping stealthily forward to close
the range from some new hiding-place. There was little tactical
control. The Boers were 'distributed to their own sweet fancy',
for they insisted on selecting their own positions. They formed
a line of individual huntsmen, sleuthing and stalking, and
moving often to fire from an unexpected place. A bayonet charge
against them would have been futile. The British would have
been shot down like so many buck before they reached them.

The plateau-bound British could take no comfort from their
position. The rocks were too small and the grass too sparse to
provide adequate cover; they were forced to lie flat on their stomachs. One soldier, finding his foot uncomfortably cramped,
shifted his position and was wounded twice while straightening
out. Although the Rifles' green jackets provided some camouflage, their white helmets made obvious targets. The girdle of
Boers fired upwards at passive targets framed by the skyline.
Standing in the centre, Colley was proud of the way his men,
many of them under attack for the first time, fired carefully and
held their ground. Their steadiness discouraged any possible
Boer rush. Exposing himself unnecessarily, the general periodically went about from point to point, speaking words of encouragement. The Boers could not help but admire his personal
courage.

The guns received the greatest attention from the Boers. The
British had unlimbered quickly, with one gun facing right and
one facing left, but by the time they had found the range, there
were nothing but boulders to shoot at. When the Boers shortened the distance, the gunners switched to case-shot. Gunner
after gunner fell. Captain Greer, commanding the artillery, fell
dead next to one of the guns and was replaced immediately by
Lieutenant Parsons. From time to time Parsons called for more
drivers to take the place of fallen gunners. Seeing that a particular party of burghers was doing the most damage, Colley ordered
Major Brownlow and his mounted men to clear the spot. As
Brownlow and his men descended, a murderous volley broke the
charge. Most of the men and nearly all of the horses went down,
though Brownlow escaped uninjured. The wounded men took
shelter behind the dead horses and gun-limbers.

A storm of bullets devastated the exposed gunners, but 'Charlie' Parsons continued to move his guns 'as if on parade'. Every officer, gunner and driver was hit. The limbers, gun-barrels and rocks about them were whitened by the splash of bullets. Just to be near the guns seemed certain death. Yet infantrymen continually volunteered to man the cannon. By mid-afternoon Colley had ordered the guns to be drawn to a less exposed position from which they fired an occasional shot under Parsons's direction. Parsons, the hero of the day, survived to win renown under Kitchener as Governor of Kassala.

At 2.30 p.m. Colley, fearing that a portion of the line on the left might be rushed because the area afforded little concealment, sent Captain Macgregor, his private secretary, with an order to Ashburnham to bring up a company of reinforcements. The colonel pointed out to the staff officer that I Company was the entire reserve. 'Wouldn't half a company do?' he asked. Macgregor merely repeated his orders, and then added that he would show them exactly where to go. But the mounted captain led the company farther than Colley had intended. Offering an ideal target at the edge of the plateau, he was killed on the spot. Lieutenant Garrett, who was in charge of the company, fell a few moments later. The men, mostly very young soldiers, gallantly 'stuck it well' for the rest of the day, although by evening all but nine were either dead or wounded. The second in command, Lieutenant Beaumont, hid behind a rock eight by ten inches in extent. Fortunately he was a very little man who had kept his weight down to less than nine stone while serving as cox in the Oxford boat for three years. He remained unhurt. The slaughter of I Company was believed to have been the afternoon's work of three well-hidden burghers located in such a favourable manner that they could enfilade the entire line of reclining greencoats.

The Boers were at close quarters in other sectors. Over to the left their proximity was such that they could be heard shouting over the roar of the musketry. They called one another by their first names—Piet, Koos, Jappie. Nicknames were often used to distinguish those with the same given name—Long Frikkie or Red Abraham. Their officers were simply addressed as 'Oom' ('Uncle') and they responded by calling the men 'Neef' ('Nephew'). The shouting of the Boers finally prompted Sergeant-Major Wilkins, a veteran of fifteen years who sported a fiery red beard, to ask Colley if he could lead a bayonet charge. The request was turned down.

While Wilkins was making his request to the general in the centre of the plateau, a single intrepid Boer on a large white horse galloped up the slope on the left, then stopped, dismounted and fired. Seeing that the range was too far, the Boer remounted and boldly rode in closer for a better shot. As the Boer was in full view of Colley and his staff, the general inquired, 'Hasn't anyone here got a rifle?' The sergeant-major saluted and said, 'Yes, Sir.' Down on one knee, Wilkins took aim and with a single round sent the burgher and his horse tumbling over and over down the hillside. Wilkins, said to be the best shot in the battalion, added to his reputation that day by potting several other Boers.[8] Afterwards he was made quartermaster and was awarded the Distinguished Service Medal for conspicuous courage.*

The fire slackened after three o'clock. Rider Haggard, who had been listening to the sounds of battle from Newcastle, thought the action had ended. But in a short time the rattle of rifles seemed more noisy than ever; it was obvious that the Boers had increased in numbers and ammunition. Parties of burghers from the Nek, dodging past the seven-pounders at the river by fording higher upstream, carried cartridges and refreshments to their comrades. As soon as Colley learned of these activities, he called for reinforcements from Mount Prospect to check the enemy's increase and to prevent the complete encirclement of his force. Few men could be spared from the base. One company of the 58th had arrived early in the afternoon to support the men and guns left at the approaches to the ford. When in mid-afternoon some Boers tried to get round to the rear of the main party they were driven off. At Colley's request, two more companies of the 58th under Captain Hornby arrived to support the first company.

Ambulances that had been brought up were not permitted by the enemy to reach the plateau. The Boers threatened to fire on them if they moved forward while the battle was in progress. The ambulances were badly needed. Well over a hundred men

* Three years later he was killed by Fuzzy-wuzzies at the battle of El Teb. Major Percy Barrow, promoted to colonel, died as a result of wounds received in the same battle.

and most of the officers were down after five hours of battle. Most of the mules (American imports) and horses were dead. Wounded animals charged about, kicking and trampling wounded men who lay in their paths. Efforts to carry the wounded men to the makeshift 'hospital' (the only protection for which was a circle of dead artillery horses) were frustrated by enemy bullets. When Mr Stewart, the interpreter, tried to lead native stretcher-bearers in response to a call for help, he was shot dead. The wounded who tried to crawl to the rear were hit again and again. 'Their blood-splashed faces', as one correspondent described it, 'presented a ghastly contrast to the whiteness of the helmets.' Another correspondent noted after the battle that most of the wounded had been struck in the right arm, which was attributed to 'the humane and accurate marksmanship of the Boers'.[9]

The hot sun contributed to everyone's misery. No water was available or procurable. Lieutenant Pixley, severely wounded in the head, managed to crawl down to the river. He pretended to be dead when some burghers found him and searched his clothes. Somehow Pixley got across the Ingogo before he collapsed. He was later found unconscious in the rushes along the bank.

Despite the lack of food, water or shade, the survivors doggedly held their ground. Ashburnham repeatedly shouted orders to conserve ammunition. The men usually had little more to shoot at than the probable source of the wispy white smoke that rose from the long grass, for the Boers were still not disposed to make any bold, headlong rushes.

The weather was fickle. In the afternoon black clouds appeared and soon the sounds of battle were mixed with those of thunder. By five o'clock the men were being pelted with rain; later the rain came down in sheets. At first it brought comfort. The thirsty men waited for the rain to accumulate in the covers of ammunition-boxes, then drank it; others chewed the bitter grass or sucked the water from blankets. In a short time, however, the rain became uncomfortable; the men caught chills and began to shiver. Still, as darkness fell, the firing continued.

At six o'clock the Boer fire suddenly slackened again. When Colley saw a white flag being raised among the burghers, he ordered a cease-fire, then sent his chaplain, Mr Ritchie, forward with a white flag in order to learn the Boer intentions. But the

Boers resumed firing. Some of the British believed it was a ruse
to discover where the general and his staff were located. Thomas
Carter, with Colley as correspondent for the *Natal Times*, suggested that since the white flag appeared on the left and the
Boers continued desultory firing on the right, 'evidently one
party was unaware of what goes on in its own lines.'[10]

Through the rain and fading light, the Boers suddenly moved
in as if to finish their work. But the British had more spirit than
the Boers had expected. Once more there was a call for volunteers to serve the guns; there was a quick response. The last few
rounds of the original 234 were carefully fired. Parsons, who was
thought by now to be bullet-proof, received a wound in the arm
and retired to have it dressed. Lieutenant O'Connell of the Rifles
fired the last artillery shots and managed to keep the Boers under
cover. The lieutenant, heir to a baronetcy and a grandnephew of
Ireland's great 'Liberator', Daniel O'Connell, was killed shortly
afterwards.

With the approaching darkness, broken only by lightning
flashes, the firing became less frequent and then ceased altogether. The burghers began to withdraw to their camp. Smit
reasoned that the British would have to surrender in the morning
—cut off from retreat by a river which had been transformed into
a raging torrent by the storm, Colley would have no alternative.
Natives who had watched the progress of the battle slipped into
Newcastle and told how the British were fighting bravely, but
that their 'arms were tired'. In their opinion, 'they would all be
killed at night.'[11]

The citizens of Newcastle were close to panic. The bad news
from Ingogo was accompanied by other information of shots exchanged between the Boers and the Mounted Police stationed
three miles from town. Fort Amiel, originally built to ward off
the Zulus, was put into a state of readiness. An attack was expected hourly. An officer was sent down the road to Pietermaritzburg to hasten forward a detachment of the 15th Hussars
which was scheduled to arrive at Newcastle the next day.

An attack was also feared at Mount Prospect—where only 150
men had been left as a guard. 'The Boers could have captured the
camp with the greatest ease,' wrote one of the officers present.[12]
Despite the odds, the burghers had no intention of storming the
fortified camp.

At 9.00 p.m. Colley made preparations for a withdrawal to camp. With no rations or water, and his ammunition nearly gone, Colley decided that the exhausted survivors of his decimated column could not repel a refreshed and reinforced enemy. Retreat was distasteful to Colley, especially as he would be forced to abandon the wounded. Since the Ingogo was in flood, stretchers could never reach the opposite bank.

The dead were counted. The wounded were collected and placed in the care of the surgeon, the chaplain, and a noncombatant volunteer. Waterproofs and blankets were collected to cover them. The general, though wearing the thinnest of summer uniforms, gave his coat to a wounded man. Those who cried out were given words of comfort; there was no medicine and only a limited number of dressings were available. The rain and the cold wind did not abate during the night, adding greatly to their misery; no fires could be lit. It was obvious that many of the wounded would not survive the night.

While discussing the recently commissioned young Haworth and his slim chances of survival with four wounds, Colley was interrupted by scouts returning from the ford with the report that there were no Boers to be seen. It was now eleven o'clock and the Boers had abandoned whatever watch they had kept on the perilous ford. They assumed that Colley would never abandon his wounded or the guns, believing that all the horses were disabled. Boer neglect, combined with heavy rain and intense darkness, gave Colley an opportunity to slip through.

The general was determined to keep the two artillery pieces from falling into Boer hands. Serviceable animals were found to pull the guns, and ropes were provided for the men so that they could help pull them over difficult places in the road. At Ashburnham's whispered orders, the line on the rim of the plateau was drawn back to make a formation with the officers and guns in the centre. Ammunition was redistributed and surplus weapons and shells were destroyed. When they moved off into the murky night, the groans of the wounded 'seemed to us to increase tenfold', as Carter wrote. 'Everyone was moody and sad.'[13]

It was a risky operation. One watchful enemy could have given away the whole show. The British kept their fingers on the trigger, for at any moment a flash of fire could be directed against any one of them as they advanced. No one spoke; no one dared to speak. Lightning flashes shocked their nerves. The sound of gunwheels bumping over rocks heightened the tension and seemed to rival the thunder. Surely a Boer scout must be hearing the noise.

To mislead the enemy, the British made a detour around the road. At one point they lost their direction. Pausing a thousand yards from the Ingogo, Colley sent out his scouts and waited. The thirsting men whispered how they would enjoy a 'skinful' at the river; those who had chewed grass found that the bitter herb had merely intensified their craving for water. The waiting was painful. At long last the scouts returned with the report that the passage was clear and the soldiers rushed precipitately towards the water.

As they entered the river the water swirled up above their waists. Hidden rocks and holes added to its treachery. The men joined hands to keep from being washed away, but despite the precaution six men were lost.

Once across the river, the march became even more difficult and trying. The nine-pounders stuck fast and the horses could pull them no farther. The remaining two men in the artillery division (there had been twenty-four in the morning) stood by with hammers and spikes, prepared to destroy the guns if necessary. 'Shall we leave them to the Boers?' the general asked. The men were adamant in their response; they again took hold of the ropes and pulled the guns free.

After more than eighteen hours, much of it spent in actual fighting, Colley's remnant stumbled into camp. Despite the fatigue they felt after the ordeal, their courage was undiminished. Colley and Ashburnham wrote dispatches attesting to the steadiness and discipline of the battalion, which they considered 'was beyond all praise'.

The companies of the 58th and those of the Rifles which were posted with the seven-pounders near the ford were missed by Colley's retreating column as it marched past in the dark. They knew nothing of the events that had occurred beyond the Ingogo. Most of the night they 'pigged it together', as one officer put it; 'officers, men, two dogs, four horses and about six mules ... I never spent such a miserable night.'14 Before dawn they began to march back. After a mile on the road, they thought they were about to make contact with the enemy. They were overjoyed to

discover that what they had encountered was actually the tail-
end of Colley's column.

Lieutenant Wilkinson, the adjutant, remained in camp only
long enough to gather medical supplies and a couple of volunteers
before starting back to the battlefield. He was swept off his horse
and drowned in the swollen river. One of the most popular of
officers, his death was deeply regretted. Colley, with whom he
had toured the Transvaal as A.D.C. the previous August,
mourned the loss of another member of his staff. He described
his passing as 'the saddest death of all—drowned returning from
an errand of mercy'.[15] Only Bruce Hamilton and 'Lucky' Essex
came through unscathed.

The loss of Wilkinson brought the total of dead officers to six,
with four wounded. Seventy men died and sixty-three were
wounded. One young soldier, Bugler Field, was taken prisoner
during the fight. It was later reported that he was captured by a
Free-Stater named Nel, who took his captive back to the Nek.
'Several of the Boers there wanted to kill him,' as Nel told it, and
they offered him 'a fine horse in exchange'; but Nel brought his
prisoner back with him to the Free State.[16]

If making fine speeches and writing dispatches could win
battles, Colley would have been one of the most successful of
generals. Shortly after his return to the shelter of Mount Prospect, the general made a brief and moving speech to the survivors
of the battle. He commended their behaviour and took the entire
blame for the set-back himself. Everyone agreed that Colley was
the most courageous, charming and courteous soldier one could
hope to meet. But one veteran officer remarked afterwards that
Colley 'ought not to be trusted with a corporal's guard on active
service'.[17]

That same morning, under a flag of truce, the general sent out
ambulances, two surgeons and a burial party to attend to the
aftermath of battle. Artillery horses were brought along to draw
back the ammunition wagon. To do all that he could to 'humanize'
this 'hateful war', Colley offered medical assistance to Joubert.
The offer was respectfully declined.

Smit and Joubert were unhappy about the outcome of the
battle. When the morning broke, they fully expected to renew
the fight and finish off the enfeebled Englishmen. Smit, who had
a force of five hundred burghers (according to Merensky) at

sunset, had greatly increased his strength by dawn. After spend-
ing the night at a farm two miles distant, he and his men raced
back at sunrise, only to find to their astonishment that Colley and
his soldiers were gone. Their amazement turned to disgust when
they found that the guns had disappeared as well. Smit was
furious to learn of the indiscipline of the young Boers who had
been posted to watch the fords. The opportunity of annihilating
Colley's force had been lost. It was a blunder the Boers did not
quickly forget.

Smit still hoped that the guns could be found. It was difficult
for him to believe that two cannon could have been taken across
the river and, without horses or mules, dragged uphill through
the mud all the way back to Mount Prospect. The Boers searched
the banks and probed the bottom of the river. For days they kept
a close watch to see if the British would come back to recover the
guns from a hiding-place.

The Boers had no objection to caring for the British wounded.
Some of the burghers came forward and assisted in placing the
disabled into the six ambulance wagons. They spoke to the
British gently and deplored a cruel war which they attributed to
injustices committed by the Imperial Government. It was simply
their duty 'to shoot all foreign soldiers who came into their
country'. Softly, but with the utmost confidence, they told the
British that this enforced conflict could end in only one way—the
rooineks would be vanquished. They insisted that the Republican
loss was a mere handful compared to the losses of those who
opposed them. The British who accompanied the wagons shook
their heads in disbelief at such 'ridiculous' statements to which
they could not give 'credence for one minute'.

Many estimates as to Boer casualties were later reported in
the press, some wildly exaggerated. Natives who lived close to
the battlefield swore they saw sixteen Boer wagons make three
trips each to carry off their dead and wounded. Merensky, an
impartial observer who was in a position to know, reported eight
dead and ten wounded, five severely. Two of them died later.[18]

Some Boers busied themselves with carrying off the booty—an
ammunition wagon, gun-limbers, and a few rifles. (Of the spoils
taken, one-quarter was supposed to go to the Government, the
remainder to the burghers.) Meanwhile Smit rode up and talked
to the British burial party. He was quiet and civil; without

bombast he spoke of ultimate victory. Understandably, the fight
at Schuins Hooghte convinced him more than ever that his
nation's independence was assured.

As the Boers rode off and the ambulances (laden with sixty-
four wounded) trundled towards Newcastle, the burial detail
finished its work. The men remarked on the multiple wounds
sustained by the dead. Many helmets were shot to pieces. One
Rifleman with a head-wound had written a letter, which later
found its way into a newspaper column. 'Can anything be more
ridiculous', he asked, 'than to clothe us in dark-green, to prevent
observation, and give us a head-dress, a staring white helmet
that can be perfectly seen a quarter of a mile off with the naked
eye, and affords a splendid target to aim at ?'[19]

Four days later Colley sent out another party to bring back
the bodies of dead officers. Thousands of vultures were now on
the scene. The 'disgusting brutes' were so gorged with their
grisly feasts of horse and mule flesh that they seemed indifferent
to the men's presence. Most of the decomposing corpses the men
dug up were already unrecognizable. 'Why the officers could not
have been left in peace on the ground where they fought so
gallantly, I do not know,' commented the officer in charge.[20]
They were reburied at Mount Prospect.

Not long after the battle, while Colley and the citizens of
Newcastle eagerly awaited reinforcements, Smit slipped his men
around Newcastle by way of the Free State and threatened the
upper districts of Natal, in the process looting wagons, taking
horses and cattle, and 'otherwise amusing themselves at the
expense of Her Majesty's subjects'.[21] The diet of the burghers at
the Nek was greatly improved with the addition of such delicacies
as marmalade and sardines. A wagon carrying sixty-eight casks
of beer was taken, but not a drop was drunk. All the beer was
poured into the nearest stream.

Newcastle prepared for an attack. Native scouts were placed
about the town to give warning if marauders should appear. Men
slept in their clothes with loaded rifles close by; their horses
remained saddled in the stable all night. Sleep was shattered by
frequent false alarms. There was little doubt that the Boers could
take the town if they wished. A large party of merchants favoured
immediate surrender rather than risk a fight because it might
hurt their trade afterwards. Neighbours began to suspect one

another of being secretly in sympathy with the Republican cause. 'We have so many treacherous friends and concealed enemies among the Natal Dutch colonists', declared the *Natal Mercury*, 'that it is high time to proclaim martial law.'

The military grew unpopular. At first it was the minor annoyance of unsightly rubbish heaps (mostly broken bottles) rising near the Mounted Police encampment. More serious was the news that DeWitt's home near Schuins Hooghte had been looted and burned to the ground by some of Colley's men. DeWitt, a Dutchman, had been guilty of nothing more than receiving Boers who passed his farm. So far, the Boers had not wantonly destroyed any house in Natal. But should retaliation take place, every outlying homestead would be in jeopardy. Colley expressed his regret for 'the disgraceful affair'.

The soldiers seemed indifferent to the welfare of the colonists. In Newcastle they had withdrawn to their forts and showed little concern for the safety of the town itself. Reports from Mount Prospect told of an Officer's Pony Race and how the Rifles played regular cricket matches with the 58th, using pick-handles for bats and ammunition-boxes for wickets. Two men indulging in horseplay were accidentally shot. The only action occurred when the Boers, lying concealed in the tall grass, fired on a vedette, killing one man and wounding another. When a mounted squadron tried a counter-surprise at the same spot the next day, there were no burghers in sight. They found instead a blue envelope addressed to the British general inviting him to try to take the Nek, and adding, 'We always thought the English were brave men, but now we think you are cowards.'[22]

All the while the mails and telegrams passed between the camp and Newcastle without interruption. Some of the Natal papers suggested that the Boers either feared electrocution or were so stupid that they believed that if they cut the line above Mount Prospect it could no longer function in the direction of Newcastle. On the strength of this and the fact that his force had remained on the field of battle well into the night, Colley telegraphed home that the action at Ingogo was a success. Though his own losses were heavy, he told Cambridge, those of the Boers were such that they 'produced a good effect'.[23] He informed Childers that obviously the Boers were chastened to the point where they would not 'undertake another similar action', either

to interfere with his communications or to attack the reinforcements as they had intended. The Boers' 'anxiety to conceal their
own losses', he observed, 'is almost comical'. He told of a burgher
who after the battle had asked one of his surgeons for a bit of
plaster for a friend who had cut his finger; 'but at last, after much
beating about, it came out that he was badly shot through the
head'.*[24]

Those immediately responsible for Colley's campaign—
Childers, Kimberley and Cambridge—found it difficult to share
his optimism. His reports began to bear a resemblance to those
of Lanyon before he was shut up at Pretoria. Colley, too, according to Kimberley, seemed 'in fact surrounded'. 'It won't do for
us to be continually beaten by the Boers,' declared the Colonial
Secretary, 'which seems to be what the fighting amounts to
practically so far.'[25] Cambridge hoped that Colley would wait for
a strong increase in his force before he attempted 'an onward
movement, for the Boers are desperate and gallant men'.[26]
Childers was apprehensive about facing Parliament before strong
steps could be taken. Meanwhile, the War Secretary's advisers,
principally Wolseley, expressed their utmost confidence in
Colley's ability to 'finish the job'. The three agreed that Colley
needed more men. It was determined to ship out two cavalry
regiments at once.

The reinforcements would hardly be sufficient if the Free State
cast its lot with the Transvaal Boers. They could muster a force
of eight thousand men, and they possessed the additional advantage of having large stores of ammunition and trained artillery.
'What will the Free State do?' was the question most commonly
asked in mid-February. The anniversary of the nation's independence would be observed on the 23rd, and it was widely held
that if a date were chosen for a pronouncement, it would coincide
with the celebration of the national birthday. On February 18th
a vigorous debate over neutrality was begun in the Volksraad at
Bloemfontein. The discussion lasted for four days, during which
time emotional appeals for assistance came 'from kindred flesh
and blood' in the Transvaal who urged the Free Staters to fight
for the common cause of liberty and religion. It took all the

---

* The Republican side suffered from the want of lint, carbolic acid and other
remedies. Aylward wrote that on one occasion a mounted messenger was sent
nearly eighty miles for leeches.

political skill and determination that Brand could summon before
he was able, on February 24th, to win a majority vote on a
neutrality resolution, despite the demands of an obstreperous
minority for a declaration of war.

Volunteers and ammunition continued to cross over to the
sister State. The Cape Government stopped the issue of permits
to bring in ammunition at Cape ports, much to the indignation of
the Free Staters. Nothing could be done, however, about the
volunteers. The Transvaalers welcomed them, but sometimes
they expressed contempt for their marksmanship. In the words
of one Transvaaler who spoke with General Buller at the conclusion of the war, 'Great girls, they can't shoot.'[27]

At the Cape, loyal subjects of the Queen could not help but
sympathize with Boer military successes. Julia Merriman (mother
of John X. Merriman, the Commissioner for Crown Lands),
commenting on the engagements of Laing's Nek and Ingogo,
wrote, 'It does seem marvellous that the Boers are able to hold
their own against not only our soldiers but our cannon.'[28]

In their 'desperate search' for allies, it was widely reported
that the Republicans had crossed 'the colour line' by seeking to
enlist the support of various tribes. Mr Osborne, the British
Resident in Zululand, advised Colley that the Boers were making
overtures to the Zulu chiefs and were circulating malicious stories
that they would 'compel the Government to restore Cetewayo'.[29]
When their advances failed to stir the Zulus, it was reported by a
mysterious correspondent of the *Natal Mercury* (he took the
name 'Junius') that if they did not give assistance now, the
Boers 'threatened to kill the Zulus as soon as they had beaten the
English'. At the same time their agents were said to have committed 'acts of infamy', such as destroying the Kambula Fort and
desecrating the graves of British soldiers who had died in the
Zulu War. Colley shared the Natal colonists' concern and warned
Kimberley of the danger of coerced Zulus 'marching against the
British'.[30]

It was also reported that Boer agents had been sent to the
Pondos and other tribes 'to organize an extensive rising'.[31]
Kruger himself was said to be encouraging the blacks in the
Transvaal to support the Republican cause. Kruger in his
Memoirs tells of visiting Magato's tribe near Rustenburg, where
the British garrison was under siege. But his stated purpose was

to ensure Magato's strict neutrality, for he had supplied the garrison and 'assumed a threatening attitude'. Insisting that this was 'a war between white men', Kruger succeeded in extracting from Magato a promise that he and his people would in no way involve themselves in the conflict.[32]

At Ingogo as at Laing's Nek, British soldiers told correspondents of the *Natal Mercury* that 'without the slightest doubt ...they saw coloured men armed and fighting' in the Boer lines; whether this was through choice or compulsion could not be determined. Aylward, having attached himself to the Boer forces at the Nek, was prompted to interview Merensky and his assistants. He announced that 'no Kaffir or coloured person, or man of mixed blood has been killed or wounded fighting on the Boer side since the beginning of the war.' The only man of colour to take the field, he added, was Joubert's own after-rider, who was completely unarmed.

Writing as a 'special' for the *Daily Telegraph* as well as his own *Natal Witness*, Aylward was happy to advise that any Europeans desiring to enter Republican service could apply to Heidelberg on terms somewhat similar to those given to von Schlickmann's volunteers during the Sekukuni War. 'To those who desire military glory, the freedom of Africa, and the defence of truth,' he declared, 'this offers a magnificent opportunity for earning, in action against the most famous nation on earth, that honourable distinction that is a soldier's best reward.' For those interested in material rewards, Aylward added that the spoils of war would be equally divided, and that the Republic would pay for any munitions, etc., which they captured. How many subscribers were inspired to join the Boer cause would be impossible to determine, but they would never have equalled the number of readers, from Natal to England, who would have enjoyed seeing 'that Fenian scoundrel' tried for treason.

To the Boers, the 'unfair assertion' that they were enlisting natives against their will was 'merely for the purpose of blinding the eyes of the civilized world' to the fact that the British themselves were arming blacks.[33] In answering these charges, the British conceded that a small body of non-Europeans (Hottentots and Coloured), formerly members of the Transvaal Police Force, were attached to Captain Nourse's Horse in Pretoria; and that 'small parties of native scouts were raised to spy on Boer activi-

ties—but not to fight them.' This subtle distinction in defining
services was lost on the Boers. Bellairs later admitted that the
'Civil Intelligence Branch' was not very dependable for obtaining
information. One besieged European, after observing the activities of the non-Europeans during the siege of Pretoria, wrote
that their information had 'always been unreliable, often totally
false', and their 'intelligence' 'appeared to be only exhibited in
successful forays upon farmyards'.[34]

With no little pride, the British marvelled at their own sense
of restraint in the employment of blacks. The Pretoria Government 'need only have spoken the word', asserted Rider Haggard,
'to set an enormous number of armed men in motion against the
Boers...Any other Government in the world in its extremity,
would have spoken that word.'[35] Lanyon, in a letter smuggled
out to Kimberley, reported that the chiefs sent frequent 'offers
of assistance to the Government in the shape of armed com-
mandoes'; but they were refused with the injunction that they
must not involve themselves 'in the white man's quarrels', even
though the Boers were not fighting 'in accordance with civilized
warfare'. He could not resist the further observation that since
the Boer farms and homesteads were at the mercy of natives, the
burghers at war 'would be compelled to disperse in order to
protect their families and property'.[36]

After six weeks of siege Shepstone got a message to Lanyon
in Pretoria, telling him that it would be a simple matter to 'raise
a native force of from 10,000 to 20,000 against the Boers' who
were trying 'to incite the natives against us'. Sir Theophilus's
eldest son, Henrique, who succeeded his father as Secretary of
Native Affairs in Natal, corroborated this view. At a signal, he
said, 'the whole border would have been alive with native invaders
from the Vaal River up to the Limpopo.'[37] Sir Morrison Barlow,
Her Majesty's Commissioner with the Swazis, wrote to Lanyon
that he had an impi numbering thousands waiting on the border
for his order 'to rush into the Transvaal to slay, burn and destroy
all and everything'. As a personal touch he added, 'There are
few things that would give me greater pleasure than to receive
such an order'. Colley, however, left no doubt that such attitudes
by British officials were not appreciated.[38]

The greatest damage to the Boer cause where the natives were
concerned was done by reports of alleged Boer brutality. After

Ingogo, stories of their misdeeds increased and began to rival the amount of space devoted to the subject prior to the annexation. Even in Germany, where nearly the entire press favoured the Boers, newspapers like the Berlin *Kreuzzeitung*, relying largely on reports from German missionaries (whose labours were never welcome to the burghers), published a series of articles describing the cruelties perpetrated by the Boers against the natives. Articles in the New York *Daily Tribune* echoed this sentiment and widened the charge of 'revolting cruelty' to include animals. British periodicals and newspapers bristled with tales of maltreatment and murder—these were not confined only to the war period but went all the way back to the Boers' arrival in Africa. The Boers, however, were not without their supporters. A bitter controversy developed in the daily newspapers as to their true character. Those who opposed the view that these simple farmers were pious, God-fearing Christians, with many virtues akin to those of Englishmen, liberally quoted the words of the revered Dr Livingstone—'brutal ... overbearing ... hypocrites ... they love slavery'. It was no secret that the Queen herself detested the Boers because of their alleged oppression of her black subjects. Even the 'popular belief' that the Boers were descended from pious Dutchmen was challenged by some correspondents. These correspondents brought forth 'evidence which proved conclusively' that the real Afrikaaners were descended from a criminal element, male and female, who sought refuge in the Netherlands during the Thirty Years' War in Germany and became such a nuisance that they were shipped out to Cape Town.

The news of the battle itself, like the one at Laing's Nek, created no undue excitement. Those who read more than one journal were undoubtedly confused: one daily reported Ingogo as 'a great victory'; to another it was 'a disaster'; others described it as a 'somewhat doubtful success', a 'bootless engagement', or simply a 'drawn fight'. But there was a general agreement with the view expressed by *The Times* that 'the resistance of the Boers cannot be indefinitely protracted against the forces which will be sent to break it down. Easy or difficult in whatever degree it may prove, the work will at last be done.'

Criticism of Colley's generalship was widespread. It was more than a mere matter of hindsight. To journals with Radical leanings, Colley's advance from Newcastle and subsequent actions

were regarded as extremely hazardous and useless. They traced
the blame to the War Office and to the Whigs in the Government. The Whigs responded with the defence that they yielded
to the superior judgment of the soldier in the field. The general
was caught between political factions in the party—fair game for
one, scapegoat for the other.

Colley was no less a target for the Conservative papers,
especially the organs of military orthodoxy such as the *Army and
Navy Gazette* and the *Broad Arrow*. They backed the traditionalists, centred in the Horse Guards, who denounced short service
with boy soldiers, promotions based on merit rather than seni-
ority, and the linked battalion system that the Secretary for War
was preparing under Wolseley's direction. It was a system which
would unite all regiments consisting of single battalions into
pairs and place them under territorial designations. Time-
honoured numbers and facings would be abolished and most of
the ancient regimental traditions would be swept away. Stalwart
old warriors were outraged. They could not help but take a
perverse delight in seeing 'that book soldier', the brightest gem
of the 'Wolseley ring' of reformers, lose a little of his lustre.
Laing's Nek and Ingogo demonstrated to the disaffected how
'the British army had dreadfully deteriorated.' Poorly led by
their officers, with non-coms and men no longer reliable under
fire, 'they are wanting in dash, and unable to force a position
defended by a few farmers, etc.'[39] The *Volunteer Service Magazine*
found it 'startling' that British soldiers were 'quite unable to hold
their own against the fire of even great numbers of men, only
partially trained—if at all—as soldiers'. The *Daily Telegraph*,
which had a reputation for a flamboyant style, asked if the 'moral
fibre of Englishmen [was] so relaxed by repeated humiliation at
the hands of an unworthy antagonist that we should exult when
a British general manages to escape in the dark from the enemy,
leaving his wounded to the mercy of the foe?...Have we fixed
Isandhlwana as the standard of strategic skill ...?'*

The general was not without his defenders. The reform-

* The *Daily Telegraph* was owned and edited by Levy Lawson, who began his
career as an admirer of Gladstone. But when the 'Grand Old Man' adopted what
Lawson regarded as 'an unpatriotic attitude', Lawson became one of his severest
critics. This patriotic posture greatly increased the circulation and influence of his
journal. Why Lawson engaged Aylward, an Irish nationalist, as the South African
correspondent of his newspaper is difficult to understand.

minded Royal United Service Institution reminded the readers of
its journal that these farmers were 'the best-trained marksmen in
the world', and when fighting on the defensive 'are more than a
match for equal numbers of the most highly-disciplined troops of
our own, or any country'. Although Colley's service in the field
was limited to fighting Asians and African tribesmen, it was felt
that 'he will profit by the experience.'[40] Several dailies adopted
Wolseley's view that Colley was 'unlucky'. They quoted Napoleon as saying that luck was more important to a general than
a thousand soldierly gifts. Others argued that, unlike Chelmsford, who had left the initiative to the enemy after Isandhlwana,
Colley continued to be aggressive. After all, it was reasoned, a
commander is justified in taking military risks rather than allowing himself to be circumvented and confronted with famine. If
Colley had remained motionless while the Boers threw up entrenchments to his front and rear, the howl of protests from his
present critics would have been far greater. 'He made the best
of a bad situation,' observed the *World*. Even those who thought
that Colley had made a mistake in leaving Newcastle without
waiting for reinforcements agreed that his vigorous measures
with a weak force had checked a serious invasion of Natal and had
effectively relieved the pressure on the garrisons in the Transvaal, not one of which had as yet been taken. Kimberley, who
feared in December that the scattered companies in the Transvaal would be quickly overpowered by the Boers, now wrote to
Colley that 'although your small force was unable to work its
way into the Transvaal, they have been able indirectly to greatly
prolong the time for which the garrisons can hold out.'[41]

[7]

THE BELEAGUERED
GARRISONS

There is nothing stirring but stagnation.
News of the Camp.

ANOTHER kind of war was fought in the Transvaal itself. In the beginning, Joubert lost no time in sending commandos to invest Pretoria and the other garrison towns. If possible, the garrisons were to be forced into submission, but most important, the investments were designed to prevent the outbreak and concentration of the garrisons. For the most part the Boer commanders were energetic and determined, but they were short of men and armaments, particularly artillery, to prepare an assault. They were further handicapped by the natural antipathy of their men to aggressive actions when confronting defence works. On the veld, the burghers' matchless mobility, deer-stalking tactics and sharp-shooting gave them strength far beyond their numbers. Siege warfare, however, greatly reduced that strength. Investment was a dull and disagreeable service. They yawned, complained of inactivity and talked of their homesteads, often far away. The impatient sometimes went home; others went to the Nek on their own. This army of farmers was one of the least stable in history. Its size was affected greatly by events in the field and at home, 'varying even with the weather, or with that mercurial mental condition of which, in irregular forces, the numbers present at the front best mark the barometer'.[1] If attacked, the Boers fought well; their intelligence was efficient, their patrols and lines made it almost impossible for a messenger to get in or out.

Cut off from the outside world and reduced to privations of every sort, the British were at their undaunted best. With colours flying, they stood by their guns night and day and faced great hardships with grim determination.

PRETORIA

Pretoria was normally a pleasant place. Nestling between low parallel ranges running east and west, it was well supplied with clean water which gave life to the quietly waving willows and handsome blue gum-trees. The one-storeyed houses of unburnt brick were surrounded by thick fences of pink briars and smothered by clusters of roses. Gardens burgeoned with an abundance of fruit and vegetables. Life was simple and relaxed. 'The inhabitants of this Arcadia', wrote Elizabeth Dietrich, 'were like one happy family.'[2]

The town was born a capital. One evening President Andries Pretorius decided (without warning his councillors) to pack up all the nation's documents and to set up headquarters in this future town, which he named after himself. Centrally situated, it became a Mecca to the farmers. Under the anglicizing influence of the merchants, however, the town drifted away from the Boers —a defection which they grew to resent. After the annexation, growth and prosperity attended the influx of officials, soldiers and traders, and the town began to even look English. Streets were built to run parallel. Emporiums, barracks, a cathedral and a large jail were built. The Boers complained that wherever the British laid out a town, the first thing they built was a hotel and canteen, 'in order to tipple and teach others to tipple, and then he builds a jail to shut up the drunkards in ... when the Boers start a village the first thing they build is a church, and the second is a school.'[3] The Boers would have agreed with Frank Oates, world traveller, when he wrote of Pretoria, 'I fear the English here are a bad lot, with few exceptions. One man who cheated me I asked if he had a conscience. He replied that no one here had them.'[4]

At first the citizens of Pretoria did not take the rebellion seriously. With reinforcements converging on the capital there seemed no need for alarm. 'How for a moment', they asked, 'could the Boers stand up to the red jackets?' This 'flattering illusion' was suddenly shattered when Conductor Egerton staggered into town late on the night of December 20th to relate the tragedy that had taken place at Bronkhorst Spruit. 'At once amazement, indignation, and sorrow were written upon the faces

of those who believed such a thing impossible,' wrote Mrs Carey-
Hobson.[5] The weeping willows seemed to mourn gracefully as
the dark clouds of war gathered.

The Royal Engineers advised Bellairs that it would be impossible to defend the sprawling town, vulnerable in a dozen places.
The inhabitants would have to be concentrated in the near-by
military camp, located on high ground. The barracks and huts,
from which the soldiers were turned out, could hardly accommodate the 975 men, 676 women and 718 children. The overflow
was therefore put into the Civil or Wagon laager to the west
near the rifle range, where there were lodgings in the form of
tents, wagons and a few lean-tos, or sheltered in the Tronk
laager, a perimeter to the south-east enclosed by sandbagged
walls which extended from the Loretto Convent to the prison.
Higher up the hill was a native camp with quarters for the 1,331
servants. The cattle were kept in a kraal below.

Night and day, working with a will, gangs of natives, civilians
and soldiers constructed eleven blockhouses, as well as walls,
trenches and wire fences. Officers and volunteers charged about
on horseback as a jumble of wagons and carts moved towards the
camp. Rifles were handed down from at least one conveyance 'to
anyone who looked as if he could deal with one'.[6] Slogging
through the mud were 'crying children and women pushing hand-
carts with half their household goods'.[7] There was a great deal
of grumbling at the thought of leaving comfortable homes only
to be crowded into the scanty accommodations of the camp. They
were consoled by the thought that it would only be a short time
before they were relieved. Outwardly, the resettlement appeared
chaotic, but it involved a nicety of organization that reflected
credit on Bellairs.

Descended from a family of great military traditions, Bellairs
was a soldier of great experience, having fought in every major
engagement in the Crimean War. Because of his flair for administrative work, he was subsequently assigned to staff work with
Chelmsford and Wolseley, and acted briefly as Administrator in
Natal. Tactful and cautious, he exercised a restraining influence
upon his impetuous second in command, Lieutenant-Colonel
Gildea, and on Sir Owen Lanyon, who daily grew more peevish
over the turn of events and, on the basis of his own military
experience, argued for more aggressive tactics. Bellairs kept a

careful account of events and later wrote *The Transvaal War*, a well-balanced and reasonably objective account in which he curiously referred to himself in the third person; the book was edited by his second wife.

Bellairs's regulars consisted of a detachment of Royal Engineers, four companies of the 21st Scots Fusiliers (plus headquarters staff and band) and two companies of the 94th, from which a small troop of mounted infantry was raised. The infantry were concentrated largely in four small forts which covered the approaches to Pretoria. Each was given a four-pounder Krupp gun. A three-pounder Whitworth was placed in the camp and manned by bandsmen. (These weapons had been part of the arsenal of the Republic before the annexation.) There was also an awesome mitrailleuse captured by the Germans from the French and given to President Burgers by old Kaiser Wilhelm I. It had been dragged by ox-team from Delagoa Bay. The twenty-five eyes of this machine-gun watched menacingly through an embrasure in a redoubt, ready to rip and shatter any unfortunate Boers who came into its sights. Two nine-pounders were operated by men of N Battery, 5th Brigade, Royal Artillery.

Bellairs anticipated an investment force of six thousand Boers. He pressed into service, therefore, every civilian capable of bearing arms. The best, many of whom had seen service in various native wars, were drawn off into two troops: the Pretoria Carbineers (one hundred horses), and Nourse's Horse (sixty horses), commonly known as 'Nourse's 'Orses' and led by Captain Henry Nourse, the experienced head of the Transvaal Mounted Police. They were distinguished from each other by the colours of their puggarees; unlike the regulars they wore full beards, slouch hats and crossed bandoliers. They might have been mistaken for Boers but for contrasting splashes of blue, yellow and red in their outfits. The regulars, from Bellairs on down, tended to regard these non-professionals with a disdain similar to that which they felt for the Boers. Nevertheless, these 'amateur cavalrymen' scouted and patrolled the area for miles around in a thoroughly efficient manner. In all attacks they took the initiative against the enemy. Their casualties were more numerous and generally of more severity, proportionally, than those of any other unit. The Carbineers had three commanders—D'Arcy, Anders and Sanctuary—successively placed *hors de combat*.

The mounted volunteers had their quarters to the north of the camp, while the Pretoria Rifles (some four hundred men) were huddled into the area of the convent redoubt. Their lively commander, Major LeMesurier, R.E., worked unceasingly to improve their shooting and to sharpen their discipline. This was a body of conscripts of differing nationalities; and although there were instances of insubordination and desertion, the views and prejudices of the men did not prevent the adequate discharge of the various duties assigned to them.

The Civil Guard (fifty men), not acceptable for various reasons in the volunteer corps, were far less reliable. Bellairs spoke critically of this nondescript body as being in a 'chronic state of grievance', for they shared with all other colonists and Boers a craving for cattle, or any other booty they could lay their hands on. Self-satisfied sentinels, they were over-zealous in discharging their duties. There were complaints of disturbed sleep and composure resulting from shouted challenges, night and day, of 'Who goes there?' Since the sentries were stationed only a few yards apart, the challenge and re-challenge became maddeningly repetitious.

There was an inherent risk in arming all of the men in Pretoria. Many 'volunteers' were Boers of doubtful loyalty who were forced to take up arms against their own people. Cases of brother pitted against brother were not unusual. (A brother of one of the Boer commanders outside Pretoria later deserted.) And there was little doubt that sympathizers inside the camp sometimes revealed to the enemy outside the nature of the defences and of various moves planned by the military. Republican records indicate that they knew almost to a man—about a thousand—the strength of the defenders. One man who was imprisoned on suspicion confessed after the war that even in jail he managed to send out information to the Boers. A group photograph of all the officers in a particular volunteer unit was shown by the Boers to a British prisoner a couple of days after it was taken. He was told that the picture was passed from one Boer post to another so that the burghers would know the officers by sight and thus be able to pick them off if they saw them.

Meanwhile, Lanyon contributed his bit to the defence of the town by raising the most distinguished and exclusive Executive Council Brigade of eight men, all of whom were members of the

Legislative Assembly. With knives in their belts and equipped with double-barrelled rifles, they were by far the fiercest-looking warriors. It was rumoured that they 'were sworn to defend the mess-room to the last sweet biscuit and glass of sherry'. Lanyon, who assumed the humble rank of lance-corporal, put the men through their drill—which one wag reported as including marching past in column and forming a square to receive cavalry.

If the Boers had ever had any serious intentions of taking Pretoria, the time to strike was before the Bronkhorst Spruit engagement. Then the defences were weak and the element of surprise would have been strong. But the Boers at that time still lacked the confidence that an initial decisive success could give them. They were undermanned and fearful of aggressive moves against their own laagers. Commandant Henning Pretorius, in charge of one of the posts, described the situation as late as December 22nd as 'miserable, yes as miserable as can be'.[8] The burghers around the town seemed too weak to protect their own families and livestock. Only a few days before, a British raid had resulted in the loss of 188 oxen and 18 horses from an outlying Boer farm. The Boers were clearly short of men, and so long as Potchefstroom, which they had hoped to take within a few days, continued to hold out, they were deprived of any reinforcements from that quarter. Once Colley made his move to the border, the Heidelberg Government decided to send what men were available to help guard the approaches through the Drakensberg. On January 12th Acting Commandant-General H.P. Malan, who directed all siege operations from Heidelberg, curtly advised Assistant Commandant-General Piet Cronje (who was conducting the siege of Potchefstroom) that Colley had a sizable force in Newcastle. '*There* is where the danger is,' he said, 'and *there* is where the outcome will be decided—not with you.'[9]

Estimates of Republican strength before Pretoria differed widely. In the case of the British, it was wholly a matter of conjecture. Even the official Republican sources vary, depending on the date. On February 4th, in a report to Kruger, Malan spoke of six hundred men. Three weeks later he mentioned eight hundred, which would have made this force roughly one-quarter of the total number of burghers in the field.[10] One thing appears certain: the Boers never outnumbered the defenders. And unless the odds changed drastically, they were prepared to follow the advice given by Bismarck during the siege of Paris, 'Let them stew in their own grease.'

Lanyon often alluded facetiously to the confinement as the 'siege of Lucknow', which might conjure up images of relentless thousands pouring an unremitting fire into the camp. Actually, the Boers never came close to the camp or to the deserted town, which was covered by cannon. Initially the Boer war plan considered the possibility of attacking under cover of darkness. Bok wrote to Cronje on January 4th that 'as soon as Potchefstroom is decided, all able-bodied must gather in Heidelberg in order to make one night attack on Pretoria, so as to have all the land cleared before England can send reinforcements to Natal.'[11] Bok had a personal interest in the capture of Pretoria, for his wife, along with Jorissen's, was being held in the camp by the British. But Potchefstroom would not fall.

Pretoria was blockaded rather than besieged. The Boers formed a rough circle of laagers six to ten miles from the town, with smaller outposts in between. Their laagers had elements of natural strength—hills and stone outcroppings—but they were not fixed and could be shifted at short notice. Patrols moved continually from one post to another. In the event of an attack at a particular point, signal fires were lit so that support could be hurried to take part in the defence, either directly or by demonstrating on the attackers' flanks or rear.

Communications, in or out of Pretoria, became virtually impossible. Only at rare intervals did a native messenger get through the tight cordon. The Boers watched not only the approaches to the town, but also every river-crossing on the borders, all the way to Griqualand West. When Gildea wrote to his father on January 8th complaining that they could 'get no message in or out', the letter was intercepted by the Boers the same day. Colley told Childers that the town was so 'closely invested' that he had no word from Pretoria between December 29th and January 10th. At the time he was writing, however, one messenger, H. L. Dacombe, who had left on January 5th, managed to elude the Republican patrols on a furtive journey from Kimberley to Pretoria. After three days of rest he got back to Kimberley, after a daring ride of 1,100 miles which took thirty days. He received a cheque for £350 as a reward for his services.[12]

Messengers moving between Pretoria and Natal encountered greater obstacles. Native kraals were scarce in this region, and their inhabitants, as Bellairs wrote, were overawed or sided with the Boers. A messenger would, therefore, have to avoid the roads and take as much food as he could conveniently carry. The documents carried were often microscopic copies made by Pretoria's leading photographer, Mr Gros (a Swiss). They were placed in a hollow stick so that if the messenger were in danger of capture, he could drop the stick in the grass and hope to recover it later. The risk of being caught and punished by the Boers did not encourage volunteers. It was generally believed—and duly reported in the English press—that the Boers put to death any natives under mere suspicion of having carried messages of any kind. It was feared that Europeans would not fare much better. Despite the dangers, a 'little, delicate lame lady' went to Gildea in the garrison office and insisted that she could run the blockade with dispatches to Colley. The offer was politely declined.

Natives sometimes came into the camp with messages that appeared to be concocted by the Boers so as to delude the British for their own purposes. If Bellairs suspected that this was the case, they 'were promptly lodged in the jail, where their services were utilized as scavengers'.[13] Other natives hoping for a reward caused considerable mischief by reporting information the besieged wanted to hear, such as that a relief army had been sighted on the road from Kimberley; often the natives brought descriptions of various actions in which the Boers were always badly routed. These tall tales were recorded in what the less credulous laughingly called the 'Book of Lies'.

On December 19th the first shots were exchanged between patrols on the Potchefstroom road. Scarcely a day passed after that without a minor clash or alarm. The Boers harassed the besieged with forays on cattle, mules, wagons, mowing-machines or anything else of value near the camp. There was no panic of the kind that gripped soldiers and civilians alike during the Zulu War, but there was plenty of excitement when Boers were sighted. The Executive Council Brigade, led by Lanyon, was often the first to appear—on the run with rifles in hand. The excitement was even greater on one occasion when it was discovered that all the rifles of the 'brigade' had been stolen. The culprit was a practical joker among the Scots Fusiliers.

False alarms were frequent, and were sometimes caused by troops of baboons. When these creatures performed outpost duty (throwing out sentries here and there), even military eyes aided by binoculars, averred Bellairs, could be deceived into believing that a party of Boers was preparing to move in.

The fights that occurred were usually due to British initiative. Their patrols constantly probed the chain of posts about them for a weak link. There was always the hope that they could break out to assist the Potchefstroom garrison. Certainly, by forcing the Boers to do battle, they would prevent them from sending burghers to assist Republican forces elsewhere.

At two o'clock on the morning of January 6th, a force that included one nine-pounder, 140 mounted men, and 289 infantry in fifteen mule wagons (which it was hoped would be filled with forage and booty on the return) sallied forth to the east. They were led by Colonel Gildea, whose combative spirit was a match for the volunteers. Captain Sanctuary took a party of sixty-five Carbineers and rode ahead to occupy a low kopje to the right rear of Zwartkopje, and thereby cut off a Boer retreat in that direction. Nourse's Horse and the infantry, after a confused march in the dark over boggy drifts, arrived at Stuben's farm near the Boer laager, shortly before sunrise. Preparations were made to execute the main attack.

The Boers, not unaware of what was afoot, came out of their laager, extended their line, and attacked the Carbineers before they had a chance to get into their appointed positions. On hearing that the Carbineers were engaged, Gildea hastened forward to begin the assault. The mounted men were thrown out to protect the flanks and rear. A shady wood before the laager facilitated the advance. The nine-pounder began pitching shells on top of the rocky hillock. Burghers remaining inside scrambled out and spread themselves out to avoid becoming targets. It was said that when the Boers saw smoke from a gun at long range, they ran forward to cover as much distance as possible before the projectile exploded.

The two companies of Fusiliers skirmished forward slowly, cautiously. They gave and received a hot fire. After twenty minutes some Boers were seen galloping to the rear; at the same time a white flag appeared near the top of the kopje. Gildea called for a cease-fire and walked forward with his orderly, carry-

1. Boers trekking to Zululand before the Transvaal War

2. Dutch Church, Pretoria, in the 1870s

3. (*left*) Reverend Thomas Francois Burgers, President of the South African Republic, 1872-7

4. (*centre*) Cetewayo, King of the Zulus

5. (*centre*) General Sir George Colley

6. (*right*) Major-General Sir Garnet Wolseley

7. (*left*) Sir Henry Bartle Frere, English statesman

8. (*centre*) Sir Theophilus Shepstone, English diplomat and colonial administrator

9. (*centre*) Field-Marshal
Sir Evelyn Wood, V.C.

10. (*right*) Sir Owen
Lanyon

11. (*left*) Petrus Jacobus
Joubert, Commandant-
General and Vice-
President

12. (*centre*) Stephanus
Johannes Paul Kruger,
four times elected South
African President

13. (*right*) Dr William
Russell, war correspondent
for *The Times*

14. (*centre*) Reverend
John William Colenso,
Bishop of Natal

15. British warships (H.M.S. *Shaw*, H.M.S. *Active*, H.M.S. *Firebrand*, H.M.S. *England* and H.M.S. *Egypt*) anchored off Durban during the Transvaal War

16. Boer tents of 2 and 3 Companies, Convent Redoubt, during the siege of Pretoria

17. (*above*) Boers practising accurate marksmanship, for which they became specially noted

18. (*right*) Boer soldiers fought a guerilla war, often in old farm clothes

19. (*below*) The British marched openly across the veld in bright red uniforms, expecting to fight according to fixed rules and proper etiquette

20. Boer commandants

21. British Army officer's tent near Pinetown

22. Lieutenant Carden and men of the 94th Regiment in the field in the Transvaal

23. Hard drinking was not uncommon among British soldiers in the few hotel bars that existed

24. Boer distribution of rations

25. A cannon made by Boers from wheel-rims, 1880

26. Captain Scrivener with a group of local volunteers for the Pretoria Rifles

27. Boer soldiers ready for action

28. Lieutenant and Mrs Long and Dr Falvey among the survivors of
the siege of Lydenburgh

29. Boer camp at Majuba Hill

30. The Southern Cone of Majuba Hill, showing the route of
General Colley's ascent

31. Majuba Hill

32. General Colley leading his men into battle on Majuba Hill

THE SCHOOL OF MUSKETRY.

33. (*left*) Cartoon appearing in *Punch* after the Majuba débâcle. Caption reads: 'Boer (to F.-M. H.R.H. the Commander-in-Chief) – "I say, Dook! You don't happen to want a practical 'Musketry Instructor', do you?"'

34. (*below*) Signing the Terms of Peace with the Boers at O'Neill's Farm near Prospect Hill Camp, March 21st 1881. From left to right in front: S. Paul Kruger, J. P. Joubert, President Brand (writing) and General Sir Evelyn Wood

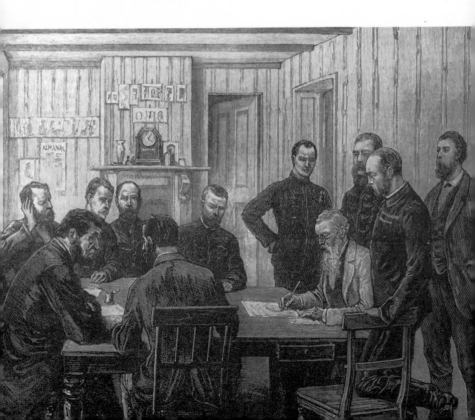

THE BOER REVOLT

1880—1881

JAMES MURRAY

(LANCE-CORPORAL)

94TH REGIMENT (NOW 2ND BATT. CONNAUGHT RANGERS)

AT Elandsfontein, near Pretoria, January 16, 1881, Murray and his comrade, John Danaher, advanced for 500 yards into the open, under heavy fire, to rescue two men of the 2nd Royal Scots Fusiliers—Byrne and Davis—who had been severely wounded. No sooner had they started forward than Murray's horse was shot under him; still, without hesitation, he proceeded on foot. "We both," writes Murray, "reached them together, and, on stooping to raise Byrne's head, I was shot through the body, the ball entering my right side and passing out near the spine. Seeing how useless it was for Danaher to remain, I ordered him to secure my carbine and escape. Byrne breathed his last, by my side, soon after. Davis and I were taken prisoners, and, together with Byrne's body, carried in a bullock hide to the Boer camp on the mountain top, where we were well treated. They kept us there twenty-six hours. By the courtesy of the Boer commandant, we were then permitted to return to Pretoria, under a flag of truce, bringing with us the body of our poor comrade. Davis died five days afterwards."—Extract from a letter dated Dublin, March 25, 1891.

265

35. Citation for the award of the Victoria Cross to Lance-Corporal James Murray on January 16th, 1881

36. British Soldiers visiting Colley's Cairn near the summit of Majuba Hill

37. President and Mrs Kruger

ing a flag of truce. The Boers on the kopje suddenly resumed fire, narrowly missing the colonel. An enraged Gildea ordered the bugler to sound the strident notes of 'charge'. Bayonets flashed into their sockets. A dozen Fusiliers fell as the rest rushed forward. Another white flag appeared, and after a few moments a hesitant burgher came forward to speak with the British commander.

Gildea demanded unconditional surrender and the Boers agreed. Seventeen of them were taken prisoner, three were found dead, along with three natives. A large number of oxen, rifles and provisions were confiscated. Eight wagons were blown up. Some seventy Boer reinforcements followed them on the return journey, but after a brief exchange of fire the burghers retired.

The British lost six killed and thirteen wounded. They claimed that they had emptied many more enemy saddles, but the Boers had dropped so quickly for cover that Bellairs admitted it was difficult to estimate their losses. Among the Boers wounded was the veld kornet, the hard-looking Hans Botha. He had no less than five wounds from shell fragments. He was a first-class marksman; it was said that at the bloody field of Bronkhorst Spruit he never fired a shot without wounding or killing a man. No one gave him much chance of recovery, but in the words of one volunteer, 'Some men are like cats—you cannot kill them.'[14] After several weeks in the hospital under the care of competent surgeons, the commander of the Zwartkopje laager was pronounced fit and was allowed to return home.

Some of the British advocated punishing the captured Boers for abusing the flag of truce: first, for having flown the flag so as to allow their mounted men to escape under a cease-fire; then, for treacherously resuming fire under a British white flag. The prisoners explained that a young burgher, thrown into a panic by the sight of an overwhelming force of British, had decided to surrender. When Botha had seen this, he angrily told him to put down this token of submission and to continue the fight. (The young burgher was killed a few minutes later.) The burghers who suddenly exercised their 'own free will' to ride home to Waterburg did so against specific orders. Most of the British, however, dismissed the Boer explanations as 'convenient'; in their eyes, they merely compounded treachery with double-dealing.

The British dead were buried in the military cemetery with full honours to the sad sounds of a Scottish lament played by the pipers. One of the dead was a volunteer lad of nineteen, another a veteran colour-sergeant who had only a few more months to serve. 'Strip war of the mantle of its glories and excitement,' wrote Charles DuVal, 'and it will disclose a gibbering ghost of pain, grief, disappointment, and despair.'[15]

Certainly Charles DuVal did his utmost to dispel the gloom. Marooned in Pretoria by the siege, this popular lecturer, musician and impersonator turned his talents to writing what *The Times* called a 'veritable journalistic curiosity', the *News of the Camp*. DuVal himself described it in the mast-head as 'A Journal of Facts, Fancies, Notifications, Gossip, and General Chit-chat'. Working with C. W. Deeker (the former editor of the *Transvaal Argus*) under a canvas roof that dripped with rain, he managed to publish the camp paper three times a week on the *Argus* presses. At sixpence a copy, the circulation rose to five hundred copies per issue; some of them, DuVal suspected, reached the Boers. After the war, in fact, he found that the Boers possessed the entire file, which—though censored—was of great value. Under his apron DuVal wore the uniform of a Carbineer. His rifle always lay near-by. Participating in all the major actions, he was easily recognized by a white top hat, the only one in camp. After the war he wrote *With a Show Through South Africa*, the best informal account of the siege.

The British success at Zwartkopje had a depressing effect on the Boers. The loss of Hans Botha, assumed to be dead, deepened their despair. Defeat accentuated the petty jealousies that divided the local leaders. Their anxiety was expressed in urgent requests to Heidelberg for more men. Reinforcements were soon forthcoming, and with them improved defences and a shake-up in command. Handsome Hendrik Schoemau, the man who rode into Pretoria and demanded that Lanyon surrender the capital, replaced D. J. F. Erasmus as Assistant Commandant-General.

On Sunday, January 16th, the British command decided to repeat its success with another sortie against the Boers. The decision was kept 'profoundly secret' among a very select circle. There was no doubt that the Boers were aware that an attack was pending, but its direction was a mystery. To confuse the enemy, the Engineers exploded dynamite to the east as artillery, infantry (riding in wagons) and volunteers dashed to the west. The attack force consisted of a total of 470 men and three guns. DuVal, riding a borrowed 'flea-bitten' old charger, had difficulty trying to keep up with Gildea and the mounted men.

They headed straight for Elandsfontein, ten miles out, a strong position held by a hundred Boers. The British almost succeeded in taking the laager, but Boer reinforcements, led by Hendrik Schoemau, began to pour in. The guns fired wildly. Their presence rather than their accuracy kept the enemy at a respectful distance. Bellairs, who had come out with an escort of Carbineers, decided that 'the game was not worth the candle.' The column retired, harried all the way to the outskirts of Pretoria. At the same time another party of burghers threatened the camp from the east. Lanyon gathered all of the available mounted men to engage the enemy as the guns of the fort opened up. There was a brief flurry, then the Boers withdrew as quickly as they had come.

Bellairs reported his casualties as two killed and eight wounded, all seriously. (Two of the wounded had been taken prisoner.) There was no way of ascertaining the Republican loss. The only sure loss to the enemy was that of four horses captured by a sergeant of Nourse's Horse. In collecting the wounded, a surgeon who spoke Dutch learned that Henning Pretorius, the Boer commander, had been hit. Several British papers and certain subsequent histories reported the Boer losses as 'at least twenty killed, with two commandants among the wounded', but Republican records indicated a total of six burghers wounded.

Deprived of what he had believed would be a victory, Gildea snappishly described the artillery practice as uniformly bad— otherwise he would have taken the laager before support arrived. While he had only the highest praise for Nourse's Horse, he blamed Captain Sanctuary for failing to employ the Carbineers in a proper manner so as to check the flanking movement of the Boers. A terrible row ensued. The Carbineers were ready to resign in a body. Neutral parties expended great effort in mollifying them.

Dr Bousfield, the Anglican bishop whom the Republican Government had allowed to enter Pretoria after the siege began, was embarrassed that the British should offer battle on the

Sabbath. 'We shame ourselves among the Boers', the good bishop wrote, 'who were surprised in their service.' They had specifically requested 'that we would not fight on this day'.[16]

The action at Elandsfontein left Bellairs discouraged. He decided that any hope of relieving Potchefstroom from Pretoria would be impractical. To march the regulars over two hundred miles, encumbered by supply wagons, would involve 'a daily running fight' there and back, against an enemy superior in numbers and supported by natural geographic advantages. And to leave Pretoria to the impetuous volunteers, many of whom were suspected of pro-Boer sympathies, was no less risky.

The only pleasure that his report gave him was in his description of the heroism of two Irish lads, Corporal Murray of the 94th and Trooper Danaher of Nourse's Horse, who both exposed themselves to prolonged fire in order to save their wounded comrades. They both received the Victoria Cross. Murray survived a severe wound to be personally invested with the honour by the Queen. Danaher joined the Connaught Rangers after the war.

For the time being, Bellairs resolved to abandon any further thrusts against the encircling Boers. Only the approach of Colley's column would induce him to try a breakthrough. On January 21st Dacombe slipped into camp with a letter from Colley intimating that a relief column was endeavouring to enter the Transvaal. If possible, Colley hoped to reach Standerton on the 21st. An infectious enthusiasm swept through the camp. Dozens of 'Sister Annes', as Bellairs described them, sat most of the day atop hills overlooking the Heidelberg road, looking 'wistfully through their glasses' in the vain hope of spotting some sign of an advancing column. On some days the look-outs in the hill-forts caught the fever and swore they could see Colley's men approaching. The heliograph, normally used to signal the appearance of Boer riders, relayed the good news to the camp.

After a month of siege, life in the camp seemed more bearable. A feeling of security prevailed. Relief was on the way and the danger of a sudden attack by the Boers appeared less likely than in the beginning of the siege. The *News of the Camp* promised that there would be 'a sharp, quick stroke of retribution ... which never failed to overtake our enemies sooner or later'. More people ventured for longer periods of time into the town, which was now deserted except for hundreds of cats. An ox-wagon omnibus, with seats inside, was run daily between the fort and the town for their convenience. Shops opened their doors for an hour or two on a serve-yourself basis. The schools were reopened for the children. There was no repetition of the incident which occurred a week before the conflict began, when a boy, in the presence of the Governor and other officials, read a piece called an Ode to Liberty that concerned itself with the 'Martyrs of Slagter's Nek'. Lanyon nearly lost his monocle.

There were amusements of every sort to satisfy every class and nationality, with celebrations for events ranging from the Kaiser's birthday to St Patrick's Day. The so-called 'Beleaguered Theatre' offered concerts by the military band and stage plays, including one by the girls of the convent which was intended to raise money for improvements to the cemetery. The witty Du-Val put on his variety show, 'Odds and Ends', after which he organized a lottery of sixty guineas for the man or woman who could come closest to predicting the exact time the relief would appear. And as always, siege or no siege, Boer or no Boer, the English arranged a cricket match.

There was always a fair share of grumbling. Thousands of fleas invaded the overcrowded quarters, often making sleep impossible. The four civilian physicians in camp went on strike, demanding at least five guineas a day. (The authorities rejected the demand and retained the rate, established during the Zulu War, of one guinea a day with rations.) The volunteers, who received five shillings a day and rations, complained that certain units were given lighter duties and better quarters.

The food rations were unappetizing. The biscuits, which were believed to have 'served' in the Zulu War, swarmed with weevils. The women complained bitterly; according to Elizabeth Dietrich, they 'quarrelled endlessly, one of the most fruitful sources of dispute being the smoke nuisance', a reference to the problem of keeping the smoke from one camp-fire from drifting into a neighbour's abode.[17] Women were on half-rations and children under twelve on a quarter allowance. So many parents claimed a full ration for children who were obviously not twelve that a visitor would have thought he had encountered a race of midgets.[18] Some women had the added difficulty of bearing children during the siege.

The young girls, on the other hand, 'thought camp life great
fun . . . there were such a lot of nice young fellows, much too
good to be sent out to be shot at.'[19] Dances were held regularly,
and several girls became engaged. One young volunteer later
tried his best to get himself killed 'as the only possible solution
of his simultaneous engagement to two ladies who had been
unable to resist the glamour of his martial achievements'.[20]

Lanyon, who selected an early date in the 'relief lottery',
placidly assured all listeners that the Republican forces could
not long prevail. As late as January 23rd he reiterated to the
Colonial Minister that the uprising was 'the result of a sudden
impulse'.[21] Five days later, by way of self-vindication for not
having anticipated events, he declared that 'many of them do not
even know why they are fighting.'[22] On the same day he wrote a
dispatch to Colley expressing the optimistic view that 'it
won't last long, for the Boers are poorly armed.'[23]

On February 7th, under a flag of truce, a Boer messenger
brought Lanyon a letter from Kruger requesting an exchange of
prisoners. The proposal was rejected. The Boer messenger
brought with him copies of the *Gazette*, which left little doubt
that Colley's advance had been halted at Laing's Nek. It was
discouraging news. Lanyon called for another attack. Bellairs
believed it wholly imprudent but, in the end he reluctantly de-
ferred to Lanyon's wishes.

Where should they attack? So far they had struck to the east
and to the west, with no small risk involved in their safe return.
To the north the defences were thought to be too strong. The
Red House laager nine miles to the south, which Gildea had
reconnoitred on January 29th, was believed to offer 'the fewest
obstacles to success'.

Very early on the morning of February 12th a strong column
of 614 men (198 of them mounted) with three guns moved
down the Heidelberg road, hoping to surprise the enemy. But
again the Boers were ready for them. As the mounted volunteers rode up towards the summit of the hill with the red house,
the Boers began to pick them off. Gildea rushed forward with
the main column and guns in support. The Carbineers tried to
take the stone cattle-kraal near the red house, but they soon discovered that it was fully occupied. Receiving volleys at short
range, the Carbineers retired to cover. Shells were dropped into

the kraal, and the burghers took to their horses. Galloping behind a ridge, they suddenly appeared, heavily reinforced, on the
left rear flank of the Carbineers. Nourse's Horse rode to support
the Carbineers, but the line caved in. Confusion followed surprise. By accident or design, a surgeon drove his ambulance
several hundred yards in front of the British line to minister to
Captain Sanctuary and other wounded Carbineers. The ambulance was fired on from both sides, as some of the British mis-
took it for a Boer wagon. The infantry, still in wagons, came
under attack. The fiery Gildea, conspicuous in mufti, stood up in
his saddle and shouted orders; he was shot in the buttocks. The
infantry barely got into action when a flanking fire caused them
to get out of hand, a fact which Bellairs later attributed to the
extreme youthfulness of the men, including the non-coms.
With some difficulty the officers succeeded in restoring order.
The Boers, with steady accretions, were emboldened by the sight.
An Engineer who had seen action in the Zulu War swore that
'all the firing at Ulundi put together, was as naught compared to
that lively quarter of an hour.'[24]

Captain Dunn, who succeeded Gildea, ordered the retreat. As
the column retired it was pursued by disaster. The mounted men,
however, checked the Boers on the flank and rear until the force
arrived safely under the guns of the forts. Bellairs now came out
to take command. He was shocked to see regulars running towards Pretoria as fast as their legs could carry them. Troops
were ordered out of camp to help discourage the enemy. A few
shots drove the Boers off. The British losses were one man killed
in action and fifteen wounded. Seven of the latter, including Sanctuary, died within a few days. Gildea, the 'verdomde colonel',
as the Boers called him, recovered slowly from his awkward
wound. Mrs Gildea, who nursed her husband and other sick and
wounded back to health, was honoured for her solicitude by the
Queen, who conferred upon her the decoration of the Royal Red
Cross. The Boers indicated no losses on their own side, but
British estimates were '65 or more killed'.

'The Red House Kraal', observed DuVal, 'helped to quicken
the trade of the surgeon and coffin-maker more than any of the
engagements' during the siege.[25] It was the last open assault by
the beleaguered.

Accusations resounded throughout the camp. While Lanyon

raved about the Boers' deliberate firing on an ambulance wagon, the Carbineers and artillerymen denounced the Fusiliers for showing the white feather. The way the Fusiliers had taken to their heels and bolted without firing a single shot was, in their opinion, not only disgraceful but an action which had endangered the lives of the men in other units. There were recriminations in which the loyalty of volunteers with Dutch names was called into question. Taunts led to blows. 'The officers had great difficulty in patching up a peace,' wrote one volunteer, 'and did not succeed in doing so till some bloody heads and noses resulted.'[26] The row began all over again when the volunteers learned that the command ascribed the defeat to their poor conduct. They were further insulted by the fact that Bellairs failed to recommend a trooper named Palmer for the Victoria Cross after Palmer had dragged a wounded comrade to safety. The regular officers may have been unimpressed, but the daring and resolution of the volunteers did not go unnoticed among the Boers.

Shortly after the battle, negotiations were begun to exchange the surgeon and two orderlies taken before the Red House laager for the prisoners the British had taken from Zwartkopje laager. When the *News of the Camp* stated that prisoners had been exchanged, Lanyon was vexed by what he believed read like an 'admission of belligerent rights'; he insisted that DuVal should insert a correction in his column. 'Exchange or no exchange,' observed DuVal, 'one thing is certain—that if the ambulance-waggon and its prisoners from Zwartkopje laager would have remained in durance vile, and daily cursed, as it was stated they did, the tyrannical and brutal treatment which compelled them to bathe every morning, wash occasionally during the day, and obey a few other sanitary conditions [was] exceedingly repugnant to their souls as free and independent burghers from the "Waterburg Distrikt" of "De Zuid Afrikans Republik".'[27]

After the Red House laager engagement, hope began to flag. Day after day there was no word from the world outside. Confinement and inaction led to boredom and depression. Excessive drinking led to further restrictions on the sale of alcohol. There were mysterious rumours that the food supply was running low, and, in fact, early in March the men were put on reduced rations. By March sickness stalked the camp: dysentery and fever victims crowded the hospital—and the cemetery. 'The line of graves just outside the burial ground', Bishop Bousfield wrote sadly, 'is fast becoming two lines.'[28]

The *News of the Camp*, its columns becoming less jovial and more abbreviated, summed up the situation with: 'There is nothing stirring but stagnation.'

The daily murmur was 'How long?'

POTCHEFSTROOM

The predicament of the small garrison at the old capital of the Transvaal was unique. Poorly fortified and ill-provisioned, it was—as Colley had foreseen—the weakest post in the land. The siege was of great concern to the Boers as well. To the Heidelberg Government, seventy miles to the east, it 'occasioned care and anxiety by night and day'. The chances of defeating the British and taking possession of their guns seemed within their grasp. But until they did, some five hundred burghers would be tied down by the investment—burghers who were needed to defend the Nek. Annoyed by the lack of progress made by the besieging forces, the Commandant General testily asked the local authorities to divert some of their men to Natal. They stubbornly refused. Correspondence between the Republican Government and the independent-minded Cronje became heated. Not until 'superior authorities' at Potchefstroom had visited Heidelberg, Jorissen wrote, did they see their error and promise 'an earnest co-operation and strict obedience to the orders of the Government'.[29] However, the small party of detached burghers sent to the Nek travelled so slowly that they arrived just as peace was being declared.

The townspeople—between two and three thousand—showed little sympathy for the Imperial cause. 'Not a volunteer is forthcoming,' reported Colonel Winsloe, 'and nearly the whole town are to all appearances on the side of the enemy'. And yet, those families that were pro-Boer were not considered as reliable by the Republicans. Virtual prisoners, they were kept under close watch by the burghers as they surrounded the fort.

Crammed into a fort some thirty yards square were 180 soldiers, a civilian conductor with 60 native drivers (nearly half of whom escaped during the first month) under his control, and 48 townspeople, along with an assortment of horses, oxen and mules. The hardships attending a close siege quickly convinced the civilians that they should return to their homes. Possible maltreatment by hostile Boers could be no worse than what was to be endured in the tiny fort. Only thirteen men and women elected to remain.

Construction of the fort had begun in mid-November when two companies of the 21st and a score of artillerymen were rushed in to quell possible disorders arising from the Bezuiden-hout affair. When the siege began, there was only a mere shelter-trench and a rampart of only four and a half feet. Working dili-gently, the men raised the parapet to ten feet, with the ditch outside dug proportionately deeper. A scorching fire from near-by trees and housetops made the work extremely hazardous and necessitated constant repairs. Two nine-pounders finally re-plied to the Boer fire, clearing brush and rooftops. The Boers brought up 'Old Griet', an ancient ship's cannon which, according to one witness, 'inflicted untold damage by knocking down a stable and killing a mule'.[30]

Thousands of sandbags—filled actually with mealies (Indian corn)—were made from tent materials. It was an unending lab-our, for heavy rains continually rotted the sacks.

For protection against attacks on dark nights, rifle-pits were dug outside. They were connected with the fort by zig-zag trenches. The Boers in turn, using large bales of washed wool (against which shells were powerless), dug trenches towards the improvised fort. The defenders cried 'foul' when they saw that the burghers were 'forcing "loyal" natives and Europeans' to work in the trenches while exposed to British fire. One man named Findlay was killed. Boer sapping activities, conceived with the greatest cunning, provoked from the British sudden night raids which sometimes had the immediate effect of destroying the burghers' advance works.

Severe wounds were at times inflicted; the British alleged that the Boers were using explosive bullets. One soldier had the entire back of his arm blown off. Winsloe, armed with the tes-timony of his surgeons, remonstrated to Cronje against this violation of 'a line of warfare established amongst civilized nations'. The protest was ignored.

Certain civilities were observed, however, which the British commander felt took 'the sting out of warfare'. The wounded were politely exchanged. The fighting was often suspended for lunch. Sundays were, by mutual consent, considered days of peace, though 'the Republicans tried to bawl down the garrison with lusty hymn-singing.'[31] On Sunday afternoons, weather permitting, townspeople strolled at a safe distance around the fort, while fathers explained to their children the fine points of siege warfare. The soldiers whistled at the young ladies. At night the Boers collected once again to sing hymns within earshot of the defenders. Winsloe was moved to write, 'They are a fine, manly, sturdy race, such as I should like to live among. Who can blame them for fighting for independence ?—we at least did not do so.'[32]

Those who visited the town after the siege concluded that the Dutch church in the Market Square would have offered a far better site for the defence, but this obviously savoured 'too much of sacrilege' to Winsloe.

It was the enemy within which gradually enfeebled the defenders. The confinement took place during the worst season of the year; heat and rain were constant companions. The first difficulty was with water. Rain-water helped to avert an immediate crisis, but unless more water could be found, capitulation was imminent. After several days of frenzied digging, good water was found fifteen feet down. 'The greatest necessity was secured,' Winsloe declared.

Food was rationed from the first day. Normally the supply would provision but one field company. Thus, a day's ration during most of the siege consisted of three pounds of Indian corn (originally intended as animal fodder), with four ounces of tinned meat on alternate days. All the animals were either killed or released, except for one horse. Everyone looked forward to a roast-horse dinner on Christmas Day, but in the end the meat was rejected as inedible.

On January 16th a man was allowed to come into the fort under a flag of truce to escort his wife home. Before leaving, he slipped a message in cipher to Winsloe which had purportedly been written by Bellairs. The message spoke of relief coming the following morning, and asked that the garrison sally forth at a signal to hasten the Boer defeat. But Winsloe believed the letter to be a clumsy forgery. At dawn, which was accompanied by a

drenching rain, heavy firing—including a cannon—was heard in
a wood a mile off. Unseen eyes watched the fort, hoping the redcoats would come out. None did. Finally the firing stopped and
Boers masquerading in British uniforms were seen drifting off to
their camp. A shell from a nine-pounder hurried them on their way.

Trusting that Colley would 'strain every nerve to reach us',
an anxious watch was kept for a signal from the hills beyond. A
heliograph was constructed and kept always ready for an instant
reply. One night a flash in the sky was mistaken for a rocket fired
by a relieving force. Many dreamed that night that they heard
bagpipes coming down the road from Heidelberg. They could
even identify the tune: 'The Campbells are Coming'. Morning
light, however, brought cruel disappointment.

Tension built up during the long nights. There was nothing to
do in the oppressive silence. Late one night, young Lieutenant
Rundle approached the colonel, saluted smartly and made a
strange request, 'Please sir, would you allow me just to give a
screech?' Wrinkling his brow, Winsloe hesitatingly assented.
Rundle scrambled to the top of the parapet and began a series of
unearthly, blood-curdling yells. Dogs barked and howled. The
startled Boers promptly opened fire. The garrison tittered in
amusement and the lieutenant, jumping down, felt all the better
for his exercise. Having thus lifted the spirits of the besieged, he
was permitted by Winsloe to repeat his performance on various
nights.* The Boers never grew accustomed to the sound that so
rent the night.

Another morale-booster was an improvised Union Jack. It was
sewn together with pieces from a sergeant's serge jumper and
the white and blue linings of an officer's cloak. A symbol of their
determination, it was displayed from the parapet throughout the
siege. After the war, the flag was inspected by Her Majesty at
Windsor Castle.

By the end of January the meagre food ration had been cut
even further. Though the corn, pounded and boiled, was comparatively nutritious, sickness became prevalent. Dysentery
spared no one. When scurvy made its appearance, the men were

* The boy lieutenant, Henry Rundle, rose to the rank of general, and served as
Kitchener's Chief of Staff in the Sudan. The *Dictionary of National Biography*, in esti-
mating his military talents, observed: 'He never took a risk, and was rewarded by
never meeting a reverse.'

ordered to boil grass and to drink the resulting broth. Typhoid and enteric fever put many into the hospital tents beside the wounded. The dead, at no small risk, were buried quickly and quietly at night outside the fort.

To dishearten the garrison further, Cronje sent in a copy of the *Staats Courant* which described British defeats. Winsloe merely replied that they would be pleased to receive the journal regularly. By now, the Boers had begun to expect a capitulation daily. They too were beginning to feel the pinch. The food and provisions which they confiscated from townspeople who were regarded as unfriendly were soon exhausted. Requisitions sent to Heidelberg for coffee, sugar and clothing were slow in coming. In addition, the Boers at Potchefstroom had been made responsible for supplying their own cartridges and powder.[33]

How long the determined little band of soldiers, hungry and fatigued, could hold their position led to a great deal of speculation abroad. Rumours that Potchefstroom had fallen and that Winsloe was dead were announced in the London press as early as January 10th. To the Victorians there was one shocking aspect to the siege: five pretty young girls of the Forssman family, without even a change of clothing, were sharing the privations of the siege with some two hundred men. Elizabeth Dietrich was 'horrified' to learn of their predicament. 'At the time their adventure was the talk of all Pretoria.'

Chevalier Forssman and his family had got into this difficulty through their friendship with the military. When the soldiers came to Potchefstroom, they were entertained lavishly with dinner parties and dances in the stately Forssman home. Young officers 'spent romantic evenings sitting on the stoop in moonlight talking sweet nothings to their friends'. Since the family's sympathies were wholly pro-British, the Chevalier advised his children to seek safety in the British compound when the Boers took over the town, and not to 'come home until things are quiet again'.*[34] A shelter of corn-cob sacks nine feet square and five feet high was made for the girls, with a small hole made at the bottom to allow them to crawl through. When the Boers used their gun, the girls were relegated to a small dug-out hole.

* Olaf Forssman had come out from Sweden in 1848 to speculate in land and to promote various projects, such as a regular coach service to Kimberley. He was ruined by the war and never recovered.

The presence of the fair sex, however, brightened the lives of the men. Every night the girls brought an element of gaiety to the officers' mess. Afterwards they led the men in the singing. Assisting the ladies back to their 'stronghold' through a hole only two feet high and one and a half feet broad required a great deal of time and care on the part of the admiring soldiers. One would have thought they were invalids, related Winsloe; the simple saying of 'good-night' was 'unnecessarily prolonged'.[35]

When privations began to undermine their health, the surgeon advised Winsloe that the young ladies should exercise. The constitutional had to be discontinued, however, when one of the youngest girls was wounded by a stray shot. Several of the others became seriously ill. The courage of 'our ladies' was an inspiration to the soldiers, but Winsloe finally asked the Boer commander to permit them to cross the lines and return home. Cronje refused; since they had sought British protection, he said, let the British take care of them.

By the end of February Cronje was content to starve the garrison into surrender. Any concession that meant one less mouth to feed would militate against these tactics. After the siege, when Cronje had a chance to study the fort, he stated that he would have stormed the place if he had known how weak it was.

Every day up to February 25th, one name or another was stricken from the roster of those ready for duty. On that day a Boer trench was only sixty yards away and the two parties were in a position to talk to each other. The words were not always friendly. One burgher wrote a message to the British soldiers on the wall of the jail which read, 'You poor devils thought to do good in this place; but go see your combrats (*sic*) bones in the back yard. Go to heaven!'

All attempts to send a messenger through with news of the garrison's condition failed. But the British felt that if they could only hold out a little longer, the long arm of Britain would inevitably reach out to save them.

STANDERTON

Visitors described Standerton as a miserable-looking place. Without trees or gardens, the fifty-odd iron-roofed houses looked to the traveller C.L. Norris-Newman 'as if they had been a mud-splash thrown at random on the bare veld'.[36] The one object of interest was the octogenarian 'General' Stander, a sturdy voortrekker who had fought the British at Bloomplaats and given the town its name.

Standerton sprawled on a slope which overlooked a ford across the broad, sparkling Vaal to the south. The fort in turn lay below rocky kopjes rising to the north and east, and the towering, flat-topped Stander's Kop which guided distant travellers on the veld.

Situated midway on the main road between Newcastle and Pretoria, Standerton's strategic importance was obvious. On December 21st two companies of the 94th and one of the 58th marched in from Wakkerstroom and began making fortifications. Major W.E. Montague was still on his way from Pietermaritzburg to take command. The assignment was not to his liking. 'I don't want to go, sir,' he had told Colley, 'I dislike the Transvaal more than I can say, but if you think there is any necessity for my going, I am ready to start at an hour's notice.' Colley thought it vital, and advised the major, who had an outstanding record in the Zulu War, 'You will find Standerton an excellent position for defence, strengthen it, take care they don't get you unawares, and hold till I come [January 20th]…we shall march together on Heidelberg'.[37]

To escape detection by Republican patrols (who had already taken two travelling officers prisoner), Montague disguised himself as a colonial bank messenger, journeying to the Transvaal in a post cart. He had bought a slouch hat, removed his collar and tie, and left his hair unkempt and his face unwashed after shaving his moustache (which by regulation was worn by all British officers). The Boers let him pass.

Arriving on December 23rd, Montague found everything 'in the wildest confusion'. The half-built fort a mile from town was 'all dirt and muddle'.[38] A strict, no-nonsense-type officer, he infused discipline and organization while more vigorous preparations were made for the defence. While the parapets of the fort were being raised, the main stone buildings in the town were loop-holed and garrisoned. Marks were laid out at certain ranges to improve the shooting. Soldiers who misbehaved were bound and lashed. Having resorted to the cat from the outset, the major had no difficulty in maintaining the strictest discipline during the rest of the siege. Even the volunteers, whose loyalty was questionable, carried out the commander's orders in exemplary fashion.

In the beginning, there were only thirty-four volunteers serving with the 350 regulars. Others 'came in but slowly, many making excuses for not joining', wrote Montague. 'Pressure became necessary.' He brought the number of 'volunteers' up to seventy-five.[39]

On finding that a firmer hand was needed than that of the local magistrate, Montague declared martial law. The food supply was ample, but when Colley did not arrive at the appointed time rationing was introduced.

Boer sympathizers were given a chance to clear out. Their deserted homes were a great temptation to looters, who were difficult to check. The small Dutch party which remained complained of, among other things, the theft of the church clock, Bibles, hymn-books and other items from their place of worship. These were later found among the effects of the men of the 94th.

The women and children were placed in a large wool-store with the windows and doors blocked up. In a few days, however, the Boers made it apparent that they were satisfied to leave the town in peace. The 'Flea laager', as it was called, was abandoned, and the women and children returned to their homes, where the only danger was an occasional stray bullet.

Operating out of three laagers, the Boer investment was complete by the New Year. They positioned themselves on the rim of kopjes and Stander's Kop in particular, and the British soon learned that the long-range rifle-fire of the Boers could be disturbingly accurate. To draw their fire away from the fort and at the same time to show the burghers how little their shooting concerned them, Montague left the tents outside standing throughout the investment. It took the Boers some time to discover that they were unoccupied. There was some difficulty, at first, in keeping the soldiers from using them. Two men were severely wounded before the order was fully obeyed. Even the officers' tents a little farther off and partially protected by walls of the fort were not entirely safe. Traverses of boxes were placed inside the tents and the officers occupied them as little as possible.

When the soldiers went to their positions, they were allowed

to run but had to keep their heads up. The military propriety of
ducking when under fire was a frequent topic for discussion
among the soldiers of that day. Some held that it was an unbecoming sign of weakness. They saw a relationship between
'bobbing' and 'bolting'. Others insisted that under fire such
movements were as involuntary as blinking the eye; and after all
it might spoil the enemy's aim and save a man's life. Nevertheless, to the major 'bobbing' was unbecoming to a British soldier.
Montague himself, while walking stiffly from post to post, received a slight wound in the leg.

If the Boer fire became too warm, Montague undertook a
sortie. But invariably within the hour, because of the Boers'
excellent organization, reinforcements rode in from distant Boer
posts to discourage any further action on Montague's part.

One night a drunken sergeant and five of his comrades boasted
that they could capture Stander's Kop. They stumbled up the
slope to a place near the top and seized a post which the burghers
left unoccupied after dark. When the unsuspecting Boers returned
in the morning, the six opened fire. The fire was returned, of
course, and the sergeant and his men quickly sobered when they
saw the seriousness of their position. Montague had to stage a
diversion to bring them down safely to the fort. The fort was
now called Alice—because 'so many of us had an Alice we loved
at home.'

To frighten the Boers from advanced positions, Montague
ordered the construction of a dummy gun. This 'gun', fashioned
from wood, painted black, and mounted on wagon wheels, was
'prepared with much ostentation'. To give it a bark, four rifles
were fixed underneath and fired simultaneously by strings connected to their triggers. The mere preparation of the dummy for
'firing' usually had the desired effect of driving off the burghers.

When the Boer patriots left Standerton on the eve of the
conflict, they vowed to return and to whip the soldiers out of
town. Unlike Potchefstroom, however, the siege was never
pushed with vigour. The Boer commander, Lombaard, was less
aggressive than Cronje, but then it appears that the men he had
at his disposal were far fewer in number than the defenders.[40]

On January 17th a person evidently of authority appeared with
a party of horsemen and rode up to the top of Stander's Kop. To
Montague it seemed as if the Boers were devising an attack. The

major learned afterwards that it was Pier Joubert himself, who
had considered attacking the fort with the bulk of his force; 'but
matters just then looked so threateningly that the men were
ordered to go on to the "Nek" instead, and we were let off.'[41]

To facilitate the siege, the Republicans had hoped to bring up
guns. 'Cannons' were made out of hoop-iron by a German
mechanic working for the Republic. Whether these were the guns
they were expecting, or others captured from the British, is not
clear. What is clear is that no artillery ever arrived.

Boer patrols kept the garrison well sealed. Only one messenger, a Zulu, got through from Pretoria. He was treated so
royally that he was reluctant to continue his journey to Natal.
After a second effort, he got through the Boer lines 'by the most
artful lies'. When he arrived at Colley's headquarters with his
precious stick filled with microscopic dispatches, the general rewarded him with £30—the value of the ten cows promised to
him. The Zulu subsequently returned to Standerton after the
siege as a servant of Cameron of the *Standard*. He deservedly
received a hero's welcome.

The progress of the relief column was indicated by unusual
Boer activities which the British, however, did not understand
until after the war was over. Each time Colley suffered a set-
back, the burghers showed their delight by jumping up from
behind the rocks they used for cover—shouting, waving and
gesticulating insultingly. One of the Republicans, who excelled
the others in this exercise, laced his words with barrack slang,
leaving no doubt that he was a British deserter. He was one of
several believed to have joined the enemy. When the war began,
one deserter marched into the fort and asked to re-join the
colours. He was jailed, but Montague took great pleasure in
handing him a pardon after the siege.

A desultory fire continued throughout the eighty-eight days
of investment. By the end of February, however, the Boer fire
began to slacken, owing perhaps to a shortage of ammunition,
much of which had been wasted. The British, while admitting to
the expenditure of 18,000 rounds, insisted that the Republican
side fired three times that number. If that is so, it took 58,000
bullets to kill five defenders, two of whom were volunteers.

LYDENBURG

The town of Lydenburg is situated on a fertile plain surrounded by the tumbled eastern ranges which taper down towards Portuguese Mozambique. It lies in the middle of the gold country, from which at the time in question it drew most of its support. The rowdy diggers and the large tribal population of the district required the constant presence of a garrison. The English-speaking diggers referred to the town as 'Bligh'. The more numerous Dutch inhabitants dubbed it Lydenburg, 'City of Sorrows', because of the hardships they had suffered before settling there. The British considered it a name well chosen, for the Dutch settlers, scrupulous in matters of religion, had a strong aversion to excessive gaiety. Parties found guilty of dancing, for example, were tried by synod. Certainly the events that transpired early in 1881 did not belie the name.

It was an unhappy little detachment which was left behind to guard the town while Colonel Anstruther marched off with most of their comrades. All that remained were eight Royal Engineers, six men of the Army Service and Army Hospital Corps (under Dr John Falvey), Conductor Parsons, and fifty-three non-commissioned officers and men of the 94th. The men were the dregs of different companies, noted for their strong tendencies to drunkenness and insubordination.

This picked lot of misfits was placed under the command of the junior officer of the regiment, Lieutenant Walter Long, recently transferred from the Inniskilling Dragoons. The soldiers, from Conductor Parsons (twenty years' service) on down, profoundly resented being placed in the care of an officer barely twenty-two years old who had never been under fire. The dust stirred up on the road by Anstruther's column had barely settled when the men began to dress improperly, steal chickens and drink to excess. Long closed the canteen and relieved Sergeant Godfrey, who was in charge, on suspicion of improperly selling liquor to the volunteers.

There is no question that Long was impulsive and wanting in tact. Under the pressures of siege conditions he became indecisive, owing to what his defenders charitably described as a 'nervous temperament'. Long later admitted as much. He excused himself on the grounds that he was inexperienced and that he was upset by the presence of his girl-wife, whose health and safety deeply concerned him. Actually, Mary Long appears to have exercised a steadying influence over her husband. The only woman in the fort, she became a universal favourite among the men. Her willing hands in constructing the fort set an example to all. 'When the men lost heart,' it was said, 'her voice encouraged and stimulated them to further exertions.'[42] Father Walsh, the soldier-priest who elected to remain with the garrison to administer to spiritual needs, declared that she was worth six soldiers.

The fort, built on a rise above the town, consisted of eight thatched huts connected by stone walls and traverses enclosing an area of seventy-eight yards by twenty yards. Outside the fort mines were laid and trenches dug. Wire entanglements and broken objects were scattered about to prevent an attack by a mounted force. The soldiers honoured the commander's wife by calling it Fort Mary; Father Walsh blessed it with a few touching words. A merchant ship's ensign was then raised 'amidst deafening cheers'.

No effort was made to hold the town. The townspeople, including Landdrost Roth, expressed their 'unqualified loyalty', but believed that the safest course for all civilians was a declaration of neutrality. If Anstruther and his men had stayed, they explained, they would have assisted in every possible way. When the citizens heard of what happened at Bronkhorst Spruit, they became even less co-operative. Only ten volunteers joined the garrison, two of them from the gold-fields, which had been left unmolested by the Boers after they took away 180 pounds of gunpowder. Once the Boers had moved in and raised the Republican banner, English storekeepers gave money and sold ammunition without objection. Even the landdrost, it was said, handed over 600 rounds to the enemy. That there was at least one secret supporter of the British in the town was demonstrated later during the siege when a dog was sent towards the fort with a note attached to it advising the soldiers that they were shooting too high.

The townspeople were intimidated by reports that Abel Erasmus, a political leader of the district whose neck Wolseley had threatened with a rope, dealt severely with those who opposed

the Republic. One Englishman guilty of loud talk was said to have
been tied to a wagon wheel and given twelve lashes. Natives
who disobeyed his commands were also given a taste of the lash.

On the whole the citizens of Lydenburg had little to complain
of during the occupation. Piet Steyne, the Boer commandant, in
the opinion of Mrs Long, was 'so gentlemanlike and well educated'. He enforced a strict discipline on his men, 'some of them
wild and untutored', and there was little loss from depredation.
Losses through requisitioning were minimal. When during the
siege a young burgher shouted into the fort, 'Come out, Mrs
Long, and make us some coffee, we are so cold,' Steyne ordered
twenty-five lashes to warm him up, and threatened to make it
fifty for anyone else repeating the offence. [43]

Before the shooting began, the Heidelberg Government sent
Mr Dietrick Muller to persuade the garrison, in the name of
humanity, to surrender. Muller was astounded by the extreme
youth of the commander, and could hardly conceal his delight in
having to negotiate with an opponent who was so obviously inexperienced. The lieutenant and his wife in turn were agreeably
impressed by the affable manners of so 'fine a specimen of a
thoroughbred Boer'. [44] Under the shade of a large marquee they
drank champagne and Long persuaded the Boer representative to
allow him time to communicate with Pretoria before he made his
decision. Muller was sure 'dat Jonker' recognized the trap he was
in and would not risk annihilation. To strengthen his argument,
Muller described in detail the disaster at Bronkhorst Spruit, in
which he had participated.

The delay gave the lieutenant five additional days to complete
his fortifications. The Boer leaders wrangled over what most of
them felt was a foolish agreement. Nor were the British in accord.
Conductor Parsons argued that what was called for was offensive
and not defensive tactics. He advised attacking the Boers as soon
as they entered the town, 'striking a blow from which they never
would probably recover from'. [45]

The message which the Boers allowed the sheriff of Lydenburg to deliver to Bellairs stated that the garrison was in excellent spirits and working earnestly on its defence. On his return,
the Boers now decided that the sealed dispatches carried by the
sheriff did not serve their interests. They were taken from him
and he was confined for several days.

The dispatch Long was permitted to send out was the only successful communication made to the outside throughout the siege. Later, on January 16th, a digger named Green came secretly into the fort. He had obtained a pass from Steyne to go to the gold-fields to look after his family. Green agreed, for the sum of £100, to carry a message to Delagoa Bay for transmission to London. 'A victim of his over-assurance and imprudence', wrote Bellairs, he was taken captive by the Boers for 'holding communication' with the enemy and was shot while trying to escape. Green's death was denounced as an atrocity by the British and the matter was investigated by the Royal Commission after the war. Commandant Steyne and Veld Kornet F. J. Marais, who had been present at the shooting, testified that Green was arrested for having gone into camp against orders and was shot as he ran off. The fact that the digger intended smuggling out a message greatly weakened the British case. The Commission considered Steyne's explanation 'to be quite satisfactory'.[46]

It was on January 6th that the Boers surrounded Fort Mary to inaugurate the siege. Under a flag of truce, an ultimatum written by Joubert was delivered; it promised honourable treatment to the British if they surrendered. Long rejected the demand and informed the Boers that the truce was at an end. The burghers moved to within 250 yards of the fort, taking advantage of whatever elevation and cover they could find among outlying houses and rocks. Firing then commenced and both Briton and Boer banged away as fast as they could fire. The only creature hit that day and the next was a soldier's pet monkey.

On the third day the Boers rolled up the first of two ship's cannon to batter down the walls of the fort. The unexpected hoarse boom of artillery startled the defenders. At first they supposed it might be an explosion of some mysterious origin, until the second shot whistled over the fort and convinced them otherwise. Long called out to Parsons who was standing close by, 'Oh! it's a cannon, run up the white flag. I won't fight against cannon.' A sentry within earshot echoed his words, 'Yes, run up the white flag.' Parsons requested that they should wait and see what damage the cannon could do; if they should knock the walls down, there would be ample cover to cut down any charging Boers. Recovering himself, Long agreed.[47]

From that day forward the garrison lost what little confidence they had had in their commander. Most of the men believed him to be a coward. Whenever the burghers opened fire with their guns, the lieutenant 'pointedly removed himself from where the round shots were striking'. Rather than direct the fire of his men, Long often remained in bed, where he received reports and issued orders. If he spoke to the men, his words and manner were discouraging. The men were convinced that he would capitulate at the first opportunity.

The Boers worked the guns regularly. An Englishman in town was kept busy making up the cartridges. The little hospital in the fort began to fill, but the mixed company set down as undesirables began to display an amazing amount of pluck. There was no dearth of volunteers when Parsons conducted grenade-tossing raids on advanced Boer positions. To disturb the enemy artillery, a cannon was ingeniously made out of the monkey of an Abyssinian pump. The improvised gun, along with a party of sharp-shooters posted to pick off Boer gunners, soon caused the enemy artillery to slacken and to draw farther back.

As time wore on the besieged became more confident. They grew accustomed to the continued noise of firing. Many were not new to siege warfare, having successfully come through the siege of Eshowe (which lasted seventy days) during the Zulu War. The courage of the smiling Mrs Long, who visited the hospital daily, made the despondent feel foolish. At night she often led the men in a merry chorus of 'Hold the Fort', adapted to a popular melody:

> We don't want to fight, but by Jingo if we do,
> We've got the pluck, we've got the men, and ammunition too.
> We've fought the Zulu king, and Sekukuni too,
> And the Boers shall never get into Fort Mary.

Equally inspiring was the presence of Father Walsh, who had served as chaplain in the Zulu and Sekukuni campaigns. One old soldier who had previously served alongside him described the big raw-boned Irishman as having 'the courage of a lion, the tenderness of a woman, and a hearty laugh that was worth its weight in rifles when...fighting in a tight corner'.[48] Walsh worked a wonderful influence over the men, and when necessary —which was often—he helped to stiffen the resolve of the lieutenant. As the water became scarce, with the men reduced to a pint a day, Walsh directed the digging of a well and blessed their efforts. At forty-eight feet an ample supply was found. Father Walsh led the soldiers in a chorus of 'Hold the Fort'.

Early in March another inspiring Irishman appeared at Lydenburg—Aylward. By now it was conceded that the Fenian was the most active man on the Republican side. The siege had been flagging for nearly a month until he arrived. Aylward instructed the burghers in chopping down gum trees to be cut to short lengths and employed as cover while the men dug a deep trench towards the fort. At the same time he tried to hire some French engineers from the gold-fields to manufacture hand-grenades, but they wanted nothing to do with it and ran off. The clever Irishman also visited the wounded to act as a surgeon. Undoubtedly the urgency behind these activities was dictated by Joubert's need for more burghers; the British were increasing almost daily in the Nek. The sooner the fort fell, the better; meanwhile, some of the burghers at Lydenburg were sent to join Joubert. How many is not known, but it could not have been a large party, for the Boers in front of the fort were never reported as numbering more than three hundred.

A fresh yet ancient element of warfare was introduced on March 9th and credited to the fertile brain of Aylward. Greek fire enclosed in small metallic tubes with perforated holes was set on the points of arrows which were apparently shot from a bow. The thatched roofs of the huts caught fire. When the Boers perceived that much of the fort was in flames, 'they opened the fiercest fire we had yet undergone.'[49] Every soldier who could be spared from the walls was sent back to put out the fires. This time Long was up to the crisis. He coolly directed the men, at great personal risk, in putting out the flames. Once the roofs were removed, the danger was lessened considerably. Heavy rains followed, however, and added greatly to the misery of the defenders.

On the morning of the 10th the garrison was 'thrown into a state of excitement' by the appearance of two men carrying a white flag. One of them was Aylward with a letter from Joubert describing how the relief column had been repeatedly defeated and was no longer forthcoming. Favourable terms of surrender were offered. Long was given three hours to consider; or, if he wished, an interview and short armistice could be arranged with

Commandant Steyne in the town. Long consulted with Father Walsh, Dr Falvey and Conductor Parsons. Parsons pointed out that the garrison still possessed 124,000 rounds of ammunition and three months' full rations. He argued strongly against a meeting with so notorious a liar as Aylward. The surgeon and the chaplain were opposed to a capitulation of any kind. The lieutenant, however, felt that if he could enter the town he might learn something of the strength of the enemy. The parley was arranged.

Long walked out of the fort, his arm in a sling from a slight wound, looking haggard and careworn, especially in the company of Walsh and Falvey who appeared none the worse for their long confinement. Parsons and the men watching Long leave were depressed, as they feared he would give up the fort. The citizens of Lydenburg 'turned out *en masse* to see the officers, as well as enjoy the pleasures consequent on the truce'.[50]

They met Aylward, Steyne and some other Boer officers in a small office building. Dr Falvey soon moved off with Dr Ashton, the surgeon with the Boers, to visit the wounded. The glib Fenian did most of the talking. At first he tried to convince Long of the futility of continuing the struggle. When this had no visible effect, Aylward became threatening, warning that if the British did not submit, 'they would be treated as murderers'.[51] The lieutenant protested that since Joubert's letter stated that the British Government recognized the Boers as belligerents, 'he could claim on behalf of his garrison the usual usages of war'. As Long returned to the fort to observe the remainder of the twenty-four-hour truce, Aylward called the chaplain aside. As one Irishman to another, the redoubtable Aylward asked what a priest was doing in the fort and suggested that he remain outside. Father Walsh gave a blistering reply 'that astonished even his nerves'.[52]

The next morning, Long sent out a written reply in which he declined to surrender. The white flags were taken down and the fighting resumed.

Inside the fort that day tempers were rising. Just before he had sent out his reply, Long had adopted the unusual course of asking his three senior sergeants their opinion regarding surrender. To a man they declared that 'they were prepared to hold the fort to the last, and, if necessary, die at their posts.' They could hardly conceal the disgust they felt for their commander. A quarrel followed between Surgeon Falvey and Long. When the former referred to Mrs Long as a 'woman', Long put him under arrest. Falvey rose, stood squarely before the lieutenant and announced that *he* was under arrest for cowardice in front of the enemy. The affair, however, was dropped. Shortly afterwards, Long put Sergeant Godfrey under arrest, and then released him. The following morning, Long put himself on the sick list and went to bed for four days. Surgeon Falvey took command.

The siege ended at noon on March 30th when Steyne reported that a peace had been signed. This was confirmed a few days later by dispatches brought into the fort by Lieutenant Baker, an officer Long had known at Eton. Three men had been killed in action and one had died of enteric fever. (The Boer losses were given as three killed and fourteen wounded.)

The soldiers went wild. Their pent-up anger exploded with baleful consequences. They rushed to the court-house and tore down the Republican flag. Long had it replaced and promised to shoot any man who touched it. Others searched for 'that black-guard Aylward'. But he had already left for Heidelberg as soon as the war was over, and from there he went on to Cape Town, 'carefully avoiding', according to one version, 'any place garrisoned by us'.[53]

In the town, many of the soldiers were plied with drink, despite Long's request that the citizens should refrain from giving them liquor. Sergeant Godfrey was arrested once more. Drunkenness led to crime and disorder. Certain townspeople were denounced for toadying to the enemy, and this often led to a brawl. Bellairs found it necessary to send a company of Fusiliers to relieve the detachment. A court of inquiry was instituted, and numerous trials by court-martial followed. Long was given the alternative of facing a court decision or of sending in his application to retire from service. The lieutenant asked to resign his commission. To Mrs Long, Bellairs sent a message of gratitude for 'the courage and example' she had shown during the siege.

Mrs Long, returning home to write down her experiences in *Peace and War in the Transvaal*, failed to mention the near mutiny and subsequent trials. Instead she described how the Boers behaved when she left the fort. Standing on all sides, many wearing crepe bands, they politely came forward, all at the same time, to shake hands. 'It seemed difficult to believe that they had been shooting at us, and we at them, for so long a time.'[54]

RUSTENBURG

Unlike the garrison at Lydenburg, the seventy-two men and ten volunteers at Rustenburg, seventy miles due west of Pretoria, were commanded by a determined and intrepid officer, Captain Auchinleck. General Wood, in a reference to Auchinleck's sagacity, concluded his official report on the siege with the pointed remark, 'At the outset he wisely got rid of the only female in the fort.'

The mud fort was only twenty-five yards square. The prospect of war caused Auchinleck to sandbag the parapets and mine the approaches. The soldiers' huts outside which might have provided cover to the enemy were torn down. Since there was no room for anything but a hospital tent, the men had to bivouac for ninety-five days, forty-five of which were wet.

The town, 700 yards below the fort, was very small, but it boasted three churches, the first of which Kruger, who had his farm near by, had helped to build. (He had been so excited at having placed the ridge-pole beam that he had climbed to the highest point and scandalized the onlookers by standing on his head.)

A Republican force occupied the town on December 27th and began a close investment of the tiny fort. This was supplemented by continual firing, night and day, until March 30th. The conduct of the men was excellent. The only behaviour problem was one with the civilian in charge of volunteers. Stricken by sunstroke, his mind later snapped under the stress of siege operations. He remained a raving lunatic until the end, tasking the nerves of those confined with him far more than anything the Boers did or threatened.

In the second week of the confinement, the burghers brought up a primitive cannon made of iron coils. Projecting a shot of six and a half pounds, they opened up at 2,000 yards. Failing to make an impression, they dragged it to within 600 yards. Though the defenders had nothing more than rifles, they made it too uncomfortable for the gunners at this distance. Three Boers were wounded.

The Boers, who already had the advantage of elevation owing to the hills around the fort, moved in closer by digging trenches. Auchinleck defiantly led a series of sorties to drive them out. On January 29th he received a wound in the head; then on February 4th a ball entered below his nose and came out of his left eye—yet that night, bandaged and half blind, he sallied forth again. In March he was shot in the thigh. The captain received more wounds than all of his men put together, for there were only three other men wounded throughout the siege.

The commander's tactics, carried out at the point of a bayonet, dampened whatever desire the Boers (about two hundred in number) had to come to close quarters. The health of the garrison remained sound, notwithstanding the half-rations, exposure, and the tight quarters which they endured for three months. Auchinleck was rewarded for his conduct by being promoted to brevet major.

MARABASTAD

Far away to the north stood another fort twenty-five yards square, the only sign of British authority for many miles. Constructed early in 1880, it was designed to maintain supremacy of the Government over some half a million or more natives in the Zoutpansberg and Waterburg districts. In Marabastad, a village of eight houses, the English of the region had gathered together and were holding a race-meeting. When the news of Bronkhorst Spruit reached them, it was therefore possible for Captain Brooke to add thirty volunteers to his small force of sixty men of the 94th. Available, too, were fifty half-castes of the Transvaal Mounted Police under Captain Thompson. In numbers the British were a match for the Boers under Commandant Barend Vorster. Various local chiefs asked to be permitted to fight the Boers, but on orders from Brooke they promised to remain neutral.

A skirmish occurred on January 19th, but not until the end of February did the Boers move in to take a commanding position on the high ground around the fort. In mid-March the garrison

was surprised by a bombardment delivered by two old ship car-
ronades using round shot made from beaten iron which had been
removed from the works of a gold-mining company in the vicinity. When Brooke learned that these were the same guns that
Captain Dahl (Native Commissioner for the Zoutpansberg district) was supposed to have brought into the fort at the beginning of the war, he was thoroughly enraged. For allowing them
to fall into the hands of the enemy, Dahl was to be relieved of his
office as soon as possible. After the war, it was decided that Dahl
was innocent of wrong-doing because Brooke's verbal message
had never been properly transmitted.

Though the Boers made good use of their guns, they had little
effect on the fort and succeeded in killing only one man. Another
man, a volunteer, was lost when he deserted to join the Boers.

There was a legend that the great chimney of the gold-mining
company would fall when the British Empire fell. At less active
times during the investment, it was said, the burghers brought
up spans of oxen, which they chained to the chimney in an effort
to pull it down. The stack like the fort, did not fall, holding fast
until the end of the conflict, in which the British had five casualties
and the Boers only one.[55]

WAKKERSTROOM

The position of the garrison here had drawbacks as serious as any
in the Transvaal. Pressures applied by the tax-collectors had put
the entire district into a rebellious state. As early as December
3rd a hundred Boers rode into town to intimidate the landdrost.
The small fort—on a plateau a mile north of the town—was
speedily completed. Thirty-three loyal inhabitants of the district
came in to join the military which consisted of two companies of
the 94th (120 men). Captain Saunders decided to hold the town
by placing thirty men in the Dutch church, which had thick walls
with loop-holes and was surrounded by a deep ditch. In front of
the church door he placed an old naval howitzer on the body of a
water-cart. The ugly piece, it was hoped, would at least frighten
the burghers. So that the garrison should be forewarned of their
coming, a 'crow's nest' was built. Communications with the fort
were maintained by telephone. The Boers, however, never came

near the town once hostilities commenced, possibly because
Saunders gave currency to a rumour that the area was heavily
mined. Recognition of the captain's ingenuity came in the form
of a promotion after the war.

A constant source of apprehension was the presence of Joubert's ever-increasing force at Coldstream, only a day's ride
away. The very sounds of battle at the Nek were clearly audible
at Wakkerstroom. Fortunately for the garrison, Joubert found it
necessary to keep the bulk of his men at the Nek.

The British at Wakkerstroom were never closely invested,
nor seriously menaced. The Boers did throw a cordon around
them and skirmishes between mounted parties were frequent.
Sometimes the Boers made a rush on the fortified places, only to
turn back when they saw the redcoats preparing to resist. Any
shooting at the fort was done from a respectful distance, though
sometimes it was wonderfully accurate. One Boer who positioned
himself on a hill, which the British later established was at a
distance of exactly 2,100 yards, was the champion. To test his
skill, the British placed a helmet on a nail on a door. Time and
again 'he put a bullet either through it or within a foot.'[56]

There were no casualties among the civilians. Three soldiers
were wounded, two of whom died.

Other towns, such as Utrecht and Middelburg, where there
were no soldiers, fell into the hands of the Boers without any
resistance on the part of the loyal inhabitants. The few Government officials still functioning in the Transvaal were left without
instruction or direction, for the 'unobtrusive competence' of the
Boers in patrolling the land was extraordinarily effective.[57]

Ill-equipped and unaccustomed to siege warfare, the Boers, as
DuVal put it, 'deserve credit for a discipline, organization, and
political and military ability, which it would indeed be difficult to
match under similar circumstances of any similar classes of
European'.[58]

The spirited defence of the British garrisons did much to save
from complete eclipse the reputation of the British Army, a
reputation which was severely damaged at Laing's Nek, Ingogo
and Majuba. Moreover, the retention of Pretoria and other
posts, as Bellairs observed, was in all probability 'useful as a
bargaining factor at the peace negotiations'.[59]

[8]

MAJUBA

What can you expect from fighting on a Sunday ?
Joubert

THE DISEMBARKING of Brigadier-General Sir Evelyn Wood
and thousands of fresh troops in February gave the Imperial cause
a tremendous boost. Wood, a man of energy and decision, belonged to the business order of British generals. Although more
experienced and one degree senior to Colley, he had agreed to
serve under him. Clearly Colley missed the strong guiding hand
of his mentor, Wolseley. Since Sir Garnet could not go to South
Africa without taking command, he had urged the Secretary for
War to send the next ranking member of his 'ring', an officer
with a flair for organization and a proven talent for handling
men. In Parliament, the minister was bluntly asked who would
command the force in Natal—Wood or Colley. Embarrassed,
Childers declined to answer on the grounds that the question was
not properly framed. Later, in the press, it was stated that Wood
would be subordinate to Colley.

Wood's appointment was a popular one. To the English
public he was second only to General Roberts in their affection.
In South Africa Wood was number one—the great hero of the
Zulu War. The shock of Isandhlwana was barely over when it
was announced that Wood had reversed the situation by defeating a force of thousands. Steadily maintaining the most advanced
position, he defeated the Zulus at Kambula, and was present at
Ulundi. His name was on every tongue. The Zulus spoke of him
as 'lukani', a hard wood used in making knobkerries. After the
war, Wood further endeared himself to the colonists by publicly
defending them in England against the charge that they had
instigated the war for their own selfish ends. Boer volunteers
who fought and died under his command admired not only his

daring and ability but also his genial and direct—sometimes blunt—manner. No respecter of persons, Wood said and wrote what he thought. In his official communications he alluded to one general as 'a blatant ass'.

Sir Evelyn's varied catalogue of military experiences included service in virtually every branch of the armed forces. At four-teen he ran away from school, where he felt he had been unjustly caned, to join the Royal Navy. During the Crimean War, in which he served ashore with the Naval Brigade, he was invalided home. Offered a commission in the army, he joined the 13th Light Dragoons, then changed to the 17th Lancers, and ended by lead-ing Indian Irregular Cavalry during the Mutiny. In the latter action he won the Victoria Cross for routing, almost single-handed, a body of rebels who had been making a determined stand. Leaving the saddle with a permanent cavalry stoop, he joined the infantry—the 90th—and then qualified as a barrister in his spare time. Wood, however, remained dedicated to the military. When he married, he asked his wife to take an addi-tional vow, that she would never interfere with his active service. In the Ashanti War, Wolseley called upon him to lead a regi-ment of coastal tribesmen. Fighting in every battle, Wood won the highest praise. The Queen herself sent him a message of approval. It was in this campaign that he formed a fast friendship with Colley. Added to all this, Wood was known to be a good practical gunner.

The man was not without his little weaknesses. To some, Sir Evelyn's methods and behaviour could be irritating. As he readily confessed in his autobiography, 'I am constitutionally nervous.' But then it was natural that he should admit it, for he was known through the service as an incurable hypochondriac. At times, his jumpiness afflicted those around him. Noted for his ability as an organizer, Wood was nevertheless personally untidy. In mufti he might have been mistaken for a tramp. His office was topsy-turvy. Wolseley complained that 'Wood never shows any of the tele-grams or letters he receives to anyone—but generally stuffs them into his pocket and apparently drops them down the "rear", for many can never be found.'[1] As to his household, the Duke of Cambridge often asked Wolseley if there was not something that could be done about 'the noise, the dirt, and the terrible meals'.[2] This and other eccentricities caused Wolseley to advise the Duke

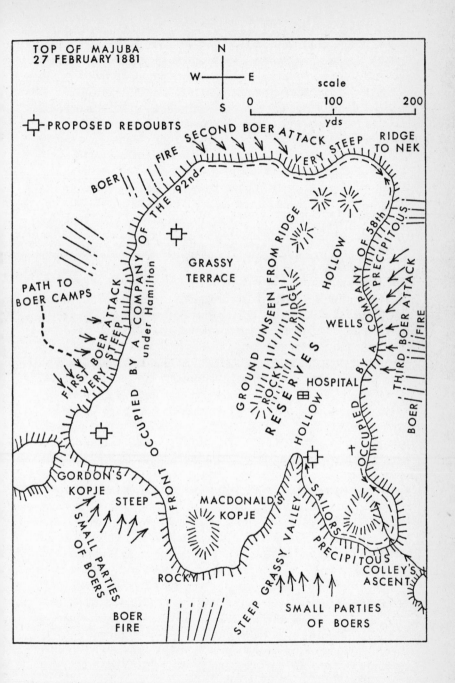

TOP OF MAJUBA
27 FEBRUARY 1881

N
W — E
S

scale
0   100   200
yds

PROPOSED REDOUBTS

SECOND BOER ATTACK

BOER FIRE

VERY STEEP

RIDGE TO NEK

OCCUPIED BY A COMPANY OF THE 92nd
under Hamilton

GRASSY
TERRACE

GROUND UNSEEN FROM RIDGE

PATH TO
BOER CAMPS

FIRST BOER ATTACK

VERY STEEP

ROCKY RIDGE

RESERVES

HOLLOW

WELLS

OCCUPIED BY A COMPANY OF 58th

PRECIPITOUS

THIRD BOER ATTACK

FIRE

BOER

HOSPITAL

HOLLOW

FRONT OCCUPIED BY A COMPANY

GORDON'S
KOPJE

STEEP

SMALL PARTIES OF BOERS

MACDONALD'S
KOPJE

SAILORS

PRECIPITOUS
COLLEY'S
ASCENT

ROCKY

BOER
FIRE

STEEP GRASSY VALLEY

SMALL PARTIES
OF BOERS

after the Egyptian campaign of 1882 that Sir Evelyn was 'a little too flighty and as the Indians say he has got too much "wind in his head" to leave him in an independent command'.[3]

Wood's most annoying personal trait was his inordinate vanity. To show off his many bright decorations, which some people believed he wore even on his pyjamas, Wood surrounded each ribbon with a small black border, so that the colours would stand out in contrast. It was suggested that this characteristic was a result of the atmosphere of adulation created by his wife and his sister. The sister, Kitty O'Shea, later transferred her affection to Parnell, a love which wrecked the Irish leader's career.

Arriving in Durban on February 12th, after Colley had been twice defeated, some believed—and many hoped—that Wood would take charge of military operations while Colley attended to his duties as Governor. Wood did not wait for a public reception; he immediately boarded a mail-cart and arrived early the next morning in Pietermaritzburg perched on a sack and looking anything but distinguished. At Government House it was a different matter. Smartly turned out in uniform, as befitted a former member of a Hussar regiment, his slight figure—which bore the slash and cut of combat—was soldier to the backbone. His clear blue eyes had the look of one accustomed to authority. In speech and gesture he was brisk but cheerful. His long face, ending in a short pointed beard, was on the ugly side. His nose was a mis-shapen lump that had been mashed by a giraffe's hoof when he tried, on a dare, to ride the beast. But 'the sweetness of his smile', wrote a correspondent of the Zulu War, 'goes to the heart, and stays there.'[4]

Lady Colley, with whom he had danced at her first ball, gave Wood a letter from her husband dated February 4th. Sir George expressed his pleasure at Wood's coming, and spoke of how each would lead a column into the Transvaal, Wood going north to Wakkerstroom and beyond, while he moved on to Pretoria. 'You will understand', Colley concluded, 'that I want to take the Nek myself.' Resuming his journey that night, Wood rushed on to Biggarsburg to lead the reinforcements on to Newcastle.

The column consisted of two squadrons of the 15th Hussars, the 2nd Battalion 60th Rifles, and the 92nd Highlanders. This was only the vanguard of a far larger force already staging in Natal, including three crack infantry regiments (the 83rd, 94th

and 97th), the 6th Dragoons and the main body of the 15th
Hussars. Other infantry and cavalry units were preparing for
embarkation from England, Ireland and India. Drafts were also
on their way to Colley's decimated regiments. Special-service
officers, artillery units and bluejackets meant to expand the
Naval Brigade were also in various stages of travel. There was
even one bellicose marine named Cooper who mixed with the
naval units, but was discovered to be an interloper. 'Deuced hard
life not to be allowed to fight the Boers,' he was quoted as saying, 'when one wants it so much.' No less exciting to the colonists of Natal was the arrival early in February of a boat-load of
women. They were sponsored by the Women's Emigration
Society 'ostensibly to assist in domestic duties', reported the
Natal Witness, 'but with an eye to matrimony as well'.

In Victorian days, an age of small wars par excellence, the
army was terribly overworked, and none more so than the regiments of the Indian contingent, which still bore the marks of
stern campaigning in Afghanistan. The 15th Hussars had seen
good service in the Kandahar column. Many of the men were
recovering from wounds, including their commander, Lieutenant-
Colonel Luck, who was renowned for his feats of swordsmanship.
The officers, as in most of the cavalry regiments, represented
wealth and rank, and regarded themselves as the elite of the
army. They followed the rule expressed by Baker Russell, outstanding leader of cavalry, when he declared that it was the duty
of every cavalryman 'to look pretty in time of peace and to get
killed in war'. The troopers were humiliated, however, by the
order to place their saddles and valises on the train to Pietermaritzburg while they tramped along like so many foot soldiers,
leading their horses.

The 2nd 60th Rifles (722 men) was made up of tough, experienced veterans who had marched from Kabul to Kandahar
and also in the subsequent expedition to the Mari country. In a
hundred days they had marched a thousand miles. Their extreme
self-reliance, together with their steadiness in tight formation,
was a subject which excited comment. The landing at Durban was
a happy occasion, for all the defaulters' records accidently fell
overboard.

But most of the kudos of the Second Afghan War went to the
92nd Gordon Highlanders. Under orders to return home, they

embarked instead for Natal because of a cable sent to Wood by
Lieutenant Ian Hamilton (in the name of the 'subalterns of the
92nd') that this 'splendid battalion was anxious to serve in
South Africa'. The senior officer knew nothing about the cable.
Wood rewarded their spirit by substituting the 92nd for the
72nd, their old rivals, who remained in India.[5]

The people of Durban were treated to a grand sight. It was
the first time that a kilted regiment had ever been seen in Natal.
Behind a brass band playing 'The Blue Bells of Scotland', they
were cheered as they tramped lightly through the broad streets
of the city. Seven hundred strong, they averaged ten years of
service—and many could boast twenty. Instinctively cocking
their caps, they fancied themselves the *crème de la crème* and they
looked forward to a frolic with the Boers. 'It was not be be
dreamed of', wrote Winston Churchill, 'that a parcel of Boers
should stand against famous soldiers.'

The officers of the regiment took pride in the fact that none of
them had ever entered for the Staff college. Traditionalists,
'they held the bullet to be fool, and the bayonet to be—the
reigning queen of battles', wrote Ian Hamilton, much to the
joy of the old Duke of Cambridge, who approved 'of all these
Bow and Arrow theories'.[6] Colley, who later spoke to the Indian
contingent in Newcastle, warned them not to underrate the
Boers, as 'they shoot straight, although not so well now as I
believe they did formerly.' But no one seemed to be listening,
remarked one bystander.[7]

Mixed in with the Indian column were sixty sailors, mostly
boys, from H.M.S. *Dido* and H.M.S. *Boadicea*. Armed with carbines, revolvers and cutlasses, they brought up more rocket tubes
and Gatling guns. The Queen, fearing that her grandsons
Prince Albert and Prince George (who were on their world
tour as midshipmen on the *Bacchante*) might join the Naval
Brigade, demanded that the young lives of the only two sons of
the Prince of Wales should not be risked. Moreover, to fight 'in
a *civil war*, would have been *wrong* in every way'. The Prince of
Wales was 'sore' over her interference.

Wood took the column from Biggarsburg to Newcastle.
With the possibility of a Boer attack, the general adopted the
unusual and exhausting procedure of making the soldiers laager
every few hours. When he met Colley in Newcastle on Febru-

ary 17th, he reported that no Boers had been visible on the road. Wood then persuaded Colley to let him reconnoitre the left flank and rear of the enemy position. With one hundred Hussars he crossed the Buffalo River and rode as far as a hill overlooking Wakkerstroom, ascertaining that there was no large commando in that direction. The military significance of his sixty-mile dash into enemy territory was exaggerated out of all proportion, but it was disconcerting to the Boers, while Wood's business-like manner and daring gave encouragement to the colonists and soldiers camped throughout the land. On his return, he and Colley agreed that no further advance should be made until more reinforcements came up. To hasten them forward, Wood asked to go back to Pietermaritzburg. Parting on February 21st, Colley riding north and Wood south, Sir Evelyn met Melton Prior, war correspondent and illustrator, on the road. No need to hurry, Wood told him, 'I have just left Colley, who has given me his word of honour that he will not move out of camp until I return.'[8]

It seemed to be only a matter of time before the Boers would be forced to leave the Nek. The Natal press printed rumours that Joubert's force was preparing to break up. After all, with the country at war for over two months, the burghers were required at their homesteads to assist their women and children, especially now that the harvest was approaching. The 'pinch of want' was being felt by them, wrote the *Natal Mercury*; 'patriotism will come in conflict with need.'

There was open grumbling in the Boer camp. The Heidelberg authorities were slow in advancing supplies. Rain and strong winds added to their discomfort and made cooking meals impossible. Joubert was obliged to speak sharply to the burghers, to remind them of the importance of their cause. To keep Boer spirits up, a leader from the Free State made a speech on the 21st 'testifying to the strong sympathy for them by their brethren in the Free State, and promising active support'.[9]

An overture for peace came from the Boers, dated February 12th. Prompted by the humane proposals of Brand, Kruger sent a letter to Colley offering to negotiate. The Triumvirate proposed a Royal Commission to settle the dispute, for they trusted in the rightness of their cause and the 'nobility of the British people'. If British troops left the Transvaal they would be given free passage and the Boers would withdraw from Natal. But if annexation were upheld, they would 'fight to the finish'.

The message arrived in London on February 14th. A special Cabinet meeting took place the next day to consider the proposal. Kimberley declared that although the terms were inadmissible, it was incumbent upon the Government to explore the position and to see whether it afforded any hope of settlement. Gladstone, with his morbid horror of war, leaned towards the annulment of annexation, but the Whigs—the Duke of Argyll, Earl Spencer, Earl Granville and Lord Selborne—were opposed. They argued that the Government would be placed 'in a very awkward position' if they deserted their stand to re-establish the Queen's authority after the reverses of Laing's Nek and Ingogo.[10] This was essentially the position also taken by the Conservatives. Disraeli, in one of his last appearances in Parliament, questioned the condition which stated that armed opposition must cease when British troops had been defeated. The credit of the nation must be preserved. The Radicals, in their turn, vigorously supported withdrawal. Chamberlain was 'out and out for negotiation', and Bright argued that England could gain nothing from conflict—not even military glory, 'which is the poorest kind'.[11] A conditional acceptance of the Boer proposal was finally agreed upon. 'Any other decision', Morley concluded, 'would have broken up the Government.'[12]

Colley was instructed to tell Kruger that if the Boers ceased armed opposition, the British Government would dispatch commissioners to arrange a settlement. Should this offer be accepted, Colley would be authorized to agree to a suspension of hostilities. Childers wrote to Colley on the same day, 'As respects the interval before reply from Boers is received, we do not bind your discretion, but we are anxious for your making arrangements to avoid effusion of blood.'[13]

Colley was confused. The dilatory and roundabout methods of the ministry, and the puzzling ambiguity of messages from the Colonial Office and the War Office, led him to ask Kimberley on February 19th to clarify the phrase 'the Boers ceasing from armed opposition'. Obviously, he observed, there could be no hostilities if no resistance was made, 'but am I to leave Laing's Nek in Natal territory in Boer occupation, and our garrisons isolated and short of provisions, or occupy former and relieve latter?'

Any armistice, he argued, which neglected these considerations would give the Boers a military advantage while implying a tacit recognition of their political demands. On the latter point, he earnestly deprecated any scheme which would divide the Transvaal, as Wood had informed him the Secretary intended. Colley advised that either a Boer republic under British protection be established or that the annexation be maintained under a liberal constitution, the latter of which he more strongly favoured.

Kimberley replied with indignation, denying that it had ever been the Government's intention to commit themselves to any schemes. If commissioners were appointed, they would decide on the 'means of a permanent friendly settlement'. As to the garrisons, they would be free to provision themselves by peaceful intercourse with the Boers, 'but we do not mean that you should march to the relief of the garrisons or occupy Laing's Nek if the arrangement proceeds.'[14]

The armistice offer, addressed to Kruger, was dispatched on February 21st, with a time-limit of forty-eight hours for reply. Acceptance would cause Colley to suspend hostilities. That same day, Kimberley went before the House of Lords and intimated that a new policy towards the Transvaal was in the making. Despite the time-limit, Colley told Childers on February 23rd that he would not 'without strong reason undertake any operations likely to bring on another engagement until Kruger's reply was received'.[15]

Two days was not time enough. General Smit, acknowledging Colley's letter at the Nek on February 24th, stated that Kruger was in Heidelberg and that, therefore, a reply would take at least four more days. Two days later, Colley learned that Kruger had gone on to remote Rustenburg in order to deal with restless tribesmen. Kruger, knowing that a reply to his overture would be forthcoming, had chosen a strange time to travel to a distant part of Transvaal. The letter from Colley did not reach him until February 28th. Within the hour he penned his acceptance, but it did not arrive at the Nek until March 7th.

As Colley had done little more than to transmit complimentary, if not unctuous, messages between Brand and Kimberley, the Boers were actively fortifying the Nek and moving their outposts forward. A couple of shells showed them that the British had them within range (5,800 yards), and sent them back to shelter.

Colley wrote to the Secretary for War that evening that he might
have to 'seize some ground which has hitherto been practically
unoccupied by either party, between the Nek and the camp, without waiting for Kruger's reply, for they have become aggressive
...and are trying to press in our vedettes'. (One of the vedettes
was killed.) But he promised Childers that he would not undertake any operation which might reach the point of hostilities until
Kruger's reply was received.[16] And no action, as Colley told the
Duke of Cambridge, would lead to a decisive success 'without the
aid of a large mounted force'.[17]

  As the war dragged on in the spurs of the Drakensberg, Colley
seemed to grow restless. One night he quietly moved out of camp
towards the telegraph office in Newcastle. He got lost in the dark,
but the exigencies of the case caused him to say the next morning
that he had merely been visiting the outlying pickets. On other
nights he was more successful. These nocturnal ventures created
some concern for his safety. There was a Boer report in circulation stating that the Republican Government would give two
farms to anyone who shot or captured a general, and one farm for
a colonel.

  Peace at this point was not a happy prospect for Colley. With
the Imperial Government eager to end the war more or less on
Boer terms, he told Wolseley that 'my failure at Laing's Nek
will inflict a deep and permanent injury on the British name and
power in South Africa which is not pleasant to contemplate ...'[18]
All the while he was convinced that the Boers, 'ill-supplied and
discontented', were growing weaker; 'they are probably decreasing instead of increasing from day to day', he informed the
Secretary for War. He told his wife candidly that he 'would
rather resign than carry out the scheme I understand is to be
contemplated'.[19]

  Among the special-service officers arriving in Newcastle was
Lieutenant-Colonel Herbert Stewart, whom Colley took on as his
Chief of Staff. Stewart, the future hero of Egyptian and Sudan
campaigns, was the latest addition to the 'Wolseley gang'. Sir
Garnet had been quick to recognize Stewart's ability when he first
met this somewhat forlorn-looking cavalry officer during the
Zulu War. Stewart was then serving on the lines of communication and was strongly considering resignation. Wolseley had
placed him on his staff, describing him as 'brilliant, yet careful

and reliable'.[20] Colley appreciated Stewart's cheery nature and sound common sense. As a 'long-headed' man who had studied architecture and who read widely in literature, Stewart was an ideal associate. In those last remaining days in February they were rarely separated and they discussed a wide range of topics. One subject earnestly pursued was the gigantic bastion which flanked the enemy's line of breastworks on the Nek. The Boers referred to it as Spitz Kop, but it became better known by its Zulu name, Amajuba—'the hill of doves'.

Early on the morning of February 24th, Colley and Stewart, with an escort of Hussars, swept round the hill and examined the reverse slopes. In addition to his personal inspection, Colley sought what information he could gain from natives who lived in the area. After several misty days, the 26th broke fine and clear, so that every scarp and crag on Majuba was clearly defined. Sitting under a tent, Colley and Stewart examined the hill with their field-glasses throughout the day as if they had never seen it before. Another native was interrogated, and when he pointed at Majuba, Colley with a nervous gesture ordered him to put his arm down immediately.

What they saw was an extinct volcano, nearly a mile in circumference, which rose steeply upwards some 2,000 feet. The saucer-like top, edged with boulders and sharp crags, was from 300 to 400 yards in diameter. The natives who had been there told the general that it dipped to a depression of from ten to forty feet in the centre, across which was a rocky reef about shoulder-high. They assured Colley that wells were to be found at very little depth. On the north end of the summit, which was directly above the Boer camp, was a grassy undulating slope that extended one hundred yards from the rim towards the reef. There was much dead ground, which was also true of the approaches to the top. Majuba, being composed of alternate horizontal strata of shale and limestone, offered deep ravines, masses of rocks and dark mimosa scrubs for those seeking cover in ascending its precipitous sides.

As the sun set, they saw the Boer picket, which went up every morning, begin its descent. Colley resolved that that night Majuba would become British.

There has been a great deal of contradictory speculation— most of it coloured by prejudice, loyalty or ignorance—as to why

Colley decided to occupy Majuba. Detractors assert that Colley's move was not only wholly unnecessary and rash but that it was an offensive one, and therefore a direct violation of his instruction. Successive defeats, the argument runs, made him anxious to recover national prestige and his own reputation before the peace party in the Government could force a capitulation to the enemy's demands. Some have suggested that Colley was desperate for a striking success before Wood or Roberts was ordered to replace him. In the latter case the situation would not seem dissimilar to that in which Chelmsford hurried to fight the battle of Ulundi before Wolseley came into the field to take charge. But the analogy is absurd, for Roberts's appointment to command in South Africa was not even considered until after the battle of Majuba, and the fact that Roberts was eventually selected over Wood seems to indicate that the latter was never seriously thought of as Colley's successor. Colley welcomed the presence of Wood; Wood was a competent general who could take over if Colley should be incapacitated in any way. Wood, it might be added, never considered the occupation of Majuba to be a violation of Colley's assurance that he would attempt no further advance until his return. In Wood's opinion, Colley's move was 'justified, in a military sense'.[21]

More difficult to refute is the argument that Colley, thirsting for success in order to satisfy a 'military ambition that literally possessed him', had had his judgment impaired by repeated failures. Before the Majuba battle, observers in camp noticed that the general did not appear to be himself. 'Another defeat will kill Colley,' remarked an unnamed officer to the correspondent of the *Natal Mercury*. Nervous and impatient, he seemed to be 'driven by a demon'—it was darkly hinted that the 'demon' was his wife. The clever and no less ambitious Lady Colley was said to have written a letter, which afterwards mysteriously disappeared, criticizing and reproaching her husband for not acting decisively before distasteful negotiations took matters entirely out of his hands.

'The enterprise was that of a madman,' was one opinion expressed.[22] But it was hardly that. Colley's letters and dispatches to the very end were characterized by the same cool detachment. There is no trace of any loss of nerve or of a mind that was unduly fevered. Colley, too good a soldier to disobey instructions, regarded his march on 'undefended' Majuba as a purely defensive manoeuvre. And surely, he reasoned, if the Boers believed that the agreement gave them the liberty to strengthen and extend their lines, he had the right to do likewise. Moreover, by the 26th the forty-eight-hour truce had long expired. By outflanking the Boers in ways which did not threaten battle, he believed he could make their position at the Nek untenable without the loss of a single man. That the surprised enemy would try to dislodge his force seemed remote. After all, the Boers were committed to fighting on the defensive, and the Sekukuni War demonstrated that they were incapable of taking a hill from even poorly armed natives.

Like Wolseley, Colley had a way of keeping his plans to himself. Nevertheless, Stewart, who was in the best possible position to know what Colley's thoughts were, corroborates this view.[23]

The action was not a sudden impulse. To allay Boer suspicions, the reconnaissance in force behind Majuba was deliberately made to the east, beyond the Buffalo River, so as to suggest that any future British action would be in that direction. And to lead the Boers to believe that if a forward move was to be made it would not be in the immediate future, the 2nd 60th Rifles was brought as far as the Ingogo and then ordered back to Newcastle, as if he were concerned about fighting another action to preserve his communications. Moreover, the presence of this unit at Mount Prospect might have caused the Boers to occupy Majuba by night as well as by day.*

That the enemy might respond to his move on Majuba by offering battle was a possibility which Colley accepted. The idea that such an untoward development could cost him his life seemed to prey on his mind before he departed. In a final letter to his wife that evening, Colley touchingly told her, 'Don't let all things be

* Colley's plan was certainly not unprecedented. During the American War of Independence, for example, when Burgoyne's advance in 1777 was blocked by Fort Ticonderoga, the British general sent a body of men up Mount Defiance, which dominated the fort. Exposed to British fire from above (which included two guns), the Americans hastily evacuated the fort without a shot being fired. Colley, an ardent student of military history, was aware of this minor victory, and more recently of Roberts's daring night march and successful attack on the Afghan position on the Peiwor Kotal. He had examined the terrain in the company of Roberts, who explained the action to him. But it is possible that Colley missed 'the vital effect... [that] Lord Roberts's feint against his opponents' centre had on the flank attacking'.[24]

dark to you if I don't come back to you ... How I wish I could
believe the mysteries of meeting again hereafter ... think of our
happiness together, and our love—not a common love I think—
and let that be a source of comfort and light to your future life,
my own much loved one, and think lovingly and sadly, but not
too sadly or hopelessly, of your affectionate husband.'[25]

After shaking hands with the chaplain, Colley told him that he
was not taking Bruce Hamilton, who was still sleeping in the tent.
'There seems a kind of fatality about my staff,' he said softly.
'If anything were to happen to him, it would kill his sister.'[26]

No one in the camp, aside from Stewart and Major Fraser, had
the slightest suspicion as to what the general had planned for that
night. The day had been fine and there had been few chores. The
men had listened to the band or amused themselves in other ways.
When 'lights out' sounded at 8.30 p.m., the verbal order was
given to prepare for a march with three days' provisions—which
could be stretched to six at a pinch. In addition the men were told
to take with them a blanket, a waterproof shelter, a greatcoat,
water, and seventy rounds of ammunition. Each company was to
carry four shovels and six picks. 'An awful load' was the way one
Highlander officer described it.

The march got under way at 10.00 p.m., with 22 officers and
627 men out of the 4,000 in camp. It was made up of two companies of the 58th (180 men), brought up to full strength from
the shattered ranks of the regiment; two companies of the 3rd
60th Rifles (140 men); the Naval Brigade (64 men); and three
companies of the 92nd Highlanders (180 men). The first orders
of the march were that no light must be struck and that absolute
silence must be maintained. The destination remained a secret.

Why the general chose companies from various units instead
of taking, say, the entire body of veteran Highlanders remains a
mystery. The only plausible explanation is that he did not consider a battle likely and that he wanted all units to share in the
glory of the occupation.

No guns, Gatlings, or even rockets capable of reaching the
laager below Majuba were taken. Later, on the summit, Colley
spoke of a Gatling being man-handled up the mountain, but none
was ordered at the time. A detail of men, spared the burden of
weapons and equipment, could conceivably have lumbered a
machine-gun or rocket trough up the mountain.

There was no plan for a general advance from the camp on to
the Nek when once Majuba was occupied. Once again, Colley's
move appeared to be a purely defensive one.

The soldiers were in high spirits as they marched off into the
warm, velvety darkness under the brilliant stars. There would be
no moon until shortly before daybreak. The 58th and 60th, with
two failures behind them, were excited by thoughts of revenge.
The confident Highlanders had that afternoon spent much of their
time discussing the number of clasps to be gained in this campaign. Now there was to be one more than they had anticipated.

They marched in close column, and the first couple of miles
were over easy, level ground. The general and his staff, along
with Zulu guides, rode out in front. An hour after the start, the
two Rifle companies were instructed to occupy Umquela Hill.

Ever-present was the fear that a Boer picket or even a barking
dog would cause an alarm, but the column continued in successful silence. As the ground grew more steep, Hay of the *Daily
News* felt his saddle-strap breaking. He was pitched on to the
rocky side of the trail. But he did not cry out, and he was not
missed. Some time later he managed to overtake the column.

A halt near Majuba led to the startling discovery that the rear
of the column was lost. The success of the mission was at stake,
for it was imperative that they reach the summit before dawn.
After an hour's search, the guides found them.

At the foot of Majuba, a company of Highlanders was told to
remain and to dig in. A small detachment was ordered to take the
horses back to camp. They considered themselves most unfortunate.

The climb began at 1.30 a.m. At first the guides were uncertain of the way, but they soon found the rough, narrow trail
which led up the south side. Colley took off his boots and put on
white tennis shoes. In single file, the men toiled up the incline
after him. Winding across the steepest part of the mountain on
little more than a sheep-path, they were confronted by boulders,
loose stones and other obstacles. 'Now and then a man would fall
with a hideous clatter,' recalls Lieutenant Ian Hamilton, 'whilst
his arms and equipment went to glory.' The sound of a fall had a
petrifying effect on the men. For half a minute they would hold
tight, expecting a volley from above. To recover those who had
strayed or fallen, there was a short blast on the whistle to signal a

halt. Before reaching the top, two men had to be sent back with sprained ankles. The brief respites provided short opportunities for the men to fill their lungs and renew their strength. Sometimes the guides themselves took the wrong track and it would be necessary to back up and start over again. The last hundred yards were the most perilous. The angle of the climb became so precipitous over slippery grass that the men had to clutch at the tufts of grass to aid them in their progress. Clambering around a projecting rock, each man would leave his rifle to the one behind until he had gained footing on the other side. One false step and the climber could have been hurled to a crippling injury or death. The kilted men, with their bare knees, suffered bruises on the rocks and were tormented by the prickly brush.[27]

Moving forward on his knees, Major Fraser reached the top with one of the guides at 3.40 a.m. He heaved a sigh of relief when he found the summit deserted. The last man, however, did not reach the top until dawn, two hours later. 'It was a fearful climb,' wrote Captain MacBean, who came up the following day, 'and it was a perfect mystery to me how men with pouches full of ammunition, carrying a rolled blanket and greatcoat, and three days' rations, could ever have got up in daylight, much less on a pitch-dark night.'[28]

On reaching the top, the men removed their gear and stretched out for a five-minute rest. To signal Mount Prospect that the hill was occupied, a flare was burned. Colley then sorted out the men as best he could in the dark and directed them to their positions. Out of the total strength of about 354 men at his disposal, half from each unit were placed along the crest while the other half acted as a reserve in the centre. The latter dug a well and set up a temporary hospital under the rocky ridge. Along the rim, the Highlanders spread out along the north and west sides, a total of over 500 yards. Two forward spurs were held by parties under Lieutenant Hamilton, the future commander at Gallipoli, and Lieutenant Hector Macdonald. Most of the steep edge to the east, about 350 yards, was covered by the 58th. The sailors, two hundred miles from their ships, were stationed for some 250 yards along the south-east, including the line of ascent.*

Straggling about in the dark, some men were separated from their comrades and mixed with units other than their own. It was

* For the plan of the battle of Majuba Hill, see map on p. 225.

obviously unsettling for men to serve with strangers under unfamiliar officers. Much of the cohesion of the clannish regimental system was lacking on the top of Majuba.

No instructions were given to dig in. When a Highlander officer asked the general if they might entrench themselves, Colley replied, 'No, the men are tired and there is no necessity for it.' Sheltered behind the rim, Colley believed that his position was impregnable and that therefore no further protection was necessary. Three places were marked for redoubts by Colley, but the work was never begun. 'We could stay here for ever,' Colley confidently told Stewart.[29] Since most of the crest was obviously inaccessible, his plan did not call for battle, but merely the forced withdrawal of the enemy from the Nek.

Ian Hamilton, who in *Listening for the Drums* wrote a highly critical account of Colley's tactics, boasted with exaggerated regimental pride that the Gordons had suffered no fatigue after the ascent, and that he personally never felt less tired in his life. He and several other Highland officers rather foolishly made their men gather stones to put up small shelters which were so thin that bullets could splash through and cause stone splinters to fly in all directions.

The British could have remained concealed for hours. At first they lay around and talked and there were occasional outbursts of laughter. But as soon as it was light, the Highlanders began to roam about; looking down at the laager below, they could observe the glitter of watch-fires. As the clear morning broke, they could plainly see the outlines of the ordered arrangement of wagons, and a few Boers bustling about to prepare for Sunday service or patrol. The Highlanders showed themselves boldly and began to shake their fists and shout, 'Ha, ha! got you this time, I think!' But they were too far away to be heard. At 5.45 a.m. Lieutenant Lucy of the 58th walked over to the crest, borrowed a rifle and sent a flying shot at some burgher below. Colley, who had hoped to avoid any provocation, instantly stood up and gave the order to 'stop that firing.' Nevertheless, other shots were fired down from the summit.

The Boers below were taken completely by surprise. Apparently none of them had looked up at Majuba or had even thought about it. 'Everybody and everything was in confusion.' wrote Assistant Veld Kornet Stephanus Roos.[30] Oxen were

quickly inspanned, tents were struck and wagons were loaded;
horsemen spread out across the plain. All eyes were now on
Majuba, for a bombardment was expected at any moment. One
of the kilted men on the skyline shouted tauntingly, 'Come up
here, you beggars!' They did not hear the challenge—but they
soon came.

Joubert, having risen early after a sleepless night, posted his
men and was busy writing reports when his wife, who had come
to the camp a few days before, told him that the British were on
the top of Majuba. Astonishment was mingled with indignation.
'Your letters on the subject of peace negotiations', he complained
to Brand, 'nearly lulled me into an unwise unsuspiciousness and
General Colley attacked us on Sunday morning whilst I was
writing to you and to him.' The Commandant-General, however,
had never discounted the possibility of an English occupation of
the mountain. Despite opinion to the contrary expressed by all
the local officers, Joubert had decided to place a picket of fifty
men on Majuba every night, beginning Thursday, February 24th.
'But by a remarkable act of Providence,' as he later saw it, 'the
picket which was told off for duty on Saturday night, being composed of burghers newly arrived from Pretoria, lost the path up
the mountain and spent the night encamped midway.'[31]

Legend has it that Mrs Joubert, no less strong-minded than
Lady Colley, vigorously urged her husband to attack rather than
to retreat. Other wives, it is said, egged their men on. Wood
later learned that the Boer women refused 'to have anything to
say to lovers or husbands until Peace was made, and it was I
believe, mainly owing to the influence of the women that the
spirit of Rebellion was maintained'.[32] Some of the young men
(often mere boys) and elders, old enough to look as if they had
better sense, were hot for battle and required little encouragement from the distaff side.

Joubert was reluctant. Only after learning that rifle-fire, not
that of artillery or rockets, was being brought to bear, and that
no other British force was near by preparing to attack, did he
resolve to storm the mountain. 'Everything was lost to us', he
later admitted to Kruger, if 'they had retained possession of the
hill'.

All preparations for retreat ceased as Joubert rode along shouting briskly, 'You are going up to fetch them.' Nicholas Smit, the

shrewd fecht general ('fighting general'), was in wholehearted agreement. As Joubert rode on in the company of his son to prepare for a possible attack on the Nek, Smit, more stern-faced than ever, made a brief, impassioned speech which ended with a call for volunteers, as was customary before an assault was attempted. 'Those who are not cowards', he shouted, 'must follow us.'[33]

When fifty or so men collected, most of whom had fought in previous engagements, they mounted and raced to Majuba. The shabbily dressed, long-haired men with their faces tanned the colour of mahogany looked puny and trivial from above as they dismounted and rushed to sit under the first ridge of rocks. A dozen or so arrived first, but others galloped up in twos and threes. The cluster of stormers looked about to see who would lead them. Smit had taken a strong force round Majuba to contain the British pickets who would be posted along Colley's line of advance. Two leaders came forward: Commandant Joachim Ferreira and Assistant Veld Kornet Stephanus Roos, who spoke of how the hill must be taken before the British brought up guns. 'Our God will help us,' he told the volunteers, 'and we shall take the kop, because there is nothing else to be done.'[34]

The Boers were not unaccustomed to storming hills. Practical experience in native wars, most of all those against the Basutos, had developed certain techniques among the Afrikaners as to how a mountain should be assaulted. The stormers would skilfully zig-zag from cover to cover up the hillside, led by burghers most familiar with the terrain. A firing-line consisting of the best shots, usually older men, was posted at the base to deliver a slow, deadly barrage on the defenders, not unlike the effects of artillery employed by European commanders.

It was about seven o'clock when Roos and Ferreira divided the stormers. With about a hundred yards between them, the parties climbed up the north and west faces of the hill. They darted from rock to rock and from bush to bush until they reached the safety of a terrace that was dead ground from above. The two climbing parties covered each other with flanking fire when either party moved. The British saw, if anything, little more than a puff of smoke here and there. As other Boers arrived from camp, they followed on behind. They usually caught up with the main parties in a short time, for the gradient on the north and west faces was

comparatively easy. A third party, to serve as spearhead, was
formed under Stephanus Trichard and D. Malan and began to
move up the east face, thus extending the assault to a third side.
According to Merensky, who was watching through binoculars,
there were about 150 men on the hillside. An equal number
maintained a storm of covering fire from below. Employing
chiefly the very fine breech-loading Westly Richards—calibre
45; paper cartridge; percussion-cap replaced on the nipple manu-
ally—they made it exceedingly dangerous for the British to expose themselves on the skyline. The fringe of the summit became
a wall of fire.

The British were astonished by the boldness of the Boers, for
they were known to have a strong predilection for the defensive.
But they saw no cause for alarm. No one imagined that the Boers
would actually come to close quarters. Colley shared and generated this confidence.

While most of the enemy bullets flew harmlessly over the
summit there was little activity. The British soldiers ate some of
their rations. As the sun was shining brightly, those forming the
reserve basked and napped in its warmth. The general busied
himself flashing messages by heliograph. At eight o'clock he
signalled the camp to send a telegram to Childers advising him
of his position. Shortly before nine, he asked that reinforcements
be brought up from Newcastle. He told Stewart that he intended
to go down the mountain later in the day, leaving Commander
Romilly, R.N., in charge, while he took charge of concentrating
the rest of the troops—for what purpose will never be known. At
half-past nine Stewart, instructed by Colley, sent a reassuring
signal: 'All very comfortable. Boers wasting ammunition. One
man wounded in foot.'

Between messages, the general calmly and cheerfully went
about encouraging the men near the rim. Hamilton came over to
him twice to report that through the curtain of smoke, the Boers
were 'getting underneath our men'.[35] Colley seemed unperturbed.
If he had risked one long look down the hill he would have seen
the Boer firing-line slowly creeping up the broken face, and
might have realized that no position was a really good one that did
not permit his men to employ their fire to advantage. Years before, he himself had indicated in his Wellington Prize Essay that
the first consideration in a defensive position, even at the sacrifice

of more perfect cover, was to have 'as clear a view and field of fire as may be'.

Colley, Fraser, Stewart and Romilly—all wearing staff dress —were having a leisurely discussion on the day's prospects when the popular, pock-faced naval officer decided to look down on the advancing enemy. 'See!' he suddenly declared. 'There's a man who looks as if he were going to try and shoot us.' Colley turned to Stewart and asked, 'I wonder what the distance is?' The latter looked through his binoculars and noted that it was about 900 yards. At that moment a bullet entered Romilly's abdomen with an exploding sound and passed out at the back of his neck. With a wild cry, Romilly fell to the ground. The wound was obviously mortal, but with 'instinctive self-possession' he said, 'I am all right.' He was taken to the hospital area, which now was rapidly beginning to fill.[36]

It was now eleven o'clock and the early-morning confidence began to wane. The fusillade of Boer bullets grew more furious and persistent. The Highlanders became anxious. Lieutenants Hamilton and Wright went to the general saying that more men were needed at their posts. Colley, depressed by the loss of Romilly, merely remarked, 'Hold the place for three days.'

Around noon, Colley made another signal to the camp. 'Send following to Secretary of State: "Boers still firing heavily on the hill, but have broken up laager and begun to move away. I regret to say Commander Romilly dangerously wounded; other casualties, three men slightly wounded." ' Regrets for the commander's wound were also sent to the commodore on the South African station. In this, his last message, Colley seems to have been curiously deluded as to the true nature of the situation. Some wagons had left the Nek, but it should have been obvious that he was the object of an attack by a large party of Boers who had no intention of withdrawing.

Below in Mount Prospect, where all was quiet, officers and men bemoaned the fact that they had been left behind. 'We could see the smoke from the volleys distinctly,' related one of the officers, 'and I have a vivid recollection of our laughing as we sat in our mess, and wishing we were up there potting "Pinheads" as they came up the hill.'[37] But there was little 'potting' of the unseen Boers. So far only one burgher, Johannes Bekker, had been lost—the only Boer to be killed that day.

At one o'clock Colley calmly stretched out for a nap, asking Stewart, who stayed near by, to rouse him should there be a change. While he was sleeping, the stormers began to scale the last hundred yards, which in some places were sheer and slippery. To keep from falling they clung to the outcroppings of thick grass. Soon they were nearly face to face with the Highlanders under Hamilton, although the opposing parties could not actually see each other. In some places the Boers were on one side of a boulder and the Scots on the other. Voices were distinctly heard and now and then each saw the muzzles of the other's rifles.

Leaving a sergeant in charge, Hamilton rushed across the summit to apprise the general and ask permission to drive them back with bayonets. Stewart told the impetuous subaltern that the general, who was still sleeping, knew what was going on and that there was no need to concern himself. When Hamilton returned to his position, it was obvious that the Boers were spreading out along the brow to establish two firing-lines, Ferreira's men to the left and Roos's to the right. (Credit for being the first to reach the top was given to a twelve-year-old boy, son of Piet Uys.)

'My courage sank for a moment,' said Roos later, referring to the moment when he cautiously lifted his head to look over the rim. With only forty or fifty men behind him, he feared the British would charge their precarious position with bayonets. He felt he must do something to raise the spirits of his men. 'I will not deny that then I made use of a lie. I hope the dear Lord has forgiven me. I waved my hat and shouted, "Come on now, you chaps! Come quickly. The English are flying." '[38] The burghers bobbed up from behind the rocks and delivered a withering fire. Highlanders tumbled all about.

The general was now awake. Stewart noted the time at 1.30 p.m. as he and Colley discussed the arrangements for the construction of redoubts. Suddenly interrupted by the importunings of the persistent Hamilton, who again asked for a bayonet charge, the general refused, saying, 'Wait till the Boers come across the open and we will give them a volley first and charge afterwards.'[39] Colley had turned to resume his conversation with Stewart when the fury of Boer volleys once more diverted his attention. Colley decided to investigate.

The Highlanders were bewildered. The fact that the Boers

were actually on the summit was difficult to comprehend. Under
fire from the front (Ferreira) and from the oblique rear (Roos),
with little cover, the kilted soldiers had begun to drop. A picket
commanding a kopje under Macdonald seemed to be destroyed in
a single moment. Some fired back at the tongues of flame, but
with little effect. Most of the British rifles, it was later discovered,
had their sights set at 500 yards or more. As the enemy emerged
from the smoke, frightened men began to bolt for the centre of
the summit.

When Colley, moving towards the point of danger, saw the
extended outer line give way, he called for support. The reserves,
many of whom had been sleeping, rushed forward in confusion.
Half dressed and half awake, they were a mob of intermixed
regimental fragments led by officers with drawn swords whose
voices and faces they did not recognize. The officers finally
organized some semblance of a firing-line composed of some
eighty soldiers and sailors, but the first volley went completely
wide of the mark. The Boers paused, flopped on the grass,
loaded, rose and, firing from the shoulder, 'let fly with a tremendous volley', knocking down nearly a score.[40] With bullets hum-
ming and dancing all around, the British broke. They were joined
in flight by others positioned near the crest. A few kept right on
running straight over the edge near to where they had ascended.
The majority rallied in a dip near the ridge which traversed the
plateau. They fixed bayonets while pipers and drummers took
rifles from the dead and wounded. The uproar was appalling.
Above the roar of rifles, the cries of the wounded mingled with
the conflicting orders shouted by officers from every side.

Standing in the centre of the line was the general, 'as cool as
on parade', doing his utmost to steady them. The attackers, still
few in number, were concealed by the uneven ground. Some dis-
engaged from the rear of their main attack, moving towards the
British right flank. Once in position a furious fire was unleashed.
The British held, but their only targets were the muzzles of
rifles appearing and disappearing in the smoke. On their left
flank, some bluejackets holding the rim came rushing in, declaring that the enemy was coming up to the top from that direction.
With bullets coming at them from three sides, the British wavered and 'a sudden piercing cry of terror ... rose from the line.'[41]
All cohesion was lost as men, as if by signal, stampeded towards

the drop behind them and leaped down the mountain. The right flank gave way completely. The centre crumbled soon afterwards, except for a small cluster around the general. The left held a little longer, but in a few moments there was only a small group holding a little kopje at the far end.

The testimony of the survivors, which is rarely in agreement regarding the details of battle up to this stage, now became more startlingly contradictory. Disaster distorted objectivity, for each survivor found it necessary to exonerate his own conduct and protect the honour of his regiment. Officers of the 92nd swore that their brave Highlanders did not panic but heard someone cry an order to retire as best they could. Major Hay (their commander), Lieutenant Hamilton and Major Macgregor (on Colley's staff) reported that the general, believing the situation to be hopeless, gave the order to retire. Others said it was Stewart. But Stewart, standing next to the general, claimed that no such order had been given, and that the men, including those of the 92nd, simply lost their nerve. According to Stewart, Colley asked him to go over and to extend the men on the left to cover the right, but he, along with other officers, found the men totally demoralized.

Carter of the *Natal Times*, supported by Cameron of the *Standard*, was unequivocal in his statements about the flight. He saw the men break, at first in groups of three and four—and then the whole line went. He heard one officer shout, 'I'll shoot you if you don't return.' Before he and Cameron, who were viewing the battle from a prone position, could get to their feet, 'the whole lot went rushing wildly over us.' On rising, it was not long before Carter was running with the rest, racing side by side with a stalwart Highlander. A bullet dropped the latter in his tracks; Carter succeeded in jumping over the edge.[42] Another who was present reported seeing an officer in desperation 'clutch the men by the throat and threaten them with a pistol'.[43]

Only one man, as Stewart told it, was moving forward—Colley. When Stewart turned round to look for him, he saw Colley alone near the hospital, walking slowly towards the enemy line and firing rapidly at the Boers some twenty yards away. After several steps, he was hit at close range by a bullet which seemed to lift him off the ground. The bullet entered his brain on the right side, just over the eye, and made a large hole in the back of his head. Corroborating Stewart's official testimony was the statement of a wounded corporal, whom Butler (in his biography of Colley) quotes as saying, 'He stood there trying to rally the men, and one of the Boers shot him straight in the forehead some time after the day was lost.' To prove that he had been present, the corporal later produced the puggaree of the helmet which Colley had worn. Without identifying his source,* Butler went on to say that Colley's last words were, 'Oh my men, do not run.'[44]

Many officers who served with Colley believed that he had deliberately courted a soldier's death. Apologists for the Highlanders' acts that day, like David and James Cromb, declared that with his reputation dissolving before his eyes, Colley was not 'strong enough to resist the temptation to make certain that he would not live to face inevitable censure and ignominy'. J. A. Froude, carried this view one step further by giving currency to the rumour that the general shot himself. Aside from the fact that Froude (who was not always too scrupulous about evidence) offered little to support this theory, there was really no need for Colley to add to his disgrace by committing suicide when any one of a hundred or more enemy rifles was quite ready to oblige him.

There was never any doubt among the Boers that they were responsible for Colley's death, but their leaders denied that they had deliberately sought him out to kill him. No one burgher ever claimed credit for the deed. Some said that the twelve-year-old son of Piet Uys did it. Merensky, in talking to Boers after the battle, stated that it was generally believed that Roos shot Colley.[45] However, in his account of the battle, Roos made no claim to the dubious honour. Oddly enough, Roos himself was fated to die with a bullet in the head while battling on another hill exactly two years later during a war with Mapoch's tribe.

A popular description of Colley's death which was accepted by many Britons was taken from the account of Captain Morris of the 58th, who felt it was 'almost murder'. Lying severely wounded near the place where the general stood, Morris swore that he saw him stand with head uncovered, 'waving a white handkerchief as a sign of truce, when the enemy, a mere boy, ap-

* Unfortunately the bulk of Butler's papers were destroyed when his home was burned during the civil war in Ireland, in the early days of the Irish Free State.

proached to within a few yards, took careful aim and shot him'.[46] Cameron in the *Standard* also claimed that he saw a white handkerchief in Colley's hand. The *Illustrated London News* embroidered on these accounts by stating that a Boer, on seeing the white flag, had called for a cease-fire, but that another Boer, obviously an officer, had shouted, 'Shoot the white flag and the man who said that.' The *Natal Witness*, never friendly to Colley, mentioned that Stewart had tied the hankerchief to the general's sword. Stewart vehemently denied it and went on to say that shortly after Colley had been killed, he was knocked down by a blow on his leg, and for the next thirty hours tried unsuccessfully to elude capture. This led to his credibility as a witness being challenged, for many of the Highland officers alleged, at least privately, that he was more interested 'in saving his own skin'. One of them wrote of how Stewart 'legged it in precious good time and before the retirement began'[47]—a curious slander in light of the pluck and daring that Stewart was to exhibit in subsequent campaigns.

In that moment of fatal confusion it seems plausible, as Major Fraser suggests, that those who thought they saw Colley with a token of surrender actually saw the white flag which was being waved in the hospital area only a few yards away. Surgeon Mahon, R.N., related how at the beginning of the retreat the Boers gained the rock just above the hospital and 'poured a tremendous fire indiscriminately into everyone they saw'. Surgeon Landon and two assistants were hit whilst attending the wounded. The fire was so hot that Mahon removed Romilly to a more sheltered place outside the hospital. Standing over Romilly, who lay in agony, Mahon fixed his handkerchief to a stick and held it over the commander. It was almost immediately shot away. He then ordered an assistant to place a piece of cloth on a bayonet. The assistant was hit twice through the helmet, so Mahon told him to lie down. When the Boers got within fifteen paces, the surgeon tried again to stop their shooting by waving a piece of bandage and shouting out to them that he was a surgeon attending the wounded. 'Two or three younger Boers wanted to shoot us,' he writes, 'but they were prevented by the older men.' While the burghers continued the pursuit elsewhere, the surgeon and his aide carried Romilly back to the hospital on a stretcher. Before they reached it, however, several Boers came up and

wanted to shoot the wounded commander, believing him to be
either Sir Evelyn Wood or Sir Garnet Wolseley. Mahon assured
them to the contrary and asked to see their leader. When Ferreira
came up, he asked for protection for the wounded, which was
immediately granted. After the action, Mahon found the Boers,
especially the older ones, 'most kind to the wounded, getting
them water, and some helping to bind up their wounds'.[48]

Meanwhile, Landon made an equally unsuccessful effort to halt
the enemy fire. Lying paralysed with a bullet in the spine, he
directed Lance-Corporal Farmer, who was only slightly wounded,
to wave a triangular bandage to indicate that this was a hospital
area. Standing up and vigorously waving the bandage, the corporal was shot in the hand. ' "I have got another arm," ' he said
gaily to the surgeon, 'as he leaned over to pick up the bandage
with his left.' As he was raising the bandage over his head, a
bullet passed through his good arm near the elbow. Several older
Boers then came forward and stopped the shooting in that direction. As Farmer rolled in pain, the Boers raised Landon up so
that he could give Farmer an injection of morphine. Farmer was
the only one to be awarded the V.C. that day.*[49]

Various white objects waved in surrender appeared on the top
and down the sides of Majuba. In groups of two and three the
British chose captivity rather than death. Some men huddled in
fear like sheep. Most did not stop running down the steep declivi-
ties until they were overtaken by bullets. One fugitive sailor,
said to have been the first man on the height, described his experience: 'It took me five——hours to get up that 'ere 'ill, but I
just touched it three——times coming down again.'[50]

But among the splintered regiments there were men, inspired
by valiant officers, who neither ran nor cowered. Lieutenant
Macdonald, holding a hillock with twenty men, refused to budge
when others on the crest gave way, although eight of his men
were killed and three wounded by firing from his right rear. When
the left of the line dissolved, his men asked, 'What shall we do?'
'Fighting Mac', as he was known throughout the 92nd, told them
to stand firm. No one moved. Remembering how he and a mere

* Lieutenant Hamilton was recommended for a V.C. for his heroism, but it was
decided that he was too young and would have other opportunities to win the covet-
ed award. Later in his career, he was recommended a second time, but this time the
decision was that he was too old, 'or at least too senior in rank'.

handful of men at the Shutar Garden had driven off a heavy body
of Afghans, the lieutenant hoped that those who had left the
crest would rally and join him in charging the enemy. Once he
saw the troops going over the hill, however, he told his men to
retire as best they could. All were shot as they came off, except-
ing Macdonald and another man who were taken as prisoners.
With Boers all around him, Macdonald drew his revolver, but
the Boers persuaded him that it would be foolish for him to resist
as they would not hurt him. After relieving him of his sword,
pistol and accoutrements, one Boer decided that his sporran
would make a most suitable trophy. As he grabbed hold of it,
Macdonald doubled him over with a kick to the stomach. A
second Boer was about to shoot him, but the one who had been
kicked intervened, saying, 'No, don't shoot—he is a brave man
and too good to kill.'

Later in the day, Macdonald met Joubert. The Boer commander had read the inscription on the sword which had been
presented to the lieutenant in recognition of his bravery, and
which told of how he had risen from the ranks. (Roberts was said
to have offered this crofter's son the choice of a V.C. or a commission.) Joubert courteously returned the weapon with the remark, 'A man who has won such a sword should not be separated
from it.' From that day forward, Macdonald, in speaking of the
Boers, would always say, 'These men are gentlemen.'[51]

'We've got to die now,' said Captain Macgregor as the line
behind Colley vanished. He and a small party of officers and men
tried to find shelter behind stones while the unequal struggle
continued for another five minutes. Old Major 'Jock' Hay looked
about and declared simply, 'The battle's over, we can't fight a
multitude; let's try and get away.' With Lieutenant Wright and
two men, he tried to make it to the crest. The two privates were
killed. Hay was shot in the upper arm and in the calf of the leg.
Wright, his helmet shot to pieces, was hit in the foot. Lieutenant
Singleton, who tried to join them, had his knee-cap smashed in
such a way that he was crippled for life. Major Fraser of Colley's
staff disappeared, having gone off in another direction.[52]

The irrepressible Lieutenant Hamilton kept insisting on a
bayonet charge until the very end. At one point, he was prepared
to undertake the move on his own account. Though the order to
fix bayonets was finally given, Colley had obviously considered

the charge impractical, as had Major Hay. Unless the Boers
themselves rushed forward, the latter testified, it would have
been 'difficult to know in what direction the charge was to have
been made'.[53] It was later vehemently argued that the moral
effect alone would have been sufficient cause for giving the order.
But it is difficult to imagine what moral effect would have been
gained from charging with a small broken line of men against
the well-directed fire of an unseen enemy in superior numbers.

Dashing about throughout the battle, Hamilton seemed to
have one encounter after another with death 'on this Hill of
Destiny', as he called it. His kilt and coat were cut by bullets.
One bullet passed a quarter of an inch from his armpit, and
another which passed between his legs missed hitting him by a
fraction of an inch. Within moments of Colley being hit, Hamilton picked up a rifle pointing up out of a tuft of grass. Searching
for a target, he spotted the broad hat and shoulders of a Boer.
Before he could press the trigger, the Boer fired and knocked him
down, the bullet shattering his wrist. The lieutenant rose again.
Turning round in the direction of his men, he saw only fugitives
shouting and disappearing off the top. Determined to rally them
and to hold the rear of the crest-ridge, he ran back, clutching his
wrist. More bullets cut his coat and grazed his knee. Then a spent
bullet or a stone hit him on the back of his head, and he dropped
to the ground, unconscious. When Hamilton recovered his senses
he found two Boers, about fourteen years old, rolling him about
in order to remove his possessions. A big, ugly, black-bearded
Boer shooed them off and then proceeded himself to take Hamilton's claymore, the same one his father had carried while serving
in the 92nd. The British officer offered him money instead,* but
suddenly Joubert, recently arrived on the summit, appeared and
shouted 'Voorwaarts' to his burghers. There was no time for
plunder while the battle was still on. Thanking the enemy commander, Hamilton added, 'This is a bad day for us.' Joubert
answered, 'What can you expect from fighting on a Sunday?'[54]

Sickened by the loss of blood and the misery of defeat, Hamilton dragged himself to the shade of a thorn bush near the ledge.
A young Boer found him there and was preparing to shoot him
when a white-bearded elder pushed his rifle to one side. Later,

---

* The sword was later recovered during the Second Anglo–Boer War and was
sent to Hamilton.

Smit had the young officer brought up to identify Colley's body. The Boers found it difficult to believe that this was in truth the Governor's body. Hamilton, a sensitive writer, later described Colley's body as 'stretched out exactly as the effigy of a knight lies in a cathedral...Had death so composed his limbs, or the pious hands of the foe?' he wondered. Looking about him, the summit of Majuba seemed to him 'a site that might have been selected by Valkyries for a hero's grave'.[55] Boers near by began to chant hymns of thanksgiving.

By now, Hamilton was covered with blood. The Boers told him that he would probably die. They dismissed him, as they did the other ambulatory wounded, who were free to go wherever they wished. The other captives were taken to the Boer camp at the Nek. Before leaving, a kindly burgher bandaged Hamilton's wrist with a red bandana handkerchief, which Hamilton considered to be the only bit of loot that any soldier brought away from Majuba.*

Stumbling and falling throughout the cold, wet night, Hamilton strayed into a marsh near Mount Prospect. Once more he fell, this time without hope of ever rising again. At daybreak, a search party which included Hamilton's fox-terrier Patch found him; Hamilton revived to find the dog licking his face.

Others were brought to identify Colley. Carter, who had escaped over the edge, was found hiding on the side of the mountain. Upon learning that he was a newspaperman who had known the general well, the Boers took him to Smit, who asked him to identify Colley's body. It was a sad sight. Carter estimated that Colley had been killed by a bullet fired from no more than four paces away. (This was supported by Surgeon Mahon.) On giving his word of honour that it was indeed Colley, Carter told the Boers, 'You have killed the bravest gentleman in the field.' They answered, 'Yes, he fought well.' One Boer said, 'He was a very nice gentleman, he dined in my house when he went to Pretoria.' Another said, 'He did not think we were wrong, but he was a soldier and must obey orders.' Others remarked without

---

* Thirty years later, while giving a speech in Harrismith, Hamilton accidentally met the donor in his audience. He sent him a handkerchief in a silver case. The wound itself nearly proved fatal. Hamilton would have spared himself dangerous fevers if he had consented to an amputation. The hand was saved but 're-mained a pathetic but neatly manicured wreck'. His friend Winston Churchill saw it as 'a glorious deformity'.[56]

exultation, 'It was no use fighting against men who had right on their side.'[57]

By mid-afternoon the drama of Majuba had shifted to the south face. The casualties suffered there were almost as great as the losses on the summit. Scores of men had jumped or had fallen down the almost perpendicular thirty-foot precipice near the top. Some had been killed by leaping headlong on to the rocks below. Tumbling and bleeding, the fugitives continued their descent. Private John Murray paused at the brow when a burgher called out in a rare Scotch for him to surrender. 'I'll see you damned first,' he replied.* (These words afterwards earned him the Distinguished Service Medal.) Jumping off, Murray was shot in the arm. Halfway down, he twisted his knee out of joint.

The Boers began to come down the mountain to the left and right of the desperate, fleeing men. Flanking fire added to the terrible toll. Many wisely sought cover in the bushes and ravines. Captain Macgregor took shelter with a few men, some of them wounded, in a clump of bushes. As soon as there was a lull in the firing they tried to move, but a volley was fired in their direction, killing one man and wounding another. When Lieutenant Wright passed by, Macgregor called for help with the wounded. The captain then announced that he had had 'enough of this carnage', and asked Wright 'to wave a white handkerchief'.[59] The handkerchief, however, only drew more fire. Private Smith then tried to signal, 'and he was wounded with buckshot by a Kaffir',†[60] so they waited until all firing had ceased and then emerged. The Boers, on seeing them, ran over and took away their rifles and ammunition. One of them exclaimed to Wright, 'Why do you fight us on Sunday?' He replied peevishly, 'I don't care whether it's Sunday or Monday. I don't want to fight you at all; but I just do as I am told.'[61] Wright and all the other officers and men taken prisoner were removed to the Boer camp, then later transferred to a camp in Heidelberg. All of these men later testified before a Court of Inquiry and stated that they were well treated.

---

* Other Scots were to be found among the enemy. James Murray, brother of the Reverend Andrew Murray who helped to organize the Dutch Reformed Church in the Transvaal, claimed that while fighting on Majuba he had discovered Colley's body and had placed a handkerchief over his face.[58]

† This report by Macgregor is the only one which mentions a black fighting with the Boers. On the British side at least one West African Kroo-man served on Majuba, but in which capacity is not known.

The sting of the Majuba disaster might have been countered
by the British by a strong stand, which would have been costly to
the Boers, before the laager at the base of the mountain. But
Captain Robertson's command, which included his own Highland
company, a company of Rifles, and fifty Hussars who had brought
in groceries and ammunition shortly before dawn, was insufficient
to resist adequately. Farther down the line, at the slope of
Imquela, were the Rifle companies which Colley had dropped off
on his march up. If they had been used to reinforce Robertson,
the outcome might have been different. Robertson, however, did
not learn of their presence behind him until daylight. He signalled and asked, 'Who are you?' The answer came back, 'Two
companies 60th, left out all night.' Robertson asked, 'What are
your orders?' They replied, 'None.' Later in the day, when the
position of Robertson's small force became precarious, he sent a
messenger back to ask for help. Still having no orders, the Rifles
refused to move.

As stragglers trickled into the laager with the news of annihilation and defeat, they were taken to the hospital or were put
into the line. Those who had lost their rifles were given new
ones. Opened ammunition-boxes were placed at regular intervals
behind the 60th, protecting the left and rear face, and the 92nd,
guarding the front and right. Boers coming down the mountain
soon drove the outposts back to their laager. Mounted Boers
appeared on the far left, driving in the Hussars, who had been
bringing in the wounded. They moved as if they meant to cut off
any retreat to Mount Prospect. A more threatening party of
Boers appeared on the left flank, but the Hussars grouped and
turned about with considerable dash to check them. 'The men
were silent, but steady,' wrote Norris-Newman. 'Every face was
set with a grave determination "to do" behind the fragile turf
walls about four feet high and two feet thick.' When the Boers
got closer, the firing was 'really heavy and sustained, and the
men began to fall fast'. Robertson then received his first order
from Mount Prospect: 'If no orders from the hill above you,
retire watching your left flank.'

The order to fall back came almost too late. The situation was
already critical. The wounded, as far as possible, were retired
first. The real retreat began with the Rifles marching out first to
the bottom of a ravine from which they could cover the withdrawal

of the Highlanders, who would then fall farther back to await the Rifles. The murderous fire of the Boers grew hotter, causing the Highlanders, carrying the last of the spare ammunition, to leave sooner than intended.

Robertson was the last to leave the laager. Arriving at the ravine, he found that some of the men, whom the officers could not control, had left. At this time the artillery in camp opened fire, accidentally killing and wounding men of the 92nd before the guns found the correct range. It looked for a time as if they would be cut off. In the end, Lieutenant Staunton and twenty-two men were captured. Robertson did not get back to camp until five o'clock. There he found that the Rifle company, along with the other two companies on Imquela, had come in long before him.

Robertson never received any recognition for his exemplary conduct in the retreat, least of all for his actions in preventing the ammunition from falling into enemy hands. (It was learned afterwards that the Boers never doubted their chances of capturing it.) On the other hand, the conduct of Colonel Bond, in charge of the camp, and Major Essex, his Chief of Staff, left much to be desired. Essex conveniently 'misplaced' Robertson's none too flattering report of the day's events; only after Wood made an inquiry was it found. The major was transferred to another station shortly afterwards.

The Boers never threatened Mount Prospect. The British believed that the appearance of a support force aiding the withdrawal, consisting of infantry, Hussars, two nine-pounders and two Gatlings, stopped the pursuit short of O'Neill's farm. Smit told Joubert that his burghers were anxious to inflict a yet more disastrous defeat, but were stopped when a sudden mist arose which concealed Mount Prospect. Joubert stood silent for a moment and then told Smit and his men, 'Look at the mist, the Lord won't allow us to go.'[62]

If the Boers had come closer, they would have seen that the perimeter of the camp was fully fortified in expectation of an attack. When Captain Vibart, after firing the last shot at five o'clock, came in with the last of the covering troops, every man was posted on the double. The Army Medical Department, which functioned splendidly throughout the war, gave speedy and careful attention to the wounded. With complete co-operation from the Republican side, medical men were allowed to go out and establish a temporary hospital at O'Neill's farm; other parties, under a flag of truce, were permitted to succour and to bring in the wounded.

The search was abandoned for the night. Darkness combined with heavy rains and it became literally impossible for anyone to see more than a few yards ahead of him. The relief sent to the small forts, thirty feet in diameter and spaced along the periphery of the camp, twice lost its way. One officer complained that more than once he had nearly been shot by sentries. All that night, and the following day and night, stragglers who had successfully eluded the enemy came into Mount Prospect, often more dead than alive. Major Fraser, who had bumped and fallen nearly two hundred feet down Majuba, came in during the second night, terribly bruised. He credited his return to glowworms which he had caught and put on his compass, thus making it possible for him to find his way back.

All through that first night an attack was expected at any moment. Major Essex, thoroughly shaken by the events of the day, added to the state of alarm by his behaviour. In the middle of the night he visited Captain Marling in one of the forts and warned him to keep 'an extra sharp look-out, as the Boers were coming down to attack the camp disguised in the 92nd's kilts, and the 58th's red coats!!!!' Marling later wrote that 'it was far and away the worst night I have ever had, I was wet through, and so covered with mud you could have grown cabbages on any part of my anatomy.'[63] At four in the morning, orders were issued that an attack was imminent. The men stood to arms until 5.30 a.m., when it was broad daylight.

The closest things to a fight that night were the quarrels between men from different units. Those of the 58th accused the 92nd of having been the first to run. The Highlanders threw the slander back in their faces and threatened to prove their point with their fists. The only thing they could agree upon was that the sailors had shown the white feather. The Rifles did not improve matters by declaring that had they been the ones on top of Majuba they would have stuck. However, everyone was sorry about the general. 'He was a most lovable person,' wrote Marling, 'but his death was a most fortunate thing for him, and, as someone said, for the Natal Field Force, too.'[64]

There was little to laugh about after the catastrophe, but the next day someone in the telegraph office revealed that an officer in charge of the commissariat, who had never been under fire at any time, sent a telegram to his wife which read, 'We are defeated, but I am saved.'[65]

Monday was a clear day and the work of bringing in the wounded began in earnest. The less serious cases were sent on to Newcastle. On top of Majuba, Surgeon Mahon remained throughout the night to care for thirty-six wounded. The Boers had helped to move them to an area near one of the wells. Luckily, enough blankets and waterproof sheets were found to cover them, for during the night it rained heavily and steadily. Towards morning it grew bitterly cold, aggravating their sufferings. Mahon had a little opium but it was difficult to administer in the total darkness. The Boers departed at sundown, leaving only a small party for observation.

At dawn a party of about a hundred men left Mount Prospect to assist Mahon and to supply the wounded with medical comforts. A Boer vedette detained them until Joubert sent word that they should be allowed to go up. Some bodies were found during the ascent; they were noted and left to be buried on the way down. Captain MacBean, one of a dozen or more officers in the war who would eventually rise to the rank of general, was one of the first to reach the summit. 'It was a horrid sight,' he declared, to see 'a long row of dead men—some forty or fifty of them'.[66] They lay with glazed eyes fixed on the sun. Entrenching tools (which had not been moved since Colley had come up the mountain) were put to good use. Some burghers helped; others watched the burial parties intently as they smoked quietly, chatted, or hummed tunes. The burial ground, in which the men were placed in three layers, was roughly walled in, and later a stone cross was raised and engraved with the words: FOR QUEEN AND COUNTRY. JESUS. MERCY. A larger stone cross was hauled up the declivity to mark the grave of the recently married Captain Maude, the only officer to be buried on the summit. Another marker was made of a small heap of stones. On one of the stones were the crudely cut words: HERE COLLEY FELL. Colley's body had been removed to the Boer camp the day before.

'There are lights as well as shades in the Boer character,' remarked the correspondent of the *Natal Mercury* who had been on

Majuba that Monday. Though Joubert had issued orders forbidding his men to plunder the dead or wounded, some of the
burghers chose to disregard them. Many of the wounded and
dead were stripped nearly naked. Here and there was a sock, part
of a puggaree or of a helmet, but nothing more. It appears that
the Boers were most interested in the kilts and sporrans. The
latter were often regarded as trophies of victory and had 'the
place of honour in their homes'. Kilts were later to be seen in the
market-square of Harrismith, where they were sold as dresses
for Boer girls.

MacBean noticed that all of the dead and many of the wounded
had been shot in the head, some as many as five or six times. Dr
Crow estimated that the bullet-wounds of the dead averaged five
per man.

Walking to that sector of the rim held by the 92nd, MacBean
found the grass matted with 'a mass of blood and brains, and red
all over'. Those who had been grievously wounded were left on
the summit to die, since it did not seem worth the effort to bring
them down; it would only have given them much pain and
brought them to their end much sooner.

The wounded spoke 'in high terms of the kindness of the
Boers towards them' since the conflict had ended. Only the very
young Boers seemed capable of cruelty. Joubert told Stewart on
the morning after his capture that if he 'had fallen into the hands
of the "Pinheads" it was as likely as not that he would have
been shot off-hand'. For this reason, commented Stewart, the
Boer leaders 'were most careful to make up patrols by mixing
old men and young men together'.[67]

Stewart found that Boer courtesy was such that they provided
him and other prisoners with every comfort, 'even down to night-
shirts'. In the camp at Heidelberg, after 'very careful inquiries',
he learned that his fellow-prisoners were receiving every consideration. With rations 'liberal in the extreme,' he reported, 'no
camp could have been more comfortable'.[68]

The Boers did not boast of victory. There was no need for
Joubert and Kruger to tell their triumphant burghers 'to put it
down to God Almighty'. Lieutenant Macdonald wrote that as
soon as the fighting was over, the Boers sang hymns for over an
hour afterwards, saying that it was not the Boers who fought but
God.[69] Other captured Britons were equally impressed by the

absence of exultation. Nevertheless, several imaginative news-
paper writers reported that when Colley had been shot, the
Boers danced around his corpse, firing their rifles into the air.
(The source of this information was never named.)

Joubert later testified that he had seen his men moved by an
'almighty power', the like of which he had never witnessed before or after. He had been doubtful of the outcome until he had
seen men whom he knew to be 'such cowards, that in Kaffir wars
even I have set them to cook the pots', behaving like heroes.[70]
Merensky, still no supporter of the Boer cause, believed that
'God's hand in a miraculous way was with them on this day.'
When they came down from the almost inaccessible Majuba and
entered the camp, the missionary found them to be sober and
quiet. As they sat around their camp fires to eat supper, 'they
spoke of the miraculous events of the day in soft, subdued
voices'.[71]

It was not the victory alone for which they were thankful, but
the fact that so few British bullets had found their marks. Only
one man—and two horses—were killed outright. Merensky
treated six wounded, only one of them severe. He found it necessary to remove this man's arm at the shoulder, but the young
burgher died within a week. For his impartial and humane
treatment of the sick and wounded at such a time of dire need, the
missionary-doctor received £20 from the Republic. Kruger declared, 'All of our lives we shall remain unable to repay Mr
Merensky for what he has done for us. Like an Angel of God he
cared for the sick and served them unselfishly.' Nevertheless,
because of his pro-British attitude since the annexation and because of his poor health, Merensky thought that he had lost the
confidence of the new Government. He returned to Germany the
next year, working there towards a better understanding between Germany and South Africa.

The British naturally believed that the Republican statistics
were a deliberate lie. Considering that the action had lasted six
or seven hours with veterans like the 92nd engaged, it was in-
conceivable that only a few of the enemy were hit. Some English
correspondents at Mount Prospect estimated Boer casualties at
close to 500 men. Obliging natives supplied 'confirmation' by
reporting the interment of burghers in mass graves. Many individual soldiers claimed to have shot, or to have witnessed the

shooting of, Boers. Calculating that between 20,000 and 30,000 rounds had been fired at the enemy, it seemed to the British mathematically impossible that such a small number should have struck among the thousand or more Boers who they assumed were on the summit. So many bullets were fired, announced the correspondent of the *Natal Witness*, that 'our men were reduced to throwing stones, tins of beef, mugs, anything they could lay their hands upon. One man struck a Boer such a blow in the face, just under the right eye, with a can of beef that it inflicted a terrible gash, and caused that Boer to drop somewhat suddenly.'

The British soldiers might have put more Boers out of action if they had in fact put their rifles aside and hurled stones at their assailants, or just rolled rocks off the edge as the Boers were ascending. Though some officers, like Captain Birkett, claimed that they held the summit 'until the ammunition was all expended',[72] official statements of other officers contradicted this assertion. Stewart reported that 'at 12.30 p.m. inquiries were made as to the expenditure, and it was ascertained that no man had expended more than half of his 70 rounds and this in very few instances.' Before the final attack, related Fraser, although a few men were very short of ammunition, 'my belief is that many had 20 to 40 rounds remaining.' The retreating men who arrived at the laager below Majuba, according to Norris-Newman, 'were offered ammunition by Captain Robertson, but declined, saying they had plenty. This was a fact, for their pouches were nearly full.'[73]

Of the 650 or so officers and men in battle that day, the losses were as follows: 6 officers and 90 men killed; 7 officers and 125 men wounded; 7 officers and 49 men captured. Nearly half became casualties *after* being driven off the summit. The 92nd lost the most men, 125; the 58th came next with 93; the Naval Brigade lost 36, more than half of its strength. Thus, in one day, if the prisoners are included, the British lost nearly a third of the total loss of the war, which Childers reported in the House of Commons on May 14th as being 24 officers and 366 men killed; 20 officers and 482 men wounded.

The day after the battle, Cameron and Carter decided to go to the Boer camp to interview the leaders. Under a white flag, they were allowed to come up to the fortifications; they were then told to wait before the Nek, which they did for some time. After nearly two hours, Joubert, Smit, a preacher and half a dozen staff officers rode up. Out in front was Aylward. When asked what he was doing there, the stout Irishman said that he was representing the *Daily Telegraph* and boasted of how, as a surgeon, he had treated the British wounded in the Boer camp, amputating the arm of one in the process. Speaking rapidly, he described in detail his report to the *Telegraph* on the battle, and told of how Joubert had sent a message of condolence to the gallant general's wife. (The authorities at Mount Prospect rejected the telegram on the grounds that it was irregular.)

One would have thought, related Carter, that Aylward was a leading general from the way he monopolized the conversation in the presence of the silent Joubert and Smit. Cameron, a high-spirited and outspoken Scot, rough in manner and speech, began to chafe angrily at the Irishman, whom he considered a traitor. Having had more than enough of Aylward, he turned to Joubert, and interviewed him directly. Joubert complained that Colley had undertaken his move at a time when negotiations were pending. Growing more excited, he spoke of his having written for three years to England in futile efforts to prevent the war. The Boers, he said, were willing to be a party to confederation, but that they insisted on having liberty. When he accused the British of firing the first shot, Cameron interrupted with, 'You fired the first shot at Pretoria.' Joubert retorted, 'Oh, no; you did,' and Cameron countered with, 'But our people there say you did.' Aylward chimed in by declaring, 'Just like the liars; I know the English.' The conversation grew more heated as Joubert, obviously annoyed, said in exasperation, 'What is the good of talking? How can you say England wants the truth? England does not want the truth from us! They want their own truth—the truth which will suit the scheme of their own ministers ... I *will* fight to the end. I know England will fight for honour, for predominance; and we will fight for liberty till we die.'

The discussion then became more general, and Cameron raised his hat to the Boers, saluting them as 'brave men, and fighting for your country but to a renegade like that [pointing to Aylward], I wish to say nothing'. Aylward called him 'impertinent' and threatened to 'make it warm' for the Scot should he ever be caught behind Boer lines. Some of the staff were amused by the exchange, but Carter, knowing Cameron's temper and fearing that he might strike Aylward, broke up the meeting. When he thanked Joubert for the interview, the general good-humouredly exchanged riding-whips with him.

As hands were being shaken all round, an ambulance appeared from the British camp and a note was handed to Joubert. It came from the chaplain, Ritchie, asking that Colley's body be given up to the British. The commandant was on the verge of agreeing when Aylward argued that the body should not be released until a request was received from the head officer of the camp. Joubert agreed. He decided to wait until the application came from a man of sufficient rank.

The Boers gave up the body the next morning. For two days a guard of captured Highlanders had watched over his remains at Republican headquarters. Aylward, who alleged that Colley was shot while running after his fleeing men, had examined the wound and put some of the brains back into the skull. He cut away some of the hair, which he sent to Burgers.* Other men had removed all of Colley's insignia, including the buttons.

There was no fuss or ceremony in the British camp. The body remained within the ambulance wagon and was watched over by Sergeant Faulkner, the general's servant. When the corpse was placed in a coffin made of packing-crates, many of the men had a last look at him. 'The features were perfectly still,' wrote Carter. 'The dead man might have been asleep, so placid was his expression.'[74] The coffin was placed on a gun-carriage and covered with a Union Jack. A procession of soldiers, led by the chaplain, moved slowly to the strains of the 'Dead March'. The grave of the general, the third general to have been killed in action since Waterloo, was dug in the military cemetery to the extreme right of the line, next to that of Colonel Deane. The service was brief and simple. No salute was fired.

Mr E. Jennings Taylor of Pietermaritzburg that same day wrote:

> He needs no tears who, in the van
>   and forefront of the fight,
> Met death as should an Englishman
>   upon Majuba's height.

* The last that was heard of Aylward was that he went to New York, where he promoted himself to the rank of colonel and gave lectures on South Africa. In 1883 he eloped with and married Miss Carrie Van Hoeson of Brooklyn. They were divorced shortly before he died in New Hampshire in 1889.

[9]

PEACE

Saving the country from sheer blood-guiltiness.
Gladstone

THE TIDINGS of Majuba created no profound shock in Britain.
'The novelty of a British army getting thrashed by niggers and
amateurs', as the *Referee* saw it, 'is wearing off'. The press,
nevertheless, gave the battle considerable space. The average
reader was still fascinated by conflict in picturesque settings,
'rather like a virtuous spinster's interest in wickedness'. It was
thrilling to read of the exploits of a 'thin red line of heroes' surprising and vanquishing a brave but slow-witted horde of barbarians. But when the situation was reversed and it was the
British who were bamboozled and routed by an altogether un-
obliging force, heralds of imperialism described the event as a
'treacherous massacre'.[1] Thus the jingoes viewed the storming
of Majuba by 'overwhelming numbers' as a betrayal of negotiations. They told how the Boers had spared neither the wounded
nor the unarmed, despite the prominent display of white flags.
'Barbarous missiles', it was reported, were used to kill poor
Commander Romilly and others. Even Ghanzi, the regimental
dog of the 92nd, had been wounded by buckshot fired at close
quarters. Colley's death was described as little short of murder.
On the other hand, the Liberal papers, which now opposed the
annexation and regarded the war as unjustified, spoke of
'creditable tactics' on the part of Joubert. They stressed how the
enemy treated the wounded with consideration. The *Irish World*
declared, 'Give thanks to God, ye starving Irish . . . the Boers
and Basutos of South Africa are fighting the battle of Ireland,
although they don't know it.'
  Liberals and Conservatives were in agreement on two points:
Majuba was a mortifying calamity, and Colley was responsible

for it. Leader-writers lavished sentimental and fulsome praise on the fallen hero, but spoke of an 'inexplicable rashness', apparently inspired by a vain desire to succeed, which had caused his blunders. Apologists for the Gladstone Government accused Colley of having 'strained his instructions so as to gain a triumph before cessation of the fighting'. Radicals charged Colley with attacking 'those splendid Dutchmen ... while lulled to a sense of security' by pending negotiations—but this duplicity had ended in the biters being bitten. It was Colley's good fortune to have atoned for his failure with a soldier's death.

Conservatives who backed the traditionalists in military matters took a different line. Colley's want of tactical skill and experience in the actual handling of troops had led him to group his men together like a herd of deer, until in the end they fell victim to undisciplined stalkers. Colley was disparaged as a mere theorist, the kind of 'scientific soldier' produced by staff colleges; he knew his lessons but was 'incompetent for the practical business of war'. Long practice with the colours instinctively led the fighting officer to victory 'where the vastly superior knowledge of the Staff man only betrays him to disaster'. Pity the poor victims of vanity, wrote the *Morning Advertiser*, who were sacrificed to a paper general's 'habitual contempt of his enemy, added to a burning desire to eclipse the memories of his former reverses'.

Anxious to discredit Childers and the army administration, the military establishment found convenient arguments for Colley's failure. The 'radical fault' of shuffling soldiers and sailors and 'long-service' and 'short-service' men—mixtures which destroyed cohesion, tradition and confidence—was demonstrated to their satisfaction on that 'mountain of misfortune'. Exaggerating its effects, the Duke of Cambridge saw the rout 'as almost unparalleled in the long annals of our Army', and told Wood that the 'dreadful mistake' was in mixing parts of various units.[2] Concerned with morale, Wood was disturbed by these attacks on soldiers. He complained to Childers that 'the hysterical complaints are more like French character than English used to be.'[3] The Secretary for War was reminded of Tacitus: 'Most unjust is this rule of war: in success all claim credit, in adversity one man bears the blame.'

The army reformers were not easily intimidated. Wolseley, though privately admitting that Colley had made a mistake, responded by writing a spirited vindication of the short-service system. And despite dire predictions by most high-ranking officers, Childers, 'with nerves of iron', introduced on March 3rd his scheme for fixing enlistment at twelve years (seven with the colours and five in reserve) and linking battalions, which Wood subsequently contended was primarily responsible for wearing down the Boers in the Second Anglo–Boer War.

The military party led by Cambridge was mollified somewhat by the appointment of Sir Frederick Roberts, the exemplary traditionalist, to replace Colley. A fighting general rather than a 'desk wallah', Roberts would surely retrieve the national honour. When Childers informed the Queen of the appointment, she answered, 'Entirely approve; had thought of this myself.'[4]

Wolseley was stunned by the turn of events. On the Monday morning after Majuba, Butler intercepted him in Trafalgar Square to break the news of Colley's death. Heartsick and low in spirit, he went to the War Office, where Childers told him that Roberts was to go to Natal. 'This decision', he wrote at the end of his career, 'was the greatest blow I had ever received. It meant to all the world that a junior officer, who had never served in South Africa, was considered better suited than I was in a country that I knew well, and in which I had already conducted a campaign.' Childers tried to soften the blow by protesting that he could not spare him; he needed Wolseley 'to help him through with military reforms he contemplated'. The Secretary for War held out to him the promise of elevation to the peerage. With Wolseley in the House of Lords, the Government would have an authoritative supporter to answer the many critics of reform. Later in the month, however, the Queen told Gladstone that Wolseley could become a peer only if he resigned his post as Quartermaster-General. The matter was dropped. As in the case of Robert's appointment, Wolseley was convinced that it was the sinister influence of Cambridge which defeated him. He was tormented by thoughts of how the 'officers of the old school would chuckle over my discomfiture'.[5]

Roberts, soon to become Lord Roberts of Kandahar, was by far the most popular choice that the Government could have made. The overwhelming national spirit, as expressed by the press, was that 'Fighting Fred' was just the man to wipe out the disgrace of Majuba. Although some humanitarians objected to his methods when executing condemned assassins in Kabul (he had them tied to cannon-muzzles), Roberts was generally looked upon as a simple, modest soldier capable of great military feats, especially in rescuing beleaguered garrisons.

And 'little Bobs', though newly arrived in England from India, was anxious for a new command. Having been 'fêted and feasted to almost an alarming extent', he thought that a long sea voyage would be just the thing for his digestive discomforts. Following a quick visit to the Queen and to Eton, where he received a Sword of Honour from the boys,* arrangements were made for him to board a train for Southampton, which was appropriately named the 'Flying Dutchman'. The thousands who gathered to cheer him on his way included Cambridge, Frere and Childers. Wolseley was conspicuously absent. The Boers, it was said, would soon discover the firm qualities which distinguished Englishmen 'as men slow to find out when they were beaten'.

Meanwhile in the Cabinet, during Gladstone's absence, the coercionist Whigs prevailed. On the night of March 1st, Kimberley stated in the House of Lords that arrangements were being made for renewed vigour in measures of suppression. He indicated that more regiments from scattered parts of the Empire would converge on Natal. The force contemplated would total over 20,000, with 10,000 already in Natal and 10,000 on the way there. In addition there was talk of a volunteer corps being formed in Natal. The War Office reported that it had received numerous applications from officers eager to serve in the Transvaal. 'Such a body of troops commanded by such a leader', declared *The Times* on March 2nd, 'can hardly fail to reassert supremacy of British arms in South Africa.'

While Whig ministers like Childers and Kimberley put on a bold front and talked war, the Radicals were thinking of peace. On March 2nd Chamberlain met Bright and urged him 'to write a strong letter about the Transvaal'. Dilke, in his diary, pointed out that the Transvaal was a convenient issue to unite the Radicals and possibly 'dish the Whigs', for the old Quaker Bright, though now strong for peace in South Africa, was only mildly interested in supporting the Radical policy of conciliation and

* Among them was his only son, who would one day be killed fighting the Boers.

concession in Ireland. With Bright and Courtney (the 'radical devil', as Dilke called him), there were at least four men prepared to resign over the matter, or 'if the Whigs yielded to us . . . Kimberley would go.'[6]

Though dimmed by age, Bright stated the case well, for on the next day Gladstone sent for him. Bright argued that despite the disaster at Majuba, 'negotiations should go on as if it had not happened—that no operations for the sake of vengeance should be adopted'. Gladstone agreed. 'Kimberley', wrote Dilke, 'at once gave in.' Bright, with obvious satisfaction, wrote in his journal, 'March 5th. Cabinet at 2 o'clock ... On Transvaal affair, no member of the Government urging war for sake of recovering the reputation of English arms—terms of pacification the same as before the conflict of Majuba Hill.'[7] The contentious coalition had survived another crisis.

Ordinarily Gladstone would have continued to base his policy on the advice of officials responsible for South Africa while he continued to concentrate on Ireland and other problems. But the Radicals persuaded him to believe that Kimberley was leading the Government in the wrong direction. Privately, his son Herbert also expressed misgivings about the Colonial Secretary. Advised by the peace-minded Donald Currie, Herbert Gladstone warned his father of the danger of letting the war spread to the rest of the sub-continent. Hating war and the almost criminal expenditures which war involved, the Prime Minister decided that it would be outrageous to fight solely for the sake of what some called national honour.

Once the shadowy caucus of Radicals had carried its point, a serious gap developed between stated policy and the ministry's intentions. Wood had no reason to doubt the Government's statements. Childers telegraphed him on March 1st to explain that although Roberts was going out with reinforcements, 'we place full confidence in you, and do not desire to fetter your military discretion.' That the Government seemed bent on continuing the war was further indicated by its offering him far more reinforcements than he wished. As for negotiations, the Colonial Office left Wood uninstructed. He assumed that the terms Kimberley had telegraphed to Colley on February 16th were unchanged, and that the first condition was that 'the Boers desist from armed opposition'. Roberts was given the same impression.

In a letter of instructions received on March 4th, Kimberley alluded to the telegram of February 16th, and stated that since no
reply had come from Kruger, he was 'unable to say anything
further on that subject at present'.[8]

As soon as news of Colley's death was received by Wood in
Pietermaritzburg, he was sworn in as Acting Governor of Natal
and High Commissioner of the Transvaal; he then made preparations for a swift departure at dawn to assume command of the
troops. He could not rest that night as telegrams were brought to
him every half-hour. Wood was further disturbed during the next
few days by the sight of thousands of troops stuck in the mud on
the road to Newcastle. 'If any person is ambitious to see mud in
perfection,' wrote a reporter of the *Cape Argus*, 'let him come
here. A kindergarten school should flourish here.'

Throughout the weary hours spent on the post-cart, Sir
Evelyn reflected much on the statement which Wellington had
made to Castlereagh during the Peninsular War: 'You may de-
pend, I shall not hurry operations, or commence them one
moment sooner than they may be commenced, in order that I
may acquire the credit of success.' With reinforcements slowed
by the rainy season, and demoralized soldiers at Mount Prospect
'outnumbered four to one', Wood chose to play for time. He
strengthened the camp and its communications, issued an extra
ration of grog, then sat down and waited. Insidious press telegrams stated that he was dead. An alarmed Lady Wood had to be
assured that her 'good and gallant husband was safe and well'.[9]

When Brand wired Wood on March 3rd that he earnestly
hoped means could 'be devised to suspend hostilities', the latter
replied that he would gladly abstain from making any forward
movement until March 10th, provided that Joubert made a similar promise. Kimberley approved, though he did not give any
fresh instructions. Brand then informed Joubert, who was amenable to the suggestion. Wood proposed a conference, to meet on
March 6th. He reasoned that he had much to gain and nothing to
lose by a temporary halt in the fighting, for he told Kimberley,
almost as an apology, that he did not expect to engage in a successful action for a fortnight.

Sir Evelyn seemed to be the ideal man to negotiate with the
Boers. Although a man of action, as Disraeli once remarked to
the Queen, he was 'always a sharp observer of men and things,

and with a mind rich with practical conclusions ... which will be
ever ready to assist him in the conduct of affairs and the manage-
ment of men'. God-fearing and plain-spoken, he was the kind of
man who could win the respect of the Boers. In addition, the
general's quick, legally trained mind and his rather convenient,
though disconcerting, deafness made him a formidable opponent
in debate. His tact and wit were legendary. (On one occasion,
while staying at Government House in another country, Wood
opened a bathroom door and saw the head of a certain general's
wife protruding from the tub. Without hesitation, Wood said,
'I beg your pardon, General——,' and closed the door.[10])

The delegations met round a small table half-way between the
lines. Wood was flanked by Major Fraser ('we'll beat them yet'),
Captain Cropper and an interpreter. Joubert came up with three
commandants, looking most uncouth. He wore a loose coat, baggy
trousers and no tie; his unkempt hair hung down to his flannel
shirt. The English commander did most of the talking; the Republicans soon relaxed from their first mood of 'severe gravity'
and became 'contaminated with his good humour and cheerful-
ness'.[11] When the Boers suggested that British troops on the
road should be halted, Wood objected. Concealing his true
motives, he declared that except for a few guns and mounted
men, who would arrive in two or three days, he had all the soldiers necessary for a fight. The object of the armistice, as Sir
Evelyn explained it, was to give Kruger time to reply to Colley's
communication. Wood then told Joubert that he would have to
leave the Nek because it was in English territory. The aroused
Joubert refused. The general then pointed to the ribbons on his
chest. Counting to nine, he said, 'and if I pitched you out, another
... will make ten'. The Boer leader pointed to his plain coat and
said, 'General, there is nothing here, and thank God, I want nothing behind that Nek there. I have not a single man to be killed
for that. We do not fight for glory, we fight for liberty, and for
liberty every English general, I know, would also yield his life.'[12]

After an hour and a half of deliberations it was agreed to suspend hostilities for eight days. Both parties promised not to engage in any forward movement during that time. The British,
however, would be free to send eight days' provisions, but no
ammunition, to the Transvaal garrisons, who would be informed
at once of the provisional armistice conditions.

A luncheon of tinned meats and champagne followed. The Boers did not seem to relish the food or drink. They were too occupied with their thoughts. Now and then they looked up towards Majuba, where exactly one week before they had been engaged in battle.

Wood was pleased at the results. He told Childers and Kimberley that he now had time to bring up more men and to dispatch eight days' rations for those of the beleaguered who were most in need. At Potchefstroom, he had heard, they would soon be reduced to eating nothing but mealies.

In England, the ministers heartily approved the cease-fire, but the Queen, suspecting that the Cabinet was anxious to be rid of the Transvaal incubus, wrote in her journal, 'I do not like peace before we have retrieved our honour.'[13]

Unaware of the Government's true attitude, Wood contemplated striking strongly and swiftly. He recommended to Kimberley 'decisive though lenient action; and I can, humanly speaking, promise victory'. But the Radicals were not interested in any promises of victory. Far more welcome were the contents of Kruger's reply (received on March 7th but dated February 28th) to Colley's letter of February 21st. Kruger suggested that representatives of both sides should meet to determine the preliminaries of an honourable peace. Kimberley informed Wood on March 8th that there would be a complete amnesty for the Boer leaders, and that Commissioners would be appointed to maintain friendly communications. In the meantime, the general was instructed to 'prolong armistice as needful'.

When Gladstone announced this agreement in the House, the Radicals cheered. To them, Kruger's reply was tantamount to an acceptance of British proposals. Gladstone's resolve was strengthened by Kimberley's report that there was a 'danger of uprising for independence among the Cape Dutch', with the Germans in the colony sympathetic. The Prime Minister cabled Hofmeyer, as leader of the Cape Dutch, for advice; Hofmeyer replied, 'Remember the example of the American Colonies.'[14]

The Cabinet met on March 12th and authorized Kimberley to say that if the Boers desisted from armed opposition and dispersed to their homes, Commissioners would be sent to consider a settlement based upon the following points: complete self-government under British suzerainty, with a British Resident;

provisions for the protection of native interests and for frontier affairs; control of relations with a foreign power to be reserved. Two days later, Wood met Joubert; they agreed to extend the armistice until March 18th so that Kruger would have sufficient time to come down to the Nek.

When Kruger, Pretorius and their advisers learned of the armistice they became uneasy. The terms obviously favoured the British, who needed time to increase their forces before the Nek. Kruger criticized Joubert; the latter defended himself 'on the ground that the burghers were manifesting dissatisfaction as they had done before Majuba'.[15] Furthermore, Joubert believed that the British Government was sincere in its desire for peace, and was therefore prepared to recognize the Republic. Kruger quoted one of his favourite mottoes: 'Be faithful but trust no one.'

The role of Kruger in the war was obscure. Joubert, on the other hand, was always in the limelight. The British began to assume that he dominated the Triumvirate. Once serious negotiations had begun, however, Kruger asserted himself and assumed the leadership. Heavy rains delayed his journey to the Nek until March 14th, but on his arrival, in the company of Pretorius, Mare and Jorissen, he was loudly cheered by the burghers.

Others came to the region of the Nek. Lady Colley, despite efforts to dissuade her, was determined to visit 'the cemetery where my husband is amongst his friends'.[16] She was accompanied by Mrs Montague, wife of the major, who in speaking of Sir George's death, declared, 'There seems no doubt he was left alone entirely; he could not run like all his men did. *This comes of commanding boys instead of men.*'[17] To make them more comfortable, a tent was pitched near the grave. The visit to her husband's tomb occurred, it was said, on the anniversary of their wedding-day. Seeing her 'was almost too much for us', wrote Melton Prior, as they watched her sink to her knees 'in a half-fainting condition'. Critics of the dead man felt embarrassed. One of them was reminded of the words of Sir George, who in writing about Colonel Deane after the defeat at Laing's Nek had said, 'I would ten thousand times rather any amount of criticism were heaped on me than one word cast at him. I can retrieve myself; he cannot.'[18]

Colonel Redvers Buller arrived on the same day as Lady Colley, riding in a post-cart filled with choice foods and excellent champagne. The big muscular man with the ruddy face, small eyes and grizzly beard was well known by reputation, if not by sight, throughout Natal. As Wood's right-hand man, he had made his mark with a reckless display of courage during the Zulu War. The Zulus called him the 'Brother of the Devil' because he had been responsible for the death of so many of their men. Referring to Buller's qualities, Gladstone once remarked, 'Joshua could not hold a candle to Sir Redvers.' His stern, brusque manner, softened somewhat by a concern for the comfort of his soldiers, made him popular throughout the ranks. When he was annoyed, Buller was not to be trifled with. He once hurled a chair through a glass door at an officer who had displeased him by watching him play billiards.

Because of the pressures of civil administration, Sir Evelyn turned military affairs over to Buller. The Boers, who admired his grim strength, said that Buller's arrival was the equivalent of a reinforcement of ten thousand men. The admiration was mutual —it was well known that Buller believed the burghers had been unfairly treated by annexation.

'Any peace now agreed to', observed Buller, 'will not be a lasting one.' He justified his statement on the grounds that the Boers would never accept his Government's intention not to return the whole of the Transvaal. Wood did not despair. He had faith in his power as a negotiator. On March 16th he and Buller and Majors Fraser and Clarke met the Boer leaders again. This time Joubert was accompanied by Kruger, Jorissen, Pretorius, Mare and Kirk Uys. United in their efforts to drive the British out, the Boer leaders were sharply divided over what concessions should be made in order to attain peace.

The negotiators met at ten in the morning in a small blue-lined marquee midway between the contending forces. Correspondents and soldiers lolling about the veld watched the proceedings through field-glasses. Some burghers climbed up Majuba for a better look.

The Boer representatives brought with them a mule-wagon which was part of the loot taken at Bronkhorst Spruit. Many carried British rifles and other equipment. Wood was disturbed by the sight, but when Joubert came forward, Wood became jocular to such an extent that one might have suspected they had grown up in the army together. Joubert, stiffened by the presence of Kruger, seemed less friendly than usual. Moreover, he felt insulted by certain articles he had seen in the British press which stated that Colley, whom the Boers held in great esteem, had been wilfully killed by a second shot fired at close quarters. These lies, he felt, were designed 'to stir up hatred between the Dutch and the English'.[19]

Unlike Wood, who regarded Joubert as the 'most far-seeing and moderate of the Boer leaders', Buller took an instant dislike to the Commandant-General. Watching with a sort of seraphic calm, he put down 'slim Piet' as a man too clever to be trusted, even by his own party. Unimpressed by what was commonly described as Joubert's fine presence and patriarchal appearance, Buller concentrated on his hands: 'I never saw any man with such cruel-looking hands.' He could well believe the stories of how in the early days Joubert was supposed to have murdered natives. His suspicions were confirmed when Joubert later told him that he would not like to kill another duty-bound English soldier, but as for burghers who remained loyal to the British, 'I would kill them all myself if I could.' The fear that crossed Buller's mind was that many loyal whites and blacks had already been put to death.[20]

The conference was one of verbal skirmishes which lasted a full eight hours. Wood, bustling and lively, did most of the talking. One minute he was affable and persuasive, the next determined and stubborn. Joubert, to whom he directed most of his words, looked on impassively, occasionally replying in his high-pitched, reedy voice. As the hours passed, Kruger began to declaim with fiery energy, discharging sentences 'like a Maxim gun'. The sarcastic Jorissen, who was believed to be strong for war, assumed the pose of a lawyer sure of winning his case. The mild-looking Pretorius said little but, in Buller's opinion, was 'mad to make peace'.

Confined to the limits of somewhat vague and incomplete instructions from the Colonial Office, Wood stood his ground. If there were to be any concessions at this juncture, the Boers would have to make them. There was no doubt in the minds of the burghers that he was anxious to fight. And as Sir Redvers put it, there was no doubt 'that we shall beat them when we do fight'.

Whenever a knotty point exposed a difference between the burghers, they moved to a spot forty yards from the tent and engaged in animated debate. There is no record of what they said. Those who watched saw Kruger doing much of the talking. At times, Joubert would quit the party and pace back and forth with his head lowered, as if he carried his problems heavily on his shoulders. He seemed caught between the persuasive charms of Wood, who appealed to his strong desire for peace, and Kruger's refusal to agree to the nebulous proposals put forth by the British.

The Boers finally accepted the general proposals of the British, but argued over the composition and powers of the Royal Commission. They asked why peace could not be established without the Commission. Wood answered curtly that he had no power to select a different course of action. Moreover, he contended, the burghers themselves had asked for a Commission. Yes, Kruger countered, but one in which the Republicans would be represented; Kruger wanted to nominate at least two out of the five members. The Boers did consent to Residents, but objected to control over interior native affairs. When Kruger asked that the Transvaal garrisons be withdrawn, Wood warned that if this were a demand, it would not only be refused but hostilities would be resumed. The burghers then agreed to put the request in the form of a hope so as to enable them to govern the Republic free of British troops who might give encouragement to various malcontents. Wood then indicated that it would be difficult to leave the Transvaal before the Commissioners defined exactly what the Transvaal was. 'The Transvaal is what you annexed!' Kruger gruffly replied. The meeting broke up with hands shaken all round.

Wood telegraphed to Kimberley that night, 'I do not think they realize they might have to yield extensive tract to native tribes and if they contemplated chance of Commission arranging this, they would not leave the Nek.' He then assured the Colonial Secretary that the 'happiest results' would follow the action he hoped to fight in fourteen days; the 'Boers should disperse without any guarantee, and then many now undoubtedly coerced will readily settle down'.[21] The Boers, however, were possibly shrewder than Wood. They recognized that it would be difficult for the British Government, having initiated the negotiations, suddenly to break off all talks without sufficient cause, as this would give the impression 'that they had been entered into solely for purposes of bad faith'.[22]

Out of office, Gladstone had never lost an opportunity to denounce the Conservatives for conducting Government business behind veils of secrecy, but negotiations with the Boers prior to Wood's armistice were carefully concealed from the public, and a general reticence was practised afterwards. Wood, also, kept his own counsel. When the conference ended, he inferentially told the reporters, who had been kept throughout the day at a specified distance of three hundred yards, that the burghers, save for two or three particulars, were in general agreement with British terms. Points of disagreement, which he did not reveal, would be discussed at a future meeting. This was hardly enough to gratify a nation's curiosity.

Speaking for the dozen or more reporters present, Carter later complained, 'We were beginning to get heartily tired of these negotiations.' Even the Boers whom they had interviewed were 'no longer objects of curiosity, or their conversation entertaining'.[23] Many correspondents privately hoped that a renewal of conflict would liven things up. They were encouraged by Wood's unofficial comment that 'unless the Boers moderate their tone, negotiations will come to nothing.' They made bets, as did soldiers and civilians throughout Natal, as to whether there would be war or peace.

Conflict was generated by the correspondents themselves. Cameron, the banker turned reporter who had quarrelled with Roberts in Afghanistan, seemed more belligerent than ever. His 2,500-word dispatch on the Majuba battle had given him a reputation for blistering on-the-spot accounts which he now found difficult to uphold. Prior and Fripp, of the *Graphic*, had grown weary of sketching the same meeting-place; Prior was angered by the disappearance of whisky from cases labelled 'drawing materials', supplies which he described as indispensable to campaigning in comfort. Quarrelling among themselves, and with officialdom, they were living up to the suggestion of Archibald Forbes, veteran war correspondent, that men of his trade 'be big and ugly enough to impress the conviction that it would be highly unwise to take liberties with [them] '.[24]

They fretted over the right of priority in the use of the telegraph service: one insisted that he represented *the* leading journal; another announced that he should have precedence because he had arrived first; a third demanded special privileges because he was considered the dean of correspondents. They fumed in chorus when the wires hummed for hours on end with messages from young ladies inquiring after the condition of their sweethearts in uniform. The words differed but the tenor was the same, 'Are you sure you are quite well, dear? Please reply at once.' The general finally ordered that all press telegrams were to be sent in the order in which they were submitted. Although he did not introduce censorship, Wood requested, 'in the nicest manner, that they refrain from speculating about military movements'.

Much of the speculation, therefore, was left to the newspapers at home. According to their political views, the papers also commented on the virtues or vileness of the Boers. The Radical press gave attention to the views of the South African correspondent for the *New York Herald*, who pitied the 'poor Boers fighting like rats in a corner . . . shot down without mercy'. They published a petition from France, signed by deputies, senators and literary men (including Victor Hugo), asking that force should not be used 'in crushing courageous little people'.

One item which offered interest seasoned with levity recounted the exploits of Lady Florence Dixie, youngest daughter of the Marquess of Queensberry, and the first woman war correspondent.* An ardent imperialist, she was engaged by the *Morning Post* to brave danger and discomfort while reporting British triumphs over the Boers. She left behind her tame jaguar but took along to South Africa her uxorious and uncomplaining husband Beau. On her departure, the London *Figaro* contributed to the general hilarity by warning that the presence of a pretty and titled female reporter might be 'the intentional cause of a battle being lost, or, at all events, of so upsetting the equanimity of a general as to render some of his plans abortive'.

By the third week in March, the sunny-faced, bright-eyed young girl reporter (she was only twenty-four) had arrived in Natal. 'With a glass of whisky in her hand,' wrote her biographer, 'she could more than hold her own in any mess tent.' A talented marksman, she once challenged a Boer to a contest. Lady Florence 'hit her bottles one after the other as if they were elephants', declared one bystander. 'The Boer', he added, 'went

---

* Her brothers, considered 'emotionally unstable', also made good copy. Francis was killed trying to scale the Matterhorn; John, the 9th Marquis of Queensberry, became famous through the rules he devised for boxing.

away signally defeated and convinced that if all Englishmen can't shoot, some Englishwomen can.'[25] With characteristic single-mindedness she smugly predicted that the so-called negotiations would come to naught, and that Wood would teach the rebels their place.

The next parley, on March 18th, took place on a disagreeably cold day, in a driving rain. (Fifty animals died that night from the bitter cold in the British camp.) Kruger and Pretorius claimed that they were too ill to attend. Only Joubert and his brother went forth to meet the British, this time in the shelter of John O'Neill's little farmhouse. While the reporters remained shivering in the kitchen, Wood told the burghers that Kimberley would not agree to Boer representatives on the Commission, or to the withdrawal of garrisons before the establishment of their Government, an estimated six months hence. Joubert, not having the power to accept or reject the Colonial Secretary's terms, asked that the armistice be extended three days (to midnight on the 21st) so that he and his colleagues might have time to consider.

All the drama was now in the Boer camp. Day and night, the burghers insisted on discussing matters with their leaders, most of all Kruger. Having won all the battles, they were not amenable to conditions. The burghers believed that Wood was stalling in order to gain the time necessary to strengthen his army. Delay could only weaken them. With the onset of winter they were needed at home to move their stock to the bushveld, and at this time of the year they ran the additional risk of sickness to themselves and their horses.*

When Joubert came back into camp to report Kimberley's intransigence, loud voices of indignation were heard. Smit held a great council in his tent and spoke of fresh military measures. The pressured Triumvirate drew up a proclamation. It described the Colonial Secretary's attitude and declared that Republican concessions were not being reciprocated. Everything was to be decided by a Commission, chosen by the British, with no time-limit set on the Commission's ultimate decision. It concluded

---

* Horse-sickness was one of the curses of campaigning in South Africa. Caused by a small night-flying gnat, it carried off horses in a matter of hours. Those few that survived the disease acquired an immunity and could be purchased only at great cost. The War Office printed special maps indicating where the disease was most prevalent.

with the statement that the armistice had been obtained by fraudulent means and that, with the help of the Almighty, the war would be resumed.

On Sunday morning, March 20th, Brand arrived determined to do everything in his power to ensure peace. After speaking earnestly with Wood, he journeyed to the Boer camp. A kindly, just man of modest demeanour, Brand was given an enthusiastic welcome. When passing some three hundred Free State volunteers, he 'went up to them and shook his finger in a reproving way. "Naughty boys," he said.'[26]

Conferring with Kruger for three hours, Brand gently urged a more conciliatory attitude, Kruger was adamant. When Jorissen read aloud the proclamation drafted the night before, Brand was shaken and cried out, 'God forbid.' The President, looking more worn and grey than usual, finally persuaded Kruger not to publish the document and to meet Wood the next day, the last day of the armistice. The plain-spoken Joubert agreed with Brand. With some heat he told the dogged, authoritative Kruger, 'I advise you to accept these terms, which are liberal; and if you refuse them, you had better nominate another Commandant-General, for I do not mean to fight.'[27]

When the leaders left the next morning, a large number of burghers decided that if nothing were settled at the last meeting, they would make an assault on Mount Prospect the following morning.

The arguments at O'Neill's began at eight o'clock in the morning and lasted until nine o'clock that night. With Brand's help, Wood succeeded in getting the Boers to withdraw their demands for a bilateral commission and for simultaneous removal of the garrisons when the burghers dispersed their forces. The general promised, in turn, that when once the Boers left the Nek no attempt would be made to occupy that position or to follow them into the Transvaal with troops.

The negotiations came close to breaking off when Wood spoke of the British retaining the eastern Transvaal. The Boers objected vigorously.

Sir Evelyn then inquired, 'Suppose we do not yield on this point, will you go on fighting?' Kruger replied, 'That is not a fair question. If we do not yield, will you go on fighting?' Wood answered, 'Yes,' whereupon Kruger took up his hat, rose and said, 'Then we need not discuss matters further.'

Taking him by the arm, Wood said, 'No, come back, you must not be so hasty.' At this point Smit intervened. 'The best thing would be to let the sword decide,' he said.

Wood, however, urged that the negotiations be continued. It was finally agreed that the separation of any territory would be left to the decision of the Royal Commission. Another forty-eight hours of armistice was agreed upon to conclude the peace negotiations. Eager to get off with verbal assurances, Wood seized the opportunity to send off an orderly with the news while Kruger was engaged in conversation with Joubert and Jorissen, but the move did not go unnoticed. Kruger, breaking off the discussion, abruptly asked Major Fraser, 'Where is the man going ?' On learning the purpose of his mission, Kruger rushed out and bellowed in English, 'Stop that man.' (Kruger no doubt understood English, but he rarely spoke it.) Realizing that any prolongation without written guarantees would give the British an opportunity to improve their military position, he went to Wood and asked him, as an honest man, to sign the agreement first. Wood refused. Kruger then turned to his men and shouted in his great bass voice, 'Burghers, saddle up.' The British general capitulated and signed.[28]

Once the provisional peace protocol was signed, the former enemies engaged in some friendly bantering. The British were told that *now* they could see the Nek. For their part, the British tried to disparage the Boers' military successes, trying to get the Boers to admit heavy losses. When Joubert was asked directly how many men he had lost at Majuba, he answered confidently, 'I myself had one killed and one wounded.'

A British officer laughed. 'But I saw more killed with my own eyes.' 'Very well,' said Joubert angrily. 'Do you go and dig one of them up and bring him here; and I promise I'll eat him, skin and all.'

The slight losses suffered by the Boers were later confirmed to their satisfaction by Merensky. He estimated the total Republican loss during the war as 35 dead, 95 wounded and 18 captured.[29] The pro-English *Friend of the Free State* in its issue of May 26th gave the official report, with names, of 43 dead and 58 recovered from wounds.

Scattered about the farmhouse was a small army of reporters

waiting to hear the news that the war was over. Their horses were saddled for the race to the military telegraph office. Captain Cropper, Wood's A.D.C., had come out now and then to smoke and to discuss the progress of events inside with his good friend Prior. The illustrator arranged to give Cameron an opportunity to beat the other correspondents to the wire. When Cropper eventually came out and carelessly whispered, 'It's all over, they have signed,' Prior raised his helmet (the prearranged signal) and Cameron was off at full gallop to Mount Prospect. Twenty minutes later, the general came out on the porch and assembled the newsmen around him. 'Gentlemen,' he said, 'we have signed the terms of peace, but I warn you that the wire is closed to all communication until a dispatch has gone to England.' What the exact terms were, Wood would not divulge. Later in the day there was great consternation among Government officials in London when a special edition of the *Standard* announced the peace before they had received any word from South Africa.[30]

Wood was proud of his achievement. Without any false modesty, he told Kimberley that the diplomatic triumph as due mainly to his personal influence with the Boer delegates. Carter concurred, saying that they 'fell in love with him from the first, and did not conceal their admiration of the man who was firm as a rock up to the utmost limit allowed him, and who was at the same time courteous, affable, good-natured, and entertaining'.[31] But Wood still hoped to fight. While telling Kimberley of his success as a diplomat, he let Childers know 'that if authorized, [he could] advance 24th, but be delayed by rivers'.[32]

'Thank God,' wrote Gladstone when Kimberley informed him of the agreement. The burghers were no less thankful. When the envoys returned that night, there were 'great rejoicings and firing of guns'. The Kriegsraad quickly approved the final terms of peace.

It was no secret that Kimberley was disgusted by the way the Radicals had won over Gladstone and carried the Cabinet on the Transvaal issue. Many of the lesser members, he found, showed little interest. The Duke of Argyll, for example, believed that the Transvaal question was a departmental matter which he knew very little about and cared even less. Privately, Kimberley did not hesitate to describe it as a 'dirty business'. It was suspected that he would resign his post when asked to support the peace treaty after the Royal Commission finished its work.

With ratification on both sides, a final meeting took place at O'Neill's for the purpose of obtaining formal signatures. Wood, by way of reward, was informed the same day that he was to continue in his present command. A message was sent to Cape Town (now connected by telegraphic cable), instructing Roberts to return immediately after his arrival. The mere presence of the great general in South Africa was considered a possible source of provocation to the Boers and their sympathizers.

When the cable was handed to Roberts, he unbuckled his sword and threw it angrily away from him. He swore he would never again serve 'such a Government'. Within twenty-four hours, Roberts and the reinforcements which had accompanied him departed for England. As they stood on the deck, 'a crowd on the quay cheered the general and loudly groaned for Gladstone'.[33] The press dubbed Roberts 'an April fool'. *Punch* announced that the Government planned to make him Earl of the Ocean, his duty being to remain at sea for ever, sailing between London and Cape Town. While on the last leg of his wildgoose chase, Roberts was said to have vowed to lead an abstemious life so that he might live long enough to efface the 'Majuba surrender'.

The news of the final signing on March 23rd was brought into the Boer camp by President Brand. Looking out of his carriage, he announced the happy news to a multitude of farmers gathered round him. Some were 'grave and quiet in demeanour, others cheered and shouted for joy waving their hats, their caps, and their rifles'. Prior, who disobeyed Wood's orders in going to the Boer camp, sketched the scene for posterity. He had fully expected that their manly pride and rowdy manner would lead to a drunken victory celebration; instead, 'the grim-looking, slovenly Boers ... grotesque rather than impressive', moved off to another part of the camp to solemnize the peace with a thanksgiving service. A pastor, dressed in a frock-coat with a hymn-book in his hand, stood before a tent; a chest was placed behind him with two candles stuck into beer bottles for lack of candlesticks. The congregation, armed to the teeth, joined in the singing of hymns. The Boer wives were generally dressed in black, but many, including their daughters, 'looked quite jolly and pretty in their print dresses'; Prior, however, confessed 'that a few whalebones would have added very much to the smartness of their figures'.³⁴

When Joubert appeared among the burghers they showed him great respect. They saluted him, and those who were sitting rose at once. At six o'clock a call from his whistle brought all the men about him. Many were dressed in frayed clothes, and though it was a capital offence to wear a British uniform, a good number of them had replaced their tattered garments with looted clothes. They listened to him with the greatest attention, lifting their caps solemnly whenever God's name was mentioned. Joubert thanked them for their good behaviour; he had not had to punish a single man. He hoped they would continue to behave well until the Royal Commission had finished its work. Joubert, however, made no effort to detail the terms of the peace. He merely assured them that they had obtained what they had been fighting for. He concluded by asking them to treat the English residents of the Transvaal as friends rather than enemies. And he warned them that they must always be prepared to sacrifice self-interest for freedom's sake, and for the liberty of the black and the white people of the Transvaal.

Kruger then came forward, saying that as Joshua had said to Israel he was now able to say to the burghers, 'To your tents'; the war was over and they had gained what they had sought.

Pretorius also spoke briefly and fluently. Dressed in fustian and clean-shaven, save for a large moustache, he tried to impress his people with the need for patience until the Royal Commission had given its decision.

The words were well received and most of the men expressed their general satisfaction, though a few dissented. They objected to garrisons being left in the Transvaal for the next six months and feared that the Royal Commission might cede some of the Transvaal to the British. One 'wretched Scottish renegade' told Prior that he did not want a peace on those terms. 'Bring over the whole British army,' he boasted, 'and we will treat it in the same way as we have the last men.'³⁵ The next morning Joubert was deeply offended to learn that several hundred men had deserted the camp that night without waiting for him to give the word to go home.

At four in the morning General Wood and his staff made their way to the Boer camp, which was on the verge of breaking up.

As Sir Evelyn appeared, word went out to the men to make preparations for a parade of honour. From all sides the Boers rushed
to their horses, trooped into the parade-ground, and in a few
minutes had formed into a hollow square. The British general
stood on a wagon to inspect them. His right hand was raised in
salute while his left gently bobbed up and down as if he were
counting—there were about 2,500 men.

After the British had departed, a long line of wagons streamed
to the north over the tall grass of the veld. They moved in a
kind of military order, each command under a leader. It was all
done simply and with celerity, with no sergeant-majors dashing
and gesticulating, or purple-faced commissariat officers on the
verge of apoplexy. The camp was a thing of the past. Only a
few scattered wagons remained amidst a great deal of debris
left by the war.

At Mount Prospect there was a totally different scene. 'A
miserable ending to a miserable war' was, according to Carter,
the general verdict of the British soldiers. Never in his life had
Carter heard an assemblage of men indulge in such strong language. 'Everyone is cursing Gladstone, the Radical Government,
Lord Kimberley,' one officer wrote.[36] Some soldiers consoled
themselves with reflection that the Gladstone Government would
be 'turned out neck and crop' when the news was received in
Parliament. Others believed that the war would most certainly be
renewed by the Boers when Britain insisted on retaining the
eastern portion of the Transvaal.

Morale had never been so low. Officers openly denounced 'the
abject surrender', and many threatened to resign. 'I am thoroughly humiliated and degraded by being a servant of the English
Government,' wrote an old cavalry officer, 'and I wish I had
never entered the service.'[37] One colonel, commander of a regiment, tendered his resignation to Wood, but the general refused to accept it. The *Natal Mercury* reported that in one crack
corps no fewer than three hundred applications for discharge were
sent in one day. In the 92nd, old servicemen were offered boun-
ties of £3 down and £1 a month if they would stay on. Only
one man accepted the offer.[38] The Highlanders were further outraged when on April 4th Stewart submitted his report, in which
he attributed the disaster to the failure to observe and report the
advance of the Boers, and then to the subsequent panic of the

troops. Major Hay denounced the report as 'utter rubbish' and 'pure invention'. At the same time great indignation prevailed among the Rifles, owing to statements in *Truth* which discredited their conduct in battle.

More than ever the soldiers sought comfort in Bass bitter and 'Cape smoke'. Serious military crimes began to occur, 'and in more than one instance sentinels were found on their posts intoxicated'.[39] A reward of £10 was offered to any person who could provide evidence leading to the arrest of civilians offering inducement to soldiers to desert.*

The soldiers were further embittered when they returned to England. There were no bands to greet them. The soldiers were kept out of sight and forgotten. 'No hand was held out to greet us,' complained one defender of a Transvaal garrison; 'if we mention the fact of our late defence, we are met with silence.' Few rewards were doled out. Only one medal, with a clasp, was awarded to those who had been engaged in all of three distinct campaigns—against the Zulus, against Sekukuni, and against the Boers.

The war changed the soldiers' attitude towards the Boers. They won the respect of officers and men who had formerly held them in contempt. As an observer in the Russo–Japanese War, Ian Hamilton found that neither the Russians nor the Japanese could 'hold a candle to the Boer when it comes to the instinctive, deadly, panther-like quickness ... A good Boer would have had an enemy on the ground for each of ten cartridges in his magazine within some twenty seconds!'[40] It was more than being 'worthy of our steel', as another officer put it. The burghers' love of liberty and their old-time chivalry (especially in their considerate treatment of wounded) put the lie to the charge of 'Boer barbarity'. Wood, in speaking before the Royal Commission, held that the Boer leaders had 'carried on a war with humanity and good feeling which has been seldom surpassed in Europe'.[41]

---

* Many of these deserters were later employed in constructing a railway at Delagoa. Known as the 'Irish brigade' because of the origin of a large proportion of them, they became notorious for their rowdy behaviour. All efforts to restrain them failed. They went too far, however, when they seized a Portuguese gunboat, battened down the crew, reversed the flag of Portugal, and stuffed clothing into the guns' muzzles. To prevent a rupture in Anglo–Portuguese relations, two British warships were dispatched to deal with the Irish brigade. When the ships arrived, however, they had fled to the interior.

One Boer leader—Cronje—was branded 'unscrupulous' by the British. In addition to his crimes of refusing to allow sick and dying women to leave the fort and of compelling prisoners of war to work in the trenches, Cronje was charged with forcing the capitulation of the Potchefstroom garrison by concealing from them the news that an armistice had been arranged and that additional rations were on the way. On March 12th Cronje had received orders from Joubert telling him to inform the British of the terms. The next day two Free State messengers arrived with terms of the armistice, terms which Brand had promised Wood would be delivered to Colonel Winsloe. Disregarding their remonstrances, Cronje would not let them pass. Determined to take the fort, he argued that Brand's letter conflicted with Joubert's. His officers agreed with him, and a request for further instructions was sent to Joubert. Two days later the *Staats Courant* containing the published terms reached the Boer commander. Cronje, however, still refused to halt the firing.

At the time, the garrison had only eight bags of rotten mealies left. To end the privations from hunger and fatigue, Winsloe sent out a flag of truce on March 19th. He asked that arrangements should be made for a surrender. The Boers pitched a tent and rolled up a cart with food, cigars and liquor. Winsloe and his officers made a good show. Their servants had spent a good part of the morning repairing the best part of the forty pounds of clothing allowed them in the field. One of the burghers asked Winsloe (who deliberately assumed an air of nonchalance), 'How are you so clean when you come out of that hole?'[42]

The 'tremendous palaver' between Cronje and Winsloe lasted two days. Cronje thundered out in a loud and imperative voice, but he was not certain of his position. Unaware of the hopeless condition of the garrison, and pressured by the dissatisfaction of his own burghers who had wearied of the siege, he made concessions. Officers and men were to keep their private property and their arms (except rifles); no prisoners were to be taken, including civilians; and the British would be permitted to march out with honours of war to Natal, surrendering only the fort and two field-guns, minus shells.

Once an agreement had been made, 'all became *couleur de rose*'. Every possible assistance was provided by way of medicine and comforts for the wounded, sick and exhausted. For the officers, the Boers arranged a round of breakfasts, luncheons and dinners culminating in a farewell banquet at which they provided dry Monopole champagne. Winsloe found the 'rough, hearty, determined-looking' burghers worthy of respect and blamed all wrong-doing on their Hollander advisers.

On March 23rd Winsloe and his men began their march from the fort to Natal, flags flying at their head and bugles playing. Cronje, 'honest Piet' to the burghers, made a touching farewell speech, and his officers crowded round to clasp hands and to wish the British Godspeed. The four hundred burghers formed up on either side of the road and saluted their former enemies.

Winsloe's command left Potchefstroom carrying fifty-four wounded and leaving behind thirty-one dead, six from disease. (The Republican side lost six killed and eleven wounded.) Along the way the burghers greeted them with kindness and generosity. Only after they were nearly at the frontier did the British learn that the war had ended on the very day they had left their fort. 'We are, one and all,' announced one of the marchers, 'ashamed of our nationality.'[43]

The British Government, including Gladstone, was seized with a sudden fit of national pride over Cronje's 'discreditable stratagem'. The British press denounced Cronje as a miscreant. The *Natal Mercury* put forth a view that 'the infusion of black blood' had produced a 'low and brutal element' in the Boer population. Joubert, speaking on behalf of his Government, apologized for Cronje's conduct. He told Wood, on his own initiative, that 'the capitulation should be cancelled'; and that the British could, if they wished, return the same military force they had had there before the surrender.[44]

Wood accepted the offer. All articles which had been taken were to be returned and sent on to Standerton. Later, in mid-June, a force under Buller reoccupied the fort (which was preserved as a memorial after the peace) and twenty-four hours later marched out again. This was an act not without deceit on the part of the British Government, for 'they pretended that Potchefstroom was to be taken back for an indefinite time.'[45] The inhabitants themselves, Boer and English alike, looked on the brief presence of the troops as a waste of time. Florence Dixie, who watched the proceedings, wrote, 'The very children jeered in imitation of the sentiments they had heard at home.' Buller called the affair 'the puppet show' of an appeasing Government, and strongly objected to 'playing the liberal ass round the Transvaal'. He reported that not a single article was ever returned. As for the two cannon, the Boers told Buller that 'they had been lost'.

What is often overlooked about Potchefstroom is that its fall was largely due to Wood's clumsy arrangements. Instead of communicating directly with the garrison commanders, he had left it to the Boer commandants to transmit the conditions of the armistice. In each instance, when informed of the armistice by the Boers, the British commanders were naturally mistrustful. Further, little practical advantage was gained from the fact that provisions were sent to the besieged. With the exception of Standerton and Wakkerstroom—garrisons which did not need provisions—the rations arrived only after the peace was declared. Those destined for Potchefstroom came in on March 25th, two days after the survivors had departed.*[46]

As for the besieged at Pretoria, 'funk' was the ugly but concise word used to describe their mood. It had begun on March 15th when the Boers sent in a newspaper containing a depressing account of what had occurred at Majuba. The flags were lowered to half-mast out of respect for Colley. There was also a sudden desire on the part of the men to consume the last of the liquor supply. Some drank to dispel the gloom; others—thought to be Boer sympathizers—appeared to be celebrating; a few others drank simply because Colley's defeat 'was another excuse to get drunk'.[47] Glasses were raised again on the next day, the one-hundredth day of the siege. 'The hearts of the defenders', wrote the *News of the Camp*, 'have sunk to zero.'

There was worse to come. On the evening of March 28th dispatches containing the terms of 'an inglorious peace' were brought into camp by a detail of three officers. The next morning a mounted party of Boers, led by Joubert, rode in. Lanyon and

---

* A great deal more was to be heard about Cronje. The surrender gave him a big name. In 1896 he became a national hero when he captured Jameson's force of raiders. During the Second Anglo–Boer War, 'dark Cronje...iron-handed ruler of natives...reviler of the British' was regarded by the British as an arch-villain. Though a man of great courage and energy, he proved less successful than in the past. When he surrendered his 4,000 men to Roberts on Majuba Day, 1900, he crashed down from his pedestal overnight and was labelled a traitor by many of his countrymen.

Bellairs (who had been promoted to brigadier-general on the
25th) greeted the victors. Joubert's eyes widened at the sight of
Bellairs's faultless attire, as if (in the words of DuVal) he regarded 'gold lace as a secondary consideration to straight shooting and good skirmishing'. Bellairs shook Joubert's hand and a
pleasant discussion followed. It was arranged that armed burghers should not enter Pretoria because, as Bellairs explained,
feelings were running so high among the besieged that a fight
might ensue.

It was a heart-breaking scene when the terms of peace were
published in camp that morning. To the soldiers it meant defeat,
but to the loyal Britons and Boers it spelled ruin and reprisals.
Women who had withstood the gruelling siege broke down and
wept, wringing their hands in grief; 'children were hushed as if
in a chamber of death, and the men were completely bowed down
with sorrow.' One distraught Englishman turned to Lanyon and
exclaimed, 'Thank God my children are Afrikanders, and need
not be ashamed of their country.'[48]

Lanyon swore to Shepstone that he would 'far rather have
remained in captivity for another ten years even, and living on
cats and dogs than that broken faith and promises should have set
us free'.[49] At the same time he told his father, 'I should dearly
like to have command for one day, just to have a slap at the
Boers.'[50] The only good news that Lanyon could report was that
he had been replaced by Bellairs; he would be glad to get out of
'wretched South Africa'.[51] The editor of *De Volksstem* fervently
wished that Lanyon would never come back! The *News of the
Camp* predicted that he would suffer heavy criticism for his role
as administrator.*

By the afternoon of March 29th the disbelief and bereavement
of the loyalists had turned to rage. They behaved like funeral
mourners gone mad with grief. A sympathetic bystander saw
men 'crying like children with shame and despair. Some went
raving up and down that they were Englishmen no longer;
others, with flushed and indignant faces, declaimed against the
treachery which led to useless sacrifice; while others again, with

---

* Like so many before him Lanyon had feared that service in South Africa would
ruin his reputation. It did. He later served unobtrusively under Wolseley in the
Egyptian campaign and in the Gordon Relief Expedition. He died of cancer in New
York in 1887, aged forty-four.

stricken and woe-begone faces, sat contemplating their impending ruin, refusing to be comforted.'[52] Even Bishop Bousfield announced that he now knew what was meant by perfidious Albion, who 'ruins those who trust her'.[53]

A mob of Englishmen hauled down the Union Jack and dragged it through the mud without a single voice being raised in protest. By evening, the mounted volunteers had joined the demonstration. They burned an effigy of Gladstone, 'scattering his well-petroleumed carcass to the winds'.[54] Discipline among the soldiers began to deteriorate. (Within the month, twenty-two soldiers absconded.) The military authorities feared the possibility of a riot. The next day some of the loyalists busied themselves in collecting their belongings. They left the camp empty and deserted, many of them swearing that they were leaving the country for good.

The siege had taken a heavy toll. Seventeen had been killed, nine from colonial units. There were also thirty-six wounded, twenty-one from colonial units. The Republican losses were five killed, eight wounded, and sixteen taken prisoner. A few suicides on the English side were suspected. DuVal ended what he called his 'somewhat eccentric career' by jumping overboard into the Red Sea on his voyage home.

The reaction to the armistice was no less intense in Newcastle. Rider Haggard told how 'every hotel and bar was crowded with refugees who were trying to relieve their feelings by cursing the name of Gladstone with a vigour, originality and earnestness that I have never heard equalled.' The refugees were joined by local colonists and raging soldiers. There were shouts of how they were no longer 'bloody Englishmen'. The natives looked on stupefied.[55]

The crowd were suddenly carried away by an idea. They gathered in the Market Square and several men erected a gibbet from which Gladstone's effigy was hung with every mark of abhorrence. As the effigy was burned, Cameron and a party of officers joined in the revelry and assisted in distributing the ashes. There were groans for the Prime Minister and cheers for themselves and Disraeli. 'Rule Britannia' was sung, or rather howled, many times. The crowd made vociferous threats against Kruger and the 'murderers' of Bronkhorst Spruit. But when Kruger and Jorissen came to town a couple of days later as guests

of Wood, no attempt was made to harm them. The once-popular
Wood, however, was hissed for having allowed himself to be
used in carrying out the Government's dirty work.[56]

Demonstrations of bitterness and contempt were made
throughout the loyal parts of South Africa. Newspapers were
edged with black, mourning bells tolled, and meetings were held
to protest against the peace in most uncomplimentary terms.
Britons felt they had lost caste in proportion to the prestige
gained by their Dutch rivals and they feared a resurgence of
nationalism. They were further frustrated by the fact that the
colonists appeared mere pawns in a political game centred six
thousand miles away. From Pietermaritzburg to Grahamstown
and Port Elizabeth, fierce mobs reversed the Union Jack or trailed
it through the mud.

That the Transvaal had been abandoned was a matter of indifference to the mass of Englishmen. Where colonial affairs
were concerned, the public memory was short. Minor wars were
almost annual occurrences, and the abandonment of territory as
being too troublesome was not novel. More sensational incidents
quickly diverted the public interest. Frere remarked in a letter to
Rider Haggard that 'dissatisfaction would have been far stronger
had not the Irish Land Bill so entirely absorbed public attentions
and the whole time of Parliament.'[57]

The Liberal journals, outside certain missionary circles, expressed feelings of relief. Retrocession was hailed as an act of
magnanimity to 'the noblest of European races'. There was not a
'single valid argument in a policy of retention', reasoned the
Evening Echo. The Government's generosity, the Liberals felt,
could only strengthen the British position in South Africa. Many
dwelt on the 'big bill' involved in an inglorious war— £2,720,000
—and in continued administration of the Transvaal.

The Conservatives waved the bloody shirt more vigorously
than ever, echoing Carnarvon's protest against 'peace with dis-
honour'. Why, they asked, did the Government first refuse retrocession, and then, after a few minor defeats and a loss of hundreds
of precious lives, conclude that there was nothing worth fighting
for? And what of the loyal blacks and whites who were left to
the mercy of Boers now flushed with vengeance and arrogance?
The high Tory Standard announced that there was to be a grand
fireworks display at the Crystal Palace to celebrate the peace,

'and that it will take the form of a monster white feather issuing from the mane of the British lion'.

The ministry, characterized by lack of cohesion during the war, was now surprisingly decisive. The Whig element seemed cowed. Forster approved of the peace, but spoke up for the philanthropic party, which was not without influence in Parliament and had the backing of the *Daily News*. He told his colleagues that where the natives were concerned 'we should not be justified in transferring them from British to Boer rule without obtaining either their assent or security for protection.' He was put off with the promise that the Royal Commission would deal properly with the matter.[58]

In a private letter, later made public, Gladstone claimed that the South African imbroglio had resulted from the misdeeds of Carnarvon. Borrowing from the Psalms, he solemnly explained his mission as simply 'a question of saving the country from sheer blood-guiltiness'. When questioned about the loss of British prestige, Gladstone frankly declared that he did not know the meaning of the word.

The Queen, however, feared that 'a humiliating peace will ruin our position in South Africa.' Kimberley failed to convince her that they had gained 'all the points of real importance to this country'.[59] Victoria curtly reminded him that the Queen's Speech on January 7th had promised a vindication of her authority, but that she could not understand how this had been accomplished. When the Cabinet members were told of her reaction, they were amused.

The military party members were obsessed with the idea of vindication. Frustrated in their vengeful desire to wipe out the stain of Majuba, they were vicious in their denunciation of Gladstone and the Radicals. Wood also felt the sting of their wrath. The army reformers joined the traditionalists in the attack on him. Wolseley said with bitterness that if Colley had had ten thousand men at his command as Wood had, he would never have made such a peace. When it was argued that Wood was chained by telegrams from London, the soldiers asked, 'Why didn't he cut the wires and fight?' It was said that he 'thought more of the wishes of the ministry than of the feelings of the nation'. Conservative journals reminded their readers that Sir Evelyn's family supported the Liberals and that his brother 'had stood for Essex, pledged up to the neck to Mr Gladstone's policy'.[60] He was, also, personally friendly with the Prime Minister, whom he taught the pleasures of 'the noble science', fox-hunting. One paper claimed that he spoke like a sergeant-major; another discovered that he had 'a foreign habit' of rolling his r's. And when leaders of the Irish party in the Commons applauded his services, Wood was made to appear as something less than a patriot.

The ministry lost no time in placing the onus of the peace terms on Wood. Craftily stated expressions of gratitude made it appear that the general had initiated the terms. Privately, the Government distrusted him. 'I have *between* ourselves', Kimberley wrote to Gladstone, 'by no means confidence in his discretion. He...half regrets the part he has played: he is very amenable to Court influence to which he looks for advancement and though he will honourably obey orders, he is very likely to unwittingly give a colour to his language which we do not intend. In short he is a soldier, not a diplomat.'[61]

Wood was crushed by the criticism. Throughout the negotiations he told his officers that he was strongly opposed to the surrender and asked them 'to witness that he was merely obeying orders'. When it was all over, he explained to the Duke of Cambridge that he was merely a soldier whose first duty was to obey. But, as Cambridge rightly pointed out to him, the cease-fire, which he had initiated because his position was not a good one, was the very thing the Government had 'needed to carry out the peaceful policy in contemplation'.[62] The Duke found it difficult to speak about the 'unfortunate peace'; he spent much of this time in bed with a severe attack of the gout. The attacks in the press went unanswered by Wood. As he told a friend, it was unwise to reply to any statement in a newspaper 'unless accused of an unnatural offence, not even then unless you have a clear alibi'.*[63]

---

* Afterwards he served with distinction in Egypt and the Sudan, and became a field-marshal, but the armistice after Majuba cast a long shadow. At the onset of the great South African War, Wolseley told him that Salisbury's Conservative ministry would never employ him in South Africa because of the part he had played in the Laing's Nek negotiations. Though Wolseley found Wood's services useful, he personally never forgave him. Nor did Butler. Although he was one of the few professional soldiers to approve of Gladstone's policy, he severely condemned Wood in his biography of Colley. Before the manuscript was published, however, Wolseley persuaded Butler to lift out the 'vituperative passages'.

On March 26th the Colonial Secretary advised Wood to visit Pretoria to explain the terms of the agreement and to arrange the provisional administration with the Boers. Arriving in Heidelberg at sunset on April 4th, he found, to his anger, the flag of the Republic flying over the court-house. When he tried to haul it down, a sentry threatened to shoot him. Wood then sent for Pretorius and Smit, telling them that there could not be two Governments in the Transvaal at the same time and demanding that the Vierkleur be brought down. The Republic's leaders argued against the flag's removal, saying that the burghers would never permit it. Sir Evelyn closed the conversation with an ultimatum: if the flag were not down by six the next morning, he would pull it down. It would, he said, be unpleasant for his family if he were shot in the act, but even Gladstone with all his great power over the English public would be unable to give the country back to the Boers.

The next morning, looking out of his hotel window, Wood saw the offending Vierkleur still flying. At precisely six o'clock he went out to the flagstaff muttering a little prayer under his breath. Before Wood had reached the pole, however, the guard took down the flag—at which point Smit came forward and admitted that his argument of the night before had been fallacious.[64]

During Wood's three-day visit to Pretoria there was little celebration. Even the farewell reception for Lanyon on April 7th fell flat. His Excellency spent much of his time attending to administrative duties and inspecting the military position. Examining the field around the deserted Zwartkopje farm, Wood realized that this ground was the scene of the sole British triumph during the entire campaign. Reviewing the evidence on the engagement at Bronkhorst Spruit, he decided that it had been a 'fair fight'.*

Addressing the volunteers, Wood was most complimentary, but throughout his speech discontented men shouted 'bunkum' and other derisive terms. Although he took no notice of the hecklers, he could not ignore the loyalist petitions, black and white. They told how they had been promised by Frere, Wol-

---

* Among those who disagreed was Roberts. When he arrived on the old battle-field during the next war with the Boers, he telegraphed that he had reached the scene where British soldiers had been victims of treachery.

seley, Lanyon and Gladstone that the British flag would never
come down and that, therefore, they had risked life and fortune
for Britain. How would she now stand by them? What of their
civil rights and claims to compensation? In reply, Wood told
them that he had little information touching these matters but
that he would forward the substance of their petitions to the
home Government. He tried to console them with the assurance
that the Commission would sit for a time in Pretoria and would
give serious consideration to every just claim placed before it.

After Wood departed, Mr Kimberley White and a loyalist
deputation went all the way to London to protest against their
abandonment. The Colonial Secretary kept them waiting for a
week; and when he did finally receive them, they were coolly
informed that they were 'too pronounced in their views'. The
memorialists received only a few signatures in the House of
Commons, where Courtney had described them as 'men from the
diggings, landjobbers, and others who are ever haunting the
borderland of civilization and [ready] to rush like unclean birds
after their prey'. Gladstone told them that it was now their duty
to respect the will of the Boer majority. However, he promised
them that he would secure for them the full enjoyment of property and civil rights.

Back in the Transvaal, wagon-loads of families streamed down
the road to Natal. 'Even the children', wrote one British officer,
'look dejected, as if they understood the circumstances as well as
the elders.'[65] Many who had been well-to-do only a few months
before, observed Rider Haggard, now hardly knew 'how to find
food for their families'.[66]

Pretoria rapidly became a ghost city. The disappearance of the
Englishman's *geld* spent by the garrison and well-paid officials
caused many shopkeepers to close their stores. Rents fell and
unfinished buildings were left unfinished. The *Transvaal Argus*
prophesied that 'there will soon be whole streets to let!' Bousfield's congregation dropped from three hundred to fifty or sixty.
Some no longer had the heart to go to church and the bishop
found it no 'exaggeration to say that nearly all would have left if
they could'.[67]

There was much speculation—and even hope—of a renewed
conflict. Wild tales circulated of bumptious Boers, intoxicated by
their success, cruelly revenging themselves on defenceless loyal-

ists. 'Active persecution is going on everywhere,' exclaimed
Lanyon. The Natal papers reported: 'Bulgarian atrocities out-
done by Boers.' Dreadful indignities, it was alleged, were suffered by ladies at Boer hands. 'Several of them were stripped
naked, nominally in order to be searched,' asserted the *Natal
Mercury*, 'but there is every reason to believe that the men had
some other purpose in view.' Major Frank Russell, on interview-
ing a number of loyalists, relayed to John Morley the warning
that there would be a contest of 'fearful ferocity' between themselves and the Boers.[68]

The 'atrocities' committed by the Boers were investigated by
Wood, but he could not authenticate a single one of them. He
found that the statements were either untrue or 'malicious exaggerations'. Other investigators, including Merriman and Bellairs,
came to the same conclusion.

The possibility of a native uprising was strong, according to
Wood. Magato, paramount chief of the Rustenburg district, told
Wood in Pretoria, 'When the British have left the country, then
we will begin.' Another chief from Swartzberg promised to fight
to the last. The Anti-Slavery Society addressed a protest against
retrocession to Kimberley on behalf of the 'true heirs to the soil'
—who outnumbered the Boers by twenty-five to one.

The Boers were equally dissatisfied. They watched with suspicion the strengthening of fortifications around the garrisons.
Once more they saw telegraph poles and wires extending into
their country, and when it was learned that certain districts in the
eastern Transvaal might be retained by the British, they were
furious. Memorials demanding that not one inch of their land
must be alienated were circulated throughout the Transvaal. At
a meeting of the Kriegsraad in Heidelberg, only three out of
twenty-seven voted to accept the peace terms. Kimberley suggested to Wood that he should march a small force into the
Transvaal for purposes of intimidation. Sir Evelyn, however,
rejected the proposal on the grounds that 'a small force would
invite an attack...a large force would confirm their opinion of
our bad faith.' Instead, he asked that he be allowed to reoccupy
the Nek. 'We are quite ready. This will give a decisive military
result, and the happiest result for the country. I guarantee we
dislodge them.'[69] In the meantime, the Boer leaders had agreed
to the opening of the Royal Commission.

The Commissioners were not a happy team. Wood, upset by criticism (and frustrated in his efforts to bring justice to the murderers of Captain Elliott), would much rather have fought his way into the Transvaal. He told Childers while they were sitting that it was essential that he should keep his large force at Newcastle 'in order if necessary to repress any outbreak' among the Boers.

Sir Hercules Robinson, the High Commissioner at the Cape who was to open the Commission, delayed his departure as long as possible. Persistent requests by Wood that he should hurry northward were brushed aside with the argument that it was necessary for him to arbitrate the costly Basuto War so as to save face for the Cape Government.* When Robinson had been appointed, Kimberley had warned him, 'We have more than fifty Colonies, and South Africa gives us more trouble than all the rest put together.'[70] After only a few weeks in South Africa Sir Hercules began to understand what the Colonial Secretary had meant. Theoretically independent, the cautious Robinson promised to be more obedient to instructions than was the impulsive Wood. Rider Haggard, who observed the work of the Commission, felt that Sir Hercules 'evidently choked down his feelings and opinions as an individual and turned himself into an official machine, merely registering the will of Lord Kimberley'.[71] After all, he was fully aware of the fate that befell his strong-minded predecessor, Frere.

Sir Henry de Villiers, Chief Justice of the Cape Colony, was entirely his own man. Though a believer in federation and the English tongue, his blood and South African sympathies caused him to be friendly to Boer interests. Shy and reserved, he was nevertheless capable of asserting his views with vigour—and almost invariably on behalf of the burghers. (But the Boers grew to distrust him.) Sir Henry owed his appointment to President Brand, the fourth member of the party who served as *amicus curiae*. Brand did little during the meetings, though he obviously leaned to the Boer side. For his invaluable services during negotiations, Brand was offered a knighthood by the Queen. His acceptance of the honour caused considerable resentment among his burghers.

* The Sprigg ministry, nevertheless, was tumbled, and subsequently the Basutos, who were permitted to keep their guns, were placed under the control of the Imperial Government.

The sessions were not held in the open as Wood had wished. As chairman, Robinson had ruled that the proceedings were to be held at the Hilldrop farm outside Newcastle. Hilldrop was the residence of Rider Haggard, which they rented for fifty pounds a week. He reserved one bedroom for his pregnant wife, who bore him a son while the Commission sat. Shepstone in his congratulations playfully suggested that he might call the boy 'Joubert' or 'Jorissen', but he felt 'Bok' would make for a shorter signature. Rider Haggard, the man who had raised the Union Jack over the Transvaal, recognized the irony of having that flag, figuratively, hauled down in his own parlour. It seemed to make him detest the Boers all the more. He now took up his pen to write volumes of disparagement. Much later in life, however, he concluded, 'I now know that there is much to admire in the Boer character, also that among them were many men of real worth.'[72]

The Triumvirate, along with Jorissen, Bok, and other Boers who attended to give testimony, appeared anything but admirable to the English who were present. The Boers eyed the Commissioners suspiciously and appeared to doubt Britain's good faith. The English who had known Kruger before now found him less conciliatory, more gruff and dour. One Englishman saw him as 'a cross between a butcher and a parson'. For much of the time Kruger sat back and enjoyed the spectacle of the Commissioners disputing among themselves.

This was largely a case of Wood pitted against the other three. First, Wood refused to recognize the Volksraad of 1877 as a legal body. De Villiers was prepared to overlook this irregularity and Robinson supported him. Wood then insisted on the establishment of a special tribunal to try parties accused of usages contrary to civilized warfare. The proposal was vetoed on the grounds that ordinary courts would suffice for the purpose. (Of the alleged murderers later brought to trial, none was convicted.) At every turn, Wood expressed his views 'with a fierceness and a vigour that was quite astonishing'. The Boers who were present quickly grew to dislike him. Robinson had a difficult time trying to get Wood to accept the reasonings which came forth from de Villiers's 'glib lawyers' tongue'. On one occasion Wood spoke so harshly to de Villiers, whose views he considered inimical to the authority of Britain, that Robinson had to take him aside and ask him to make an effort to get along.

Shortly afterwards, Wood asked the chairman to be allowed to resign. 'Don't say that,' Robinson cried. 'I have just spent half the morning persuading de Villiers to stay on!'[73]

Tempers reached a new high point during the Commission's efforts to determine future borders. The unsurveyed boundaries had always been vague. Of the east, for example, seven maps had been printed between 1870 and 1877, each showing a different Zululand border, varying by as much as seventy miles. To the west, the Boers disputed the line of the Keate Award. More serious was the plan to retain for Britain all the land east of the 30th meridian. Kimberley, sensitive to philanthropic pressures, sought 'to interpose a tract of territory under British rule between the Zulus and Swazis and the Boer state', so as to 'render it much easier to maintain peace'.[74] It was a region with a large native population, and included the gold-bearing territory of Lydenburg with its British subjects. It was argued in some circles that by retaining at least some territory it would demonstrate, at least symbolically, that the English had not been forced out of the Transvaal.

All the Commissioners except Wood opposed Kimberley's original scheme as impractical. Wood battled to keep at least an insulating strip to the south-east. Bellairs, who was most conciliatory towards the burghers, then testified that any detachment of land would cause more, rather than less, 'discord and evil' in the future. When it came to Lanyon's turn, he cynically remarked that 'the sooner we get rid of contingent responsibilities the better for imperial interests. The recession ... should be prompt and complete without any fresh responsibilities.'[75]

The most telling argument came from the Boer leaders, who warned that their people would never accept the idea of a mutilated Transvaal. The burghers would fight. This was a prospect which did not disturb Wood. Earlier in the negotiations, Wood had taken Joubert aside and suggested that since Joubert disliked British reservations about native territories, they should settle the matter with another fight. 'Oh,' Joubert declared, 'I do not want any more bloodshed.' Somewhat fatalistically, he added, 'We shall not win again now, and I am in favour of a peaceful settlement.'[76]

Again, however, Wood was outvoted, as the others feared that by interposing a buffer there would be another war sooner or later. Even the western border was adjusted in a way that was more favourable to the Transvaal. The Triumvirate, for their part, conceded the appointment of a British Resident with the power to veto on the proposed Native Locations Commission which was designed to guarantee native land-rights.

Over the head of the chairman, Wood protested against the decision to Kimberley, who could overturn the work of the Commission at any point. But Kimberley, too, felt that the risk of renewed hostilities was too great. Wood offered his resignation. Attaching 'much importance' to his service, the Colonial Secretary protested that he must stay on. Kimberley defined this 'importance' to Gladstone: 'His leaving it would greatly encourage all those, both whites and natives, who wish to disturb the settlement.' In addition, he feared that Her Majesty, who 'throws so much obstruction in the way of everything I do—may take it into her head that Wood ought to be allowed to get out of a discreditable business'.[77] Wood, meanwhile, went on to Pretoria, working out his anger by chasing wild ostriches with a hunting-crop.

Although Kimberley was prepared to acquiesce on political issues, he haggled to the last pound over the financial settlement. In the beginning he had still hoped to collect the arrears of taxes which had provoked the revolt! On the advice of de Villiers, however, he waived this and other claims, the largest of which was the cost of the Sekukuni War (£383,000). To burden the Transvaal State financially (with little hope for obtaining credit), it was argued, would merely limit the chances for recovery by the British. The total debt was finally calculated at £457,000, but the Imperial Government decided to be content with little over half (£265,000), which they agreed to lend at 3½ per cent.

The loyalists found the home Government less generous. The European settlers, who owned nearly half of the property in the land, had hoped to be fully compensated for their losses. The Commission, however, decided first that indirect losses resulting from depreciation of land and other property after retrocession would not be recognized. Next, the Commission (with de Villiers dissenting) agreed to compensation for war losses and damages. Requests for such compensation were investigated by a sub-commission which dragged on until March 1882. The British officials required witnesses, certificates, sworn inventories and other kinds of legal evidence before the promised compensations were authorized. Many claims were therefore declared inadmissible, and some claimants were reduced to poverty. Others established fictitious claims, 'not forgetting to inflict telling jokes at the expense of less astute people'.[78] In the end, only one pound in six of the amounts claimed was allowed. The total amount granted was £959,590. When the Republic stated that it was unable to pay, the British agreed to defray the costs.

It was now the loyalists' turn to complain about official *hauteur* and indifference against which the Boers had previously protested. More representatives went to London and were ignored. In the House of Commons claims for compensation were ridiculed by Radicals as attempts at extortion by 'interested contractors and stockjobbers'. It was related how one claimant went so far as to ask for £50,000 on the basis that his feelings had been wounded by retrocession. By rejecting the vengeance which passion demanded, the Gladstone Government acquired moral stature at home and abroad, but to the Transvaal loyalists, 'Majubanimity' was an act of crushing betrayal.

The natives put it another way: 'The English protect us only to eat us.' They were confused by the constant shift in policy. One day the English took their side against the Boers; the next they were sacrificed to Boer interests. Robinson called a meeting of the Transvaal chiefs and tried to explain to them that the 'great white Queen' had annexed the land 'under a misapprehension', and since Britain was 'a justice-loving nation', the country was to be returned to the Boers. The chiefs immediately answered that if the English loved justice so much why did they not give the land back to its original owners, the natives?

The English were embarrassed by some of the chiefs' unabashed wailing as they rose to protest against the transfer. 'I am English, I belong to the English,' they announced. Why, they asked, were they being passed from hand to hand 'as a stick or piece of tobacco'? Robinson had no ready answer, but in private he expressed his distaste for the humiliating affair.

When it was learned that a Convention, the fruit of the Commission's labours, was to be signed on August 3rd, a rowdy party of loyalists held a mock-trial at the European Hotel. After some deliberation, Gladstone was given the death sentence for having murdered the British flag. The next day, while the document was being signed, nearly 600 Europeans and 200 natives walked in solemn procession behind a hearse which carried a coffin with the Union Jack inside. Within full view of the signers at Government House, they halted and dug a grave. There was a funeral oration, and then the flag was placed in its grave. A tombstone placed over the mound carried the inscription:

In Loving Memory of the
British Flag in the Transvaal
who departed his life
August 2nd 1881
in his Fifth Year

In other climes none knew thee but to love thee

Resurgam

The following morning, however, the grave was empty. The coffin was discovered hanging at half-mast from a near-by flag-pole. Colonel Gildea, who was probably responsible for the deed, had taken possession of the flag (it had belonged to the 94th).*

'The dear Vierkleur', as Kruger called it, was raised by Joubert on August 8th. It was the 38th anniversary of the Boers' abandonment of Natal to the English. Several thousand burghers were expected, but only a couple of hundred turned up, behaving 'in a most moderate and quiet manner'.[79] Bok, as State Secretary, read a proclamation from the Triumvirate thanking the burghers for their zeal and obedience, and promising equal rights for all. Joubert then spoke and reiterated that there would be full protection for all, 'whether burgher, foreigner, or Kaffir'.

But those who remained feared that 'Verdomde Engelsman' would become a battle cry for repression. Instead, to their surprise, 'conciliation and magnanimity were practised as well as preached' by the new Government.[80] Property and person, as laid down by the Convention, were respected. According to the testimony of a staunch loyalist, there was barely a word of

* He later took it back to England, where he kept it until his death in 1898. When war broke out in 1899, his widow gave the flag to her husband's old regiment, the 21st, before it embarked for South Africa. Buller promised that the historic piece of bunting would be hoisted over a captured Pretoria. He never quite managed this, but General Hunter later suggested that it should be raised over Potchefstroom in memory of the heroic defence which had been made there. The tombstone was preserved as a curiosity in a near-by saloon.

reproach: there was no boycott of renegade shopkeepers, and officials who had served the British were not recalled; even those who had fought against the Republic later served as members of the Volksraad. 'We were treated', he went on to say, 'with generosity which is unparalleled in history.'[81] The slump which overtook them, save for the gold-fields, lasted no more than a few years.

Gladstone was pleased to be rid of the Transvaal. 'For forty years,' he admitted, 'I have always regarded the South African question as the one great unsolved and perhaps insoluble problem of our colonial system.' The separation of self-governing colonies from the mother country was, as he saw it, a moral obligation. The problem was for the Government to determine the proper time to sever its ties. In the case of the Transvaal, which had become the hairshirt of the Empire, it was not necessary to ask permission of Parliament for withdrawal, as Parliament had never legislated for the Transvaal under the South Africa Act. As in the case of the Free State, which had been an 'emphatic precedent', autonomy and independence could be granted by the Crown.

But Parliament need not have been silent. Perhaps fortunately for the Government, Disraeli was stricken with a final illness in March, and when he died on April 19th, many believed that Gladstone behaved shamefully when he failed to attend the funeral. Nor could he find at first the proper words for the eulogy. (After prayer for guidance, he eventually succeeded.) 'For some days,' wrote his biographer, 'Gladstone's passion for sincerity caused him mental anguish which brought on a sharp attack of diarrhoea.'[82]

Acrimonious debate in the Commons was postponed. This was the result of an appeal made by Gladstone to Hicks Beach requesting that time be given the Commission in order to deliberate in the best possible political climate. The moratorium did not extend, however, to the House of Lords, where on March 31st the stately Lord Cairns led a spirited attack. A gifted lawyer and eloquent speaker, he presented a strong condemnation of Government policy. A flaccid Kimberley conceded that 'to be connected with a failure is now the unfortunate lot of this country.'

Chamberlain, the ministry's leading apologist, spoke in Birmingham on June 17th and defended the retrocession by admitting that the previous policy had been a mistake, but that after Majuba the Government preferred justice to revenge.

When the debate began in the Commons on July 25th, Gladstone, with Olympian presence, still refused to concede that there was any error in refusing retrocession before Majuba. During the subsequent exchange on the floor, Hicks Beach struck at the heart of the matter when he exclaimed, 'You have given to men with arms in their hands what you denied in their peaceful prayers...a policy which could be fatal in a country that had domination over so many alien and ignorant races.' As for the natives, he went on, the same ministers who had condemned the Zulu War without regard for the white colonists in Natal were now prepared to turn over to the Boers eight hundred thousand natives who preferred English rule. Chamberlain replied that the Boers had been 'persistently maligned' as to their treatment of the natives. According to the evidence before him, the Dutch were anything but 'fierce and unjust aggressors'. Gladstone added his praise for the Boer character as 'in some respects not unlike what we boast of for ourselves'. As for the peace, he concluded, 'We have endeavoured to cast aside all feelings of false shame...to do right and eschew wrong.' Gladstone's high moral stance and Chamberlain's forceful arguments held the Liberals firm in beating back a vote of censure.*

Retrocession was either the most magnanimous or the most cowardly act in British history—depending upon which side the public listened to. But, in general, the public showed little if any interest. The Convention was accepted as the best possible solution under the circumstances. *The Times* reflected this attitude: 'The Empire is big enough without the Transvaal.'

It proved easier to annex the Transvaal than to restore it. The old Volksraad, which dissolved in August, had been noted for its carefree and sometimes prankish behaviour. Members tripped each other up and tossed paper gliders. In the new Volksraad,

* There is an interesting sequel to these remarks. On October 19th, 1899, Chamberlain, now 'Minister of Empire' and the most fervent imperialist, told the House of Commons, 'The treatment of the natives of the Transvaal has been disgraceful...unworthy of a civilized Power.' Speaking before the same House on March 19th, 1903, after his return from South Africa, Chamberlain freely admitted, 'They [the Boers] seem somehow or other to have understood the native character. They have not been regarded on the whole as hard or severe masters by the natives, and no great amount of ill-feeling has ever sprung up between them.' Which one then was the real Joseph Chamberlain?

elected on September 15th, the atmosphere was charged with violent language. The Convention of thirty-three articles was spoken of as a cup of milk with thirty-three flies. The members were unanimous in their resolve to alter the more objectionable clauses. As one member put it, if he dared to approve the Convention his constituents would stone him to death. Their most vociferous protests were made against the acknowledgment of the suzerainty of the Queen, which the British defined as the right to appoint a Resident, to conduct foreign relations, and to send troops across the country in time of war. Kimberley had even changed the name from the South African Republic to the Transvaal State.

Fretful deliberations gave rise to ominous rumours. In mid-October telegrams from Gladstone informed the burghers that there would be no further concessions, and if ratification did not take place by November 3rd, British forces would move into the Transvaal. Wood, who had refused to sign the Convention of Pretoria, made elaborate plans for invasion.* He and Buller were certain that the Boers would fight rather than ratify.

The Triumvirate, most of all Kruger, after much persuasion got the Volksraad to ratify rather than to risk war. It was, however, stated for the record that they were submitting to force and trusted that, in view of their submission, the British would eventually correct certain clauses, most of all the matter of suzerainty. As it developed, the Resident in Pretoria had no means of enforcement and merely reported acts of disobedience to the High Commissioner, Sir Hercules Robinson, whom Kruger found to be a 'good friend'. Later, by the terms of the London Convention signed on February 27th, 1884, the third anniversary of the Majuba battle, the inexact concept called suzerainty was virtually sacrificed to keep the expanding Boers out of Bechuanaland. The South African Republic, as it was now allowed to call itself, agreed not to extend its borders, restrict freedom of trade, or conclude treaties with other Powers unless sanctioned by Britain. At the time, a conciliatory attitude was said to have been exhibited by the Queen herself, for when Kruger dined at Windsor and poured coffee into his saucer to cool, she too drank from her saucer.

---

* His dissent was published in the Blue Book, C.3114 (1882), but omitted from a subsequent edition of the Royal Commission's Report.

The sword was returned to the scabbard. Thousands of British troops were marched back to their transports, while fifteen thousand burghers gathered once more at Paardekraal in mid-December to give thanks to God for the restoration of their land. Joubert, his hair noticeably greyer, said, 'The world says, the Boers are good shots, and therefore they have gained the victory. But how to account for the good shooting on the other side? That at least we could not prevent. No, it is not the good shooting of the Boers that has procured for us the victory, but the Lord's help. The Lord has done it.'

THE AFTERMATH

Winston Churchill once described battles as punctuation-marks on the pages of history. Rated by the combatants engaged, Majuba was a mere skirmish, but few battles have had more immediate and far-reaching effects. The Boers not only won back the Transvaal but made it the centre of intensified Dutch national feeling. They vigorously expressed their faith in the future with the toast: 'United Free South Africa—sooner or later, and the sooner the better'. Majuba also made it possible for the Radicals, with the Irish question and, certainly, power uppermost in their minds, to defeat the Whigs and philanthropists. (Further injury was inflicted on Kimberley when he was forced to accept Court-ney as Under-Secretary at the Colonial Office, despite 'very strong objections'.) Radical success once more demonstrated how Imperial policy was often subject to the vagaries of domestic programmes, even at a time described as the New Imperialism. No doubt the reversal of Government policy in the Transvaal encouraged Parnell and the Irish Nationalists, who supported the Radicals, to hope for Home Rule.

To the imperialists, Majuba was a comma, not a full stop. Carnarvon, who saw his cherished dream of confederation dis-integrate between his translations of the fifth and the eleventh books of the Odyssey, promised a future war 'for Empire and very existence'. Others too believed that surrender after defeat would encourage the Boers in an anti-British and anti-native policy which would lead to a second and greater war. Hicks Beach spoke of 'infinitely worse trouble'. Wood observed that 'in a few years ... we shall have to take over the country.'

The standards of the age of exaggerated nationalism de-manded vengeance—whether it was for Sedan or the death of Gordon at Khartoum. Majuba was a blot upon England's honour. Speaking in Parliament, Salisbury, who led the nation up to and through the Second Anglo–Boer War, said that in 'every contest which the Government have to wage—military, diplomatic and domestic—the stain of that defeat will be upon them, and they will feel that they are fighting under the shadow of Majuba Hill'.

The defeat seemed to rankle more and more as the years passed. When President Kruger later declared the anniversary of Majuba a public holiday, on which to give thanks to the Almighty for preserving their independence, Englishmen assumed that it was 'merely an annual occasion for crowing over the defeat of British troops and boasting of their own prowess'. Yet it was only natural, as Bellairs pointed out, that a young nation should hand the victory down to succeeding generations of South Africans 'as a grand achievement performed by their ancestors'. The press and popular writers of blood-stained fiction, such as Haggard and Henty, heated memories with stories of Boer cruelty and intolerable arrogance. It was told how the Boers, with Majuba in mind, taunted Englishmen, with the question 'Now do you call us cowards?' Carter, who wrote a more objective account of the war, recalled derogatory remarks made by the English about Boer courage during the annexation period and concluded that 'the guilt, if any, does lie with us.'

In his *Memoirs*, Kruger wrote that there were two causes for a second Boer War, the first being the wealth of the gold-fields in the Transvaal, the second 'revenge for Majuba Hill'. When Anglo–Boer tensions exploded in 1899, British soldiers of every rank spoke of erasing the contempt that the Dutch had expressed after Majuba. The brooding Gordons, before whom no one ever dared mention Majuba, vowed that they would allow themselves to be hacked to pieces rather than retreat a single step before the enemy. Hector MacDonald, who led the Highland Brigade, told a bugler whose father had been killed at Majuba, 'You are now on the right road for your father's grave, but I hope my lad, you'll see it all wiped out.'[1] As British soldiers approached the old battlefields of the Nek, a variety of oaths were to be heard. One officer told of how he 'became impregnated with that "fierce, red-looking feeling" which is an absolute ally of the offensive spirit'. The cry 'Remember Majuba' was to be heard in one engagement after another.* The Gordons shouted the words as

* Majuba itself was not the scene of bloodshed. In the 'thirties, however, five persons were murdered on its slopes in one day by a madman named Swarts.

they charged up the hill of Elandslaagte, led by Colonel Ian
Hamilton, and drove off the Boers at the point of the bayonet.
After the war there was the general feeling, as expressed in *The
Times History*, that Imperial Britain had 'worthily avenged, or
rather redeemed, the national disaster that followed so soon after
Majuba'.[2]

The second war, oddly enough, followed many of the same
lines as the first, with most of the same main actors—Kruger,
Joubert, Cronje, Buller, Roberts, and others who rose in rank like
DeWet, Delarey, MacDonald,* and Hamilton.† In the British
army, hidebound outdated methods and traditions still took
precedence over marksmanship. The individual soldier continued
to be allotted only 300 rounds a year for rifle practice. Even then
the emphasis was placed on mechanical firing of volleys which
did little to improve individual accuracy. Colonial wars, most of
all in the Sudan, encouraged neglect, for the stress was on
defensive and shock tactics necessary to repel spear-wielding
hordes. The art of concealment as practised by the Boers was
still held to be beneath the dignity of a British soldier. Wolseley,
who had that irritating habit of knowing too much too soon,
laboured to update the army but enjoyed only partial success.
Recognizing that lack of cavalry and most of all the lack of a
mounted infantry had contributed heavily to Colley's defeat, he
succeeded in getting the military to accept the mounting of
infantrymen.

In 1881 the Boers enjoyed the advantage of not having to face
Wolseley, master of the small war. And in 1899 Buller rather
than Wolseley (who was now the Commander-in-Chief) was
sent to command in South Africa. Buller, who would much rather
have served under his old chief, committed one blunder after
another. He issued such anachronistic orders as 'The men must
get to close quarters with the enemy—that is the way to victory
and to safety.' As one student of military history wrote, 'At

---

* 'Fighting Mac', honoured as one of Scotland's greatest heroes, committed
suicide in 1903 after being confronted by an 'opprobrious accusation'. There seems
little doubt that the alleged crime involved the charge of homosexuality. The other
party was believed to have been the son of the Governor of Ceylon. Years later a
rumour persisted that he slipped off to Germany where he assumed the name von
Mackensen and became one of Germany's most brilliant generals in World War I.

† Herbert Stewart, who in only five years rose from captain to major-general,
took the place of Colley in the affections of Wolseley and also died the death of a
hero while leading an advance column in an effort to save Gordon at Khartoum.

Waterloo he would have been magnificent.' The Government, passing over Wolseley once more, replaced Buller with Roberts. Wolseley did his part by organizing the man-power and *matériel* for Roberts to overwhelm the enemy. It was assumed that when Roberts drove the Boers from the field the war was over, and he was recalled, leaving the command to Kitchener. But the burghers only took to the hills. As Smuts observed on the eve of conflict, as guerrillas the Boers could hold out in the hills for six or seven years, if necessary, and 'long before that', he added, 'there will be a change of opinion in England. Other things will crop up, they will become tired and lose interest ... and *this time* we shall get all that we want.'[3] Kitchener, however, adopted a plan forecast by Buller himself in 1881. Since there were so few points of any strategic importance to occupy or destroy, Buller wrote, the British would have 'to reduce them by harrying their farms and burning their homesteads; cruel work at the best of times and very cruel against a much-married and much-scattered population like the Boers ... a war from which little credit would be gained'.[4]

For the Boers, nothing failed like success. They were still masters of fire and movement, but Majuba had made them overconfident. When war was declared in 1899, the State Secretary of the Transvaal said, 'God help poor Tommy.' And the commanders (like Joubert), having grown cautious with age, adopted the same strategy that had brought them victory in the previous contest. Once more they surrounded the British garrisons— Ladysmith, Kimberley, Mafeking—and waited for relieving forces which could be destroyed in defensive battles. The siege strategy failed, for the British were far more numerous and relentless.

There was much condemnation and abuse in Britain directed towards Gladstone, who died in 1898, for having brought on a second war with his policy of surrender. A better case for censure could have been found in the fact that he did the right thing at the wrong time. As Kruger explained, if it had not been for the annexation and the policy of retention, 'there would have been no Majuba Hill, and no revenge for Majuba Hill' would have been called for.

NOTES

Chapter 1 — Annexation

1. Ernest B. Iwan-Müller, *Lord Milner and South Africa* (London, 1902), p. xiii.
2. D. F. Ellenberger and J. C. MacGregor, *History of the Basuto, Ancient and Modern* (London, 1912), 224–5.
3. John Kotze, *Biographical Memoirs and Reminiscences* (Cape Town, 1934), I, 26.
4. John Robinson, *A Lifetime in South Africa* (London, 1900), 37.
5. Garnet Wolseley to Richard Wolseley, June 2nd, 1875, Wolseley Papers, Hove.
6. Carnarvon to Wolseley, July 14th, 1875, Carnarvon Papers, P.R.O., 30/6, No. 18.
7. George Pomeroy-Colley, *Report on the Neighbouring Dutch Republic*, Aug. 10th, 1875, Archives, Pietermaritzburg.
8. Wolseley to Carnarvon, May 7th, 1875, Carnarvon Papers, P.R.O., 30/6, No. 18.
9. Ibid., July 8th, 1875.
10. Wolseley to Shepstone, Nov. 11th, 1876, Shepstone Papers, Archives, Pietermaritzburg.
11. Ibid., loc. cit.
12. Cornelis J. Uys, *In the Era of Shepstone* (London, 1933), 441.
13. Olive Schreiner, *Thoughts of South Africa* (London, 1923), 88.
14. Wolseley to Shepstone, Oct. 11th, 1876, Shepstone Papers.
15. Ibid., loc. cit.
16. S. P. Engelbrecht, *President Thomas François Burgers: A Biography* (Pretoria, 1946), 305–6.

Chapter 2 — Retention

1. *The Times*, Feb. 15th, 1881.
2. Ibid., June 27th, 1881.
3. Engelbrecht, *Burgers*, 301–2.
4. Henry Rider Haggard, *Days of My Life* (London, 1926), I, 95–6.
5. J. P. R. Wallis, *Fitz: The Story of Sir Percy Fitzmaurice* (London, 1955), 67–8.
6. Shepstone to Hicks Beach, May 8th, 1878, Minute by Herbert, June 26th, 1878, P.R.O., C.O. 291/ID 47; Frere to Hicks Beach, May 14th, 1878, Minute by Herbert, June 13th, 1878, P.R.O., C.O. 48/485 D116.
7. Hicks Beach to the Governor of Malta, July 17th, 1880, P.R.O., C.O. 158/257.
8. John Martineau, *Life and Correspondence of Sir Bartle Frere* (London, 1895), II, 30.
9. Owen Lanyon to Charles Lanyon, March 20th, 1880, xv, Lanyon Papers, Archives, Pretoria.
10. Ibid., Jan. 30th, 1880.
11. Victoria Alexandra Hicks Beach, *Life of Sir Michael Hicks Beach* (London, 1932), I, 166.
12. Garnet Wolseley to Louisa Wolseley, Sept. 15th, 1879, Wolseley Papers, Royal United Service Institution Library (R.U.S.I.).
13. Garnet Wolseley to Matilda Wolseley, Oct. 3rd, 1879, Wolseley Papers, Hove.

14. Wolseley to Hicks Beach, Sept. 25th, 1879, Wolseley's Private Letterbook on South Africa, 1879–1880, R.U.S.I.
15. William Francis Butler, *Life of Sir George Pomeroy-Colley* (London, 1899), 224.
16. Garnet Wolseley to Louisa Wolseley, Sept. 29th, 1879, R.U.S.I.
17. Ibid., July 31st, 1880.
18. Ibid., Oct. 31st, 1879.
19. Wolseley to Hicks Beach, Nov. 11th, 1879, Private Letterbook, R.U.S.I.
20. Ibid., Wolseley to Lanyon, Nov. 11th, 1879, R.U.S.I.
21. Ibid., Wolseley to Hicks Beach, Oct. 28th, 1879.
22. Ibid., loc. cit.
23. Ibid., Nov. 11th, 1879.
24. Garnet Wolseley to Louisa Wolseley, July 16th, 1895, R.U.S.I.
25. Blanche St John Bellairs, *The Transvaal War, 1880–1881* (Edinburgh, 1885), 21.
26. Garnet Wolseley to Louisa Wolseley, Nov. 10th, 1879, R.U.S.I.
27. Wolseley to Cambridge, Jan. 21st, 1880, Royal Archives, Windsor.
28. J. W. Matthews, *Incwadi Yami, or Twenty Years' Personal Experience in South Africa* (London, 1887), 440.
29. Garnet Wolseley to Louisa Wolseley, April 11th, 1880, R.U.S.I.
30. Wolseley to Cambridge, Jan. 2nd, 1880, R.A.
31. John Black Atkins, *The Life of Sir William Howard Russell* (London, 1911), ii, 306.
32. Wolseley to Hicks Beach, Sept. 25th, 1879, Private Letterbook, R.U.S.I.
33. Garnet Wolseley to Louisa Wolseley, Jan. 21st, 1880, R.U.S.I.
34. Wolseley to Hicks Beach, Jan. 16th, 1880, Private Letterbook, R.U.S.I.
35. Ibid., March 12th, 1880.
36. Wolseley to Cambridge, March 13th, 1880, R.A.
37. Garnet Wolseley to Richard Wolseley, April 21st, 1880, Hove.

Chapter 3 — Rebellion

1. Wolseley to Cambridge, Feb. 16th, 1880, R.A.
2. John Morley, *The Life of Gladstone* (London, 1903), iii, 3.
3. Cabinet Memo. 37/5, August 20th, 1880, P.R.O.
4. Owen Lanyon to Charles Lanyon, Sept. 4th, 1880, xv, Lanyon Papers.
5. Ibid., Nov. 8th, 1880.
6. Wolseley's unpublished memoirs, no page-number indicated, R.U.S.I.
7. Julia Merriman to Agnes Merriman, Jan. 9th, 1881, Merriman Papers, South African Public Library, Cape Town.
8. Lt Commeline to father, Sept. 5th, 1880, Commeline Papers, Gloucester Record Office.
9. Colley to Cambridge, Aug. 26th, 1880, R.A.
10. Martineau, *Frere*, ii, 112.
11. Thomas Fortesque Carter, *A Narrative of the Boer War: Its Causes and Results* (London, 1896), 103.
12. Bellairs, *Transvaal War*, 129.
13. Owen Lanyon to Charles Lanyon, Sept. 25th, 1880, xv, Lanyon Papers.
14. Bellairs, *Transvaal War*, 39.
15. Douglas Blackburn and Walter Waithman Cadell, *Secret Service in South Africa* (London, 1911), 124.
16. B.M.Hart-Synnot (ed.), *Letters of Major-General Fitzroy Hart-Synnot* (London, 1912), 212.

17. Blackburn and Cadell, *Secret Service*, 108–9.
18. Ibid., 114.
19. Lanyon to Colley, Nov. 26th, 1880, C–2740.
20. William E. G. Fisher, *The Transvaal and the Boers; A Brief History* (London, 1896), 211.
21. Kimberley to Lanyon, Dec. 30th, 1880, xv, Lanyon Papers.
22. Cabinet Memo. 37/5, Dec. 5th, 1880, P.R.O.
23. Alfred Aylward, *The Transvaal Today* (London, 1881), 24.
24. Alfred Kinnaer, *To Modder River with Methuen* (London, 1900), 152.
25. R. W. Schikkerling, *Commando Courageous: A Boer's Diary* (Johannesburg, 1964), 5.
26. Butler, *Colley*, 268.
27. Charles DuVal, *With a Show Through Southern Africa* (London, 1882), ii, 280.
28. Lanyon to Kimberley, Jan. 7th, 1881, v, Lanyon Papers.
29. Ibid., Jan. 3rd, 1881.
30. Ibid., Jan. 5th, 1881.
31. Strahan to Kimberley, Memo. by Herbert, Jan. 11th, 1881. P.R.O., C.O. 48/499, D 27.

Chapter 4—Bronkhorst Spruit

1. David M. Wilson, *Behind the Scenes in the Transvaal* (London, 1901), 259.
2. James Cromb, *The Majuba Disaster: A History of Highland Heroism* (Dundee, 1891), 49.
3. 'Boer War of 1881: By an English Officer', *Forum* (Jan. 1900), 600–14.
4. Arthur Cunyngham, *My Command in South Africa, 1874–1878* (London, 1879), 208, 241.
5. Schikkerling, *Commando*, 169.
6. W. H. Tomasson, *With the Irregulars in the Transvaal and Zululand* (London, 1881), 232.
7. H. E. Pegg and W. Talbot Evans, *South Africa: A History* (Cape Town), 1960 249.
8. G. Tylden, 'The British Army and the Transvaal, 1875 to 1885', *Journal of the Society for Historical Research*, xxxx (1952), 159.
9. G. Tylden, 'The Development of the Commando System in South Africa, 1715 to 1922', *Africana Notes and News*, xiii (1959), 306–7.
10. W. E. Montague, *Campaigning in South Africa* (Edinburgh, 1880), 79.
11. *Natal Witness*, March 2nd, 1881.
12. Joubert to Merriman, April 3rd, 1881, Merriman Papers.
13. DuVal, *With a Show*, ii, 195.
14. J. J. F. Hume, 'A Narrative of the 94th Regiment in the Boer War, 1880–81', *The Ranger*, iv (Sept. 1925), 163–78; Regimental Papers, Connaught Rangers, R.U.S.I.
15. Mary Anne Carey-Hobson, *At Home in the Transvaal* (London, 1884), ii, 315.
16. Regimental Papers, Connaught Rangers, R.U.S.I.
17. Percival Scrope Marling, *Rifleman and Hussar* (London, 1931), 30–31.
18. Charles L. Norris-Newman, *With the Boers in the Transvaal and the Orange Free State in 1880–1881* (London, 1882), 124.
19. Crow's dispatch quoted in Matthews, *Incwadi Yami*, 451.
20. DuVal, *With a Show*, ii, 276.
21. Martineau, *Frere*, ii, 408–10.
22. Butler, *Colley*, 275.

23. Arthur Conan Doyle, *The Great Boer War* (London, 1900), 16.
24. DuVal, *With a Show*, II, 226.
25. Morton Cohen, *Rider Haggard; His Life and Works* (London, 1960), 68.
26. Goschen to Granville, Feb. 12th, 1881, Granville Papers, P.R.O., C.O. 291/3.
27. Ibid., Fenton to Granville, Jan. 4th, 1881.
28. Charles Mallet, *Herbert Gladstone: A Memoir* (London, 1932), 82.
29. Morley, *Gladstone*, III, 33.

Chapter 5—Laing's Nek

1. Colley to Childers, Dec. 26th, 1880, C–2866.
2. Ibid., loc. cit.
3. Ibid., Jan. 1st, 1881.
4. Ibid., Jan. 19th, 1881.
5. Ibid., Dec. 26th, 1880.
6. William Charles Frances Molyneux, *Campaigning in South Africa and Egypt* (London, 1896), 190.
7. Colley to Cambridge, Jan. 9th, 1881, R.A.
8. Ibid., Cambridge to Leister Smith, Jan. 20th, 1881.
9. George White to wife, Dec. 23rd, 1880, White Papers, India Office Library, MSS Eur. F.18.
10. Donald R. Morris, *The Washing of the Spears* (New York, 1965), 303.
11. Quoted in 'Machine Guns: Their Status in Warfare', *United States Magazine*, Oct. 1881, 129.
12. Montague, *Campaigning*, 79.
13. Butler, *Colley*, 277.
14. Ibid., 279.
15. Colenso to Colley, Jan. 6th, 1881, Government House Papers, Cape Town.
16. Wolseley to Childers, Jan. 14th, 1881. Wolseley Papers, War Office Library.
17. Ibid., Alison to Childers, Feb. 18th, 1881.
18. Marling, *Hussar*, 31.
19. Alison to Childers, Feb. 18th, Wolseley Papers, W.O. Library.
20. Charles E. Callwell, *Stray Recollections* (London, 1923), I, 180.
21. DuVal, *With a Show*, II, 237.
22. Telegram in Merriman Papers.
23. Edwin Mole, *King's Hussar* (London, 1903), 249.
24. Kimberley to Robinson, Jan. 26th, 1881, C–2837.
25. Herbert Gladstone, *After Thirty Years* (London, 1928), 218, 236.
26. Colley to Kimberley, Jan. 2nd, 1881, Gladstone Papers, #44226, British Museum.
27. Butler, *Colley*, 325.
28. Alexander Merensky, *Erinnerungen aus dem Missionsleben in Transvaal, 1859–1882* (Berlin, 1899), 391.
29. Marling, *Hussar*, 36.
30. John Frederick Maurice, *Official History of the War in South Africa* (London, 1906–10), I, 76.
31. Quoted in Norris-Newman, *With the Boers*, 171.
32. James Ritchie, *Brighter South Africa* (London, 1893), 33.
33. H.P.Holt, *The Mounted Police of Natal* (London, 1913), 101.
34. 'Boer War of 1881: by an English Officer', *Forum* (Jan. 1900), 600–14.
35. John James Aubertin, *Six Months in Cape Colony and Natal* (London, 1963), 123.

36. Wolseley to Bury, July 17th, 1878, Wolseley Papers, W.O. Library.
37. John Buchan, *History of the Royal Scots Fusiliers* (London, 1925), 244n.
38. E. Spencer Childers, *The Life and Letters of the Right Honourable Hugh C.E. Childers, 1827–1896* (London, 1901), II, 16.
39. Joubert to Kruger, Jan. 28th, 1881, Boeren Voormannen Papers, Archives, Pretoria. (Indicated as B.V.)
40. Ibid., loc. cit.
41. Merensky, *Erinnerungen*, 391.
42. Butler, *Colley*, 289.
43. Cambridge to Colley, Feb. 3rd, 1881, R.A.
44. Morley, *Gladstone*, III, 34.

Chapter 6 — Ingogo

1. Eric Walker, *Lord de Villiers and His Times* (London, 1925), 151–2.
2. Hicks Beach, *Life*, I, 141.
3. Fairfield to Kimberley, Feb. 5th, 1881, P.R.O., C.O. 48/499.
4. Colley to Brand, Feb. 8th, 1881, C–2782.
5. Carter, *Boer War*, 197.
6. Butler, *Colley*, 312.
7. Ian Hamilton, *When I Was a Boy* (London, 1939), 15.
8. Carter, *Boer War*, 205.
9. Brian Roberts, *Ladies in the Veld* (London, 1965), 92.
10. *Natal Times*, Feb. 12th, 1881.
11. Henry Rider Haggard, *The Last Boer War* (London, 1899), 143.
12. Marling, *Hussar*, 51.
13. Carter, *Boer War*, 213.
14. Marling, *Hussar*, 45.
15. A. Theodore Wirgman, *Life of James Green* (London, 1909), I, 136.
16. Norris-Newman, *With the Boers*, 178.
17. Marling, *Hussar*, 41.
18. Merensky, *Erinnerungen*, 390n.
19. James Grant, *British Battles on Land and Sea* (London, 1897), I, 357.
20. Marling, *Hussar*, 49.
21. Haggard, *Boer War*, 146.
22. *Natal Mercury*, Feb. 23rd, 1881.
23. Colley to Cambridge, Feb. 12th, 1881, R.A.
24. Childers, *Life*, I, 22.
25. Ibid., 19–20.
26. Cambridge to Colley, Feb. 10th, 1881, R.A.
27. Childers, *Life*, I, 29.
28. Julia Merriman to Agnes Merriman, Feb. 12th, 1881, Merriman Papers.
29. Osborne to Colley, Jan. 30th, 1881, C–2950.
30. Kimberley to Granville, Feb. 20th, 1881, Gladstone Papers, #44226.
31. *Graphic*, Jan. 8th, 1881.
32. Paul Kruger, *The Memoirs of Paul Kruger* (London, 1902), I, 155–6.
33. Norris-Newman, *With the Boers*, 115.
34. DuVal, *With a Show*, II, 28.
35. Haggard, *Boer War*, 137.
36. Lanyon to Kimberley, Jan. 3rd, 1881, v, **Lanyon Papers**.
37. Lt Linmitte's Report, C–2950.
38. Ibid., Colley's Report.

39. Quoted in a Retired Field Officer, 'Our Disaster in South Africa', *Colburn's United Service Magazine* (March 1881), 303.
40. Ibid., 303–6.
41. Kimberley to Colley, Feb. 24th, 1881, C–2866.

Chapter 7—The Beleaguered Garrisons

1. J.F.Maurice, no date, Maurice Papers.
2. Elizabeth (Dietrich) Smithers, *March Hare* (London, 1935), 33–4.
3. J.Slater, *Birth of the Bond* (London, 1900), 10.
4. Frank Oates, *Matabeleland and the Victoria Falls* (London, 1889), 10.
5. Carey-Hobson, *At Home*, 344.
6. Johannes Meintjes, *DeLaRey: Lion of the West* (Johannesburg, 1966), 49.
7. Smithers, *March Hare*, 70, 115.
8. H.Pretorius to C.G.Malan, Dec. 22nd, 1881, Joubert Collection, 25, No. 2424, Archives, Pretoria; B.V. 433, 21, p. 81.
9. Malan to Cronje, Jan. 4th, 1881, B.V. 17, p. 44.
10. Joubert Collection, 26, No. 2424; B.V. 433, 21, p. 81.
11. Bok to Cronje, Jan. 4th, 1881, B.V. 17, p. 44.
12. *Diamond News* (Kimberley), Feb. 3rd, 1881.
13. Bellairs, *Transvaal*, 172.
14. DuVal, *With a Show*, II, 73.
15. Ibid., II, 80.
16. H. B. Bousfield, *Six Years in the Transvaal* (London, 1886), 92.
17. Smithers, *March Hare*, 116.
18. Thomas Victor Bulpin, *Lost Trails of the Transvaal* (Cape Town, 1953), 276.
19. Carey-Hobson, *At Home*, 347.
20. Carl Jeppe, *The Kaleidoscopic Transvaal* (London, 1906), 108.
21. Lanyon to Kimberley, Jan. 23rd, 1881, C–2783.
22. Lanyon to Kimberley, Jan. 28th, 1881, C–2921.
23. Lanyon to Colley, Feb. 1st, 1881, v, Lanyon Papers.
24. DuVal, *With a Show*, II, 137.
25. Ibid, II, 142.
26. John Nixon, *The Complete Story of the Transvaal* (London, 1885), 204.
27. DuVal, *With a Show*, II, 141.
28. Bousfield, *Six Years*, 25.
29. E.J.P. Jorissen, *Reminiscences and Warnings* (Pretoria, 1885), 5.
30. Jeppe, *Transvaal*, 2.
31. Bulpin, *Lost Trails*, 282.
32. R. W. C. Winsloe, 'Siege of Potchefstroom', *Macmillans*, XLVII (1882), 453.
33. A.M. Davey, *The Siege of Pretoria* (M.A. Thesis, University of South Africa), 249.
34. Smithers, *March Hare*, 119, 120.
35. Winsloe, 'Potchefstroom', 449.
36. Norris-Newman, *With the Boers*, 42.
37. W.E. Montague, 'Beseiged in the Transvaal (The Defence of Standerton)', *Blackwood's Magazine* CXXXX (July–August, 1881), 2.
38. Ibid., 8.
39. Bellairs, *Transvaal*, 311.
40. 'Number of Boers in Engaged in Siege Warfare', Feb. 21st, 1881, B.V., v.13, 423.
41. Montague, 'Standerton', 6–7.

42. John Scoble and Hugh Romilly Abercrombie, *The Rise and Fall of Krugerism. A Personal Record of Forty Years in South Africa* (London, 1910), 58.
43. Mrs Walter H.C. Long, *Peace and War in the Transvaal: An Account of the Defence of Fort Mary* (London, 1882), 41.
44. Ibid., 39.
45. Conductor Parsons's Report, W.O. 33/38, 305.
46. William Johannes Leyds, *The First Annexation of the Transvaal* (London, 1906), 285–7.
47. Parsons's Report, W.O. 33/38, 304.
48. G.B. Hamilton, *The Lost Legionary in South Africa* (London, 1192), 44.
49. Long, *Peace and War*, 85.
50. Letter to the *Advertiser*, March 25th, 1881.
51. Carter, *Boer War*, 437.
52. *Advertiser*, March 25th, 1881.
53. Carter, *Boer War*, 437.
54. Long, *Peace and War*, 101.
55. Bulpin, *Lost Trails*, 280.
56. Melton Prior, *Campaigns of a War Correspondent* (London, 1912), 143.
57. Davey, *Pretoria*, 305.
58. *News of the Camp*, March 30th, 1881.
59. Bellairs, *Transvaal*, 232.

Chapter 8 — Majuba

1. Wolseley to Buller, Jan. 31st, 1885, Buller Papers, W.O. 132/2.
2. Note by Frances Wolseley, no date, Wolseley Papers, R.U.S.I.
3. Wolseley to Cambridge, Oct. 6th, 1883, R.A.
4. Archibald Forbes, *Souvenirs of Some Continents* (London, 1885), 358.
5. Ian Hamilton, *Listening for the Drums* (London, 1944), 41.
6. Ibid., 119–20.
7. *Natal Mercury*, Feb. 24th, 1881.
8. Prior, *War Correspondent*, 128.
9. Manfred Nathan, *Paul Kruger: His Life and Times* (Durban, 1944), 164.
10. Dilke Papers, Feb. 15th, #43935.
11. James Louis Garvin, *The Life of Joseph Chamberlain* (London, 1932), I, 440.
12. Morley, *Gladstone*, III, 35.
13. Childers to Colley, Feb. 16th, 1881, C-2837.
14. Ibid., Kimberley to Colley, Feb. 19th.
15. Childers, *Life*, II, 24.
16. Ibid., loc. cit.
17. Colley to Cambridge, Feb. 18th, 1881, R.A.
18. Colley to Wolseley, Feb. 21st, 1881, Wolseley Papers, Hove.
19. Butler, *Colley*, 339.
20. Wolseley's unpublished memoirs, Wolseley Papers, R.U.S.I.
21. Henry Evelyn Wood, *From Midshipman to Field-Marshal* (London, 1906), II, 112.
22. David L. and James Cromb, *The Highland Brigade and Its Heroes* (Sterling, 1902), 290.
23. Arthur Ponsonby Ponsonby, *Henry Ponsonby, Queen Victoria's Secretary: His Life from His Letters* (London, 1942), 333–4.
24. D. Fairfax, *Sound of the Guns* (New York, 1958), 51; C. Callwell, *Small Wars, Their Principles and Practice* (London, 1899), 293–4; C.O. Head, *The Art of Generalship: Four Exponents* (London, 1929), 115–16.

25. Butler, *Colley*, 367–8.
26. Ibid., 369.
27. Hamilton, *Drums*, 131–2.
28. Cromb, *Majuba*, 35.
29. Douglas to White, April 5th, 1881, White Papers.
30. G. Tylden (trans.), 'Majuba. A Contemporary Boer Account' (Stephanus Roos), *Journal of the Society for Army Historical Research*, XVII (1938), 9.
31. Matthews, *Incwadi Yami*, 335.
32. Wood, *Midshipman*, II, 120.
33. Eric Rosenthal, *General DeWet: A Biography* (Cape Town, 1946), 25.
34. Tylden, 'Boer Account', 10.
35. Douglas to White, April 5th, 1881, White Papers.
36. 'Private Letters of Major T. Fraser', *Royal Engineers Journal* XI (June, 1881), 115; *Natal Mercury*, March 1st, 1881.
37. Butler, *Colley*, 389.
38. Tylden, 'Boer Account', 11.
39. Douglas to White, April 5th, 1881, White Papers.
40. Ibid., Hamilton to White, no date.
41. Carter, *Boer War*, 276.
42. Ibid., 276–7.
43. Rosenthal, *DeWet*, 26.
44. Butler, *Colley*, 404.
45. Merensky, *Erinnerungen*, 396n.
46. Cromb, *Majuba*, 27.
47. Douglas to White, April 5th, 1881, White Papers.
48. Surgeon Mahon's Report, C-2950; Fraser, *Engineers Journal*, 117.
49. Henry Evelyn Wood, ed., *British Battles on Land and Sea* (London, 1915), II, 843.
50. Callwell, *Recollections*, 192.
51. Macdonald to White, April 20th, 1881, White Papers; J. H. Settle, *Anecdotes of Soldiers in Peace and War* (London, 1905), 309; J. Montgomery, *Toll for the Brave* (London, 1963), 46.
52. Macgregor to White, May 6th, 1881; Hay to White, May 12th, 1881; Douglas to White, April 5th, 1881, White Papers.
53. Cromb, *Majuba*, 24.
54. Winston S. Churchill, *Ian Hamilton's March* (London, 1900), 119–20; I. B. Hamilton, *The Happy Warrior: A Life of General Sir Ian Hamilton* (London, 1966), 42; Hamilton, *Drums*, 141–4.
55. Hamilton, *Happy Warrior*, 45.
56. Churchill, *March*, 122.
57. Carter, *Boer War*, 285.
58. Johannes DuPlessis, *The Life of Andrew Murray of South Africa* (London, 1919), 331n.
59. Cromb, *Majuba*, 30.
60. Report of Capt. Macgregor, April 3rd, 1881, C-2950; Macgregor to White, May 6th, 1881, White Papers.
61. Cromb, *Majuba*, 31.
62. Matthews, *Incwadi Yami*, 337–8.
63. Marling, *Hussar*, 54.
64. Ibid., 55.
65. Ibid., loc. cit.
66. Cromb, *Majuba*, 35.
67. Ibid., loc. cit.

68. Leyds, *Annexation*, 278.
69. Macdonald to White, April 20th, 1881, White Papers.
70. Matthews, *Incwadi Yami*, 337.
71. Merensky, *Erinnerungen*, 397.
72. *Graphic*, April 9th, 1881.
73. Norris-Newman, *With the Boers*, 214.
74. Carter, *Boer War*, 304–13.

Chapter 9 — Peace

1. E. T. Raymond, *Portraits of the Nineties* (London, 1921), 73–4.
2. Cambridge to Wood, May 26th, 1881, R.A.
3. Childers, Life, II, 24.
4. Ibid., 25.
5. Wolseley's unpublished memoirs, R.U.S.I.
6. Dilke Papers, #43934.
7. Ibid., loc. cit.; G. M. Trevelyan, *The Life of John Bright* (London, 1913), 431.
8. Kimberley to Roberts, March 4th, 1881, C-2866.
9. Harman to Lady Wood, March 8th, 1881, Wood Papers.
10. Horace Lockwood Smith-Dorrien, *Memoirs of Forty-eight Years' Service* (London, 1925), 353.
11. Carter, *Boer War*, 226; Fraser, *Royal Engineers Journal*, 116–17.
12. Matthews, *Incwadi Yami*, 338–9.
13. George Earle Buckle, ed., *The Letters of Queen Victoria*, 2nd series (London, 1926–32), III, 331.
14. Scoble and Abercrombie, *Krugerism*, 34.
15. Nathan, *Kruger*, 172–3.
16. Edith Colley to Wood, March 5th, 1881, Wood Papers.
17. Norris-Newman, *With the Boers*, 301.
18. Henry Brackenbury, 'Sir George Pomeroy-Colley: Some Personal Recollections', *Blackwood's Magazine*, CLXV (March 1899), 568.
19. *Daily Telegraph*, March 16th, 1881.
20. Charles Henderson Melville, *Life of General the Right Honourable Sir Redvers Buller* (London, 1923), II, 148–9.
21. Wood to Kimberley, March 16th, 1881, C-2783.
22. Bellairs, *Transvaal*, 407.
23. Carter, *Boer War*, 329.
24. Forbes, *Souvenirs*, 2.
25. Roberts, *Ladies*, 106, 114–15.
26. Rosenthal, *DeWet*, 27.
27. Wood, *Midshipman*, II, 121.
28. Kruger, *Memoirs*, 159–60.
29. Ibid., 161.
30. Prior, *War Correspondent*, 137.
31. Carter, *Boer War*, 331.
32. Wood, *Midshipman*, II, 120.
33. John Buchan: *Lord Minto: A Memoir* (London, 1924), 60.
34. *Illustrated London News*, May 14th, 1881; Prior, *War Correspondent*, 140.
35. Prior, *War Correspondent*, 138.
36. Marling, *Hussar*, 55.
37. Hugh McCalmont, *The Memoirs of General Sir Hugh McCalmont* (London, 1924), 196.
38. Douglas to White, April 5th, 1881, White Papers.

39. Wood, *British Battles*, II, 387.
40. Ian Hamilton, *A Staff Officer's Scrap-Book* (London, 1905), II, 254.
41. Report of Conference with Boer Leaders on April 19th, 1881, C-3219.
42. Winsloe, 'Potchefstroom', 458.
43. Carter, *Boer War*, 431.
44. Wood to Joubert, April 8th, 1881, C-3098.
45. Charles Williams, *The Life of Lieutenant-General Sir Henry Evelyn Wood, V.C.* (London, 1892), 142.
46. Melville, *Buller*, II, 151.
47. Bulpin, *Lost Trails*, 287.
48. Martineau, *Frere*, II, 417.
49. Lanyon to Shepstone, March 30th, 1881, XVII, Shepstone Papers.
50. Owen Lanyon to Charles Lanyon, March 24th, 1881, XVI, Lanyon Papers.
51. Ibid., April 14th, 1881.
52. Nixon, *Transvaal*, 298.
53. Bousfield, *Six Years*, 96.
54. Carter, *Boer War*, 383.
55. Haggard, *Boer War*, 116.
56. Haggard, *My Life*, I, 194.
57. Ibid., 191.
58. Cabinet Memo., P.R.O. 35/5.
59. Buckle, *Victoria*, III, second series, 202, 204.
60. Williams, *Wood*, 136–7.
61. Kimberley to Gladstone, Sept. 30th, 1881, Gladstone Papers, #44226.
62. Cambridge to Wood, June 15th, 1881, R.A.
63. Wood to Mitchell, March 26, 1881, Wood Papers.
64. Wood, *Midshipman*, II, 122.
65. Hart-Synnot, *Letters*, 192.
66. Martineau, *Frere*, II, 415.
67. Bousfield, *Six Years*, 62.
68. Russell to Morley, May 6th, 1881, Morley Papers, #48266, XLIX, British Museum.
69. Wood, *Midshipman*, II, 124.
70. Francis R. Statham, *South Africa As It Is* (London, 1897), 123.
71. Haggard, *Boer War*, 181.
72. Lilias Rider Haggard, *The Cloak That I Left* (London, 1951), 159.
73. Walker, *De Villiers*, 157–9.
74. Cabinet Memo., P.R.O. 37/5, 17–20.
75. Wood to Kimberley, May 30th, 1881, P.R.O., C.O. 291/18.
76. Wood, *Midshipman*, II, 121.
77. Kimberley to Gladstone, June 7th, 1881, Gladstone Papers, #44226.
78. G. Nicholson, *Fifty Years in South Africa* (London, 1898), 158.
79. Norris-Newman, *With the Boers*, 268.
80. Davey, *Pretoria*, 304.
81. Nicholson, *South Africa*, 158.
82. Philip Magnus, *Gladstone: A Biography* (London, 1960), 280.

The Aftermath

1. Settle, *Anecdotes*, 309.
2. *The Times History of the War in South Africa* (London, 1900–5), 66–7.
3. James Percy Fitzpatrick, *South African Memories* (London, 1932), 168.
4. Melville, *Buller*, II, 153.

INDEX